FREEDOM OF COMMERCIAL EXPRESSION

Freedom
of
Commercial Expression

ROGER A. SHINER

OXFORD
UNIVERSITY PRESS

OXFORD
UNIVERSITY PRESS

Great Clarendon Street, Oxford OX2 6DP

Oxford University Press is a department of the University of Oxford.
It furthers the University's objective of excellence in research, scholarship,
and education by publishing worldwide in

Oxford New York

Auckland Bangkok Buenos Aires Cape Town Chennai
Dar es Salaam Delhi Hong Kong Istanbul Karachi Kolkata
Kuala Lumpur Madrid Melbourne Mexico City Mumbai Nairobi
São Paulo Shanghai Taipei Tokyo Toronto

Oxford is a registered trade mark of Oxford University Press
in the UK and in certain other countries

Published in the United States
by Oxford University Press Inc., New York

© Roger A. Shiner

British Library Cataloguing in Publication Data
Data available

Library of Congress Cataloging in Publication Data
Data available

ISBN 0–19–826261–2

1 3 5 7 9 10 8 6 4 2

Typeset by Hope Services (Abingdon) Ltd.
Printed in Great Britain
on acid-free paper by
T.J. International Ltd, Padstow, Cornwall

For Sharon, Emma, and Kira

Acknowledgements

This book has been a long time in the writing. The project began in 1990. I happened to have been reading an article which talked about freedom of commercial expression and which quoted the famous 'shampoo' epigram of Justice Rehnquist (as he then was) in the *Virginia Board* case (see Chapter 1.2 below). Intuitively, Rehnquist seemed to me correct, that freedom of expression does not have anything to do with marketing shampoo. But obviously this was then, and still is, a minority view, and thus a challenge to defend. Just about that time Wilfrid Waluchow telephoned to invite me to present a paper at a conference he was organizing on Freedom of Expression. Was there any aspect of this problem I was interested in? Yes, I said: I will give a paper on freedom of commercial expression. And so the journey began. A revised version of that paper eventually appeared in the published proceedings of that conference (W.J. Waluchow, ed., *Free Expression: Essays in Law and Philosophy* (Oxford: Clarendon Press 1994)). It was very much a first pass at the issues. Although my basic belief that the Rehnquist intuition is correct has not changed, my reasons for holding it have developed greatly. So little of that paper survives in this book that it was not worth asking the Press for permission to use it. All the same, I am deeply grateful to Wil for the impetus to get me thinking and writing about freedom of commercial expression; without that fillip, I would not have embarked on what has been an intriguing piece of research.

Two individuals must be specifically thanked for their part in this project. Fred Schauer provided advice, encouragement, and support at many stages in the first few years of this work, commenting on draft material, writing references, and the like. As will be clear from the text that follows, the influence on me of his ideas about freedom of expression and about the justification for constitutional protection of freedom of expression is enormous. I am very grateful to him both as person and as authority. Scot Powe also has contributed a great deal by way of advice and encouragement. He gave freely of his time when I was working in Austin, read drafts of chapters, and willingly put up with many specific questions on freedom of speech in the U.S. submitted by e-mail. His own writings set a standard of clarity and accessibility which the present book will not emulate, though not from a lack of trying. In both cases, and perhaps especially in Scot's, it will need to be emphasized that they do not necessarily agree with the views defended in this book.

I am grateful to the Canada Council for the award of a Killam Senior Research Fellowship for 1992–4. The importance of the freedom to pursue scholarship which such an extended period of leave allows needs no reminder. This research has also been supported by the Social Sciences and Humanities Research Council of Canada, through grant #410-93-1269, and I am grateful to that Council too. I would also like to thank the Social Sciences Research Network for a free waiver, which enabled me to continue to receive abstracts from a number of their mailing lists, and thus to keep up with current research.

The Killam Fellowship allowed me to spend time in 1993 and 1994 as a Visiting Scholar in the School of Law at the University of Texas at Austin (the winter terms, naturally; I am from Canada). The array of First Amendment specialists there is remarkable. Then-Deans Mark Yudof and Michael Sharlot and his colleagues made me very welcome, even though a Canadian philosopher must have been something of an oddity. I should especially thank David Anderson, Cindy Estlund, Dennis Patterson, David Rabban, and Charles Silver, all of whom were very willing to be patient with any question I might have had, however simple-minded.

The research grant led me to be able to work collaboratively with a fine set of research assistants at the University of Alberta. Guangwei Ouyang did a great deal of background research in the theory of organizations, and of corporate structure and personality. This work provided solid ground for the construction of much of Chapter 9. Dale Dewhurst also researched carefully the treatment of corporations by courts under the Canadian Charter of Rights and Freedoms, and that research also provided valuable background to Chapter 9. Chapter 14 is based on work done jointly with Matthew Stephens, and is in fact an extended and revised version of a paper co-authored with Matt, which was presented to the IVR World Congress at Bologna in 1995, and published in its proceedings; I am grateful for permission to use that material here.

Others who must be thanked for reading and commenting on drafts of chapters, in addition to people already mentioned, are Annalise Acorn, Joakim Nergelius, June Ross, and Carl Wellman. An anonymous reader for the Press was especially helpful as regards the chapter on European law. I am grateful to audiences at Okanagan University College, the University of Alberta, the University of Kansas, Massey University, the University of Victoria, and at meetings of the Western Canadian Philosophical Association, for their comments on versions of material in this book. I would also like to thank Faith Peyton of the Inter-Library Loan section of the North Campus library at Okanagan University College, for the efficiency and friendliness with which she has in the last two years put up with an endless stream of requests.

Much of this book is about the state of the law. To the best of my knowledge, the statements of the law are correct as at 31 December 2002.

Completion of this book was seriously delayed by the arrival into our family of Emma Mi Ann Shiner and Kira An Yang Shiner, and the sudden departure therefrom of the much-loved and lamented Dorothy Ann Birtles. I can only hope that Emma and Kira continue to be as impressed by Daddy's ability to write chapter books as they are now, and that they come to understand why Daddy's books have no pictures. Wherever Dorothy may be, I know she will be bursting with pride; it would be nice if she deserved so to be. My debt to my wife, Sharon Pfenning, is huge. Her support for this project has been unconditional. As important, her unphilosophical practicality has been a constant and valuable reminder of the real world outside the ivory tower, something which a person who aspires to write a work of applied ethics like this one deeply needs. And the last paragraph of the book was her idea too.

Kelowna, British Columbia

Contents

Table of Cases

Both Canadian and United States cases are Supreme Court cases unless otherwise indicated at the end of the citation.

1

Introduction

1 THE COMMERCIAL EXPRESSION DOCTRINE

Watching beer commercials on Canadian television is a strange experience. All manner of wonders pass before the eye (to sketch those appearing in the last few weeks alone)—beavers catching hunters in man-traps, mannequins attending rock concerts, grungily dressed youths making terrible puns, self-consciously inept attempts at putting ships into bottles, and of course the usual crowd of incredibly attractive and healthy-looking young people engaged in eco-friendly and energetic pursuits such as canoeing or swimming in mountain lakes, cycling, rock climbing, sitting round camp fires, and so forth. But rarely will you see a bottle or a can or a glass of beer itself. And never, never will you see any-one actually *drinking* beer. The reason is straightforward. The Canadian federal law, which regulates beer advertising, forbids the showing on television of per-sons drinking beer during the advertisement.

Such statutory regulation of advertising in broadcast and printed media is entirely common in western liberal democracies. Some examples of such regu-lation seem sensible, even obligatory, in a society with concern for the common good. It is quite appropriate (in my opinion, at any rate) that a proper regula-tory framework be created for advertising on television programmes aimed at children. Moreover, a central government which cares for the physical well-being of its citizens will quite appropriately regulate advertising of products with a potentiality for causing physical harm—tobacco, for example. Other examples of restrictions on advertising have been quite silly. Before they were struck down by the Supreme Court of Canada in *Rocket*,[1] the rules controlling the dental profession in Ontario forbad dentists to advertise even when their offices were open and what languages they spoke—in what is in its urban areas at least a thoroughly multicultural province.

The economic, or policy, or even ethical grounds for regulation of advertis-ing, at the level of general principles and of particular cases, however, are not the main focus of this book. This book is concerned specifically with what I shall call the *commercial expression doctrine* or the *commercial speech doctrine*.[2]

---

[1] *Royal College of Dental Surgeons of Ontario et al v Rocket et al* [Indexed as Rocket v Royal College of Dental Surgeons of Ontario] (1990) 71 DLR (4th) 68.

[2] A terminological note: the First Amendment to the U.S. Constitution talks of 'freedom of speech'. The Canadian Charter of Rights and Freedoms and the European Convention on Human Rights refer to 'freedom of expression'. As a Canadian with a U.K. publisher, I cast this book as far as possible in the 'expression' idiom. The use of the term 'expression' rather than 'speech' in the newer constitutional documents is not a coincidence: see Chapter 4.1, 7.4, 8 below.

This doctrine is the thesis that so-called commercial expression (commercial advertising, for example) deserves the same, or sufficiently similar, constitutional protection as any other form of constitutionally protected expression or speech, because it serves essentially the same purposes in essentially the same way.

The reasoning behind the doctrine may be sketched as follows. Advertising is brought about by the use of words and images. Advertising, in other words, is in a broad sense a case of expression or of speech. As such, advertising is the paradigm example of so-called *commercial expression* or *commercial speech*.[3] Freedom of expression or freedom of speech has for some considerable time been regarded in western liberal democratic thought as a fundamental value of the polity. Section 2(b) of the Canadian Charter of Rights and Freedoms, the First Amendment to the U.S. Constitution, Article 10 of the European Convention on Human Rights all give to freedom of expression some measure of constitutional protection: courts have the power to invalidate legislation either as such or as applied on the ground that it limits freedom of expression. Commercial expression so called is expression like any other. The right of beer manufacturers, therefore, for example, to say whatever they wish in advertising their product—a right infringed by the Canadian regulations alluded to above— is, according to the commercial expression doctrine, essentially no different from the right of artists to paint whatever picture they wish, of newspaper columnists to express whatever opinion they wish, and so on. There may be reasons in different cases for varying the burden placed on the state to justify regulation of different kinds of expression, or to deal differently with different contexts of regulation. But nonetheless freedom of commercial expression is a good like any other kind of freedom of expression, and merits constitutional protection as just such a good.

The aim of this book is to demonstrate that the commercial expression doctrine so understood is wholly indefensible. The extension of constitutional protection to so-called commercial expression was not an inevitable consequence of the case law which preceded it. The normative arguments offered to justify such an extension are unsound.

The argument that a certain activity should receive constitutional protection is, crudely speaking, an argument within normative political morality that the activity at issue is so important to human flourishing that not even a legitimate government should be allowed to restrict its pursuit. There is no justification within normative political morality for thinking that so-called commercial expression is such an activity. To put, for example, the peddling by a multi-billion dollar industry of a product known to cause a variety of illnesses and often death on a par with artistic creativity and political oratory is absurd.

Let me emphasize again that I am not discussing here the merits of this or that case of, for example, regulation of advertising as such. As I have noted, taken

---

[3] For more on the definition of commercial expression see Chapter 1.3 below.

piecemeal, some seem sensible, some seem silly. Taken apart from any issue of constitutional rights, and viewed solely by whatever standards are proper for judging government regulation of commercial activity, there is not going to be any general answer to whether commercial advertising or other so-called commercial expression should be regulated. Different regulations will have to be taken piecemeal, and many of them will involve enormously complex issues of empirical and normative truth. To what extent, for instance, restriction on tobacco advertising is a sensible way of responding to tobacco consumption seen as a public health problem is a very difficult policy matter. Legislatures hopefully are in a position to judge such things; I am not, even if (clearly) I Have Views. In rejecting the commercial expression doctrine, I am not to be taken to be approving thereby of every piece of government regulation of advertising that has ever been proposed.

Rather, I am concerned here with the commercial expression doctrine as an attempt to derail or divert government decision-making with constitutional side constraints. I am concerned with the thought that saying what one wishes in an advertisement, for example, is a *fundamental human right*—a right of free expression—or a matter of *fundamental human freedom or liberty*. These latter thoughts are the ones which seem to me mistaken. A government should not be called upon to defend its regulation of advertising in a court *of human rights*, however much and however appropriately it may be called upon to defend any such regulation in the court of policy think-tanks or political opinion.

I do not believe that such a project is as narrow or as technical as it might seem. Corporations wield an immense amount of political and economic power in the present world as it is. Individual governments are rendered by multinational corporations almost as helpless to make policy within their own borders as are the individual citizens to retain control of their own lives. It makes a bad situation worse to allow corporations to pre-empt and pervert for their own ends the sources of protection for personal autonomy at the heart of our political life as individual persons and as citizens. A work of jurisprudential theory such as this book does not have immediate practical and political implications. Nonetheless, the goal of preserving the integrity of fundamental human values in an increasingly corporate world is an important one. Behind the respect traditionally given in liberal democratic thought to freedom of expression as an ideal lies an attractive picture of human beings as autonomous choosers, and of human flourishing as relying on freely chosen sociality. The corporate domination of both the real market and the market-place of ideas defaces this attractive picture. The predatory attempt by corporations to appropriate the picture in order to justify constitutional protection for the contribution made by corporate expression to that domination needs to be exposed as the conceptual and normative fraud that it is. The extension of constitutional protection to corporations and corporate advertising through the commercial expression doctrine is a dilution of a fundamental human value. The task undertaken here of exposing the problems in the putative justifications for the doctrine is a significant one.

2 THE INTUITIVE OBJECTION TO THE DOCTRINE

It is not difficult to show how the hard questions of justification for the commercial expression doctrine arise. Traditional liberal theory identifies three grounds for the constitutional protection of expression. The Supreme Court of Canada has formally stated these for Canadian juridical purposes as:

1. Seeking and attaining the truth is an inherently good activity.
2. Participation in social and political decision-making is to be fostered and encouraged.
3. The diversity in forms of individual self-fulfillment and human flourishing ought to be cultivated in an essentially tolerant, indeed welcoming, environment.[4]

The wording is a variation on the well-known four-part analysis of the value of free expression by T. Emerson. The four 'values' that freedom of expression protects work as follows. Maintenance of a system of free expression is necessary (1) as assuring individual self-fulfilment, (2) as a means of attaining the truth, (3) as a method of securing participation by the members of the society in social, including political, decision-making, and (4) as maintaining the balance between stability and change in society.[5]

Each of the three grounds mentioned by the Supreme Court of Canada, it should be noted, bases constitutional protection of expression on some value of such protection to _the individual_. At first sight, however, constitutional protection for freedom of so-called _commercial_ expression protects the self-benefiting activities of organizations or of corporations, and not the self-benefiting activities of individuals. Moreover, such protection guards not the scientific, or artistic, or political activities of corporations, but aspects of their strictly commercial activities—that is, activities whose motivation is to improve the position of the organization or corporation in the real economic marketplace, not to seek truth, participate in political decision-making or cultivate diversity. The initial intuitive question therefore is fairly raised—if the point of constitutional protection for expression is to protect the truth-oriented, or political, or self-realizing activities of individuals, why are courts protecting aspects of the commercial activities of organizations and corporations? The question was pointedly raised by Rehnquist J (as he then was) in dissent in the U.S. Supreme Court case in which constitutional protection was first extended to so-called commercial speech, _Virginia Board_:[6]

---

[4] _Attorney-General of Quebec v Irwin Toy Ltd_ [Indexed as Irwin Toy Ltd v Quebec (Attorney-General)] (1989) 58 DLR (4th) 577, at 612.

[5] Thomas I. Emerson, 'Toward a General Theory of the First Amendment', _Yale Law Journal_ 72 (1963): 878–9. See also Robert J. Sharpe, 'Commercial Expression and the Charter', _University of Toronto Law Journal_ 37 (1987): 232.

[6] _Virginia State Board of Pharmacy et al v Virginia Citizens Consumer Council Inc et al_ 425 US 748 (1976).

The Court insists that the rule it lays down is consistent even with the view that the First Amendment is 'primarily an instrument to enlighten public decision-making in a democracy'. I had understood this view to relate to public decision-making as to political, social, and other public issues, rather than the decision of a particular individual as to whether to purchase one or another kind of shampoo. [at 787]

Of course, at this stage of my argument, I am opposing this roughly-hewn intuition against the commercial expression doctrine simply as a starting-point. The intuition needs much refinement. The arguments made on behalf of the commercial expression doctrine must be presented and analysed. All the same, by the end of this book I hope to have shown that the intuition is jurisprudentially sound, and deserves adoption in carrel, cafe, and court alike.

As noted above, however, the supporters of the commercial expression doctrine can offer an equally simple argument: advertising is expression; all expression should be constitutionally protected; so advertising should be constitutionally protected. We have the stage set, that is to say, for a classical philosophical conundrum—the radical opposition of two equally plausible pre-philosophical intuitions. The opposition is not superficial: it reaches back to fundamental issues in jurisprudence and political theory. The actual reasoning used on the bench and in the ivory tower by supporters of the commercial expression doctrine is rhetorically powerful, and claims the high moral ground of the best ideals of liberal democracy. To deconstruct the rhetoric, and display the inadequacy of the argumentation as putatively rational, is not a simple task. It will involve careful analysis of just exactly what steps the argument takes, and just exactly where it falters. The analysis that occupies the bulk of this book will be very detailed. But angels, not devils, lie in the details.

3 WHAT IS COMMERCIAL EXPRESSION?

I will shortly distinguish two ways in which the issue of the definition of commercial expression may be raised. But one important point must be made first. One central issue to be discussed[7] is whether to call advertising, for example, 'expression' in the first place begs relevant theoretical questions. In fact I do think it is question-begging. For this reason I have to this point always qualified my use of the term 'commercial expression' with 'so-called'. However, this practice rapidly becomes stylistically tedious and ugly, and I shall now cease to do so. But I ask the reader to bear in mind that I do think the use of the term is theoretically problematic, and to await patiently my explanation of why I think this. The fact that I will go along with current usage in order to be able to write this book at all should not be taken to imply that I think current usage is normatively justified.

---

[7] See Chapter 7.4, Chapter 8, below.

What, then, is current usage for 'commercial expression' or 'commercial speech'? I am going to discuss the matter in terms of 'definition', even though it is clear that the term 'commercial expression'/'commercial speech' inevitably has fuzzy edges and a penumbra of uncertainty to its application. I hope to show that a clear enough core notion can be identified to make the term tractable enough for the purposes of this book. There are two ways to approach the issue of definition. The first way is abstract: how should the term be defined for the purposes of a theoretical enquiry into the merits of a thesis concerning constitutional protection for freedom of commercial expression? The second way is concrete: how is the term defined in the jurisprudence of a particular court or jurisdiction? The two ways may or may not be related. Suppose that a particular court has struggled with the task of defining the term. It may have succeeded in finding a definition which meets its own institutional needs but does not meet the needs of the theoretician. Or it may have succeeded in finding a definition which both meets its own institutional needs and also is valuable to the theoretician. The two ways have to be distinguished, because a particular court may claim that its institutional needs are best met by not defining the term. It does not follow that the theoretician can do without a definition for the purpose of assessing the jurisprudential merits of decisions taken by that court.

I state the issue in the above elaborate way for an obvious reason. As I will indicate in Chapter 4, the Supreme Court of Canada has not felt the need to produce a definition of 'commercial expression', since it does not wish to be bound doctrinally to the creation of categories of expression. The European Court of Human Rights and the European Court of Justice have followed the same path. The U.S. Supreme Court, on the other hand, has approached freedom of expression jurisprudence in terms of identifying categories of speech, including the category of commercial speech. The present book requires that commercial expression doctrine can be identified in a way which permits the term 'commercial expression' to be meaningfully used for purposes of evaluating the commercial expression doctrine, even when talking about a Court that claims to have no special category of 'commercial expression'. As the Supreme Court of Canada said, '[w]hile the words "commercial expression" are a convenient reference to the kind of expression contemplated by the provisions in issue, they do not have any particular meaning or significance in Canadian law'.[8] So the term has to be defined abstractly in order to be such a 'convenient reference'. But it would be foolish not to make use of the ground gained by a Court which has over time set itself to lay out the boundaries of the notion.

As I shall show in Chapter 2, the U.S. Supreme Court took some time to zero in on the specific question of whether a form of speech that could be called 'pure commercial speech' was within the scope of the First Amendment. Several instances of what might have seemed intuitively to be 'commercial speech' were

---

[8] *Attorney-General of Quebec v La Chaussure Brown's Inc et al* [Indexed as Ford v Quebec (Attorney-General)] (1988) 54 DLR (4th) 577, at 610.

said not to be. The Court in *Virginia Board*[9] concluded that (i) speech is not 'commercial' merely because money is spent to project it; (ii) speech is not 'commercial' merely because it is carried in a form that is 'sold' for profit; (iii) speech is not 'commercial' merely because it may involve a solicitation to purchase or otherwise pay and contribute money. It is not until the later case of *Bolger*[10] that the Court discusses the concept of commercial speech in a positive way. The discussion is not concise. Its conclusions were concisely, and so conveniently, summarized in a later case thus:

The [U.S.] Supreme Court has identified three characteristics of commercial speech, while being careful to note that none is necessary or sufficient for speech to be classified as commercial. According to the Court, speech that is *concededly* an advertisement, refers to a specific product, and is motivated by economic interest may properly be characterized as commercial speech.[11]

In addition to this characterization, the U.S. Supreme Court often picks up on a phrase first used in *Pittsburgh Press*,[12] speech that does 'no more than propose a commercial transaction', a way of thinking about commercial expression which culminates in the famous paradigm of 'I will sell you the X prescription drug at the Y price' in *Virginia Board* (at 761).

It is a common-place among commentators that the characterization 'does no more than propose a commercial transaction' raises questions. Often, there is no 'reference to a specific product' which is offered at a specific price in what otherwise seems clearly commercial expression—in generic advertising, for example, such as that for agricultural produce at stake in *Wileman*.[13] The claim that California summer fruits are wholesome and delicious does not offer a specific product for sale at a specific price, although it would surely be commercial expression. Moreover, the kind of commercial expression being assumed as a paradigm features prominently the role of such expression as a carrier of information. That is hardly surprising, as many of the arguments used to defend the commercial expression doctrine rely on this function of commercial expression. This will be evident from the discussion of the case law in Chapters 2–5. The strength of such information-based arguments will be assessed later: see Chapter 13. But many kinds of commercial expression do not in any obvious sense convey information: see Chapter 14.

Whatever the difficulties are in theory of characterizing commercial expression accurately, a look at the actual decided cases as discussed in Chapters 2–5 reveals that courts do not seem to have found the difficulties insoluble in practice. Of all the cases heard in the U.S. Supreme Court, only one does not concern

---

[9] At 761: for more detail see Chapter 2.4 below.

[10] *Bolger v Youngs Drug Products Corp* 463 US 60 (1983).

[11] *Securities and Exchange Commission v Wall Street Publishing Institute Inc dba Stock Market Magazine* 851 F 2d 365 (USCA DC Cir 1988), at 372; original emphasis.

[12] *Pittsburgh Press Company v Pittsburgh Commission on Human Relations et al* 413 US 376 (1973), at 385.

[13] *Glickman v Wileman Brothers and Elliott Inc et al* 117 SCt 2130 (1997), at 2135.

directly advertising, promoting or soliciting for business: that is the *Coors* case,[14] which concerns product labelling, and that is not so far from product advertising. The Supreme Court of Canada and the European Court of Human Rights have been somewhat more accommodating. Although still the vast majority of cases concern advertising, the Supreme Court of Canada has also considered letters of reference, product colouring and 'counter-advertising' posters as commercial expression. The European Court of Human Rights has contemplated requests for consumer feedback and magazine articles on product safety as putative commercial expression.

This analysis suggests that the idea of 'doing no more than proposing a commercial transaction' is at the heart of the concept of commercial expression.[15] If that phrase is taken narrowly to refer only to examples like 'I will sell you product X at price Y', then it will be hard to fit much advertising and expression that solicits the purchase of goods or services into the characterization. The practice of the courts, rather, seems to be to interpret the phrase widely as including cases which are clearly advertising or solicitation, but are psychologically more complicated than the simple case of informational advertising. I would hazard a guess that it is in the regulation by government of advertising and solicitation that by far the greatest danger lies to the economic interests of those regulated. Hence such cases are prominent in the jurisprudence of commercial expression.

Most of the subsequent discussion in this book will focus, therefore, on cases of government regulation of advertising and selling/solicitation. The reason for that is not the tidy one that we have been able to find a strictly valid definition of 'commercial expression', which demarcates cleanly just this range of cases. The reason is rather the untidy, if pragmatic, one that this range of cases is where the action has been in the courts. Expressing plaintiffs, regulating governments, and adjudicating courts alike have in practice seen this range of cases as those raising most sharply the plausibility and applicability of the commercial expression doctrine. I am in no position to disagree.

4 The roads not travelled

As I will bring out in this Chapter 1.5 and 1.6, the project of this book is tightly focussed. It is focussed on one particular way of handling the issue of the normative status of the commercial expression doctrine. I am not at all supposing that my way is the only way; it is not. But it is an important way. It also must not be confused with other legitimate approaches to the issue. Furthermore, my aim in the argument that follows is to be primarily positive, not negative. That is to say, I want to focus on defending my own view, rather than criticizing the

---

[14] *Rubin v Coors Brewing Company* 115 SCt 1585 (1995).
[15] Cf. Nat Stern, 'In Defense of the Imprecise Definition of Commercial Speech', *Maryland Law Review* 58 (1999): 89–109.

views of others. True—I will criticize arguments made in the courts, and to some extent in the academic literature. But I am not going to spend time defending my approach against others, and I cannot spend time anticipating and rebutting every objection that could be or has been brought against the general line that I take. In order to prepare the way for the exposition of the way that I shall follow, I want to spend this section in briefly outlining other possible approaches to the commercial expression doctrine, which I shall neither take nor directly confront in this book.

The Libertarian View. From the libertarian political perspective, all regulation by government of anything is at least presumptively and in all likelihood actually unacceptable from the point of view of political morality. In the area of commercial expression, the view makes its appearance in believing that the government has the same deep obligation not to be involved in the expressive aspects of social life as it has not to be involved in the economic aspects. Economic markets should be free from all forms of government regulation in the name of maximizing social good, and so should all exchange of expression. Concretely, in the area of freedom of commercial expression, the view appears as the claim that commercial expression should receive exactly the same high level of protection as political and other forms of fully protected expression. Corporations are seen as the main agents of citizen welfare in a free enterprise economic system, and corporate expression deserves the same freedom from government interference as does other corporate wealth-producing activity. The view has received its fullest and most sophisticated defence to date in Martin Redish's recent book *Money Talks*.[16] The gulf between one who thinks that governments are presumptively illegitimate and one who is willing in principle to listen to the claims of government to justify its action is a wide one, and is not going to be bridged in this book by a general argument about fundamental political values. Given specific arguments against specific cases of government regulation of commercial expression are a different matter, and some of those will appear in this book. But I am not here going to attempt to show *a priori* that libertarianism about freedom of commercial expression is wrong.

A variation on the idea that governments should not regulate commercial expression because they should not regulate anything is the idea that commercial expression should be constitutionally protected because commercial expression is really political expression. All advertising is a contribution to political debate, and should be protected as such. When governments regulate advertising, they are stifling, or biassing, political debate. To tell a tobacco manufacturer what it can and cannot say in an advertisement for its products is as bad as requiring citizens to vote for no other political party than that of the rulers,

---

[16] Martin Redish, *Money Talks: Speech, Economic Power, and the Values of Democracy* (New York: New York University Press, 2001). Other versions of the view may be found in Aaron Director, 'The Parity of the Economic Market Place', *Journal of Law and Economics* 7 (1964): 1–10; R.H. Coase, 'Advertising and Free Speech', *Journal of Legal Studies* 6 (1977): 1–34; Richard A. Epstein, 'Property, Speech, and the Politics of Distrust', *University of Chicago Law Review* 59 (1992): 41–89.

and controlling news media so that they broadcast only what the government wants the citizens to hear. Redish and others defend at length such an approach to regulation of tobacco advertising.[17] The government's 'suppression' of advertising is as much of an unconstitutional sponsorship of one side of a public debate as would be the government's 'seeking to maintain itself in power by stifling political opposition'.[18] Regulation of truthful advertising 'inescapably amounts to governmental censorship and the imposition of mind control'.[19] Scott Joachim speaks approvingly of tobacco advertising as a 'political crusade'.[20] Jef Richards goes so far as to make the government responsible for turning tobacco advertising into political speech, because the government, by regulating tobacco advertising, made the matter a topic of political debate.[21] Others have similarly questioned the appropriateness of any distinction between commercial and political expression.[22]

Stern, properly in my view, characterizes such an approach as 'the Romantic Fallacy', the mistaken belief that 'any ostensibly commercial advertisement carries deeper overtones'. Such a line of reasoning, he says, 'proves too much':

> It converts the unexceptionable observation that at least some noncommercial message can be teased out of all commercial speech into an instrument for prying lofty but contrived commentary out of any advertisement.[23]

Over-interpretations are over-interpretations, whether they are of advertisements or more literary forms of discourse.

The Anti-Corporate View. The complement to the pro-corporate libertarian view is the anti-corporate view from, broadly speaking, the political left. In this view, the modern business corporation is not an instrument of great social benefit and wealth. Rather, it is an instrument of social evil and disaster. Corporations corrupt democracy, manipulate the worker and the citizen, and function only to line the pockets of the rich from the exploitation of the poor. Corporate advertising plays an essential role in the creation and maintenance of corporate power. Government intervention in the form of regulation of corporate advertising therefore has an essential role to play in curbing the power of corporations. George Wright has recently made an argument of this style at

---

[17] Martin H. Redish, 'Tobacco Advertising and the First Amendment', *Iowa Law Review* 81 (1996): 589–639. Redish acknowledges that this article was supported by a research grant from a tobacco manufacturer (at 589).

[18] Ibid., 606–7.   [19] Ibid., 610.

[20] Scott Joachim, 'Seeing Beyond the Smoke and Mirrors: A Proposal for the Abandonment of the Commercial Speech Doctrine and an Analysis of Recent Tobacco Advertising Regulations', *Hastings Communications and Entertainment Law Journal* 19 (1997): 544.

[21] Jef I. Richards, 'Politicizing Cigarette Advertising', *Catholic University Law Review* 45 (1996): 1147–212.

[22] Alex Kozinski and Stuart Banner, 'Who's Afraid of Commercial Speech?', *Virginia Law Review* 76 (1990): 627–53; Kenton F. Machina, 'Freedom of Expression in Commerce', *Law and Philosophy* 3 (1994): 375–406; David F. McGowan, 'A Critical Analysis of Commercial Speech', *California Law Review* 78 (1990): 359–448.

[23] Stern, 'In Defense of the Imprecise Definition of Commercial Speech', 133–4.

length.[24] Other ringing declarations may be found elsewhere.[25] The difficulty with the anti-corporate view is ultimately of a piece with that of the libertarian view, for the purposes of my project here. In neither case are the rights and wrongs of the commercial expression doctrine as such at issue. Government regulation of commercial expression simply becomes yet another battle-ground in the great and never-ending war between the political right and the political left. The debate is a matter of the exchange of grand and familiar rhetoric and slogans, and not the examination of the justification for the commercial expression doctrine itself. My project here aims to be much more, and more suitably I believe, nuanced than that.

The Determinist View. I mean by this view the thought that the development of commercial speech doctrine is just the playing out of deep twentieth-century cultural forces. Edward White has recently defended a complex and sophisticated account of the development of First Amendment jurisprudence in the U.S., including the jurisprudence of commercial speech as a special case.[26] White takes as a central theme the commitment of twentieth-century First Amendment jurisprudence to what he calls 'the bifurcated review project', the thought that constitutional challenges to economic activity receive a lower level of judicial scrutiny than constitutional challenges to legislative infringements of non-economic rights (at 301–2). White associates the progress of the bifurcated review project with the rise in the twentieth century of modernism. Modernism is associated with rationalist approaches to public decision-making, approaches that are deferential to government economic regulation. But modernism is also associated with a deep commitment to human freedom, an approach that leads to careful protection of such a freedom in areas like political or artistic expression. The cultural innovation of constitutional protection for commercial speech represents a 'severance of the concept of freedom from democratic theory' (at 369). The commercial speech doctrine exploits the self-realization value in order to claim for an economic right the privileged position of rights associated with democratic freedom. White says of *Virginia Board*, however:

The Court, straining to demonstrate that the regulation affected 'public decision-making in a democracy', suggested that because information about the price of drugs might enhance the individual economic choices of consumers, that information would necessarily also enhance the collective political choices of communications who would then

---

[24] R. George Wright, *Selling Words: Free Speech in a Commercial Culture* (New York: New York University Press, 1997).

[25] Allan C. Hutchinson, 'Money Talk: Against Constitutionalizing (Commercial) Speech', *Canadian Business Law Journal* 17 (1990): 2–34; M. David Lepofsky, 'The Supreme Court's Approach to Freedom of Expression—*Irwin Toy v Quebec (Attorney General)*—and the Illusion of Section 2(b) Liberalism', *National Journal of Constitutional Law* 3 (1993): 37–98; Ronald K.L. Collins and David M. Stover, 'Commerce and Communication', *Texas Law Review* 71 (1993): 697–746; Mark V. Tushnet, 'Corporations and Free Speech', in David Kairys (ed.), *The Politics of Law: A Progressive Critique* (New York: Pantheon Books, 1982), 253–61.

[26] G. Edward White, 'The First Amendment Comes of Age: The Emergence of Free Speech in Twentieth-Century America', *Michigan Law Review* 95 (1996): 299–392. The summary here has all the defects (but hopefully at least some of the virtues) of the short version of a long argument.

have an enhanced basis for evaluating policies directed towards deregulation of the pharmaceutical industry. But one just as well could have argued that by electing representatives who chose to regulate commercial speech for the protection of consumers, individual citizens had already signaled their political choices. [at 370–1]

I am not going to discuss further White's analysis, except incidentally, although there is much to admire in it. His focus is that of the historian, albeit the historian of ideas, and of legal ideas. My focus is that of the philosopher. My occupational concern is with argument and justification, not with historical explanation. My enquiry is into whether the commercial expression doctrine can be defended by sound jurisprudential argument, rather than with whether the doctrine represents an explanatorily coherent evolution of the seminal intellectual themes of the twentieth century.

The Communication Theory. Some theorists hold that valuing freedom of expression is a way in the end of valuing communication. Communication is of prime importance to human beings, both collectively and individually. Freedom of expression as a value protects communication. Communication as a central concept in political theory is associated primarily with the work of Jürgen Habermas. As Lawrence Solum rightly points out, the literature there is huge—both the primary literature of Habermas' own work, and especially the secondary literature in interpretation and debate of it.[27] 'The theory of communicative action is rich with implications for interpretation of the freedom of speech.'[28] The key distinction seems to be that between 'communicative' and 'strategic' action. 'If the participants adopt the attitude that they will attempt to achieve success without the rational agreement of those persons whose actions they seek to influence, then they are engaged in strategic action. If they are oriented to reaching understanding, they are engaged in communicative action.'[29] Commercial advertising is most plausibly construed as 'strategic', not 'communicative'. If Solum is correct that 'the distinction between communicative and strategic action grounds the line between protected and unprotected speech',[30] then Habermas' theory repudiates the commercial expression doctrine.

The fullest explicit development of a communication theory of freedom of expression is by Richard Moon.[31] Communication properly understood is something which is essentially social, relational, interactive, dialogic, participatory, equal. Communication connotes much more than one speaker, one listener, and comprehension. Moon takes a strong position on the essentially

---

[27] Lawrence B. Solum, 'Freedom of Communicative Action: A Theory of the First Amendment Freedom of Speech', *Northwestern University Law Review* 83 (1989): 86.

[28] Ibid., 106. See also R. Randall Rainey and William Rehg, 'The Marketplace of Ideas, the Public Interest, and Federal Regulation of the Electronic Media: Implications of Habermas' Theory of Democracy', *Southern California Law Review* 69 (1996): 1923–87.

[29] Solum, 'Freedom of Communicative Action', 91.   [30] Ibid., 134.

[31] Richard Moon, *The Constitutional Protection of Freedom of Expression* (Toronto: University of Toronto Press, 2000).

social character of language and meaning: 'In expressing him/herself to others, a speaker employs a language that is created and shaped in discourse. In an important sense, language precedes the individual user. It is produced intersub-jectively. . . . The creation of meaning is a shared process, something that takes place between speaker and listener. A speaker does not simply convey a mean-ing that is passively received by an audience. Understanding is an active, creative process in which listeners take hold of, and work over, the symbolic material they receive' (at 21, 23). The three traditional ends promoted by freedom of expression—the search for truth, participation in the political process, and indi-vidual self-fulfilment and self-realization—can be served only if expression is conceived of as 'communicative' in Moon's thick sense. The utility of truth is not to the individual, but to the community, and the search for and attainment of truth is not private, but communal and participatory (at 12). Free expression as an essential part of the search for truth implicates communication. Democracy is not a matter of merely aggregating individual preference rank-ings; it has to do with public discourse. 'Democracy requires that public action be founded upon a public opinion formed through open and interactive processes of rational deliberation.' Democracy is inherently communicative. Finally, 'the value we attach to freedom of expression makes sense only if we recognize that the creation of meaning (the articulation of ideas and feelings) is a social process, something that takes place between individuals and within a community. Freedom of expression is central to self-realization and autonomy because individual identity, thought and feeling emerge in the social realm' (at 21).

Moon is not shy of emphasizing one extremely important consequence of the cogency of the communication theory of freedom of expression. If what matters is communication understood in this thick sense, then constitutional protection for freedom of expression must include, wherever it is appropriate, action, whether civic, judicial, or legislative, to protect communicative opportunities for all. That means taking a stand against creating and protecting concentra-tions of economic communicative power, and that in turn implicates questions of redistribution of wealth. It is not hard therefore for Moon to argue against the extension of constitutional protection to commercial expression, as he does in his Chapter 3. The root problem is 'the near-complete commercialization of culture' (at 79). 'The underlying message of advertising, that self-realization is achieved through consumption, is an almost unchallengeable cultural assump-tion' (at 81). The significant challenge to our commitment to freedom of expres-sion comes from systemic features of public discourse, such as commercial domination (at 82–3). Advertising is part of a system of public discourse that is one-sided or one-directional in character. The advertisement comes to the indi-vidual not as a part of an active dialogue or exchange with the advertiser. The structure of public discourse means that the audience has no real opportunity to respond to the advertisement, except to tune out or to decline to make a pur-chase (at 94). In short, the communicative function of expression which freedom of expression as a value protects cannot be found in the discourse of commercial advertising, dominated as it is by the interests of the corporate expressers. Commercial expression is exactly not the form of discourse which the value of freedom of expression is there to protect.

Again, although there is much for one taking my view of the commercial expression doctrine to admire in Moon's position, I shall not consider it except incidentally in what follows. The reason is that Moon's view is based on a premise which is the opposite of one of mine. As I shall indicate in Chapter 1.5, I am willing to repudiate the commercial expression doctrine while leaving in place one standard assumption of liberal democratic thought, that the 'freedom' in 'freedom of expression' is, in Isaiah Berlin's famous terminology, a 'negative', not a positive freedom.[32] Moon thinks that freedom of expression cannot be understood as the value it is unless the assumption of negative liberty is rejected (at 3, 7). Even Habermas' view emphasizes the value of the end-state of actual communication over the process value of free individual participation. It is not that there have not been periods in the history of constitutional protection for freedom of expression when that freedom has been interpreted more 'positively' than 'negatively': see for example the discussion of the *Red Lion*[33] case below, in Chapter 10.8. But I believe it is more important to undermine the commercial expression doctrine from within, by showing that its soundness does not follow even from normative premises, which the doctrine itself officially accepts.

The Liberty Theory. One of the best-known modern theories of freedom of speech is the so-called Liberty Theory defended by Edwin Baker.[34] Baker claims that the First Amendment protects 'a broad realm of nonviolent, non-coercive, expressive activity', the realm of liberty (at 47). He argues that the justification for valuing freedom of expression does not end at the traditional values thought immediately to underlie it. Rather, those values are an intermediate stage of justification; they have value because they serve to protect the realm of liberty. The separation of liberty from the traditional values is crucial to the account subtended by the Liberty Theory of commercial speech.[35] Baker is willing to accept that freedom of commercial speech can serve those values in principle as well as freedom of any other kind of speech. So, if serving those values were all that mattered, there would be no objection in principle to constitutional protection for freedom of commercial speech. Since Baker opposes freedom of commercial speech, then, the ground for such opposition must lie elsewhere. It lies in the fact that commercial speech is a part of the economic marketplace, and Baker's view is that this marketplace is inimical to liberty. His argument, briefly, is that market behaviour, and *a fortiori* speech in the market, is unfree because it is

---

[32] Isaiah Berlin, *Four Essays on Liberty* (Oxford: Clarendon Press, 1969), 121 ff.

[33] *Red Lion Broadcasting Co v FCC* 395 US 367 (1969).

[34] C. Edwin Baker, *Human Liberty and Freedom of Speech* (New York: Oxford University Press, 1989).

[35] Ibid., Chapter 9.

determined by the demands of the market. The standards for market behaviour are 'externally imposed' (at 201) on market actors. There is no 'freedom' in the market; there is only the inevitability of subjecting one's will to market-based constraints.

Baker first published a version of this view at the time of the crucial decision in *Virginia Board*, and has fine-tuned rather than radically revised it since. It seemed to critics then,[36] and it seems to me now, that the view depends on taking an unappealing view of what counts as a determined decision. It is true that, if the position of a participant in the economic market is regarded as ineluctably profit-seeking, then principles of economic rationality determine the correct decision. The decision-maker does not, except contingently in the case of indifference curves, have a choice as to the rational decision. But no more does the logical decision-maker when confronted with a problem of whether a theorem is validly derivable within a system. We do not feel that the force of the logical 'must' removes the logician's freedom and autonomy. Why then should things be any different in the case of economic rationality? I will have occasions more than once in what follows to draw on Baker's ideas about freedom of commercial expression taken piecemeal. My doubts here are only about the fundamental assumptions of the Liberty Theory.

Rational Reconstruction. By theories of this kind I mean those which take a particular institutional context and history as a given, and seek to find a theory which best explains that history, given certain assumptions about the values underlying the history. Much, and perhaps most, academic commentary on Supreme Court decision-making takes this form, often resulting in the critical view that no such reconstruction is possible. As long as the institutional doctrine is in flux, rational reconstructions are condemned to short lives and obsolescence. But once a doctrine appears to have reached a point of stability, then it is worthwhile to undertake such a task of assessment and review. With respect to the doctrine of freedom of commercial speech as applied by the U.S. Supreme Court, that point seems currently to have been reached. Apart from *Wileman*,[37] the decisions from the mid-1990s onwards have seen little variation in doctrine, but have more been a matter of applying a standard doctrine to different actual regulations. Commercial speech as a category is granted constitutional protection, but a lower level of protection. Commercial speech occupies a middle position between, for example, political speech as fully protected and, for example, obscenity as not protected at all.

But now the rational reconstructer faces a difficulty—how to explain this middle position. If commercial speech serves the same values as other forms of speech, why is it not given the same level of protection? If it does not serve these

---

[36] Steven Shiffrin, 'The First Amendment and Economic Regulation: Away from a General Theory of the First Amendment', *Northwestern University Law Review* 78 (1983): 1243–4; Martin H. Redish, 'Self-Realization, Democracy, and Freedom of Expression: A Reply to Professor Baker', *University of Pennsylvania Law Review* 130 (1982): 686–7.

[37] See Chapter 3.6 below.

values, why is it protected at all? An important attempt to provide a rational reconstruction of the U.S. Supreme Court's current jurisprudence on commercial speech has been recently made by Robert Post.[38] Post argues that commercial speech can be seen as 'the set of communicative acts about commercial subjects that within a public communicative sphere convey information of relevance to democratic decision-making but that do not themselves form part of public discourse'.[39] Because commercial speech is not part of public discourse, it is not entitled to the full level of protection accorded to political speech. But because it 'conveys information of relevance to democratic decision-making', it merits some level of protection. In the remainder of his article, he applies this formula to the details of the U.S. Supreme Court commercial speech doctrine as evidenced in the series of holdings in the last few years.

My purpose here is not to debate the merits of Post's or anyone else's rational reconstruction of the jurisprudence of the U.S. Supreme Court or any other court. Such reconstructions, whatever their merits as reconstructions, must in the nature of the case beg the theoretical questions which interest me here. Institutional history, if it is taken as a given, constrains the theoretical enquiry. My enquiry is not so much how to make the institutional history we have the best it can be. My enquiry is more like what would be the best institutional history to have from the point of view of normative political morality? The matter of any actual institutional history, whether rationally reconstructed or not, conforming to such an ideal is a different issue.

The above brief survey does not do justice to the amount of theoretical commentary on the commercial expression doctrine, although I do believe it covers the main variants. As I will go on to explain below, I exercise an author's right to choose the premises of his or her own discussion. Such an exercise, of course, carries the risk that the resulting enquiry courts irrelevance, but I have confidence that in the case of this book the risk is negligible.

5 Negative liberty and the traditional values

The main reason I choose not to travel any of the roads mentioned in the previous section has ultimately to do with argumentative strategy. Suppose that, in mounting an argument against a certain thesis—the commercial expression doctrine, for example—a person makes use of premises that supporters of the thesis are wont to reject. Then it does not really matter whether the argument deploying those theses is valid, or even sound. The immediate response will be that the critique is making assumptions that the thesis being criticized does not

---

[38] Robert Post, 'The Constitutional Status of Commercial Speech', *UCLA Law Review* 48 (2000): 1–57; see also Robert Post, 'Reconciling Theory and Doctrine in First Amendment Jurisprudence', in Lee C. Bollinger and Geoffrey R. Stone (eds.), *Eternally Vigilant: Free Speech in the Modern Era* (Chicago: University of Chicago Press, 2002), 170–2.

[39] Post, 'Constitutional Status', 45–57.

make. The only way to avoid this difficulty is not to make such assumptions—to found the critique, that is to say, on assumptions that the thesis or doctrine being criticized manifestly accepts. If this methodological strategy is sound, then what might seem some of the more attractive bases for attacking the commercial expression doctrine—that freedom of expression is valuable because it fosters communication, and commercial expression does not foster communication, for example; or that the capitalist commodification of social life is to be deplored—are thereby ruled out. It would be easy, for example, for defenders of the commercial expression doctrine to dismiss criticisms of the doctrine which assumed that hearers' rights to receive information legitimated extensive control of broadcasting and print media, in order to guarantee the availability of necessary information.[40] It would be claimed that such a view interprets freedom in a different way from the commercial expression doctrine, and so does not meet its challenge to government regulation of corporate expression.

The argument I shall make in this book, therefore, begins from two premises that are fundamental to the commercial expression doctrine itself. The first is that the kind of freedom which freedom of expression, and *a fortiori* freedom of commercial expression, involves is so-called 'negative freedom', not so-called 'positive freedom'. As Berlin elucidates negative freedom or liberty, 'I am normally said to be free to the degree to which no man or body of men interferes with my activity. Political liberty in this sense is simply the area within which a man can act unobstructed by others.' Positive freedom, by contrast, has to do with 'the source of control or interference that can determine someone to do, or be, this rather than that'.[41] Famously, Berlin goes on (at 133 ff) to argue that positive freedom is compatible with a very narrow area of negative freedom, and considerable government interference with social and private life. As Gerald MacCallum has plausibly argued, these two are not so much two systematically different kinds of freedom as two different ways of instantiating the general formula that 'x is (is not) free from y to do (not do, become, not become) z'.[42] The philosophical disagreements are better seen as turning on the proper range of the different variables in the formula—does x range over only natural persons; does y range over only the actions, rules, or institutions of natural persons? Does z range over actions, or characters as well as actions? In MacCallum's view, we do not have any grip on the idea of types of freedom independently of the answer to these questions of range.

Freedom of expression, or freedom of speech, is very plausibly seen as the friends of so-called 'negative liberty' will see it—a freedom from restrictions imposed by governments to express or speak, or not, as and how one wishes. We shall see that many of the crucial issues raised by the commercial expression

---

[40] See Chapter 10.5 and 10.7 below. [41] Berlin, *Four Essays*, 122.
[42] Gerald C. MacCallum Jr, *Legislative Intent and Other Essays on Law, Politics, and Morality*, edited by Marcus G. Singer and Rex Martin (Madison, Wis.: University of Wisconsin Press, 1993), 87, 91 ff.

doctrine fit MacCallum's profile of the proper range of the variables. Can the value for '*x*' be a corporation, as opposed to a natural person? (See Chapter 9 below.) Can the value for '*y*' be a restriction imposed by a corporation as well as by a government? (This question we shall not address, as a limitation imposed by the strategy of meeting the commercial expression doctrine on its own turf.) Can the value for '*z*' include the receiving, as well as the imparting, of expression, or speech, or information? (See Chapters 10 and 13 below.)

Questions of that sort, to turn to the second issue for this section, cannot be answered in a vacuum. Nothing in the concept of freedom or liberty as such determines the answer; here, MacCallum's reorientation of the issue is significant. Theories of freedom of expression determine the answer—not analytical theories, but normative theories, theories, that is, of the value that freedom of expression has and why it has it. As I indicated in Chapter 1.2 above, constitutional protection for commercial expression has largely been defended on very traditional grounds. Freedom of commercial expression, or so it is argued, is valuable because it promotes some or all of the search for truth, democratic self-government, and individual self-realization and self-fulfilment. I am willing to evaluate the commercial expression doctrine in those terms. My argument is not that freedom of commercial expression incorporates or brings about some social or individual disvalue, which outweighs any good it might do by promoting the values mentioned. My argument is simply that the commercial expression doctrine is mistaken; freedom of commercial expression does not promote the ends which make freedom of expression valuable. It has no claim on our attention for that reason.

The shape of my project, in short, at the most general level is this. Let us assume that the kind of freedom involved in freedom of expression is so-called negative freedom, or, if you prefer, that the range of the values in the MacCallum formula is pretty much that which would be chosen by theorists who are friends of so-called negative freedom. Let us further assume that freedom of expression is valuable because it promotes some or all of the search for truth, democratic self-government, and individual self-realization and self-fulfilment. The commercial expression doctrine is a mistake, because freedom of *commercial* expression, even assuming that it is a form of negative freedom, does not promote those values. If sound, this argument does not of course show that freedom of commercial expression is unjustifiable on every possible ground. It shows only that it cannot be justified on those grounds to which its supporters have traditionally appealed. But that is an important result, for its supporters do believe that it is justified on those grounds.

Even so construed, there are two further distinguishable ways of interpreting the project of normative theory undertaken here. The political theorist John Rawls proposed as a methodology for normative theorizing what he called 'reflective equilibrium'. He wrote that in the process of balancing considered judgments against principles 'we work from both ends'. When there are discrepancies between our judgements of principle and our considered particular convictions 'we have a choice. We can either modify the account of the initial situation or we can revise our existing judgments.' By 'going back and forth' in this way we arrive at a 'reflective equilibrium' in which our principles 'match our considered judgments duly pruned and adjusted'.[43] Theoretically, either may give way in the search for reflective equilibrium. Later, the state of having arrived at a theory of justice is said to be 'one reached after a person has weighed various proposed conceptions and he has either revised his judgments to accord with one of them or held fast to his initial convictions (and the corresponding conception)'.[44]

Ronald Dworkin in a review of *A Theory of Justice* observed that 'we have a choice between two general models that define [such] coherence and explain why it is required'. One of these he calls a 'natural' model, and the other a 'constructive' model. On the natural model, the significance of coherence in a normative theory is instrumental. Such a theory, according to this model, putatively describes an objective normative reality. The theory is related to particular intuitions of this reality as a physical theory is related to observation statements. 'Moral reasoning or philosophy is a process of reconstructing the fundamental principles by assembling concrete judgments in the right order, as a natural historian reconstructs the shape of the whole animal from the fragments of its bones that he has found.' The 'constructive' model, on the other hand, 'treats intuitions of justice not as clues to the existence of independent principles, but rather as stipulated features of a general theory to be constructed as if a sculptor set himself to carve the animal that best fits a pile of bones he happened to find together . . . It does not assume that the animal it matches to the bones actually exists'.[45]

Dworkin's distinction may be applied to the present project. How should we take my claim that the derivation of the commercial expression doctrine from the combination of negative freedom and the traditional triad of values justifying freedom of expression does not succeed? Should we take it 'constructively'— that is, should we say simply that we do not as yet here have an equilibrium between the commercial expression doctrine and the principles? Or should we take it 'naturally'—that is, that the principles are part of a genuine normative reality, and the incompatibility of the commercial expression doctrine with them is a sign that the doctrine is not part of any normative reality at all? I myself believe that the natural model is appropriate. But that is a decision I can take only for myself. Even if others prefer to take the argument of this book constructively, still the argument is important.

[43] John Rawls, *A Theory of Justice* (Cambridge, Mass.: Harvard University Press, 1971), 20.
[44] Ibid., 48.
[45] Ronald M. Dworkin, *Taking Rights Seriously* (2nd edn., Cambridge, Mass.: Harvard University Press, 1978), 160–1.

6 THE PROJECT OUTLINED

In detail, then, here is the way that the project of dismantling the justification for the commercial expression doctrine will proceed. In order to set the scene for the more theoretical arguments of the main body of the book, in *Part I* I will examine in more detail the institutional history behind the commercial expression doctrine in the United States, Canada, and Europe. *Chapter 2* will deal with the case law in the U.S. up to and including *Virginia Board*, and *Chapter 3* will cover the case law in the U.S. after *Virginia Board* to the present. *Chapter 4* will discuss the case law in Canada, and *Chapter 5* the case law in Europe. Apart from the obvious purpose of acquainting readers with the case law, the discussion will serve two further purposes. It will provide some introduction to the issues of normative justification on which the remainder of the book will focus. It will also reveal that the institutional history of the commercial expression doctrine is full of historical accidents and contingencies. It does not in any way represent a working out of some 'inner logic'[46] or 'inner morality'[47] of that history. In *Chapter 6*, I will briefly summarize and comment on eight different arguments for the commercial expression doctrine that can be found in the case law. I will identify those arguments that have been the most prevalent in judicial opinions and theoretical commentaries alike, and point the way to the places where these arguments will be more fully examined.

Part II will achieve two things. In *Chapter 7*, I will elucidate the basic theoretical assumptions I am making and concepts I am deploying in this book. The first three sections of the chapter will deal with aspects of the analysis of the concept of a right. The remaining section considers the form a justification for a doctrine of free expression will have to take. My claim is that the justification must be 'top-down', from principles concerning the normative value of freedom of expression to a conclusion that this or that form of expression is one that should be free, should be the subject of a negative freedom from government restriction, for example. *Chapter 8* will pursue this general methodological claim further, by examining some controversial examples of the intrusion of freedom of expression principles into adjudication of a 'commercial' matter.

Part III then focusses on the actual arguments that courts and commentators have appealed to to justify the commercial expression doctrine. The arguments in various ways presume the classic liberal model of a human right as belonging intrinsically to the autonomous human person. *Chapter 9* looks at the issue of whether a corporation may be held to be an autonomous person of the relevant kind. I will show that there are severe obstacles to any such claim. Many defenders of the commercial expression doctrine will not disagree. The predominant

---

[46] The phrase is Joseph Raz's: see Joseph Raz, *Ethics in the Public Domain: Essays in the Morality of Law and Politics* (Oxford: Clarendon Press, 1994), Chapter 11.

[47] The phrase is Lon Fuller's: Lon L. Fuller, *The Morality of Law* (2nd edn., New Haven, Conn.: Yale University Press, 1964), 42.

way to root constitutional protection for freedom of commercial expression in some right of an autonomous person is by appealing to a supposed right to hear or receive information. The next three chapters explore different ramifications of this thought. *Chapter 10* considers the very idea of hearers' rights to receive information, and how far the plausible cases of such rights are available to support the commercial expression doctrine. My conclusion is not very far, if at all. *Chapter 11* looks at the claim that freedom of commercial expression merits constitutional protection because it promotes the freedom of expression value of self-realization and self-fulfilment. My conclusion is that it does not. *Chapter 12* examines the claim made by supporters of the commercial expression doctrine that government regulation of commercial expression is inherently paternalistic, and so objectionable on such grounds. Again, I show that the claim has no force.

The next two chapters approach freedom of commercial expression from a different direction, that of the supposed social utility of such freedom, especially as exemplified by the so-called 'free flow of commercial information', which flow regulation of commercial expression will allegedly constrict. In *Chapter 13*, I argue that it is a naïve construal of the relevant economic issues to suppose that an unregulated market in information invariably realizes the social value of information. I show also that to assign powers of economic regulation to courts, as the constitutionalizing of advertising regulation would effect, poses serious normative issues of proper institutional design from both a political and a practical perspective. *Chapter 14* considers a different kind of argument for the social value of freedom of expression. It has been argued by Joseph Raz[48] that freedom of expression has value as a public good in ways not reducible to aggregated good to individuals. In theory such an argument might also apply to freedom of commercial expression. I shall argue, however, that it does not, and that commercial expression cannot be a 'public good' of the relevant kind. *Chapter 15* concludes the project. It provides an 'executive summary', if you will, and some reflections on the outcome of the project.

---

[48] See Chapter 7 of *Ethics in the Public Domain*.

PART I
THE CONTINGENCIES OF
INSTITUTIONAL HISTORY

2

Commercial Speech in the United States 1900–76

In this Part I shall present a reading of the institutional history of constitutional protection for freedom of expression in the U.S., Canada, and the European Community. I put my intentions in the guarded terminology of 'a reading' advisedly. I shall not attempt a detailed and complete history; that would be an ambitious, and an entirely separate, project. All histories, though—even a 'detailed and complete' one—are partial. My history is partial in two senses. In the case of the U.S. and Canada, I will focus on decisions of the Supreme Courts, and refer to lower court decisions only in so far as they raise issues otherwise not covered. Moreover, this Part is designed to lead to the Parts of jurisprudential analysis that lie beyond it.

The aim of the Part is indicated by its title, 'The Contingencies of Institutional History'. As already announced, this book is sceptical about the jurisprudential soundness of the commercial expression doctrine. I want to present the cases I mention so as to reveal a pattern of arbitrariness in them. In all three of the U.S., Canada, and Europe, the cases that led to the establishment of constitutional protection for commercial expression have other features which led to their being tempting candidates for the invalidation of the laws at issue. I shall show that any impression of a linear and rational progression towards a sound commercial expression doctrine is at best misleading, and at worst illusory. The reading in this Part of the institutional history will, I hope, engender a receptive mood for the jurisprudential critique of the commercial expression doctrine, which follows in the remaining two Parts.

I turn first in this and the next Chapter to the history of commercial speech in the U.S. In this Chapter, the story will be told up to and including the landmark case of *Virginia Board*.[1] In Chapter 3 we will journey from the aftermath of *Virginia Board* to the present day. I begin with the U.S. because the history there of constitutional protection for commercial expression begins notably earlier than in Canada and Europe, and U.S. constitutional jurisprudence casts a long shadow over the other two. In the U.S., constitutional protection for freedom of speech[2] is based on the First Amendment to the U.S. Constitution, which came

---

[1] *Virginia State Board of Pharmacy et al v Virginia Citizens Consumer Council Inc et al* 425 US 748 (1976).
[2] Throughout Chapters 2 and 3 I shall use the term 'speech' rather than the term 'expression', since the U.S. Constitution is so worded.

into force in 1791, four years after the Constitution itself.[3] The Amendment reads as follows:

Congress shall make no law respecting an establishment of religion, or prohibiting the free exercise thereof; or abridging the freedom of speech, or of the press; or the right of the people peaceably to assemble, and to petition the Government for a redress of grievances.

Freedom of speech, therefore, is only one of several aspects of social life covered by the Amendment; neither the other clauses, nor elements of First Amendment jurisprudence not to do with commercial speech, are dealt with in this book.

1　Pre-1940 history

The First Amendment did not come to occupy a central position in constitutional litigation until the second decade of this century. The bare bones of the historical facts are not in dispute.[4] The U.S. Congress passed the Espionage Act in 1917,[5] a bill that, in the fourth year of World War I, extensively criminalized speech that could be held to be against the country's war-related interests. A number of cases challenged the Act on First Amendment grounds, and reached the Supreme Court for final determination in the period 1919–27. The jurisprudence that evolved over this period set the foundation for First Amendment adjudication for the rest of the century.

I mention this period for a reason. The focus of these two Chapters is specifically commercial speech under the First Amendment, and not the First Amendment generally. Standard histories of the commercial speech doctrine place the origin of that doctrine in the 1942 case of *Chrestensen*[6] and its immediate predecessors.[7] *Chrestensen* clearly is crucial, and I shall come to it shortly. But on my reading the roots of the commercial speech doctrine are also right

---

[3] See John E. Nowak and Ronald D. Rotunda, *Constitutional Law* (6th edn., St. Paul, Minn.: West Group, 2000), 1055–9.

[4] Detailed scholarly studies of the issue abound, as do scholarly disagreements about the details. I have especially profited from reading David M. Rabban, *Free Speech in Its Forgotten Years, 1870–1920* (New York: Cambridge University Press, 1997) and G. Edward White, 'The First Amendment Comes of Age: The Emergence of Free Speech in Twentieth-Century America', *Michigan Law Review* 95 (1996): 299–392. Footnotes to these two essays will serve as excellent trailheads for documentary exploration.

[5] Act of June 17, 1917, 40 Stat 219.

[6] *Valentine v Christensen* 316 US 52 (1942).

[7] See, e.g., Edwin P. Rome and William H. Roberts, *Corporate and Commercial Free Speech: First Amendment Protection of Expression in Business* (Westport, Conn.: Quorum Books, 1985), 11 ff; Nowak and Rotunda, *Constitutional Law*, 1137 ff. An exception is Alex Kozinski and Stuart Banner, 'The Anti-History and Pre-History of Commercial Speech', *Texas Law Review* 71 (1993): 747–75. However, they discuss different pre-1940 cases from those that I discuss, in accord with their belief that constitutional protection for commercial speech is a most welcome development in the law.

there in the post-World War I cases. In one of those cases, *Abrams*,[8] Justice Wendell Holmes produced his famous image of a 'free trade in ideas' and 'competition in the market' of ideas:

But when men have realized that time has upset many fighting faiths, they may come to believe even more than they believe the very foundations of their own conduct that the ultimate good desired is better reached by free trade in ideas—that the best test of truth is the power of the thought to get itself accepted in the competition of the market, and that truth is the only ground upon which their wishes safely can be carried out. [at 630]

This image of laissez-faire economics applied to intellectual exchange itself, especially in Brennan J's later 'market-place of ideas' variation ('It would be a barren market-place of ideas that had only sellers and no buyers'[9]), has certainly been successful in its eponymous market.[10] The image of a 'free trade in' or 'market-place of' ideas is not a jurisprudentially innocent image, and I will discuss its deceptiveness for the present project below (Chapter 13.8). The power of the image, however, undoubtedly plays a part in the eventual development of the commercial speech doctrine.

2 THE 1940s TO THE 1960s

And so to *Chrestensen*. Chrestensen owned a submarine, which he moored at a pier owned by New York State on New York's East River in order to make money from it as a tourist attraction. He printed advertising handbills, but the police stopped his distribution of them as being in conflict with a city ordinance forbidding distribution in the streets of commercial advertising, though not of handbills solely devoted to information or political protest. A revised version containing almost the same advertisement on one side and a protest on the other against the city not allowing him to moor his submarine at a city wharf was also stopped. Such anti-handbilling ordinances were at that time by no means uncommon. Three years earlier, in considering a group of similar cases all concerning the distribution of religious or political literature, the Court invalidated broad ordinances, which covered any kind of handbill as being in conflict with the First Amendment. The Court commented, however, in one, *Schneider*, that it were 'not to be taken as holding that commercial soliciting and canvassing may not be subject to regulation'.[11] In *Chrestensen* the Court took its own hint. States and municipalities, while they may regulate, may not forbid the dissemination of information and opinion. 'We are equally clear that the Constitution

---

[8] *Abrams et al v United States* 250 US 616 (1919).

[9] *Lamont v Postmaster General of the United States* 381 US 301 (1965), at 308.

[10] According to David Cole, 'Agon at Agora: Creative Misreadings in the First Amendment Tradition', *Yale Law Journal* 95 (1986): 857, the economic image in Holmes's form occurs in 14 Supreme Court cases since 1925, and in Brennan's form in 33 since 1965 (at 893, n. 160). An updated total would be significantly higher.

[11] *Schneider v State of New Jersey, Town of Irvington* 308 US 147 (1939), at 165.

imposes no such restraint on government as respects purely commercial adver-tising' (at 54). As for Chrestensen's ingenious dual-purpose handbill, the Court ducked the issue on the ground that it was obviously no more than a gimmick to 'evade the prohibition of the ordinance' (at 55).

The Court decided this case not long after *Chaplinsky*,[12] the case in which the First Amendment was held not to cover so-called 'fighting words'. Presumably the Court was in a period of receptiveness to arguments that sought to limit the Amendment's scope. However, in the case of 'fighting words', it took very little time for the expansiveness of *Chaplinsky* to be reined back.[13] In the case of com-mercial speech, the line was drawn more clearly in the sand—no constitutional protection for commercial speech under the First Amendment. For some thirty years, the course of commercial speech cases is an odd combination of clear adherence to the *Chrestensen* precedent, while fine-tuning the Court's holdings on the issue to pave the way for later re-examination. The chronologically next significant case would certainly be placed in the latter category. In *Thomas*,[14] a Texas statute requiring union organizers to register with the state and acquire a licence was invalidated. The Court was well aware that union organizers are paid for their work, and indeed that labour unions are part of the economic sec-tor of society. It commented that 'the idea is not sound therefore that the First Amendment's safeguards are wholly inapplicable to business or economic activ-ity', and rebuked Texas for urging that engagement in 'business activities' and receiving compensation were sufficient to rule out First Amendment protection (at 531). The Court's approach, however, marked a break from *Chrestensen* in that it characterized the commercial connection as a relevant factor to be entered into the balance of reasons, not as a factor which in itself was decisive against constitutional protection for the speech in question.[15]

This change of direction from a ban to a balance became clearer in the next case. In *Breard*[16] the Court considered an ordinance prohibiting door-to-door selling, in Breard's case of non-religious magazine subscriptions. The Court distinguished Breard's commercial canvassing from religious canvassing,[17] and upheld the ordinance because of the commercial character of the speech restrained—that is to say, the *salesperson*'s speech; the magazines in themselves would have been protected if the city had tried to ban their distribution as such. 'The solicitors for gadgets or brushes' cannot appeal to the First Amendment as can 'the press or oral advocates of ideas' to protect their speech (at 641). That is

[12] *Chaplinsky v New Hampshire* 315 US 568 (1942).

[13] *Terminiello v Chicago* 337 US 1 (1949).   [14] *Thomas v Collins* 323 US 516 (1945).

[15] The Supreme Court in *Virginia Board* relies heavily on *Thomas* as a precursor to its holding there. However, I shall show below (Chapter 2.4) that the Court's reasoning on this matter is seri-ously problematic.

[16] *Breard v City of Alexandria* 341 US 622 (1951). In its opinion the Court does not refer to its prior holding in *Thomas*, but that case is a clear precedent for the approach taken.

[17] Cf. *Martin v City of Struthers* 319 US 141 (1943), shortly after *Chrestensen*, in which religious canvassing was held to be protected.

to say, the speech aspect does not automatically guarantee First Amendment protection because the speech is commercial. But the commercial aspect, *contra Chrestensen*, does not automatically guarantee absence of protection. 'By adjustment of rights, we can have both full liberty of expression and an orderly life' (at 642). Nonetheless, 'it would be, it seems to us, a misuse of the great guarantees of free speech and free press to use those guarantees to force a community to admit the solicitors of publications to the home premises of its residents' (at 645). The Court gives no further examination to, or explication of, the principles at issue. In particular, it does not reveal what kind of 'misuse' this would be of the 'great guarantees', and why.

Chrestensen seemed to slam the door shut against constitutional protection for commercial speech. These two cases, despite their apparent disparaging of the commercial aspect, leave the door ajar. There is a world of difference between an exclusionary rule and a rule assigning scant weight in the balance of reasons.[18] An exclusionary rule has an intrinsic mandatory force which a consideration to be weighed in the balance of reasons does not and cannot have.

The point I would like to highlight about these two cases is this. In each case, the speech in question, while being in some sense 'commercial', occurs in association with other forceful freedom of speech values. In *Thomas* it is the speech of a union organizer, and is integrally linked to workers' rights in relation to labour organizing, discussion of working conditions, and the like. Other cases as well as *Thomas* around the same period underlined the role of the First Amendment in the protection of workers' free-speech rights.[19] In *Breard* the speech is associated with published magazines, and so with the freedom of the press. So the appearance of the Court being pushed in the direction of constitutional protection for commercial speech by the fact that the cases involve speech in some sense 'commercial' is misleading. The speech in question occurs in the context of other, historically more protectable speech. This is clear even from the opinion of Black J in dissent. He would have invalidated the ordinance because, in his view, 'the freedom of the people of this Nation cannot survive even a little governmental hobbling of religious or political ideas' (at 650). He adds, though, in a throwaway footnote: 'Of course I believe that the present ordinance could constitutionally be applied to a "merchant" who goes from door to door "selling pots"' (ibid.). Just because of the admixture of workers' rights and press freedom, these cases are not 'pure' commercial speech cases. Thus, rather than pointing towards constitutional protection for commercial speech, they point away from it.

[18] For the argument for this view see Joseph Raz, *Practical Reason and Norms* (London: Hutchinson, 1975), Chapter 4. For the contrary view see Stephen R. Perry, 'Judicial Obligation, Precedent and the Common Law', *Oxford Journal of Legal Studies* 7 (1987): 215–59; Frederick F. Schauer, *Playing By The Rules: A Philosophical Examination of Rule-Based Decision-Making in Law and in Life*, Clarendon Law Series (Oxford: Clarendon Press, 1991), Chapter 5.3.

[19] *NLRB v Jones & Laughlin Steel Corporation* 301 US 1 (1937); *Associated Press v NLRB* 301 US 103 (1937); *Thornhill v Alabama* 310 US 88 (1940); *AFL v Swing* 312 US 321 (1941); *NLRB v Virginia Electric & Power Co* 314 US 469 (1941).

As we shall see, the U.S. Supreme Court was very conscious when it came eventually to consider 'pure' commercial speech that it was facing an analytically new issue, and rightly so. My claim, however, is that nonetheless the Court was misled by the series of 'mixed' cases that preceded a 'pure' case into taking the 'mixed' cases to show the plausibility of extending constitutional protection under the First Amendment to 'pure' commercial speech. Too much attention was paid to the shared characteristic of being in some sense 'commercial speech', when attention should have been paid to the differentiae in the 'mixed' cases of being as well, and more importantly, other kinds of speech.

The facts of *Thomas* and *Martin*, above, would have entitled the Court to rule that the commercial aspect of otherwise fully protected speech did not detract from such full protection. As noted, the Court did not in fact so rule on those occasions, thus leaving a space for its holding in *NY Times*.[20] Sullivan was a Commissioner of Montgomery, Alabama, with responsibility *inter alia* for the police force. He claimed he was libelled by a full-page paid advertisement in the *New York Times* describing harsh treatment of anti-segregationist protesters in Montgomery in early 1961.[21] The *Times* received almost $5,000 for this advertisement. Sullivan argued that the putative status of the allegedly libellous speech as protected by the First Amendment was vitiated, following *Chrestensen*, by its 'commercial' nature. The Court flatly rejected this argument, ruling that:

the publication here was not a 'commercial' advertisement in the sense in which the word was used in *Chrestensen*. It communicated information, expressed opinion, recited grievances, . . . That the Times was paid for publishing the advertisement is as immaterial in this connection as is the fact that newspapers and books are sold . . . [I]f the allegedly libelous statements would otherwise be constitutionally protected . . . , they do not forfeit that protection because they were published in the form of a paid advertisement. [at 266]

The effect of the ruling is to prepare the way for the notion of 'pure commercial speech' by narrowing down what the term 'commercial speech' could denote. *NY Times* made explicit what earlier cases had left only implicit, that the mere fact of being speech for which remuneration was received did not prevent speech from being fully protected by the First Amendment.

The case, of course, is famous for other reasons—for introducing the requirement that a public official must prove, not merely falsehood, but actual malice, that is, knowledge of or reckless disregard for the falsity of the statement (at 279–80)—if he or she is to succeed in a libel suit. I offer no comment on the rights and wrongs of the decision as regards libel. But the Court is right about the following. If the aim of constitutional protection for freedom of speech is to promote wide debate about matters of public interest, then a rule which allows

[20] *New York Times v Sullivan* 376 US 254 (1964).
[21] For a thoroughly readable and non-technical account of this case see Anthony Lewis, *Make No Law: The Sullivan Case and the First Amendment* (New York: Random House, 1991).

only the defence of truth to persons seeking to criticize public officials will tend to chill such debate. Not only that, in the context of the civil rights struggle of the 1950s and 1960s against segregation, endorsing Sullivan's attempt to silence criticism would have been wrong from the point of view of political morality. But these facts show only that *NY Times* too fits the profile of *Thomas* and *Breard* sketched two paragraphs above. A form of speech which is eminently protectable but happens to be 'commercial' draws speech with a commercial character in general towards the protective canopy of the First Amendment.

In their discussion of the origin of the commercial speech doctrine, Rome and Roberts make another claim for the contribution of *NY Times* to the history of the doctrine.[22] The following is a (justly) famous passage from Brennan J's majority opinion:

> Thus we consider this case against the background of a profound national commitment to the principle that debate on public issues should be uninhibited, robust, and wide-open, and that it may well include vehement, caustic, and sometimes unpleasantly sharp attacks on government and public officials. [at 270]

'The modern commercial speech doctrine', say Rome and Roberts,[23] 'rests primarily not on the rights of the speaker, but on the rights of potential recipients of information and opinion. The *New York Times* case recognized this important source of constitutional protection' (at 35). The present book, as I have already emphasized, is not an empirical history of psychological processes. I do not dispute that Rome and Roberts might well be right empirically in stating that later judges and commentators have taken *NY Times* this way. My concern is with the movement of thought as a would-be valid inference. Is there a defensible train of thought connecting *NY Times* with constitutional protection for advertising? Rome and Roberts make two major steps in their analysis; each seems to me problematic. First, they regard the above quotation from Brennan J's opinion as authority for the claim that the First Amendment primarily protects 'not private rights, but a public power', *viz.* 'the system of freedom of expression' (ibid.). By virtue of protecting a system, the rights of (would-be) hearers are protected as well as the rights of speakers. Secondly, they infer that 'the system of freedom of expression' thus protected obviously includes commercial speech.

Both of these steps are problematic. In the first place the form of words, 'the system of freedom of expression', is not mentioned in Brennan J's text: that talks only about 'uninhibited, robust, and wide-open' debate on public issues. The form of words is Thomas Emerson's.[24] Brennan J's wording is entirely compatible with the view that the First Amendment protects those who participate *as speakers* in 'uninhibited, robust, and wide-open' debate. Argument would

---

[22] Rome and Roberts, *Corporate and Commercial Free Speech*, 35–7.
[23] With some doctrinal or institutional validity: see below Chapters 9–12, although I shall there be arguing that the claimed ground is jurisprudentially inadequate.
[24] It is the title of his book: Thomas I. Emerson, *The System of Freedom of Expression* (New York: Random House, 1970).

have to be made that the opinion aims also to protect an activity, public debating, which has a normatively protectable status independent of the rights of speakers. Moreover, the context of the *NY Times* case leaves very little doubt that the Court is thinking of essentially *political* debate. So even if we can conclude that in some sense a 'system' of robust debate is being protected, it is another step to argue that the relentless pounding of the human mind by commercial advertising is part of such 'robust debate'.

These comments are not intended to be conclusory. Attempts have been made to supply the arguments that are overlooked here by Rome and Roberts. I shall return to these issues later, in Part III. I want simply at this point to underline how much has to be read into *NY Times* to treat it as authority for the commercial speech doctrine, whatever it was later held to imply.

3 PAVING THE WAY FOR *VIRGINIA BOARD*

The Court in *Virginia Board* finally and unambiguously overruled *Chrestensen*. But the Court advanced towards its holding in this landmark case slowly, and an analysis of the progression will prove instructive.

The city of Pittsburgh had an ordinance prohibiting *inter alia* employment notices which discriminated by sex. The *Pittsburgh Press* newspaper had a practice of publishing employment advertisements separated into 'Male Help Wanted' and 'Female Help Wanted'. The city found the newspaper in breach of this ordinance. In *Pittsburgh*,[25] the city's finding was challenged as a violation of the newspaper's First Amendment rights. The fact that paid advertisements were involved raised the issue of the status of commercial speech under the First Amendment. The Court deemed the newspaper's editorial decision to publish employment advertisements in that form to be as much 'commercial speech' as the advertisements themselves (at 387–8). The Court therefore had to decide whether to accept the invitation by the newspaper to depart from *Chrestensen*:

Insisting that the exchange of information is as important in the commercial realm as in any other, the newspaper here would have us abrogate the distinction between commercial and other speech. *Whatever the merits of this contention may be in other contexts*, it is unpersuasive in this case. Discrimination in employment is not only commercial activity; it is illegal commercial activity under the Ordinance. [at 388; my emphasis]

Any *First Amendment interest which might be served* by advertising an ordinary commercial proposal and *which might arguably outweigh* the governmental interest supporting the regulation is altogether absent when the commercial activity itself is illegal and the restriction on advertising is incidental to a valid limitation on economic activity. [at 389; my emphasis]

[25] *Pittsburgh Press Company v Pittsburgh Commission on Human Relations et al* 413 US 376 (1973).

The Court did not therefore have to decide whether to accept the proffered abrogation, and it did not. Nonetheless, it left an opening, as is illustrated by the emphasized phrases. The newspaper's contention about the value of the exchange of commercial information *might* be of value; ordinary commercial proposals *might* serve a First Amendment interest, and one with the capacity to outweigh a governmental interest at that. But these are musings, not rulings.

It is important not to misrepresent the Court's holding in *Pittsburgh*. Rodney Smolla, for example, avers that the Court here 'evidenced a concern for the protection of commercial speech, noting that "the exchange of information is as important in the commercial realm as in any other".'[26] But the Court itself does not speak those words in its own voice; it reports in indirect speech the claim as made by the litigant newspaper. Nowak and Rotunda state correctly that the Court relied on the narrow test of 'if an activity is illegal, the state may prohibit advertising or touting' that activity. But then they go on: 'The negative implication of this reasoning is that if the activity is legal, the state may not prohibit advertising the activity'.[27] The proposed test is, in the first place, doctrinally highly implausible; it is illegal to overthrow the government, but not illegal to advocate such an overthrow, in the absence of any clear and present danger of success. The test also represents the straightforward formal fallacy of Denying the Antecedent: 'If not-P, then not-Q' does not imply 'If P, then Q'. The test does imply that, if the state may not prohibit advertising of the activity, then the activity is legal. That proposition, though, infers the legality from the inability to prohibit, not the inability to prohibit from the legality. Again, the holding is no authority for the commercial speech doctrine. Even the Court itself is not immune to rewriting history. In *Bigelow*,[28] the Court quoted the second passage above with the claim that it there indicated that 'the advertisements *would have received* some degree of First Amendment protection if the commercial proposal had been legal' (at 821; my emphasis). If one goes by the plain meaning of the words, the claim is simply false.

I would like to draw attention, however, to the idiosyncrasies of the advertisements in this case. We are dealing here with issues of sex discrimination in employment. The case came about because the National Organization for Women Inc filed a complaint with the Pittsburgh Commission on Human Relations. As the Court itself remarks, the 'issue is a sensitive one, and full understanding of the context in which it arises is critical to its resolution' (at 378). The Court does align the case with *Chrestensen* as 'no more than a proposal of possible employment' rather than with *NY Times* as expressing opinion, reciting grievances, etc. (at 385). But it also shows itself highly conscious of the issue of sex discrimination and the justified proscription of such acts (at 388–9). Sex discrimination is not merely a conventional illegality. Its illegality

---

[26] Rodney A. Smolla, *Smolla and Nimmer on Freedom of Speech* (3rd edn., Deerfield, Ill.: Clark Boardman Callaghan, 1996), 20–5.

[27] Nowak and Rotunda, *Constitutional Law*, 1146.

[28] *Bigelow v Virginia* 421 US 809 (1975); this case is discussed in more detail very shortly.

has to do with fundamental normative issues of how men and women should be treated by the public institutions of their society. The fact that the proscribed discrimination is carried out by what seems in some sense 'commercial speech' is coincidental. But this coincidental aspect becomes the focus. The case becomes a speech case, not a discrimination case.

Jeffrey Bigelow edited a weekly newspaper. He ran in the paper an advertisement stating the legality of abortions in the state of New York and the lack of residency requirements, and the availability of services to arrange placements for out-of-state women in appropriate clinics. He was convicted under a Virginia statute making it a misdemeanour to encourage by the sale or circulation of any publication the processing of an abortion. He challenged the statute as a violation of his First Amendment rights. The state of Virginia in defending the conviction relied on the authority of *Chrestensen* as removing commercial speech from First Amendment protection. The Court not only pointed to later decisions, holding, as noted already, that the remunerated character of speech did not automatically forfeit First Amendment protection. The Court also by a deft process of distinguishing narrowed the authority of *Chrestensen* to a concern with reasonable regulation of the manner of distribution of commercial advertising (at 819). It repudiated the theory that *Chrestensen* stood for the claim that commercial advertising is *per se* unprotected (at 820).

These *viae negativae*, though, are familiar. *Bigelow* is important for taking some steps in a positive direction. The Court argued:

The advertisement published in the appellant's newspaper did more than simply propose a commercial transaction. It contained factual material of clear 'public interest'. Portions of its message . . . involve the exercise of the freedom of communicating information and disseminating opinion. . . . [T]he advertisement conveyed information of potential interest and value to a diverse audience . . . .. [at 822]

Here we have a different line of thought from previous cases. As with *Pittsburgh*, the Court looks at the content of the speech in question. Unlike *Pittsburgh*, the Court finds here that the speech is of public interest. The speech conveys information, which normatively ought to be in the public domain, rather than speech that normatively ought not. So the Court moves away from the paid aspect of otherwise political or religious speech not preventing First Amendment coverage towards the positive value of otherwise commercial speech securing coverage.

The Court is still cagey: 'We need not decide in this case the precise extent to which the First Amendment permits regulation of advertising that is related to activities the State may legitimately regulate or even prohibit' (at 825). This sentence has attached to it a long footnote (n. 10) alluding to a variety of lower court cases on which the Court declines to comment. These are cases in which the U.S. Court of Appeals upheld seeming restrictions on commercial speech and the Court did not take the case on further appeal. The subject-matter of these cases is significant. *Hunter*[29] had to do with prosecuting a newspaper for racially discriminatory housing advertisements in violation of the Civil Rights Act. *Lawrence*[30] had to do with violations of anti-block-busting provisions of the Fair Housing Act. The Court comments: 'In those cases there usually existed a clear relationship between the advertising in question and an activity that the government was legitimately regulating' (at 825, n. 10).

The Court also refers to two cases relating to Federal Communications Commission controls of broadcast tobacco advertising, *Capital Broadcasting*[31] and *Banzhaf*.[32] These are both cases in which forms of regulation of tobacco advertising were held not to violate the First Amendment. The cases elegantly illustrate the jurisprudential flexibility of the tobacco industry. *Banzhaf* concerned the FCC requirement of fairness in broadcast presentations of public policy issues. Acting on a complaint from John Banzhaf, a leading anti-smoking activist, the FCC required radio station WCBS which carried cigarette advertising to devote a significant amount of broadcast time to presenting the case against cigarette smoking under the fairness requirement. These anti-smoking 'advertisements' were very effective in reducing levels of smoking. The tobacco manufacturers therefore strenuously sought to have tobacco advertising officially declared *not* to state a position on a matter of public interest, so that the fairness requirement would not apply to them. *Capital Broadcasting* concerned a total ban on broadcast tobacco advertising imposed by the Public Health Cigarette Smoking Act of 1969. The tobacco manufacturers in this case equally strenuously sought to have tobacco advertising officially declared *to be* speech on a matter of public interest, so that they could claim the protection of the First Amendment. The Court in *Bigelow*, however, declined to draw inferences from these cases as regards Bigelow's advertisements because of the special connection with broadcast media.[33]

Whether one is for or against the commercial speech doctrine, one has reason to find footnote 10 to the majority opinion in *Bigelow* tendentious. If one is for the doctrine, one will complain about the bald appeal to the special characteristics of the electronic media, when the justification for such an appeal is controversial. If one is against the doctrine, one will deplore the refusal to face the lower courts' sense that the cases alluded to in the footnote have everything to do with ridding society of the evil of racial discrimination, combating a severe public health problem, and the like, and little to do with freedom of speech.

---

[29] *United States v Bill R. Hunter dba The Courier* 459 F 2d 205 (1972) (USCA 4th Cir).

[30] *United States v Bob Lawrence Realty Inc et al* 474 F 2d 115 (1973) (USCA 5th Cir).

[31] *Capital Broadcasting Co v Mitchell* 333 F Supp 582 (USDC DC 1971).

[32] *Banzhaf v FCC* 405 F 2d 1082 (USCA DC 1968).

[33] The history of the differential judicial treatment under the First Amendment of broadcast and print media is a topic all to itself. For an erudite and lively history, together with powerful criticism of the distinction, see Lucas A. Powe Jr., *American Broadcasting and the First Amendment* (Berkeley and Los Angeles, Cal.: University of California Press, 1987); see also Thomas G. Krattenmaker and Lucas A. Powe Jr., *Regulating Broadcast Programming* (Cambridge, Mass.: The MIT Press, 1994).

The crucial side-issue, and a non-speech-related issue, bearing on the Court's decision in *Bigelow* is the fact that two years earlier the Court decided the landmark abortion case of *Roe*.[34] In that case the Court held that the due process clause of the Fourteenth Amendment implied a right of privacy broad enough to cover a women's decision whether or not to seek an abortion. In *Bigelow* the Court is well aware it is venturing on to the same normative territory (at 822). It is highly unlikely that the Court would have been tempted to move towards the idea that commercial advertising constituted speech relating to a public interest if Bigelow and his newspaper had been advertising the availability in New York of a distinctive kind of fur coat or fast car, or if *Roe* had been decided the other way. In a state as repressively against abortion as Virginia seems then to have been, the advertising of the availability of abortions in New York indeed seems to be in the public interest. A decision to uphold the Virginia statute criminalizing such advertising would be a major retreat both normatively and doctrinally from the decision taken two years previously in *Roe* to support a privacy right to seek an abortion. But what does the provision of information in Virginia about the availability of abortions in New York have to do with commercial speech? Yet again, the Court is led by its justified desire to do the right thing from a public policy perspective into mistakenly thinking that it has reason to develop a general doctrine of constitutional protection for commercial speech.

Bigelow is also important for a further reason. Blackmun J's opinion speaks of the advertisement as 'convey[ing] information of potential interest and value to a diverse audience' (at 822), and this thought plays a role in the decision-making. Although the right of Bigelow as speaker is clearly the focus, the interests of Bigelow's potential audience give weight to this right, never mind its commercial aspect. There is mention of hearers' First Amendment rights in earlier decisions,[35] but no development of the idea occurred. The issue of hearers' rights will be discussed more extensively below (Chapter 10). I note here only the following point. One would not have to press the Court's text very much to find a serious conflation between 'the public interest' and 'the interest of some member of the public'. It does not follow from the fact that publication of a certain speech is 'of public interest' that therefore the interests of hearers have constitutional status. It is especially important to mark this distinction when, as in *Bigelow*, the undoubtedly felt public interest of the advertisement has some weight in the Court's decision on whether to invalidate the restriction on its publication.

---

[34] *Roe v Wade* 410 US 113 (1973).

[35] *Martin*: 'This freedom [sc. that protected by the First Amendment] embraces the right to distribute literature . . . and necessarily protects the right to receive it' (at 143). 'The First Amendment contains no specific guarantee of access to publications. . . . I think the right to receive publications is such a fundamental right' (*Lamont v Postmaster General of the United States* 381 US 301 (1965), at 308, per Brennan J). The cases will be considered in detail in Chapter 10.

4 *VIRGINIA BOARD*

In 1976 the Court finally confronted the issue of constitutional protection for 'purely' commercial speech. A Virginia statute declared it to be unprofessional conduct for a licensed pharmacist to advertise the prices of prescription drugs. The Virginia Citizens Consumer Council, the state organization of labour unions (AFL-CIO) and a state resident began proceedings to have the statute declared unconstitutional on First Amendment grounds. The consumer interest in the public availability of prescription drug pricing information was clear. Prices for precisely the same drug were shown to differ widely from one pharmacy to the next, and consumers could save a considerable amount of money if they were able to patronize the cheaper pharmacies. At issue here was no lofty form of political or artistic speech: 'the "idea" [the pharmacist] wishes to communicate is simply this: "I will sell you the X prescription drug at the Y price"' (at 761). Such a statement is the paradigm of 'purely' commercial speech (see Chapter 1.3 above). The Court asked itself 'whether this communication is wholly outside the protection of the First Amendment' (ibid.), and answered resoundingly in the negative.

It might be that, as a recent article has put it, 'after *New York Times*, *Pittsburgh Press* and *Bigelow*, explicit recognition of First Amendment protection for commercial speech seemed inevitable'.[36] Certainly, it seemed that way to the Court. Nonetheless, the step did need actually to be taken, and the Court[37] constructed what seems to be a careful and thorough argument for its conclusion. Both the Court itself and commentators subsequently have taken *Virginia Board* to show that commercial speech does merit constitutional protection under a right of freedom of speech. However inevitable the step seemed psychologically, it is not logically inevitable. Argument was needed, and, for all its apparent thoroughness and care, the Court's argument is in fact wholly unsound. I will first present the argument in its entirety, on the Court's own terms, before making any comment. For purposes of analysis, I will separate the argument into three parts. Part A consists of the opening two paragraphs of section V of the opinion on political process (at 761–2). Part B goes from the beginning of the second complete paragraph at 762 ('Focusing first on the individual parties . . .') to the end of 765. Part C consists of the first complete paragraph on 762. The linear order of the Court's exposition on paper thus does not follow the logical order of its argument. Parts A and B are premises from which Part C as conclusion is held to follow.

---

[36] Arlen W. Langvardt and Eric L. Richards, 'The Death of *Posadas* and the Birth of Change in Commercial Speech Doctrine: Implications of *44 Liquormart*', *American Business Law Journal* 34 (1997): 491.

[37] I will examine the majority opinion of Blackmun J only. Although Burger CJ and Stewart J added concurring opinions, they do not raise new issues of relevance to this study.

Part (A) of the argument:

(A1) The Court begins with 'several propositions that are already settled or beyond serious dispute' (at 761). It refers to past decisions in support of its claim. The 'several propositions' are:

(i) Speech does not lose its First Amendment protection because money is spent to project it: *Buckley*[38] (political speech); *Pittsburgh Press* (civil rights); *NY Times* (political speech);

(ii) Speech does not lose its First Amendment protection because it is carried in a form that is 'sold' for profit: *Smith*[39] (retail book selling), *Burstyn*[40] (commercial movies), *Murdock*[41] (religious literature);

(iii) Speech does not lose First Amendment protection because it may involve a solicitation to purchase or otherwise pay and contribute money: *NY Times* (political speech); *NAACP v Button*[42] (civil rights); *Jamison*[43] (religious literature), *Cantwell*[44] (religious literature).

(A2) If there is a form of commercial speech that lacks all First Amendment protection, therefore, it must be distinguished by its content (ibid.).

So then the Court tries to identify the content in question.

(A3) The speech whose content deprives it of protection cannot simply be speech on a commercial subject: the speech of a pharmacist who expressed an opinion on the regulation of pharmaceutical prices would be protected (at 761–2).

(A4) That the speech simply reports a fact or is non-editorial cannot be enough to remove the speech from protection: cf. *Bigelow* (abortion); *Thornhill* (labour relations).

Part (C) Conclusion: The Court then concludes:

Our question is whether speech which does 'no more than propose a commercial transaction' is so removed from any 'exposition of ideas', and from 'truth, science, morality, and arts in general, in its diffusion of liberal sentiments on the administration of Government', that it lacks all protection? Our answer is that it is not. [at 762: citations omitted]

Let us review the form of argument so far. Part (A), (1) to (4), argues that commercial speech has several features which in other cases have not prevented speech with those features from being protected. The Court's conclusion (C) is then that commercial speech is not so different from those other forms of speech that it should be denied First Amendment protection. But there is a missing step. A person opposed to the Court's view might say, 'But those cases are different from commercial speech, because they are not *purely* commercial speech; they

---

[38] *Buckley v Valeo* 424 US 1 (1976). [39] *Smith v California* 361 US 147 (1959).
[40] *Joseph Burstyn Inc v Wilson* 343 US 495 (1952).
[41] *Murdock v Pennsylvania* 319 US 105 (1943). [42] *NAACP v Buton* 371 US 415 (1963).
[43] *Jamison v Texas* 318 US 413 (1943). [44] *Cantwell v Connecticut* 310 US 296 (1940).

are cases of speech which is traditionally protected by the First Amendment that happens to have a commercial dimension'. This response undoubtedly has force, as I have already suggested (Chapter 2.2 and 2.3 above). The cases the Court cites involve such elements as speech about civil rights, political speech, movies as part of 'the press', religious literature, all of which are within the scope of traditional accounts of the First Amendment.

To meet this potential objection, the Court needs to give some positive argument, independent of the *viae negativae* of (A1)–(A4), that will bring commercial speech within the traditional scope of the First Amendment. This in fact the Court then tries to do.

Part (B). The Court offers some features that 'pure' commercial speech of the 'X product for Y price' kind has in common with central First Amendment cases, and so which will ostensibly count as reasons for commercial speech not being 'so removed from any expression of ideas . . . that it lacks all protection'. The Court mentioned five such candidate features:

(B1) Protection has been extended to speech in a context of labour relations, even though the speech was specifically directed to the promotion of the speaker's economic self-interest; it was not speech about the 'merits of unionism in general'. Advertising speech is just as much directed to the promotion of the speaker's economic self-interest (at 762–3).

(B2) Political speech is protected because of the citizen's interest in the existence of such speech. The particular consumer's interest in the free flow of commercial information may be as keen as, if not keener by far than, his interest in the day's most urgent political debate (at 763).

(B3) Generally, society as a whole has an interest in robust political debate.[45] Society also has a strong interest in the free flow of commercial information (at 764).

(B4) Even an individual advertisement, though entirely 'commercial', may be of general public interest.

So long as we preserve a predominantly free enterprise economy, the allocation of our resources in large measure will be made through numerous private economic decisions. It is a matter of public interest that those decisions, in the aggregate, be intelligent and well-informed. To this end, the free flow of commercial information is indispensable. . . . And if it is indispensable to the proper allocation of resources in a free enterprise system, it is also indispensable to the formation of intelligent opinions as to how that system ought to be regulated or altered. Therefore, even if the First Amendment were thought to be primarily an instrument to enlighten public decision-making in a democracy, we could not say that the free flow of information does not serve that goal. [at 765]

(B5) The Court's final argument (at 766–70) considers arguments put forward by the Virginia State Board of Pharmacy concerning the professionalism of pharmacists, and the need to trust such professionals. The Court acknowledges that perhaps there are dangers in removing regulation, but it remarks:

---

[45] This sentence is not explicit in the opinion, but it is surely implicit.

It is precisely this kind of choice, between the dangers of suppressing information, and the dangers of its misuse if it is freely available, that the First Amendment makes for us.

Finally, as a coda to the opinion, the Court does deny its holding to be that no regulation is possible, for four reasons:

(i) Time, place, or manner restriction may be possible.
(ii) Untruthful commercial speech is not protected, nor deceptive or misleading speech.
(iii) If an illegal activity is advertised, the advertisement is not protected.
(iv) Special conditions may apply to electronic broadcast media.

Moreover, albeit in a footnote (at 771, n. 24), the Court indicates that there are 'common sense differences' between commercial speech and other varieties of protected speech. These differences 'suggest that a different degree of protection' may be required in the case of commercial speech, as indeed turns out to be the doctrine adopted by the Court.[46] The claimed differences are that commercial speech is more verifiable and more durable. Despite the amount of criticism this approach has received from commentators, the Court still adheres to it even in more recent commercial speech opinion.[47]

Assessment. Let me now turn to assessing the Court's argument. In Part (A), (A1), the assertion of the distinct propositions that speech does not lose its First Amendment protection because money is spent to project it, because it is carried in a form that is 'sold' for profit, or because it may involve a solicitation to purchase or otherwise pay and contribute money is surely unexceptionable both severally and conjunctively, at least as a statement of enduring doctrine. So also is (A4), the claim that the speech simply reporting a fact or being non-editorial cannot be enough to remove the speech from protection.

One might ask two different questions about (A2), the claim that 'If there is a form of commercial speech that lacks all First Amendment protection, *therefore*, it must be distinguished by its content' (my emphasis). *First*, how are we to read the 'therefore'? Is the Court's thought that (A2) is then a consequence of (A1)? (A2) is not a consequence of (A1) as (A1) stands. For (A2) to be a consequence, (A1) would have to list all the possible grounds for exclusion from First Amendment protection except content; content would have to be the, and to be the sole remaining, ground for exclusion. But of course (A1) is not comprehensive; there are many other grounds for exclusion from First Amendment protection—that the speech is obscene, poses a clear and present danger of harm, has to do with a whole variety of topics that have never been thought to be the business of the First Amendment (see here Chapter 7.4 below), and so on. So (2) in

---

[46] Cf. the discussion of *Central Hudson Gas & Electric Corporation v Public Service Commission of New York* 447 US 557 (1980) below, in Chapter 3.2.

[47] 44 *Liquormart Inc v Rhode Island* 116 SCt 1495 (1996), at 1506. Since the aim of this book is to argue that commercial speech should not be within the ambit of constitutional protection at all, I am not going either to defend or to criticize the Court on the claimed 'common sense differences', and on whether the differences would justify a lower level of protection for commercial speech than for other forms of protected speech.

point of logic is not a consequence of (A1). Moreover, using content as a ground for exclusion from First Amendment protection might be thought to be firmly against the whole point of the Amendment. For this reason, it is somewhat surprising that the Court asserts (A2).

Secondly, is (A2) nonetheless true, even if it does not follow from (A1)? If it is true, then it may well serve as a premise from which to draw further conclusions. In fact, (A2) plausibly is true. The most obvious difference between a statement like 'Pharmacists ought to be able to advertise the price of prescription drugs' and one like 'I will sell you the X prescription drug at the Y price' is one of content. Like it or not, the Court's approach to the issue of commercial speech is content-based.

In (A3), we see why the Court is not discombobulated by this basis in content. The Court argues that having a commercial content cannot be in itself a reason for denying constitutional protection. Speech about drug advertising policy is 'speech on a commercial subject'—speech with a commercial content, therefore—and it clearly is speech that merits constitutional protection. The argument, however, is tendentious, for reasons that are getting boringly familiar. The reason the comment on drug advertising policy would likely be protected is that it is a form of *political* speech, not of commercial speech. The Court in fact wants to have it both ways in this part of its argument. The Court tacitly appeals to the political character of the comment on drug advertising policy in order to get the comment in play as an example of protected speech. The Court then appeals to the commercial aspect of the comment as a potential reason for extending constitutional protection to speech which is commercial without being political. The comment on drug advertising policy has a double character, as both political and commercial. But the comment presents itself as a good candidate for protection in virtue of the feature that it does not share with paradigm commercial speech—being political—and not in virtue of the feature it does share—being commercial. Consider the following argument: 'The fact that an activity is horse-riding does not count against it receiving constitutional protection, as is shown by the fact that, when it occurs as part of a civic pride parade, the horse-riding is constitutionally protected. Therefore, horse-riding as carried out by professional jockeys deserves constitutional protection.' That argument, it hardly needs saying, is absurd. But the Court's argument about commercial speech here is exactly in that form.

In short, if the scope of the expression 'speech on a commercial subject' is broad enough to encompass the case of a comment on drug advertising policy, then what the Court says is true. Being speech on a commercial subject in itself does not disqualify speech from constitutional protection, as is shown by cases that are both political and commercial, and which are protected because they are political. But that's all; nothing follows from such 'mixed' cases for the normative propriety of constitutional protection for commercial speech, which has no political dimension.

The Court therefore in Part (A) of its argument secures the truth of its 'several propositions', but at a price. In each of these propositions, the underlying reason the speech mentioned is protected has nothing to do with the connection of that speech with anything 'commercial' *in the sense of 'purely commercial'*. The Court does not stick with its paradigm of 'I will sell you X product at Y price'. Instead, the Court selects cases where, although there is a plausible reason for calling the speech 'commercial' because it has a commercial aspect, not only is the speech also arguably 'political'; there are also appealing public policy reasons for thinking that the impugned legislative restriction is a bad thing from the point of view of public policy. *Virginia Board*, in fact, fits right into such a selection; there are good public policy reasons for abolishing the impugned restriction. But we are not debating public policy in such a diffuse sense, or concerned about the propriety of protecting political speech. We are debating whether 'purely commercial speech' merits constitutional protection under the First Amendment.

If the Court is to secure its conclusion (C), therefore, it must provide some positive argument. The most that can be concluded from Part (A) is indeed that having a commercial aspect does not in itself bar speech from constitutional protection. The reason, though, is that some speech, even if 'commercial', merits constitutional protection under the First Amendment in virtue of other characteristics that it has. If the Court is to show that speech that is 'commercial' without also being some other form of speech merits constitutional protection, then the Court has to produce some positive argument on the point. And the Court, as noted, tries to do just that, in what I have identified as Part (B) of its overall argument in the case. But the argument in Part (B) is too weak to bear the load that the logic of the Court's argument puts upon it. I will deal with each point made in turn.

(B1) The Court draws attention to the economic character of both commercial speech and the speech protected in *Thornhill* and analogous cases. Put schematically, the Court's argument about the labour relations cases is this:

(a) In *Thornhill et al*, the speech at issue was solely economic in character, with no political dimension.
(b) In *Virginia Board*, the speech at issue was solely economic in character, with no political dimension.
(c) If therefore the speech in *Thornhill et al* merits First Amendment protection, and it does, then so does the speech in *Virginia Board*.

The reply to this argument is thus. Point (a) is just false; the labour relations cases are different. These cases are part of the First Amendment's traditional concern to protect a specific kind of speech: speech in the context of picketing, discussing wage offers, working towards union recognition, and other similar activity. The force of the First Amendment in these contexts draws acknowledgment on the value of workers' rights as well as the value of freedom of speech. The Court's comment in footnote 17 at 763 is misleading and self-serving. The Court remarks that the labour relations cases show that 'in some circumstances speech of an entirely private and economic character enjoys the protection of the First Amendment'. 'Private', I take it, is intended to imply exactly that the speech does not deal with matters of public policy. But it is also clear that the Court in cases such as *Thornhill* decided those cases the way it did because the Court analogized the workers' speech at issue as closely as possible to political speech.

These cases belong to the late 1930s and early 1940s, the period of Franklin Roosevelt's New Deal and the National Labour Relations Act. The cases are important representative sites of the struggle of the workers to unionize in the post-Depression period, and of the opposition of corporations, their owners, and management to such efforts. The Court begins in *Thornhill* with traditional, and mellifluous, rhetoric about the exposure of falsehood being 'essential to free government', and about 'the confidence of those who won our independence' in 'the power of free and fearless reasoning and communication of ideas' (at 95). The Court urges later that:

freedom of discussion . . . must embrace all issues about which information is needed or appropriate to enable the members of society to cope with the exigencies of their period. In the circumstances of our time the dissemination of information concerning the facts of a labour dispute must be regarded as within that area of free discussion that is guaranteed by the Constitution. . . . Free discussion concerning the conditions in industry and the causes of labor disputes appears to us indispensable to the effective and intelligent use of the processes of popular government to shape the destiny of modern industrial society. [at 102–3]

The feature that 'purely commercial speech' cases have in common with labour relations cases—that the speech is on an economic subject—is not the feature which protects the speech in the latter cases. *Thornhill* and the rest stand for the proposition that it is not the case that if a speech is on an economic subject it is not constitutionally protectable. The truth of that proposition is altogether logically independent of the truth of the proposition the Court needs to infer to support its story about commercial speech, that if speech is on an economic subject then it is protectable.

The Court seems to entertain a second line of argument, which is no more plausible. The Court points out (at 763) that in *Thornhill* it was observed that there might well be widespread economic repercussions from a labour dispute at one single factory. The Court comments that 'the fate of such a "single factory" could as well turn on its ability to advertise its product as on the resolution of its labor difficulties', and thus sees 'no satisfactory distinction' between the two cases. Perhaps not, in the very respect identified. But so what? Are we to take the purpose of the First Amendment now to include the provision of protection from economic hardship? In this line of argument, the Court finds the cases to have in common a feature which does nothing at all to suggest that *either* kind of case falls within the scope of the First Amendment, let alone that First Amendment protection is merited.

The Court's first attempt to provide a positive reason why commercial speech merits constitutional protection fails. The cases to which the Court analogizes *Virginia Board* do involve speech for an economic purpose. But they involve further elements also, and it is those further element—elements lacking in 'I will sell you product X for Y price'—which implicate the First Amendment.

(B2) The Court's second argument is based on the thought that 'the particular consumer's interest in the free flow of commercial information may be as keen, if not keener by far, that his interest in the day's most urgent political debate' (at 763). First, we need to clarify what is being here compared to what. Suppose I am buying a new car while an election is on. It might well be that it matters far more to me in such circumstances that I buy the car which fits my needs best at a price I can afford than that I vote for the candidate I support. So it will also matter more to me that I get the fullest information possible about the kind of car I am interested in, about its features and performance, than I get about the political platforms of the respective election candidates. That is one possible comparison which would explicate the Court's thought. Here is another: I may generally be someone who takes much more interest in consumerism, in buying things, getting bargains, etc., than in politics. I am far more likely to be watching the Shopping Channel than CBC Cable News. From the wording, it seems more likely that the Court has the second in mind.

But what do these truisms have to do with freedom of speech? Nothing. From the fact that I as an individual have certain priorities in my life-plan, nothing follows about what my, or anybody else's, constitutional rights ought to be. Suppose, though, we transfer the issue to a more abstract level. Let us assume that 'the free flow of commercial information' promotes economic welfare, and so I have in its existence whatever interest I have in living in a society that has economic well-being. Let us assume also that I have an interest in living in a society in which there is extensive freedom of political speech.[48] 'I' in these formulations essentially means 'anyone': I am taken to be typical of any representative citizen. Now, it might be that, from some external point of view from which we can assess interests of this degree of generality, the former interest outweighs the latter. But it would then be perverse in the extreme to argue that the point of the First Amendment is to protect that former interest and not the latter interest in freedom of speech.

We have canvassed three different ways of explicating the Court's comment about the 'particular consumer's interest in the free flow of commercial information'. Each of them makes plausible the thought that 'the particular consumer's interest in the free flow of commercial information may be as keen, if not keener by far, than his interest in the day's most urgent political debate'. But none of

[48] Joseph Raz has argued that this interest is weighty, and may indeed be the basis for a strong argument in favour of constitutional protection for freedom of expression. See Joseph Raz, *Ethics in the Public Domain: Essays in the Morality of Law and Politics* (Oxford: Clarendon Press, 1994), Chapter 7. I discuss Raz's argument, and its implications for freedom of commercial expression, in more detail in Chapter 14 below.

them shows that the thought has any implications for First Amendment protection of commercial speech.

Here are some other ways of taking the Court's remark:

(i) For all X, if the consumer has as weighty an interest in X as in a protected category of speech, then X deserves First Amendment protection.

This cannot be what the Court intends. Far too much would be included within the scope of the principle. It is no part of the First Amendment to protect interests which, however weighty, do not have anything to do with the freedoms of religion, speech, press, or assembly. Alternatively, consider:

(ii) For all X, if the consumer has as weighty an interest in X as in a protected category of speech, *and X is a kind of speech*, then X deserves First Amendment protection.

This surely comes much closer to what the Court must have in mind. The 'free flow of commercial information' looks like a kind of speech. But the italicized clause is tricky. What does the term 'speech' mean in (ii)? Is 'speech' a technical term of constitutional law? Or is it the term in the ordinary meaning of everyday discourse? Frederick Schauer has claimed that, in its use in the First Amendment and in constitutional law, the term 'speech'

is a functional term. It must be defined by the purpose of a deep theory of freedom of speech, and not by anything the word 'speech' might mean in ordinary talk.[49]

If Schauer is right, and if the Court's argument is accurately expressed by (ii) above, then the Court's argument begs its own question. The question whether commercial speech is a kind of 'speech' is just the original question whether commercial speech is so removed from any exposition of ideas and so on that it lacks all protection[50] asked a different way. Argument (ii) is valid, substituting 'commercial speech' for 'X', if and only if the italicized clause is true. But whether it is true on such a substitution is the issue at stake.

What I have identified as proposition (B3) in Part (B) of the Court's argument fares no better. The thought here is that society's interest in robust political debate and society's interest in the free flow of commercial information are both real. Relatively uncontroversial assumptions about the kind of society we live in need to be made, for the Court's claim to be true that we do, as the Court says, 'live in a predominantly free enterprise society', and that 'the allocation of our resources . . . will be made through numerous private economic decisions' (at 765). But the same question as in (B2) arises: why is the fact that our society has both these interests a reason for granting some level of constitutional protection to commercial speech? The principle,

---

[49] Frederick Schauer, *Free Speech: A Philosophical Enquiry* (Cambridge: Cambridge University Press, 1982), 91. That Schauer is right about the term 'speech' is crucial to the position developed in this book. I present and defend Schauer's view at greater length in Chapter 7 below.
[50] Cf. *Virginia Board* at 762.

(i) For all X, if society has a strong interest in X, then X deserves First
     Amendment protection,

is clearly ludicrous. At the very least, the First Amendment covers only speech-
related interests. The alternative principle,

(ii) For all X, if society has a strong interest in X, *and X is a kind of speech*,
      then X deserves First Amendment protection,

raises the same doubts as the analogous version in (B2). 'Speech' is a term of art.
We first need to know whether economic speech is speech of the relevant kind.
The Court's argument begs the question in assuming that economic speech is
speech of the relevant kind.

Now, it may be that the preservation of the free flow of commercial information is, for quite independent and idiosyncratic reasons—reasons, that is, other
than its purported similarity to speech that is properly protected—a value which
implies constitutional protection for commercial speech, and one to which the
commercial expression doctrine can properly appeal. I have not shown here that
it is not, although I shall show it in Chapter 13 below. My argument here is narrower. My aim has been to show that there is no plausible way to interpret the
way that the Court appeals in *Virginia Board* to the supposed fact of someone's
interest in consumer affairs as by itself a premise from which the commercial
expression doctrine may be validly inferred.

Note also that the cases the Court mentions to support its claim of a strong
societal interest in the free flow of commercial information are abortions
(*Bigelow*), artificial furs as an alternative to the slaughter of animals (*Fur Info
and Fashion Council*),[51] and the fear of job losses overseas (*Chicago Joint
Board*).[52] The Court then, and yet again disingenuously, comments:

Obviously, not all commercial messages contain the same or even a very great public
interest element. There are few to which such an element, however, could not be added.
Our pharmacist, for example, could cast himself as a commentator on store-to-store dis-
parities in drug prices, giving his own and those of a competitor as proof. We see little
point in requiring him to do so, and little difference if he does not. [at 764–5]

The Court begins by mentioning clear cases of issues of high public interest,
issues in relation to which full disclosure of all relevant information would be

---

[51] *Fur Information and Fashion Council Inc v EF Timme and Son* 364 F Supp 16 (1973) (SDNY).
[52] *Chicago Joint Board v Chicago Tribune Co* 435 F 2d 470 (1970) (USCA 7th Dist), *certiorari
denied* 402 US 973 (1971). The Court's mention of this case is puzzling. The Amalgamated Clothing
Workers of America requested an injunction to compel Chicago newspapers to accept a full-page
advertisement, paid for by the union, explaining why the union was picketing the Marshall Field
store. The store was retailing imported clothing. The union argued in support of its request *inter alia*
the public interest of the issue. The Court of Appeal, however, firmly denied the request, saying no
state action was involved and that there were no constitutional grounds for compelling a privately
owned newspaper to publish an advertisement against its wishes. So the case hardly illustrates that
the issue has been found to be one of constitutional significance. Perhaps the Court's point in
Virginia Board is simply, and hardly contestably, that some members of the class of paid advertisements are members of the class of speech on a topic of public interest.

important. Then it goes on to cases with a 'political' dimension but lacking in high public interest, and concludes with 'I will sell you the X prescription drug at the Y price', the actual case in point. That case is grouped with the original examples by two moves—the weakening of the 'great public interest' requirement and the statement that the pharmacist *could have* offered political commentary even though he did not. Neither step is convincing, especially the second. I doubt the Court would be impressed if the maker of an obscene movie argued that he could have made the same movie without the obscenity, but as it happens did not, and so the movie he actually made should have the same degree of constitutional protection as the one he could have made.

(B4) I quoted at length above the Court's fourth argument about the role of the free flow of commercial information in a free enterprise society, since it is an argument that has found much subsequent favour. For all that, I find it a problematic argument. I will, as noted, consider the argument at greater length in Chapter 13. Here I confine myself to narrower problems with the argument. In the first place, is it two arguments or one? That is, how do we interpret the argument's claims made prior to the ellipsis of omission in the quotation, the claims that the allocation of resources will be made through numerous private decisions, that society has an interest in these decisions being well informed, and that to that end the free flow of commercial information is indispensable? Are they just factual background? Or are they an independent argument for constitutional protection of commercial speech? If the latter option is chosen, the response to be made is that propping up the free enterprise economic system is not obviously a First Amendment value. That is, it would be a radically new interpretation of the First Amendment to claim that a given form of speech merits protection simply because it serves the goal of efficient allocation of resources in a free enterprise economy. Likewise, in dismissing later the state's claim that the advertising restriction preserves the integrity of the pharmacy profession, the Court comments that 'the only effect the advertising ban has on [the pharmacist] is to insulate him from price competition and to open the way for him to make a substantial, and perhaps even excessive, profit' (at 769). The Court is doubtless correct. The anti-competitive character of advertising restrictions in the professions is well known. But since when were strictly economic considerations such as these the foundation of the First Amendment?

It is more plausible to take the whole paragraph as constituting one argument:

(a) The free flow of commercial information is indispensable to the proper allocation of resources in a free enterprise system.
(b) If the free flow of commercial information is indispensable to the proper allocation of resources in a free enterprise system, then it is indispensable to the formation of intelligent opinion about how that system ought to be regulated or altered.
(c) If the free flow of commercial information is indispensable to the formation of intelligent opinion about how a free enterprise system ought to be

regulated or altered, then it is indispensable to enlightened public decision-making in a democracy.

(d) The First Amendment protects everything which is indispensable to enlightened public decision-making in a democracy.

Therefore,

(e) The free flow of commercial information is protected by the First Amendment.

This argument has the undoubted advantage of formal validity. But still we need to be careful. The conclusion (e) will be shown true by the argument only if each of (a) to (d) is true. (d) is a very plausible theory of, or at least one main purpose of, the First Amendment.[53] But what of the remaining premises? They are all claims of fact, but disputable claims. (a) makes an assumption about the role of information in the promotion of economic efficiency which is not necessarily correct. Economic theory has raised doubts both about whether information is a market commodity at all, and about whether the free flow of information really does promote efficiency.[54] Moreover, the argument from information as economically efficient would apply, if it applied, only to forms of commercial speech which contain factual information. Much, even most, contemporary advertising is not straightforwardly informative (see Chapter 14 below).

Note, furthermore, the conditional character of (b) and (c). At first blush, what is needed for enlightened public decision-making are general statistics about social trends, economic indicators, and so forth. Footnote 20 on page 765 of the Court's opinion, in which the Court illustrates the kind of information it has in mind, is about only general statistics. Whatever the facts are about advertising and its effect on consumption, for example, those are the facts that are needed. Constitutional protection of the free flow of facts such as these stems from their status as social scientific facts with a direct political relevance. It does not follow, however, from the fact that the public needs the general information that therefore at the level of the particular advertisement there should always be no government restriction. As I will discuss at greater length in Chapter 13.3, some advertisements have the effect of promoting market failure. From the need to protect general economic factual information nothing immediately follows about the legitimacy or otherwise of regulation of the first-order 'speech' on which the information about general trends is based. Protection of sociological surveys of the use of pornography does not imply protection of pornography.

Note also that even if we grant that an efficient market in information is indispensable to the proper allocation of resources in a free enterprise system, it does not follow that all government regulation of the free flow of information should

---

[53] The Court (at 765, n.19) acknowledges Meiklejohn as a leading exponent of the theory. See Alexander Meiklejohn, *Free Speech and Its Relation to Self-Government* (New York: Harper and Row, 1948).

[54] I discuss so-called 'public good' arguments in favour of freedom of expression, of which the Court's seems to be one, at greater length in Chapters 13 and 14 below. I explore more fully there the role of information in particular.

be constitutionally forbidden. Even if the, or a, purpose of the First Amendment is to promote an efficient market in information, then would not the First Amendment support government attempts to *compel* speech? That is, suppose it was determined that a particular corporation, or a particular (segment of an) industry, was, without being deceptive or misleading, not disclosing information whose disclosure would improve efficiency. The company that was being required to disclose information about its products could not then complain on First Amendment grounds about a restriction of its commercial speech. Prime examples might be a labelling scheme which required the listing of nutritional content, or alcohol content, or tar content. It cannot be automatically within the scope of the First Amendment, even if interpreted to be performing an economic function, to imply that no government regulation of information of any sort should be allowed. Of course, instead of a goal-based argument on grounds of economic efficiency, one might prefer a right-based ground for minimal government intervention in the economy. But it is not clear that it should be the purpose of the First Amendment to be the servant of such a view.

In short, the above seemingly attractive argument (B4) for First Amendment protection of commercial speech based on the value of the free flow of commercial information faces several obstacles.

(i) At its best, the argument would not cover all commercial speech, but only such speech as contained neither deceptive nor misleading information. The Court in fact soon comes explicitly to acknowledge this in *Central Hudson*, though its stance there is foreshadowed by the comment in *Virginia Board* that the state may legitimately ensure 'that the stream of commercial information flow[s] cleanly as well as freely' (at 772).

(ii) The argument applies most plausibly to general economic and similar social-scientific information; however, even if First Amendment coverage of such information is proper, nothing is thereby implied about coverage of 'purely commercial speech' of the 'Product X at Y price' type.

(iii) The argument applies most plausibly to a market in information, which is regulated to whatever degree is necessary to attain efficiency. It has to be a *separate* argument that what is needed for efficiency is minimal government regulation of the flow of information, leaving it entirely up to the economic marketplace what information gets out there and what does not.

The Court comes closest to a right-based ground, as opposed to an efficiency-based ground, for minimal government intervention in the economy in its fifth argument, (B5) above, where the Court places the First Amendment's thumb on the balance between suppression of information and risk of harm. It is hard to see how the argument that one set of risks is preferable to another set of risks can be a cogent empirical, goal-based argument, when scant attempt is made to consider empirical information. The argument that we must be allowed to make our own mistakes, and the condemnation of the paternalistic state, is an argument based on autonomy, not on instrumental good.[55] But even if the First Amendment is construed as privileging autonomy, it remains to be argued that it comprehends strictly economic autonomy. Here too, as in the places already observed, whether the First Amendment protects commercial speech is already assumed by the argument the Court puts forward to support the conclusion that it does.

5 CONCLUSION

I have examined the Court's opinion in *Virginia Board* at such great length, because it is historically such a pivotal opinion. For my sceptical purposes, it is important to show that the Court does not have sound arguments for the conclusion to which it comes. The Court sets up the issue with admirable clarity, when it sets itself the task of showing that commercial speech is sufficiently like traditionally protected forms of speech that it merits constitutional protection. The Court's rhetoric, and the Court's prior commitment to the decision it wants to reach, disguise from itself and from those who, then and since, have applauded the Court's decision the fact that the Court fails in its self-appointed task. Whatever may be the intrinsic merits of the commercial expression doctrine, and I hope that we are in a position to see by the end of this book that there are none, there is no sound basis for the doctrine laid down in the U.S. Supreme Court's opinion in *Virginia Board*. The opinion presents what looks like complex and cogent argumentation. The arguments, however, fall apart as soon as they are examined with any care. Their appeal to prior First Amendment decisions is spurious and question-begging; their intrinsic validity as arguments is evanescent.

Nonetheless, the ideas expressed in the argumentation caught on. The asserted conclusions developed a life of their own, both within the U.S. Supreme Court itself and, as we shall see in Chapter 6 summarizing Part I, in the Supreme Court of Canada and the European Courts of Justice and of Human Rights. It will be necessary eventually to deconstruct the rhetorical appeal of these ideas, and that is the task I attempt in Part III of this study. In the meantime, we must turn to further examination of the contingencies of institutional history.

---

[55] I examine in detail the soundness of the appeal to anti-paternalism in Chapter 12 below.

3

Commercial Speech in the United States 1976–2002

The U.S. Supreme Court was not slow to apply the new doctrine of constitutional protection for commercial speech, albeit in somewhat of a tentative manner. *Linmark*[1] concerned a township's ordinance prohibiting the posting of 'For Sale' or 'Sold' signs on real estate. The township's motive was the laudable one of promoting racially integrated housing by slowing panic selling by whites. A real estate agent and property owner sought to have the ordinance overturned on First Amendment grounds as an unjustifiable restriction on commercial speech. Despite its sympathy for the township's aims, the Court agreed with the petitioners. The Court nonetheless reaffirmed the comment in the (in)famous cautionary footnote from *Virginia Board*[2] that there are 'common sense differences' between commercial speech and other varieties of constitutionally protected speech, which differences may suggest a different level of protection for commercial speech.

The Court in *Virginia Board* in a further footnote acknowledged that, though *Virginia Board* dealt with a profession, that of pharmacy, generalization to other professions would be premature. Physicians and lawyers might have to be treated differently (at 773, n. 25). Perhaps not surprisingly, there then followed three more cases to do with professional advertising, specifically by lawyers. In *Bates*,[3] the Court struck down the state's prohibition on any advertising by attorneys. It reiterated the economically based arguments for constitutional protection for commercial speech, in language taken directly from *Virginia Board* (at 353–4). However, it more directly balanced the state's interest in the regulation against the interests represented by the First Amendment: the arguments advanced by the Arizona State Bar were analysed and rebutted in some detail (at 368–81). It is worth pointing out that the fourth of these arguments the Court headlines as an argument from 'the undesirable economic effects of advertising' (at 377). The Court solemnly opines that 'neither [of two versions of the argument] appears relevant to the First Amendment' (ibid.). I cannot see how the Court can distinguish in a principled way between these economic

---

[1] *Linmark Associates Inc v Township of Willingboro* 431 US 85 (1977).
[2] *Virginia State Board of Pharmacy et al v Virginia Citizens Consumer Council Inc et al* 425 US 748 (1976) at 771, n. 24.
[3] *Bates v State Bar of Arizona* 433 US 350 (1977).

arguments in *Bates* whose relevance it excludes and its own arguments in *Virginia Board* about the economic effects of advertising, about whose relevance it has no doubt. The *Bates* decision has also been hailed as a high point of economic sophistication by the Court, from which point the quality of economic analysis has been all downhill.[4] I find that remarkably ironic, in that the sophistication in *Bates* is evinced in a realization that market regulation as much as market de-regulation may serve economic efficiency. It is what we shall see is the Court's later mindless commitment to the 'free flow of commercial information' which marks the lack of sophistication (see Chapter 13 below).

The Court also itself added a fifth ground for possible legitimate restriction of lawyer advertising, that restraints on in-person solicitation by attorneys might be justifiable (at 384). In *Ohralik*,[5] the Court then held that indeed there was a distinction between commercial in-person solicitation and published commercial advertising, and that the former could legitimately be restrained. Those 'common sense differences' were emphasized again (at 455). For the first time, commercial speech was formally said to deserve 'a limited measure of protection, commensurate with its subordinate position in the First Amendment scale of values' (ibid.). There might be allowable 'modes of regulation that might be impermissible in the realm of non-commercial expression' (ibid.). In *Primus*,[6] a different form of solicitation was permitted, on the grounds that it was by mail, not in person, and was not for pecuniary gain (the lawyer was providing her services *pro bono*). The Court thus saw the case as not so much 'commercial' as involving political speech and the civil liberties which were the concern of the American Civil Liberties Union, by whom Ms Primus was employed.

Friedman v Rogers[7] provides a perfect example of the point that making the promotion of economic efficiency the goal of the First Amendment can cut both ways. At issue was a section of the Texas Optometry Act prohibiting the practice of optometry under a trade name. The Court somewhat implausibly claimed that trade names were a different form of commercial speech, since they lacked intrinsic meaning (at 12). As the Court immediately noted, they still do have meaning, albeit from established associations. As a result of this difference, the Court said, there were far more extensive possibilities for deception in the use of trade names in advertising. The Court concluded that:

Rather than stifling commercial speech, [the impugned regulation] ensures that information regarding optometric services will be communicated more fully and accurately to consumers than it had been in the past. [at 16]

The Court thus acknowledges that the economic interests claimed to underlie First Amendment protection for commercial speech may in theory be as well

---

[4] Fred S. McChesney, 'De-Bates and Re-Bates: The Supreme Court's Latest Commercial Speech Cases', *Supreme Court Economic Review* 5 (1997): 81–139.

[5] *Ohralik v Ohio State Bar Association* 436 US 447 (1978).

[6] *In re Primus* 436 US 412 (1978).   [7] *Friedman et al v Rogers et al* 440 US 1 (1978).

served by regulation as by no regulation. It could hardly be clearer that in reality we are not dealing with freedom of speech at all, but with regulation of the economy, the traditional province of the legislature, not the courts. It could also hardly be clearer that any market in information, viewed from an economic perspective, must be a regulated, not an unregulated, market (again, see Chapter 13 below for more detailed analysis).

This set of cases suggests, especially in the light of the overt hesitancy in *Ohralik*, that the Court has not endorsed, and does not wish to be seen as endorsing, full-scale First Amendment protection for commercial speech. One might even hazard that the Court decided *Virginia Board* without first working through all the implications of what it had done. The Court, however, was not slow to take a step back and re-group. In 1980, no more than four years after *Virginia Board*, the Court systematically revisited its commercial speech doctrine in the *Central Hudson* case.[8] The framework laid down in this case still today governs the Court's approach to freedom of commercial speech, and to this case we must now turn.

2 CENTRAL HUDSON

In 1973, the Public Service Commission of the State of New York responded to a severe winter and the resultant fuel shortage by banning all advertising promoting the use of electricity. In 1977, despite the shortage being long over, the Commission continued the ban as applied to so-called promotional, rather than informational, advertising for the use of electricity. The ban was challenged by the Central Hudson utility as an interference with its First Amendment rights. The decision of the Court to strike down the ban is important, not for introducing any new elements to its approach to commercial speech under the First Amendment, but for its operationalization of doctrine hitherto somewhat vaguely expressed. Nonetheless, two points should be noted. The Court characterizes commercial speech here as 'expression related solely to the economic interests of the speaker and its audience' (at 561). This is certainly much broader than the 'Product X at Y price' type of example, and is one of those comments that has provoked much discussion over definitions. As I have suggested, however, this concern has little practical significance (Chapter 1.3 above). Secondly, the Court declares explicitly that 'the First Amendment's concern for commercial speech is based on the informational function of advertising' (at 563). All well and good, but we face then the difficulty that so much advertising is not at all, or only minimally, the providing of information. (For more on this see Chapter 14 below.)

The Court presents what it calls a 'four-part' or 'four-step' analysis to determine whether a regulation commercial speech should be invalidated:

---

[8] *Central Hudson Gas & Electric Corporation v Public Service Commission of New York* 447 US 557 (1980).

[1] At the outset, [the commercial speech] must concern lawful activity and not be misleading. [2] Next we ask whether the asserted governmental interest is substantial? If both inquiries yield positive answers, we must determine [3] whether the regulation directly advances the government interest asserted, and [4] whether it is not more extensive than necessary to serve that interest. [at 566; my numeration]

The first step represents the Court's decision to restrict itself to commercial speech that is truthful and not misleading, and that concerns a lawful activity. I will comment on this step shortly. The second step assesses the weight of the interest the government asserts that its regulation promotes. The third and fourth steps in different ways assess the relation between the interest asserted and the regulation in question.

The first step seems an intuitively reasonable restriction, especially in the light of any economic cast to the commercial speech doctrine; false statements have no value as information. But it already is a clue to the anomalous nature of freedom of commercial speech. After all, as Powell J famously remarked, '[u]nder the First Amendment there is no such thing as a false idea. However pernicious an opinion may seem, we depend for its correction not on the conscience of judges and juries but on the competition of other ideas.'[9] It is true that immediately after the passage quoted, Powell J continued: 'But there is no constitutional value in false statements of fact.' But then he also continued, 'Neither the intentional lie nor the careless error materially advances society's interest in "uninhibited, robust and wide-open" [*NYT v Sullivan*] debate on public issues' (ibid. at 340). It is not the lie as such, but its being 'intentional' which makes the constitutional difference; it is not the error as such, but its being 'careless' which makes the constitutional difference. The parenthetical reference is to *New York Times*;[10] the quotation is from the opinion of Brennan J at 270. In this case the Court laid down a very strict standard for the defamation of public figures to meet in order to override First Amendment protection of freedom of speech, resulting in constitutional protection for many false statements, although not for those maliciously made. Even though we are dealing here with false statements of fact, not false ideas, and despite the apparent attribution of no constitutional value, still the interests of robust political debate are held to be of supreme importance. But commercial speech has nothing to do with political debate. False statements in product advertising, for example, cannot be defended as contributions to robust and uninhibited debate on public issues. What makes speech special does not apply to commercial speech.

It is true that apparently the Court itself offers a different explanation of the lack of protection for false statements. The Court speaks in *Virginia Board* of 'the greater hardiness and objectivity of commercial speech' (at 771, n. 24 (again!)). But it is not clear either what the Court has in mind here, or why those features should make a difference. After all, it is a commonplace that much, and

⁹ *Gertz v Robert Welch Inc* 418 US 323 (1974), at 339–40.
¹⁰ *New York Times v Sullivan* 376 US 254 (1964).

even most, commercial advertising is not 'objective', but rather rhetorical, emotional, and persuasive. Moreover, it is clearly possible to portray 'I will sell you X product at Y price', or, 'This product will produce X effect if used in manner Y', as 'hardy' and 'objective', compared with 'Where do you want to go today?' and the like. But then most theses advanced by science are in some sense variations on the form 'This substance will produce X effect if used in manner Y'. Moreover, many typical campaign statements take the form of 'I will build you X schools at Y price', or 'I will order X stealth fighters at Y price', and seem comparably 'hardy' and 'objective'. Yet in the case of scientific or political statements, we do not take the supposed hardiness or objectivity of some such statements as reasons for denying others of such statements—false ones, for example—full First Amendment protection. Why then do these features in the case of commercial speech supposedly underwrite an exclusion of false or misleading speech, and a lower level of protection for the rest?

The remaining parts of the test I will leave for later comment (see Chapter 13.5–9 below). The *Central Hudson* test taken as a whole substantiates the Court's earlier implication that commercial speech deserves *some* protection under the First Amendment, but a lower level of protection. In the case of judicial review of legislation under the due process and equal protection clauses of the Fourteenth Amendment, the Court normally requires only that the legislation classifying individuals for the purposes of differential treatment is *rationally related* to a *legitimate* government interest. That is an easily satisfied requirement, and so much legislation will pass the test. Where legislation infringes upon the exercise of fundamental rights,[11] the legislation is subject to so-called 'strict scrutiny'. This requires that the legislation aims at a *compelling* or *overriding* government interest, and that it is *necessary* or *narrowly tailored*, that it represents the *least restrictive means*, to the furthering of the interest. This standard aims to be a difficult one for legislation to satisfy. As compared with these two tests, the *Central Hudson* test, in requiring in its second part that the government interest be '*substantial*' requires more than the first, but less than the second, of the other two tests. As it stands, the same thing seems to be true of the fourth part of the *Central Hudson* test—more than a rational relationship, but less than a narrow tailoring. As we shall see, it fell to the later *Fox* decision[12] to clarify the matter.

3 THE APPLICATION OF *CENTRAL HUDSON* IN THE 1980s

The Court in *Bolger*[13] backtracked in one important respect from the enthusiasm of *Virginia Board*. The Court did strike down a federal statute prohibiting

---

[11] Or where it creates a suspect classification—but this aspect is outside the scope of the present book.
[12] *Board of Trustees of the State University of New York et al v Todd Fox et al* 109 SCt 3028 (1989). The case will be discussed shortly.
[13] *Bolger v Youngs Drug Products Corp* 463 US 60 (1983).

unsolicited mailing of contraceptive advertisements. Among the items mailed, however, were informational pamphlets about condoms; these pamphlets did not propose any commercial transaction. Some made specific reference to Youngs' own products, some did not. The Court made it clear that 'the mailings constitute commercial speech notwithstanding the fact that they contain discussions of important public issues such as venereal disease and family planning' (at 67–8). These mailings were 'statements made in the context of commercial transactions' (at 68). 'A company has the full panoply of protections available to its direct comments on public issues, so there is no reason for providing similar constitutional protection' for such statements (ibid.). In *Virginia Board* (at 764–5), the Court flirted with the conclusion that a public interest commentary attached to otherwise purely commercial speech would give the latter the character of political speech. *Bolger* firmly rejects any such thought. Public interest commentary that in itself has no element of advertising is still commercial speech if it occurs in a commercial context. That is, such commentary would in principle receive the level of protection appropriate for commercial speech, not for political speech.

The way to *Fox* was paved by *Posadas*.[14] Although casino gambling was legal in Puerto Rico, a statute of the Commonwealth of Puerto Rico, administered by the Tourism Company of Puerto Rico, banned all advertising of gambling to the public of Puerto Rico. Advertising was permitted through publicity media outside Puerto Rico. A casino hotel that had frequently been fined under it for violating the ban challenged the statute. The decision is significant for the way that the majority, per Rehnquist J (as he then was), applied the *Central Hudson* test in upholding the legislation, not for any formal interpretation of the test. In focussing on the third part, on whether the restriction on commercial speech directly advanced the government's asserted interest, the Court said that clearly it did. The reason was:

The Puerto Rico legislature obviously believed, when it enacted the advertising restrictions at issue, that advertising of casino gambling aimed at the residents of Puerto Rico would serve to increase the demand for the product advertised. We think that the legislature's belief is a reasonable one . . . [at 341–2]

With respect to the fourth part of the test, on whether the restriction imposed is no more extensive than necessary to serve the government's interest, the hotel argued that the government could as well have proceeded by countering speech with more speech as by banning speech. The Court's response was:

We think it is up to the legislature to decide whether or not such a 'counter speech' policy would be as effective in reducing the demand for casino gambling as a restriction on advertising. The legislature could conclude . . . [at 344]

---

[14] *Posadas de Puerto Rico Associates dba Condado Holiday Inn v Tourism Company of Puerto Rico et al* 478 US 328 (1986).

These two quotations illustrate an approach of considerable deference towards the legislature's view of the matter. The Court does not ask the legislature for positive argument in favour of the view it holds; the Court simply deems the legislature's belief reasonable, and that its approach is a possible approach. *De facto*, therefore, while supposedly applying the *Central Hudson* test, the Court demands little, if any, more than would be required by the weak 'rational relationship' test described above (Chapter 3.2). Doubtless, the fact that the product being advertised was the seemingly dubious one of gambling played a role here.

In *Fox*, the State University of New York had regulations restricting commercial activities on its campuses to a prescribed list—selling food or books, laundry services, banking, and the like. Todd Fox and other students wanted to host sales parties for American Future Systems Inc, marketing housewares to students. They were banned from doing so under the university regulations, and sought to have the regulations invalidated on First Amendment grounds. The Court, acknowledging the conflicting dicta in previous cases (at 3033), used the case to clarify exactly what the fourth step of the *Central Hudson* test amounted to. The Court verified that, to satisfy the fourth step requirement, 'something short of a least-restrictive-means standard' (ibid.) would suffice:

What our decisions require is a ' "fit" between the legislature's ends and the means chosen to accomplish those ends' (*Posadas* 341)—a fit that is not necessarily perfect, but reasonable; that represents not necessarily the single best disposition, but one whose scope is 'in proportion to the interest served' (*In re RMJ* 203);[15] that employs not necessarily the least restrictive means but . . . a means narrowly tailored to achieve the desired objective. Within those bounds we leave it to governmental decision-makers to judge what manner of regulation may best be employed. [at 3035]

The Court maintains that the requirement of some form of narrow tailoring means that the government has to do more than it does under the 'rational relationship' test, and therefore that the *Central Hudson* test even under this interpretation constitutes a form of protection under the First Amendment for commercial speech. For all that, it is a very low level of protection.

4 THE EARLY 1990s

The fundamental framework for First Amendment protection of commercial speech is now clearly the four-part test established in *Central Hudson*. But, as Chapter 3.3 has just indicated, the test does not wear its application to specific cases on its face. Different interpretations of the stringency of the test's requirements are possible, especially the third part to do with 'directly advancing' the stated government interest, and the fourth part to do with the degree of impairment of the speech in question. Decisions after *Fox* have revealed that *Posadas*

---

[15] *In re RMJ* 455 US 191 (1982).

and *Fox* marked the low point of the Court's standard for constitutional protection of commercial speech. Although there has not exactly been complete consistency in the jurisprudence of post-*Fox* cases, a trend is evident upwards from the low level of protection seemingly condoned by *Fox*.

With respect to the third part of the *Central Hudson* test, the Court began in *Discovery*[16] to require that the government present some real empirical evidence that the proposed restriction of speech would directly advance the stated interest. The City of Cincinnati proposed to ban from its streets vending boxes for commercial advertising newspapers, but not ordinary newspapers, in the interests of safety and aesthetics. The City presented no argument for how such a move would advance these ends in the light of the fact that commercial vending boxes were only a tiny proportion of the total number of such boxes on city streets. The Court concluded that it had not satisfied the third part of the *Central Hudson* test (at 1510). In *Edenfield*[17] (at 1800) and *Florida Bar*[18] (at 2377), the government was deemed to have passed the third element of the test in part precisely because of its provision of empirical information. In *Coors*,[19] the third part of the test was taken to be the requirement that the Federal Alcohol Administration Act is conceptually and logically coherent, a test which, as Thomas J for the Court gleefully pointed out (at 1590 and 1592), the Act miserably failed. Only *Edge*[20] breaks the pattern. The Court baldly announces that it has 'no doubt that the statutes directly advanced the governmental interest at stake in this case' (at 2704). It seems plausible to attribute this *insouciance* to the fact that the interest in question was lottery regulation.

While the requirement of real evidence is welcome, if in fact genuine constitutional rights are at issue, it might be too optimistic to suppose that the requirement will move courts a long way from simply exercising their own discretion. In his dissent in *Florida Bar* (at 2384), Kennedy J is loath to accept that the third element of the *Central Hudson* test has been met:

This document [the summary of the research] includes no actual surveys, few indications of sample size or selection procedures, no explanations of methodology, and no discussion of excluded results. There is no description of the statistical universe or scientific framework . . .

It is arguably absurd to expect petitioners to meet the standards required by professional peer-reviewed journals of social science. Courts are far more likely to fudge the application of such a high-level test than invariably to find against every government that fails to meet it.[21]

---

[16] *City of Cincinnati v Discovery Network Inc et al* 113 SCt 1505 (1993).
[17] *Edenfield v Fane* 113 SCt 1792 (1993).
[18] *Florida Bar v Went For It Inc* 115 SCt 2371 (1995).
[19] *Rubin v Coors Brewing Company* 115 SCt 1585 (1995).
[20] *United States v Edge Broadcasting Company* 113 SCt 2696 (1993).
[21] Such a connection has become extremely important in the case of strict regulation of tobacco advertising on public health grounds. The Supreme Court of Canada in particular has struggled with the issue, as has the European Court of Justice. See Chapters 4.5 and 5.2 below.

The same pattern is evident in the Court's handling of the fourth part of the *Central Hudson* test, the requirement of a 'reasonable fit' between the government interest at stake and the means used to forward it. In *Discovery* (at 1516) the Court rejected Cincinnati's bare assertion that commercial speech was of lower value as sufficient justification for the banning of commercial vending boxes. In *Florida Bar*, the thirty-day ban on in-person solicitation by lawyers was held to pass the test. The Court determined it to be sufficiently 'narrowly tailored' because information about the availability of attorneys to consult could be obtained from many sources other than in-person solicitation (at 2380–1). By similar reasoning in *Coors*, the availability of many other ways to promote an interest in controlling the consumption of alcohol without restricting speech meant that the ban on printing alcohol strength on beer labels could not be regarded as 'narrowly tailored', and failed the test (at 1593).

This rebounding from the *Posadas–Fox* minimalist view on commercial speech is accompanied all the same by clear signals at the level of principle that the Court intends to maintain its balancing act as regards the level of constitutional protection. *Discovery* explicitly affirms the doctrine of a lower level of protection for commercial speech (at 1510), and leaves open the possibility that some acceptable way of banning commercial but not non-commercial vending boxes might exist (at 1516). *Edenfield* also draws attention to the appropriateness of a different test for constitutionality than for non-commercial speech (at 1798). *Florida Bar* revives the terminology of 'core', and by implication 'peripheral', categories of speech from the point of view of the First Amendment, and quotes with approval the language of *Fox* ascribing a 'subordinate position in the scale of First Amendment values' to commercial speech.[22] As against this emphasis, the Court also affirms the positive value to society of commercial speech, in *Discovery* (at 1512) and *Edenfield* (at 1798).

5 44 LIQUORMART

44 Liquormart merits separate consideration. The decision has the formal hallmarks of being thought by the Court to be a major decision—several different opinions and extensive reasoning in the major opinion. However, those very characteristics result in the doctrinal implications of the case being hard to pin down. Four different judges write opinions; the main opinion by Stevens J is in eight parts, which attract differing numbers of judges in support. The bottom-line judgment itself, that Rhode Island's total ban on advertisements of liquor prices is unconstitutional, is unanimous. Eight judges accept that the *Central Hudson* test is the appropriate test for commercial speech, even if Scalia J does so reluctantly and only because he sees no other test currently available (at 1515). Seven of the nine judges believe that the ban does not pass the fourth part

---

[22] *Florida Bar* at 2375, quoting *Fox* at 3033.

of the *Central Hudson* test. Part VI of Stevens J's opinion discusses the status of *Posadas*. Stevens J presents for examination three different doctrines found in *Posadas*—strong deference to the legislature where commercial speech is concerned; the argument that the greater power to regulate an activity implies the lesser power to regulate the promotion of that activity; the argument that there is a 'vice exception' to the *Central Hudson* test, resulting in a negligible level of protection for speech in the context of an activity such as gambling. Stevens J repudiates all three doctrines. In the other detailed opinion in *44 Liquormart*, by O'Connor J, in which three colleagues join her, she also explicitly rejects the *Posadas* defence of a deferential approach. This part of Stevens J's opinion also therefore has the support of eight judges.

Beyond this, not much is clear. The ninth judge is Thomas J. In his opinion, he urges rejection of the *Central Hudson* test for commercial speech:

I do not see a philosophical or historical basis for asserting that 'commercial' speech is of 'lower value' than 'non-commercial' speech. . . . I do not believe [the *Central Hudson* balancing test] should be applied to a restriction of 'commercial' speech, at least when, as here, the asserted interest is one that is to be achieved through keeping would-be recipients of the speech in the dark. [at 1518]

The last sentence might seem to be less than a complete rejection of commercial speech as a special category, but it is not. Thomas J's opposition is to any case where true and non-misleading commercial speech is regulated. If we subtract from the total of commercial speech false or misleading commercial speech (which Thomas J still seems willing to exclude from constitutional protection), only true and non-misleading speech is left. Thomas J essentially therefore reduces the *Central Hudson* test to its first part. There would still be a difference between commercial speech and non-commercial speech. As Powell J remarked in *Gertz*, 'under the First Amendment there is no such thing as a false idea'.[23] The societal interest in robust political debate militates against a strict requirement of truth.

Thomas J does not attract any support for such a strong view. Nonetheless, given Scalia J's comment that he shares Thomas J's discomfort with the *Central Hudson* test (at 1515), it seems likely that, on a formal vote on the matter, the remaining two aspects of *Posadas* picked out by Stevens J in Part VI of his opinion would be supported by at least a bare majority of the Court. Only three other judges formally join Part III of Stevens J's opinion, in which he endorses the importance to 'our' culture of advertising, and gives a history of previous commercial speech cases, but again it seems likely that Thomas J and Scalia J would be on side too. The remaining argumentative Part IV of the opinion is another piece of kite-flying. Stevens J argues that complete bans on speech should require a stricter standard of review than other commercial speech regulations. But only two others join him in this.

---

[23] *Gertz v Robert Welch Inc* 418 US 323 (1974), at 339–40.

Two things are clear from *44 Liquormart*. First, the four-part *Central Hudson* test, with its built-in lower level of protection for commercial speech than for non-commercial speech, still remains the Court's device of choice for dealing with commercial speech cases. Secondly, though, the Court has abandoned the weak interpretation of the test suggested by *Posadas* and *Fox*, and expects the government to make a real case for regulation, notwithstanding the lower level of protection. These trends were evident in the immediately preceding decisions, *Edge* excepted.

6 THE MOST RECENT CASES

The recent cases have been marked chiefly by the continued adherence to the four-part *Central Hudson* test as the primary doctrinal device for deciding commercial speech cases. This has naturally disappointed commentators (and doubtless Thomas J himself) who hoped that Thomas J's call for full First Amendment protection for commercial speech in *44 Liquormart* set the Court's future direction.[24] At the time of writing, four further commercial speech cases have been decided, as follows.

Two of the cases concerned an issue that had not previously come before the Court: the constitutional status of so-called compelled commercial speech. In the case of the kind of political or religious speech given full First Amendment protection, it is well established that to be forced to say what one does not want to say is as much a violation of the right of free speech as is being prevented from saying what one does wish to say. Both amount to intrusions into, and even repudiations of, personal autonomy—'in a free society one's beliefs should be shaped by his mind and his conscience rather than coerced by the State'.[25] The two chief U.S. precedents illustrate the issue well—Jehovah's Witnesses who for religious reasons did not wish to be compelled to salute the U.S. flag every morning in school assembly;[26] residents of New Hampshire, also Jehovah's Witnesses, who did not wish to be compelled to show the motto 'Live Free or Die' on their automobile licence plates.[27] The Court later supplemented these precedents with a line of cases beginning with *Abood* in which compelled contributions for expressive activities that conflict with personal beliefs could also be declared unconstitutional. A framework thus existed which required little, if any, change to be applied to appropriately chosen restrictions on commercial speech. The candidate restrictions concerned producers in the agriculture industry being required to fund generic advertising for the industry as a

---

[24] Cf., for example, Arlen W. Langvardt and Eric L. Richards, 'The Death of *Posadas* and the Birth of Change in Commercial Speech Doctrine: Implications of *44 Liquormart*', *American Business Law Journal* 34 (1997): 542–53.

[25] *Abood v Detroit Board of Education* 431 US 209 (1977), at 234–5.

[26] *West Virginia Board of Education v Barnette* 319 US 624 (1943).

[27] *Wooley v Maynard* 430 US 705 (1977).

whole, a common scheme in the industry. There have been two such cases in the last five years, with differing results.

The first case, *Wileman*,[28] concerned marketing orders promulgated by the Secretary of Agriculture pursuant to the Agricultural Marketing Agreement Act of 1937 to compel growers, handlers, and processors of California tree fruits to fund generic advertising for any and all California tree fruits. Some producers challenged the mandatory contribution as a violation of the right of free speech. The Court had ample reason independent of any devotion to freedom of commercial speech to take this case, as there had been inconsistent decisions in the Court of Appeal (at 2137). The Ninth Circuit, the court below in the instant case, had decided in favour of the fruit producer,[29] but the Third Circuit, in an earlier case concerning a similar scheme for beef producers, had upheld the scheme.[30]

The Supreme Court also upheld the scheme, departing from its recent pattern of government-bashing and paeans to the free flow of commercial information, as Souter J's spirited dissent in the case made clear. The Court distinguished the case from precedents such as *Barnette* and *Maynard*. Although the Court did not give background reasons for their analysis, they laid down as distinguishing the facts in *Wileman* that the marketing orders at issue 'do not compel the producers to endorse or to finance any political or ideological views' (at 2138). The Court noted that 'requiring respondents to pay the assessments cannot be said to engender any crisis of conscience' (at 2139), and concluded that 'what we are reviewing is a species of economic regulation that should enjoy the same strong presumption of validity that we accord to other policy judgments made by Congress' (at 2142). The Court did not even reach the applicability of the *Central Hudson* test (at 2141), having determined that First Amendment scrutiny was not warranted.

The decision was narrow, by five to four, and roundly criticized by Souter J in his spirited dissent. The Court smartly returned to the issue in *United Foods*[31] and this time upheld an apparently similar scheme for mushroom producers. Stevens J and Kennedy J from the *Wileman* majority changed sides, to provide a six to three vote to invalidate the scheme. The scheme in question was pursuant to the Mushroom Promotion, Research and Consumer Information Act.[32] The Court was careful to present itself as distinguishing, and not overruling, *Wileman* (at 2339ff). The fundamental ground for the distinction was that the compelled advertising regulations in the latter were 'part of a comprehensive statutory agricultural marketing program' (at 2339), whereas the scheme in *United Foods* was simply a programme of compulsory subsidy for generic

---

[28] *Glickman v Wileman Brothers and Elliott Inc et al* 117 SCt 2130 (1997).
[29] *Wileman Brothers and Elliott Inc v Espy* 58 F 3d 1367 (1995) (USCA 9th Cir).
[30] *United States v Frame* 885 F 2d 1119 (1989) (USCA 3rd Cir).
[31] *United States v United Foods Inc* 121 SCt 2334 (2001).
[32] Mushroom Promotion, Research and Consumer Information Act 1990, 104 Stat 3854, 7 US Constitution 6101.

advertising.[33] The Court followed *Wileman* in declining to apply the *Central Hudson* test, and viewing the issue of compulsory subsidy for generic advertising as belonging to the doctrine of compelled speech, rather than commercial speech, even though commercial speech was involved.

That the distinction the Court makes is a valid one can be argued. The relation between speech and a regulatory scheme is different in the case where the scheme regulates a group or an industry overall, and impacts on speech relatively minimally, and where the scheme does nothing except regulate speech. If 'coercion' is a relevant factor in the analysis, arguably the latter kind of scheme really does 'coerce' speech more than the former kind. But the Court's analysis in *United Foods* wholly fails to confront the issue raised by the majority in *Wileman*, of whether conceptually the issue of compelled speech is relevant at all. The main reason for granting constitutional protection against being compelled to speak lies in the preservation of personal autonomy; hence the reference in *Wileman* to 'engender[ing] a crisis of conscience' (at 2139).[34] There is no difference in this respect between the fact situation in *Wileman* and that in *United Foods*. United Foods Inc is, as the Court itself acknowledges, 'a large agricultural enterprise based in Tennessee' (at 2337). It is absurd to paint 'a large agricultural enterprise' as capable of suffering from crises of conscience. That United Foods has to subsidize generic claims about the value of any mushroom as such, when it believes that its mushrooms are superior to any others (cf. 2336), is not the stuff of which crises of conscience are made.

The Court implicitly tries to anticipate this objection:

The fact that the speech is in aid of a commercial purpose does not deprive respondent of all First Amendment protection, as held in the cases already cited. The subject matter of the speech may be of interest to but a small segment of the population; yet those whose business and livelihood depend in some way upon the product involved no doubt deem First Amendment protection to be just as important for them as it is for other discrete, little noticed groups in a society which values the freedom resulting from speech in all its diverse parts. First Amendment concerns apply here because of the requirement that producers subsidize speech with which they disagree. [at 2335–6]

A 'large agricultural enterprise', which heavily markets its products in the western United States, is hardly a 'discrete, little noticed group'. Moreover, as Breyer J notes in his dissent (at 2347), in any case small mushroom producers who might lay a claim to being discrete and little-noticed are exempt from the requirements of the Act.

Stevens J in his concurring opinion is embarrassed enough to concede that true freedom of conscience cases like *Barnette* and *Maynard* are not germane to the matter (at 2342). Yet he does agree that *Abood* is relevant. The Court latches

---

[33] As also was the case in *Frame*; but the Court did not hesitate in *Wileman* to agree with the Third Circuit's disposal of *Frame*.

[34] I will say more about corporations and autonomy, and about autonomy-based arguments for freedom of commercial expression, in Chapters 9, 11, and 12 below.

on to a comment in that case that speech need not be characterized as political before it receives First Amendment protection (at 232). As the above quotation shows, the Court then couples this comment with reiteration of the claim that a commercial dimension does not rule out the possibility of the speech being protected. The Court then concludes that the doctrinal mechanism established in *Abood* is in principle applicable to United Foods Inc, and applies it to hold the compelled subsidy for generic advertising unconstitutional. The Court here, as it did in *Virginia Board* (see Chapter 2.4 above), argues invalidly. It does not follow simply from the fact that *Abood* opens the door to the protection of non-political speech that the speech in *United Foods* and the speaker in *United Foods* are of a kind to make *Abood* a proper precedent. Nor does it follow from the fact that some speech with a commercial dimension is protectable speech that the speech in *United Foods* and the speaker in *United Foods* are protectable.

In between the two cases on generic advertising, the Court also decided *GNOBA*,[35] another case concerned with regulation of lottery and casino advertising. The Court had upheld in *Edge* (see Chapter 3.4 above) the constitutionality of federal regulation 18 USC §1304 as applied to broadcast advertising of Virginia's lottery by a radio station located in North Carolina, where no such lottery was authorized. In *GNOBA*, the Court ruled that §1304 could not be applied to advertisements of private casino gambling broadcast by radio or television stations in Louisiana, where such gambling is legal. The Court avowedly does not 'break new ground' (at 1930), applying the *Central Hudson* test. Stevens J's opinion focuses on the idea that 'the operation of s.1304 and its attendant regulatory regime is so pierced by exemptions and inconsistencies that the Government cannot hope to exonerate it', including *inter alia* an exception for tribal casino gambling to the regulation, and an exemption for state-run, rather than privately run, lotteries (at 1928). The Court refers back to its demand in *Discovery* and *Edenfield* that the third part of the *Central Hudson* test, that the impugned regulation materially advances the government interest, 'is not to be satisfied by mere speculation or conjecture' (*Edenfield*, at 1792). The Court concludes that the rag-tag of regulations concerning casino advertising cannot meet the demand. The Court does concede that, 'had the Federal Government adopted a more coherent policy, or accommodated rights of speakers in States that have legalized the underlying conduct . . . this might be a different case' (at 1936). But they didn't, and it wasn't. Thomas J repeats his call to abandon the *Central Hudson* test and accompanying lower standard of review, but attracts no concurrers (at 1936).

---

[35] *Greater New Orleans Broadcasting Association Inc v United States* 119 SCt 1923 (1999).

7 TOBACCO AND DRUG ADVERTISING

The next commercial speech case decided by the U.S. Supreme Court, *Lorillard*,[36] finally plunged the Court into one of the major issues of public policy in the last two decades, that of government regulation of tobacco products. It is now beyond dispute that the consumption of tobacco products is a major cause of physical ill-health in the population and, it must be acknowledged, a major source of taxation revenue. As a result, the manufacture and distribution of tobacco products are everywhere to greater or lesser degree regulated. Beyond that, much less is clear. The pros and cons of tobacco regulation constitute a tangled Sargasso Sea of principles and policies, rights and goals.[37] Only one thread of this complex set is at issue in this book, that of the regulation of tobacco products by means of regulating the advertising of them. But it is an important thread. Tobacco manufacturers understandably (they make billions of dollars in income from the sales of their products) seek to relieve themselves of regulatory burdens by every means that the legal and political systems that regulate them provide. Among those resources is certainly the commercial expression doctrine. In the United States, Canada, and Europe, there have been major challenges under the heading of freedom of commercial expression to government restrictions imposed on the advertising and promotion of tobacco products.[38] In this chapter our concern is with the U.S.

The Food and Drug Administration (FDA) in 1995 promulgated a set of regulations for the tobacco industry, including restrictions of various kinds on the advertising of tobacco products. These regulations were immediately challenged by the industry on many grounds, including constitutional grounds under the First Amendment. The industry won the first round.[39] The ruling related only to the FDA's powers under the Federal Food, Drug and Cosmetic Act, and declared that tobacco was not a 'drug' such that it was within the FDA's powers to control it.

The Clinton Administration was simultaneously pursuing the strategy of a negotiated settlement with the industry on the regulatory framework within which it operates, as opposed to the imposition of such a framework by legislation. Such a strategy culminated in the Master Settlement Agreement of November 1998, into which nearly all the states entered. Notwithstanding that the Agreement incorporated some level of regulation of tobacco advertising, the state of Massachusetts promulgated in 1999 much more restrictive regulations aimed at limiting tobacco consumption by minors.[40] These regulations were

[36] *Lorillard Tobacco v Reilly* 533 US 525 (2001).

[37] For a valiant, and important, attempt to unravel the tangle see Robert L. Rabin and Stephen D. Sugarman (eds.), *Regulating Tobacco* (New York: Oxford University Press, 2001).

[38] For Canada see Chapter 4.5 below; for Europe see Chapter 5. 2 below.

[39] *U.S. Food and Drug Administration v Brown and Williamson Tobacco Corp* 529 US 120 (2000).

[40] 940 Code of Mass. Regs. §§21.01–21.07, 22.01–22.09 (2000).

promptly challenged by the tobacco manufacturers on several grounds, including specifically these two—that the Federal Cigarette Labeling and Advertising Act,[41] with its clause forbidding restriction on the advertising and promotion of cigarettes (§1334(b)), pre-empted the Massachusetts regulations, and that the regulations violated the First Amendment protection of commercial speech.

The Court held for the manufacturers on the federal pre-emption issue. However, as noted, the federal Act related only to cigarette advertising. The Massachusetts regulations covered smokeless tobacco and cigars as well. The Court was therefore forced to assess the First Amendment claim as it applied to these categories of tobacco products. The Court affirmed the applicability of the *Central Hudson* test (Thomas J again dissenting and calling for strict scrutiny) (at 553–5). By stipulation, the impugned regulations passed the first two parts of the test. The Court's analysis therefore focussed on the third and fourth parts: material advancement and minimal impairment. The Court had no difficulty finding that the restrictions on advertising and promotion satisfied the constraint of not being 'mere speculation or conjecture'. The Court was willing to accept statistics from a variety of sources as to a causal connection between tobacco advertising and underage tobacco use. The Court, however, ruled that the Massachusetts regulations failed to satisfy the fourth prong of the *Central Hudson* test. A complete prohibition on smokeless tobacco and cigar advertising within 1,000 feet of schools and playgrounds was too broad (at 562). The definition of 'outdoor' was so wide that it amounted to a virtual ban on any advertising, even to adult consumers (ibid.). The point-of-sale regulations failed both the third and fourth parts (at 566). The requirement that individuals wishing to handle and purchase tobacco products do so through a salesperson was, however, deemed not to violate the First Amendment (at 567–9). Given the apparent political will of states to come to terms with tobacco consumption as a drain on public resources, and the deep pockets and commitment to its self-interest of the tobacco manufacturing industry, and given too the persistence of the belief that commercial speech merits constitutional protection, it is unlikely the last has been heard in the courts of these issues.

There has been much litigation in the last few years concerning the FDA's attempt to include as part of its regulatory repertoire for monitoring the pharmaceutical industry restrictions on pharmaceutical drug advertising. Most of this litigation has been confined to the lower courts. The litigation raises, in my view, very sharp questions for the commercial expression doctrine, and I will discuss it in more detail in Chapter 8.2 below, once the theoretical context has been defined. One issue, however, has reached the U.S. Supreme Court, and constitutes the most recent commercial speech case: *Western States*.[42] Drug compounding is a process by which a pharmacist or doctor combines, mixes, or

---

[41] 79 Stat. 282, as amended, 15 USC §1331 (1970).
[42] *Thompson v Western States Medical Center* No. 01-344 (April 2002).

alters ingredients to create a medication tailored to an individual patient's needs. The Food and Drug Administration Modernization Act of 1997 (FDAMA) exempts compounded drugs from the FDA's standard drug approval requirements under the Federal Food, Drug, and Cosmetic Act (FDCA), so long as the providers of the compounded drugs abide by several restrictions, including that the prescription be unsolicited (21 USC 353a(a)) and that the providers not advertise or promote the compounding of any particular drug, class of drug, or type of drug (353a(c)). These restrictions were challenged by a group of licensed pharmacies that specialize in compounding drugs. In yet another five to four decision, the Court invalidated the restrictions. The Court relies on three arguments. First, the regulatory scheme fails the fourth prong of the *Central Hudson* test since, in the Court's opinion, 'several non-speech-related means' exist of ensuring that drug compounding remains a niche activity, and not a way for pharmaceutical manufacturers to escape the reach of new drug approval requirements (at 10–15). Secondly, the Government relies unconstitutionally on the fear that people will make bad decisions if given true information (at 15–18). Thirdly, the regulations are broad enough to cover what seems like quite appropriate conveying of information: for example, a pharmacist serving a children's hospital where many patients are unable to swallow pills would be prevented from telling the children's doctors about a new development in compounding that allowed a drug that was previously available only in pill form to be administered another way, or that the flavour in medications could be changed (at 18–19). The opinion tracks the argumentation in *Virginia Board* quite closely (unsurprising, perhaps, in that both concern pharmaceutical advertising), down to the appeal to a class of persons worthy of much sympathy (in this case, children), who will be starved of needed information by the wicked Government's restraints. Breyer J in his dissent reminds the majority that the issue here is really public health and not freedom of speech:

An overly rigid commercial speech doctrine will transform what ought to be a legislative or regulatory decision about the best way to protect the health and safety of the American public into a constitutional decision prohibiting the legislature from enacting necessary protections. [end of Part III]

'As history in respect to the Due Process Clause shows', he continues, 'any such transformation would involve a tragic constitutional misunderstanding', an argument I will return to in Chapter 13.6–9 below.

8 TELEMARKETING

There is one specific issue involving commercial speech on which the Supreme Court has decided, so far at least, to act by not acting. It has not so far decided to hear any cases, despite inconsistency of decisions in lower courts. The dispute is with regard to telemarketing, and centres mainly on so-called ADADs,

Automatic Dialling-Announcing Devices. These machines are essentially computers with the capacity to dial telephone numbers automatically and deliver a recorded message when the telephone is answered. Most states have legislation controlling the use of these devices, and the federal Telephone Consumer Protection Act (1991) also regulates the use of ADADs. From the point of view of businesses which wish to use such telemarketing to advertise themselves and their products or services to consumers, these regulations appear clearly to be a restriction on their commercial speech. Thus the regulations become obvious potential targets for challenge under the First Amendment.

The cases litigated so far show no consistency. State regulations have been challenged four times. In Oregon[43] and New Jersey[44] the state regulations have been overturned as unconstitutional. In Minnesota the state regulations have twice been upheld.[45] The federal Act has been challenged twice, and upheld twice.[46] As noted the Supreme Court has declined to hear appeals both from the Ninth Circuit's decision on the federal Act and from the first Minnesota Supreme Court decision on the state statute. The Court's strong support for a privacy interest in *Florida Bar* doubtless underlies the refusal. But there is still plenty of potential for the issue to come before the Court again.

Even in the case of telemarketing by a solicitor for a charity, at least one court has ruled that there was no violation of First Amendment rights. Charitable solicitation is fully protected by the First Amendment.[47] However, in *NFAB of Arkansas*,[48] the charity challenged a state statute which provided that 'if the person receiving the telephone call indicates that he or she does not want to hear about the charity, goods, or services, the caller shall not attempt to provide additional information during that conversation about the charity, goods, or services'.[49] The Eighth Circuit ruled the provision not to be in violation of the First Amendment. It acknowledged that 'most households in today's society are plagued by a flood of unwanted telephone solicitations', and said that it was 'unwilling . . . to second-guess the Arkansas legislature's judgment that many citizens have difficulty dealing with these intrusions' (at A.2).[50]

---

[43] *Moser v Frohnmayer* 345 P 2d 1284 (1993) (Oregon SC).

[44] *Lysaght v New Jersey* 837 F Supp 646 (1993) (US Dist Ct Dist NJ).

[45] *State v Casino Marketing Group* 491 NW 2d 382 (1992) (Minn SC), *certiorari denied* 507 US 1006 (1993); *Van Bergen v Minnesota* 59 F 3d 1541 (1995) (USCA 8th Cir).

[46] *Moser v FCC* 46 F 3d 970 (1995) (USCA 9th Cir), *certiorari denied* 115 SCt 2615 (1995); *Szefcek v Hillsborough Beacon* 668 A 2d 1099 (1995) (NJ Sup Ct, Law Divn).

[47] *Riley et al v National Federation of the Blind of North Carolina Inc et al* 487 US 781 (1988), at 787–8.

[48] *National Federation of the Blind of Arkansas v Mark Pryor*, No. 00-2324 (July 31, 2001) (USCA 8th Cir).

[49] Ark. Code Ann. § 4-99-201 (a) (2).

[50] As this book went to press, the Federal Act survived a challenge by companies objecting to regulation of unsolicited fax advertising: *Missouri v American Blast Fax, Inc et al* 02-2705/2707 March 21st 2003 (USCA 8th Cir).

9 Conclusion

Far more cases have been covered in this chapter, and in far less space, than was so in Chapter 2. There is a clear reason. From a strict doctrinal or institutional perspective, freedom of commercial speech is now an established constitutional right in the United States. The doctrine has been in place for almost twenty-seven years. It is twenty-three years since the main continuing framework for adjudication under the doctrine was established. It has become routine to speak of corporations' rights under the First Amendment. There have been ups and downs within a fairly narrow band of taking governments seriously, but an intermediate level of constitutional protection for commercial speech has become standard operating procedure. It would be a brave person who, from the point of view of political realities, forecast that anything would change.

The fact remains, although I acknowledge that the argument of Parts II and III of this book will be needed to demonstrate it, that the U.S. Supreme Court has erected its doctrinal structure on a flimsy or non-existent jurisprudential foundation. The tough questions that, in my view, were left open by the jurisprudential inadequacy of the Court's arguments in Virginia Board, have simply not been faced in the subsequent years to date. How come business corporations have ascribed to them a right of free speech that belongs primarily to natural persons? How come the free flow of commercial information is touted as an unequivocal good, when economists acknowledge the importance of regulation of information in maintaining efficient markets? Or when most of what is protected is not in fact carrying information at all? What is it about *commercial* speech, as opposed to political speech, which means it has to weigh so heavily in the balance against other social needs like public health? And so on. We do not find answers to any of these questions in the cases since *Virginia Board*, but only a reiteration of arguments made in that case as if they were assertions whose patent truth transcended enquiry. But they are, as I shall show, not true at all.

4

Commercial Expression in Canada

1 INTRODUCTION

Constitutional protection in the full sense (that is, a right the enforcement of which may lead to invalidation of legislation) for freedom of expression in Canada is relatively recent compared with that in the U.S. Prior to April 1982, the formally written constitution of Canada was essentially the British North America Act of 1867,[1] an act of the United Kingdom Parliament in Westminster establishing the Dominion of Canada as a federation of provinces. The Act focussed mostly on the governmental structures of the provincial and federal governments and the distribution of powers between the two levels of government. Protection of fundamental rights and freedoms was left to legislation and the common law, following the United Kingdom tradition. The Canadian Bill of Rights[2] was enacted in 1960, applying only to federal legislation. Alberta, Quebec, and Saskatchewan also enacted Bills of Rights with respect to provincial legislation. All of these instruments, however, are themselves ordinary Acts of parliaments. The extent of their authority *vis-à-vis* legislation is not clear.[3]

All that changed with the enactment in April 1982 of the Canada Act 1982.[4] This was an Act of the United Kingdom Parliament terminating the authority of the Westminster Parliament over Canada, and designating its own Schedule B as having the force of law in Canada. This Schedule is comprised by the Constitution Act 1982. The relevance of the Constitution Act 1982 to the present context is threefold. (i) Section 52(2) of the Act, among other provisions, defines the Constitution of Canada as including the Constitution Act 1982 and the renamed (from the 'British North America Act') Constitution Act 1967. (ii) Section 52(1) states that 'any law that is inconsistent with the provisions of the Constitution is, to the extent of the inconsistency, of no force or effect.' (iii) Sections 1–34 of the Act are explicitly designated the *Canadian Charter of Rights and Freedoms*, and thus form a Bill of Rights for Canada with the authority to invalidate legislation.

The two sections which concern us here are sections 1 and 2(b). These sections read as follows:

---

[1] 30 & 31 Vict, c.3 (U.K.).   [2] RSC 1985, Appendix III.
[3] On the specific issue of Bills of Rights in Canada see Peter W. Hogg, *Constitutional Law of Canada* (Loose-leaf edn., Toronto: Carswell, 2002), Chapters 31 and 32 ; on the history of Canadian constitutional law generally, see Chapters 1–4.
[4] U.K. 1982, c.11.

1. The *Canadian Charter of Rights and Freedoms* guarantees the rights and freedoms set out in it subject only to such reasonable limits prescribed by law as can be demonstrably justified in a free and democratic society.
2. Everyone has the following fundamental freedoms:
    (a) freedom of conscience and religion
    (b) freedom of thought, belief, opinion and expression, including freedom of the press and other media of communication;
    (c) freedom of peaceful assembly;
    (d) freedom of association.

The contrast with the First Amendment to the U.S. Constitution is clear. First, the term 'expression' is used instead of 'speech'. This change reflects the Canadian drafters' perception that much of what merits protection under such a clause as section 2(b) is not literally *speech* in the sense of words uttered in a language with and as with a sense and reference. Rather, any plausible right of freedom of expression comprehends also silent expressive behaviour such as wearing an emblem or marching in protest. Secondly, the absolutist language of the First Amendment is gone; section 2(b) simply acknowledges the possession by everyone of a certain protected normative position characterized as a 'freedom'.[5] Thirdly, and perhaps most obviously, the Canadian Charter explicitly acknowledges in section 1 the possibility of valid limitations on Charter rights and freedoms under certain conditions. Section 1 authorizes courts where appropriate to balance governmental interests against those represented by the rights and freedoms defined in subsequent sections of the Charter.

Section 2(b) is obviously the focal point of my discussion in this book, and I shall turn to it shortly. First, though, let me say more about section 1. Its statutory form is quite general in content, and it does not wear on its face any instructions for the application of the section to actual litigation. The Supreme Court quite properly took time to develop a practical test for the justification of legislative impairment of a Charter right or freedom. The test was eventually laid down early in 1986 in the case of *R v Oakes*,[6] and unsurprisingly is known for short as 'the *Oakes* test'. The test is as follows:

(1) The objective of the limitation must be sufficiently important to warrant overriding a constitutionally protected right or freedom. As a minimum, it must represent a pressing and substantial concern.

(2) The means employed must be reasonable and demonstrably justified. The assessment of this takes the form of a three-part test of proportionality:
    (i) The measures employed must be rationally connected to the objective.
    (ii) The measures should impair the freedom no more than is necessary to accomplish the objective.
    (iii) The effects of the impugned limit must not be disproportionate to the importance of legislative objective sought.

[5] L.W. Sumner, *The Moral Foundation of Rights* (Oxford: Clarendon Press, 1987), Chapter 2.
[6] *R v Oakes* (1986) 26 DLR (4th) 200, at 224–8. See also Hogg, *Constitutional Law*, Chapter 35.

A brief comparison with the *Central Hudson* test (see Chapter 3.2 above) in U.S. Supreme Court jurisprudence is in order. The *Oakes* test, of course, applies to infringements of any Charter right or freedom and *a fortiori* to commercial expression, while the *Central Hudson* test is specifically for commercial speech. That said, there are clear similarities. The *Oakes* test comes into play only once it has been determined that a Charter right or freedom has been infringed: likewise the first part of the *Central Hudson* test asks whether the speech in question comes within the scope of the First Amendment. The first part of the *Oakes* test proper concerning the importance of the objective of the government limitation corresponds to the second part of the *Central Hudson* test concerning the weight of the government interest behind the legislation. Part 2, step (i) of the *Oakes* test, requiring a rational connection between the objective and the measures employed, corresponds to the third part of the *Central Hudson* test requiring that the regulation directly advance the government interest. Part 2, step (ii) of the *Oakes* test, concerning minimal impairment of the right or freedom, corresponds to the 'no more extensive than necessary' criterion of part 4 of the *Central Hudson* test. There is no complement in the *Central Hudson* test to part 2, step (iii) of the *Oakes* test. As I shall discuss later (Chapter 4.5), there are questions to be asked about whether the Supreme Court of Canada's actual handling of freedom of commercial expression respects jurisprudential constraints implicit in the institutional separation of section 1 from the subsequent sections, including section 2(b), of the Charter.

A determination of the constitutional status of commercial expression by the Court was a long time in coming, in 1989 in the *Irwin Toy* case.[7] Before that case, attempts to have legislation invalidated on the ground of freedom of commercial expression had mixed success in lower courts. It is jurisprudentially as well as institutionally important to review those decisions, as they both demonstrate well the issues that need discussing and throw into needed relief the stance on commercial expression later taken by the Supreme Court.

2 FREEDOM OF COMMERCIAL EXPRESSION 1982–89

As I indicated above, at first sight there are two stages to the determination under the Canadian Charter of Rights and Freedoms of the constitutional validity of legislation. The first stage is to determine whether a Charter right or freedom has been infringed. The second is to determine whether the infringement is justified or not using the *Oakes* test. As we shall see (Chapter 4.3 below), the Supreme Court's eventual view, at least as regards freedom of expression, makes the first stage of little significance. But that was not so in the period under review in this section. As regards commercial expression, some courts were

---

[7] *Attorney-General of Quebec v Irwin Toy Ltd* [Indexed as Irwin Toy Ltd v Quebec (Attorney-General)] (1989) 58 DLR (4th) 577.

quite prepared to find, notwithstanding familiarity with the decision of the U.S. Supreme Court in *Virginia Board*,[8] that legislation regulating commercial expression did not constitute an infringement of section 2(b), although some courts did find commercial expression to be within the scope of the section 2(b) freedom of expression. The cases may be grouped by subject-matter, and within each section are presented chronologically.

Professional advertising. As in the U.S., many of the early commercial expression cases concerned restrictions placed on advertising by professional persons. In *Klein*,[9] concerning advertising by lawyers, the court was divided on whether commercial expression fell within section 2(b). The majority excluded it, on the grounds that freedom of expression in section 2(b) had to do with protection of the democratic political process. U.S. cases from *Virginia Board* onwards were reviewed, but the court chose to adopt the reasoning of the dissenters in such cases. The dissenting judge in *Klein*, by contrast, appealed to the role of commercial expression in supporting a free enterprise economy as a reason for including it within section 2(b). In *Grier*,[10] concerning advertising by an optometrist, the court was quite clear that 'the dissemination of product information is a valued activity in our society' (at 336), and included commercial expression within section 2(b). In *Griffin*,[11] restrictions on advertising by dentists were held to be outside the scope of section 2(b), on the ground again that section 2(b) had to do with protection of the political process. In *Rocket*,[12] the majority held commercial expression to be within section 2(b) on the ground of the importance to society of the free flow of commercial information. The dissent excluded the expression in question from section 2(b), distinguishing commercial expression in general from professional advertising in particular; the latter was held not to be a protected form of expression because of the importance to society of a high standard of professionalism.

Product advertising. The issue in *Halpert*[13] was provoked by Canada's conversion from the imperial system of weights and measures to the metric system. The legislation made it illegal to continue after a certain date to advertise gasoline in imperial gallons, which the defendant was doing. The court referred to the U.S. Supreme Court's reasoning in *Virginia Board* and *Bigelow*,[14] and concluded that commercial expression fell within section 2(b). *Irwin Toy*[15] concerned provisions of Quebec's consumer protection legislation regulating

---

[8] *Virginia State Board of Pharmacy et al v Virginia Citizens Consumer Council Inc et al* 425 US 748 (1976).

[9] *Re Klein and Law Society of Upper Canada: Re Dvorak and Law Society of Upper Canada* (1985) 16 DLR (4th) 489 (Ont HCt).

[10] *Re Grier and Alberta Optometric Association* (1987) 42 DLR (4th) 327 (Alta CA).

[11] *Re Griffin and College of Dental Surgeons of British Columbia* (1988) 47 DLR (4th) 331 (BC SC).

[12] *Re Rocket et al and Royal College of Dental Surgeons of Ontario et al* (1988) 49 DLR (4th) 641 (Ont CA).

[13] *R v Halpert et al* (1983) 9 CCC (3d) 411 (Ont Prov Court, Cr Div).

[14] *Bigelow v Virginia* 421 US 809 (1975).

[15] *Irwin Toy Ltd v Quebec (Attorney-General)* (1986) 32 DLR (4th) 641 (Que CA).

advertising aimed at children. The court held such advertising to be clearly within section 2(b). *Ford*[16] revolved around the requirements of Quebec's *Charter of the French Language*,[17] specifically the requirement that commercial advertising be in French only. La Chaussure Brown's Inc, Valerie Ford as sole proprietor of a wool shop, and other businesses challenged the legislation as, *inter alia*, an infringement of their freedom of commercial expression. The court found that there was an infringement of section 2(b). Finally, in *Edible Oil*,[18] the requirement of the Ontario Oleomargarine Act that margarine be coloured differently from butter was held to be a restriction of a form of advertising, and as such an infringement of section 2(b) freedom of commercial expression.

Solicitation by prostitutes. There were several cases relating to section 195.1(1)(c) (now section 213.1(c)) of the Canadian Criminal Code. The section makes it an offence to communicate or attempt to communicate with any person for the purpose of engaging in prostitution.[19] In *McLean*,[20] the court alluded to the only existing precedent at the time on commercial expression, the *Klein* case mentioned above, and its split decision on whether commercial expression fell within section 2(b). The court ruled that, even if other forms of commercial expression were within section 2(b), solicitation certainly was not. It would 'demean the grand concept of freedom of opinion and expression' (at 184) to hold otherwise. In *Skinner*,[21] the majority held that freedom of expression in section 2(b) should be interpreted generously and not moralistically, and as extending, 'by necessary inference, to negotiations between buyers and sellers of goods and services other than labour' (at 211). The dissent refers to the judgment in *McLean*, and holds that solicitation is not within section 2(b). In *Jahelka*,[22] the court held (at 108) that freedom of expression must include communication for the purpose of earning a livelihood, including the sale of one's body, for after all what else is done by professional athletes. The court placed solicitation within the scope of section 2(b). In *Cunningham*,[23] section 195.1(1)(c) was held to be a violation of section 7 of the Charter, the section that guarantees 'life, liberty and security of the person', and not justified under

[16] *Attorney-General of Quebec v La Chaussure Brown's Inc et al* [Indexed as Ford v Quebec (Attorney-General)] (1987) 36 DLR (4th) 374 (Que CA).

[17] R.S.Q. 1977, c. C-11.

[18] *Re Institute of Edible Oil Foods et al and the Queen* [Indexed as Institute of Edible Oil Foods v Ontario] (1987) 47 DLR (4th) 368 (Ont HCt).

[19] There has been virtually no similar case law in the U.S. But see *Morgan et al v City of Detroit* 389 F Supp 922 (1975) (US Dist Ct, E Dist Mich, SD), 'thought-provoking' commercial speech would be within the scope of the First Amendment, but solicitation would not be (at 928); *State v Allen* 424 A 2d 651 (1980) (Conn Sup Ct), 'speech incidental to solicitation for prostitution' is not 'within the protective embrace of the First Amendment' (*sic!* at 654). A corporation advertising its brothels is, naturally, a different matter: such speech comes under the protective shield of the First Amendment, although it fails to pass the *Central Hudson* test (*Princess Sea Industries Inc v Nevada* 635 P 2d 281 (1981), *certiorari denied*, 456 US 926 (1982), per Manoukian J, concurring).

[20] *R v McLean, R v Tremayne* (1986) 28 CCC (3d) 176 (BC SC).

[21] *R v Skinner* (1987) 35 CCC (3d) 203 (NS SC, App Div).

[22] *R v Jahelka* (1987) 36 CCC (3d) 105 (Alta CA).

[23] *R v Cunningham* (1986) 31 CCC (3d) 223 (Man Prov Ct).

section 1. The court declined to speculate on the status of the section in relation to section 2(b) of the Charter. In response, the Manitoba provincial government referred the constitutionality of section 195.1(1)(c) to the Manitoba Court of Appeal. That court[24] ruled that solicitation does not fall within section 2(b): 'I think that Milton and Mill would have been astounded to hear that their disquisitions were being invoked to protect the business of whores and pimps' (Huband JA at 413).

Newspaper vending box cases. The publishers of *The Globe and Mail*, Canada's largest national newspaper, decided to pursue the possibility of using the Charter's protection of freedom of expression to overturn ordinances in various cities across the country which controlled or forbade newspaper vending boxes on city streets. Initially, their attempts met with success. In Quebec City, the court held that the placement of vending boxes on city streets came within section 2(b), and the restrictions were not justified under section 1.[25] In Victoria, however, the court was less co-operative.[26] The ordinance was said not to be a prohibition against the distribution of newspapers which would offend against the Charter. It was said to be instead a prohibition aimed at preserving the unique character of Victoria for reasons of tourism, and so there was no infringement of section 2(b). In Montreal, the newspaper lost again.[27] The court construed the newspaper's claim that the city could not tell it where to place vending boxes as a claim to have a right to use public property as it wished. It could not fall to a freedom of expression clause to protect such an impossible claim.

Miscellanea. Two further cases should be mentioned. In *Slaight*,[28] in a dispute between a radio station and a salesman unjustly fired, the station was ordered by a labour tribunal to provide a specified letter of reference for the salesman, and to respond to requests for a reference with nothing but that letter. The court had no doubt that the section 2(b) freedom of expression of the radio station was infringed, but voted to uphold the tribunal's order under section 1. The court did not, though, acknowledge the case specifically as one of freedom of *commercial* expression. In *Reid*,[29] a farmer who failed to file tax returns for five successive years claimed that the requirement under section 151 of the Income Tax Act that in his return he 'estimate' the amount of tax payable was an infringement of his freedom of expression under section 2(b). The Provincial Court judge agreed with the farmer, and invalidated section 151. The Alberta Court of Queen's Bench allowed the inevitable appeal by the Crown,

---

[24] *Reference re ss. 193 and 195.1(1)(c) of the Criminal Code* (1987) 38 CCC (3d) 408 (Man CA).
[25] *Re Canadian Newspapers Co Ltd and Director of Public Road and Traffic Services of the City of Quebec* [1987] RJQ 1078 (Que Sup Ct).
[26] *Re Canadian Newspapers Co Ltd and City of Victoria et al* [Indexed as Canadian Newspapers Co v Victoria (City)] (1989) 63 DLR (4th) 1 (BC CA).
[27] *Canadian Newspapers Company Ltd c Ville de Montréal et le procureur général du Québec, mis en cause* [1988] RJQ 482 (Que Sup Ct).
[28] *Slaight Communications Inc (Operating as Q107 FM Radio) v Davidson* [1985] 1 FC 253 (Fed CA).
[29] *R v Reid* (1988) 40 CCC (3d) 282 (Alta CA).

and the Court of Appeal agreed. The court remarked that 'in their widest sense, the words "thought, belief and opinion" would encompass virtually every mental process . . . Yet the section [section 2(b)] cannot have been intended to protect, as a "fundamental freedom", the mental aspect of every human activity' (at 286–7).

Analysis. In the U.S., after *Central Hudson*,[30] there was essentially no dissent from the basic idea that commercial speech merited some level of *prima facie* protection under the First Amendment. It is clear, however, that the lower courts surveyed above evince two contrasting approaches to the status of commercial expression under section 2(b). The first is to construe the meaning of 'expression', and the associated freedom, narrowly. Such an approach sees freedom of expression as primarily related to preserving the integrity of the democratic political process, as related to positive or 'grand' social values. On that basis, advertising, solicitation, siting of vending boxes, and so on are remotely, if at all, connected to the integrity of the political process, and so limitations on the freedom to pursue such activities cannot be within the purview of section 2(b). The second view construes the meaning of 'expression', and the associated freedom, generously and broadly. On this view, commercial expression has social value, in its guise of the provision of information. It is part of the free enterprise economy and the pursuit of economic well-being. Even if some forms of commercial expression are of little social worth, the value of free expression precisely forbids their exclusion from constitutional protection on such grounds. Note again that this is not a difference of opinion on how to weigh legislation restricting freedom of commercial expression in section 1 analysis. It is a difference of opinion on whether commercial expression falls within freedom of expression as protected by the Charter.

Although the Supreme Court had not yet decided any commercial expression cases in the period under review, lower courts were not entirely without guidance from the Supreme Court on how to go about determining whether there was an infringement of the section 2(b) freedom of expression. The guidance came (the opinion is referred to in several cases) from the opinion of Dickson J (as he then was) in *Big M Drug Mart*,[31] a freedom of religion case. He wrote:

Freedom in a broad sense embraces both the absence of coercion and constraint, and the right to manifest beliefs and practices. Freedom means that, subject to such limitations as are necessary to protect public safety, order, health, or morals or the fundamental rights and freedoms of others, no one is to be forced to act in a way contrary to his beliefs or conscience. [at 354]

The interpretation [of a Charter right or freedom] should be . . . a generous rather than a legalistic one, aimed at . . . securing for individuals the full benefit of the Charter's protection. At the same time it is important not to overshoot the actual purpose of the right or freedom in question. [at 359–60]

[30] *Central Hudson Gas & Electric Corporation v Public Service Commission of New York* 447 US 557 (1980).
[31] *R v Big M Drug Mart Ltd* (1985) 18 DLR (4th) 321.

The difficulty is clear. Dickson J's advice can be embraced by supporters of each of the approaches distinguished above as authority for their view. The first approach emphasizes the recognition of limitations in the first passage quoted. The second highlights the emphasis on generosity of interpretation in the second passage.

The final point I wish to make in Chapter 4.2 is to argue that this range of Canadian cases displays the same characteristic as we have seen in the U.S. cases, which established the commercial speech doctrine. The cases in which courts, or individual judges, held that commercial expression should be within section 2(b) are ones where *for independent reasons* of policy or political morality it seems plausible to side with the commercial expresser.

As in the U.S., a number of the key cases in the area of commercial expression have been constitutional challenges to statutes regulating the professions, which typically have put restrictions of some severity on the ability of such professionals to advertise their services. In Canada, lawyers, dentists, optometrists, all have litigated such cases. These cases all involve commercial corporations of a quite idiosyncratic kind—the individual natural person who for pragmatic reasons of taxation status incorporates himself or herself as a professional corporation. Part of the way in which an autonomous natural person may promote self-realization is through the choice and pursuit of a career, especially one as intellectually complex (and financially profitable) as a traditional profession. There is a lot of not wholly misplaced hand-wringing by Henry J in dissent in the *Klein* decision about the travails of a struggling young lawyer and the need to advertise to obtain a foothold in the profession (at 505–6). Contrast the Ontario Court of Appeal in *Rocket*; it is rudely dismissive of the crude self-promotion of the principals in that case, despite upholding their appeal. The advertisements in question 'serve no public interest' (Dubin ACJO at 659); they are 'distasteful, pompous and self-aggrandizing' (Cory JA (as he then was) at 679). All the same, the underlying approach is still thoroughly economic: advertising regulation of the kind impugned is a very effective entry barrier for new professionals, and as such serves considerably to reduce the level of competition for the services provided and thus to reduce economic efficiency.[32]

Nonetheless, if the paradigm of self-expression and self-realization is, as it traditionally is, the artist, then these professional advertising cases are misleadingly borderline. Compare the status of an individual professional corporation with an ordinary business, small or not, which has the taxation status of a sole proprietorship. Valerie Ford, after whom the celebrated case is indexed, operated a wool shop as a sole proprietorship. However much sympathy one may have with her personally, and no matter how much personal satisfaction she

---

[32] David A. Strauss, 'Constitutional Protection for Commercial Speech: Some Lessons from the American Experience', *Canadian Journal of Business Law* 17 (1990): 52; Fred S. McChesney, 'A Positive Regulatory Theory of the First Amendment', *Connecticut Law Review* 20 (1988): 362–5, 376; Fred S. McChesney, 'Commercial Speech in the Professions: The Supreme Court's Unanswered Questions and Questionable Answers', *University of Pennsylvania Law Review* 134 (1985): 59–60.

derived from running her wool shop, the wool shop is still a commercial business, and so part of the economic marketplace, not the 'market-place of ideas'. And so it is with the professional corporation. The personally expressive aspects of the professional corporation are contingent. The situation in the case of the artist is the reverse. Artistic expression is intrinsically non-commercial, and becomes so only by choice. In fact, the more that art becomes commercialized, the more suspicious people become of its artistic status. We forgive Margaret Atwood her material success, because her art seems in no way to have suffered. We do not forgive the successful lawyer his or her material success; we give such lawyers our business.

As for the vending box cases, it is a commonplace that the fact that a newspaper company makes a profit from selling newspapers in no way interferes with any constitutional right it may have to freedom of expression or of the press. But does it follow that any restriction on the sale of newspapers is a restriction on freedom of expression, it not being disputed that the freedom to publish is in part the freedom to have one's publications purchased and read? While a complete ban on newspaper circulation clearly would be an infringement of freedom of expression, restrictions like those of Quebec City, Victoria, and Montreal seem to affect only, if at all, the economic interests of the newspaper publisher. While the presence of a profit motive cannot be a bar to constitutional coverage, the distinguishing feature of these cases is that the only motive is the profit motive of increased circulation.

Finally, there is plenty of opportunity for being misled by the Quebec Language Charter case of *Ford*. There are sound reasons in Canada why there should be protected freedom of expression in both of our two official languages, and that choice of language itself should be protected. A law that proscribes the use of one of those two languages in the public arena is therefore immediately, and rightly, suspect. But note that the paradigm application is again primarily to natural persons. I find it hard to see how a shoe shop, a wool shop, a tailor and dry cleaner, a florist, and a cheese distributor (the challengers in *Ford*) each have the kind of personal identity and sense of individuality which gives them a right to advertise in the language of their choice. The political demands to strike down a repudiation of one official language should not seduce a court into an unjustified extension of constitutional coverage to commercial expression under section 2(b).

3 1988–90: THE SUPREME COURT DEVELOPS DOCTRINE

As the above account indicates, the variation between provincial jurisdictions, and courts within the same jurisdiction, on the status of commercial expression under the Charter created a situation where settlement of the matter by the Supreme Court was indispensable for judicial certainty. In fact the build-up of issues needing resolution was such that over the eighteen-month period from

December 1988 to June 1990 the Court decided five different kinds of commercial expression cases on appeal from provincial courts of appeal (see the previous section for details of the cases). Only the vending box issue was not heard. In this period, the Court developed the doctrine of freedom of commercial expression under the Charter that has been the law in Canada ever since.

The Canadian Supreme Court, however, unlike the U.S. Supreme Court and, as we shall see in Chapter 5, like the European Court of Human Rights and the European Court of Justice, has in a sense not developed a freedom of commercial expression doctrine at all. The Court in the period in question develops a doctrinal approach to the interpretation of section 2(b) quite generally, even though several of the key cases are in fact cases of commercial expression. The Court's commercial expression doctrine is simply a matter of the application to commercial expression cases of its approach to freedom of expression generally. The Court is quite self-conscious about this. As we shall see, the Court considers it important to develop a different approach to freedom of expression from the one it finds south of the border.

The first case was *Ford*,[33] the case dealing with language rights and the Quebec *Charter of the French Language*. Among the important constitutional questions identified by the Court as raised by the case was: does the freedom of expression guaranteed by section 2(b) of the Canadian Charter extend to commercial expression? The Court's answer is 'It is apparent to this court that the guarantee of freedom of expression in s.2(b) of the Canadian Charter . . . cannot be confined to political expression' (at 616). The Court referred to its earlier decision in *Dolphin Delivery*,[34] in which so-called secondary picketing (picketing of a business which is not a party to a given labour dispute) was recognized to be expression within section 2(b). The *Dolphin Delivery* court acknowledged that the primary motivation of the picketing at issue was economic, but said that there was always an element of expression in any picketing, and therefore that the picketing was within section 2(b) (at 187). The Court in *Ford* concluded:

There is no sound basis on which commercial expression can be excluded from the protection of s.2(b) of the Charter. . . . Over and above its intrinsic value as expression, commercial expression which, as has been pointed out, protects listeners as well as speakers plays a significant role in enabling individuals to make informed economic choices, an important aspect of individual self-fulfilment and personal autonomy. The court accordingly rejects the view that commercial expression serves no individual or societal value in a free and democratic society and for this reason is undeserving of any constitutional protection. [at 618]

---

[33] *Attorney-General of Quebec v La Chaussure Brown's Inc et al* [Indexed as Ford v Quebec (Attorney-General)] (1988) 54 DLR (4th) 577.

[34] *Retail, Wholesale & Department Store Union, Local 580 et al v Dolphin Delivery Ltd* (1986) 33 DLR (4th) 174.

However, on the issue specifically of commercial expression that was as far as the Court went in this case. The section 1 analysis in the decision related solely to the requirement that only French be used in advertisements, and to the freedom to express oneself in one's own language as an element of freedom of expression.

The Court also laid down what turned out to be a crucial methodological principle. It said:

It must be kept in mind, however, that while the words 'commercial expression' are a convenient reference to the kind of expression contemplated by the provisions in issue, they do not have any particular meaning or significance in Canadian constitutional law, unlike the corresponding expression 'commercial speech,' which in the United States has been recognized as a particular category of speech entitled to First Amendment protection of a more limited character than that enjoyed by other kinds of speech. [at 610]

The Court went on to say that the issue should not be whether section 2(b) extended to a certain category of expression; that inquiry would give rise to 'definitional problems' (ibid.). Rather, the issue should simply be whether the constitutional guarantee should be extended to some particular kind of expression in its own right—that is, without subsuming it under some pre-selected category. Thus did the Court start down on what, in my opinion, has turned out to be a very slippery slope (see this Chapter 4.4–5 below).

The Court then turned its attention to *Irwin Toy* and the challenge to the Quebec Consumer Protection Act's[35] regulation of advertising to children. In this case, as the Court was aware (at 605), there were no language rights issues to confuse the matter. While advertising to children is hardly a paradigm case of the classic 'I will sell you the X product at the Y price', in that it typically stretches the bounds of acceptable manipulativeness, it is undoubtedly pure 'commercial expression'. As such it provided a better test case for the status of commercial expression under the *Charter* than could be provided by litigation relating to the Quebec Language Charter.

Even so, the Court begins its enquiry narrowly: 'does advertising aimed at children fall within the scope of freedom of expression?' (ibid.) But the scope soon broadens:

We cannot, then, exclude human activity from the scope of guaranteed free expression on the basis of the content or meaning being conveyed. Indeed, if the activity conveys or attempts to convey a meaning, it has expressive content and *prima facie* falls within scope of guarantee. Of course, while most human activity combines expressive and physical elements, some human activity is purely physical and does not convey or attempt to convey meaning. [at 607]

---

[35] SQ 1978. c.9 (R.S.Q., c. P-40.1).

The Court then in a justly notorious passage goes on to present an elaborate scenario to demonstrate how, contrary to what a person might think, parking a car can be an expressive act—if it is a protest against a policy of reserving an area for the spouses of government employees (ibid.).[36] The only exception the Court acknowledges is that violence as a form of expression receives no protection. The Court here quotes again from *Dolphin Delivery*, a passage where McIntyre J for the Court said that 'violence or threats of violence' were excluded from Charter protection. This view was repeated in cases subsequent to *Irwin Toy*. However, in *Keegstra*,[37] the Court realized the anomalous nature of excluding mere threats of violence from the scope of section 2(b), when it had laid down such broad principles of inclusion, and ruled that threats of violence were protected by section 2(b). Only violence officially remains excluded. The Court concludes: 'Surely it [sc. advertising aimed at children] aims to convey a meaning, and cannot be excluded as having no expressive content' (at 608).

There are further complexities in the *Irwin Toy* test for whether there is an infringement of section 2(b). After the enquiry into whether the activity restricted falls within the scope of freedom of expression, 'it must next be determined whether the purpose or effect of the impugned governmental action was to control attempts to convey meaning through that activity' (at 608–9). This enquiry has two distinct phases, into the purpose and into the effects of the governmental activity. With regard to freedom of expression,

if the government has aimed to control attempts to convey a meaning either by directly restricting the content of expression or by restricting a form of expression tied to content, its purpose trenches upon the guarantee. Where, on the other hand, it aims only to control the physical consequences of particular conduct, its purpose does not trench upon the guarantee. [at 612]

The mischief aimed at cannot consist of the meaning or the influence of the meaning on behaviour. If it is established that the purpose was to restrict the conveying of a meaning, then infringement of section 2(b) is demonstrated. If that is not established, then the court has to consider whether nonetheless the effect of the governmental activity is to restrict attempts to convey a meaning. Here the burden is on the plaintiff to demonstrate such an effect, and the plaintiff must do that by showing that the restricted activity promotes one of the three values which underlie freedom of expression—seeking the truth, participation in social and political decision-making, individual self-fulfilment (ibid.). It has not been often that this latter two-stage part of the *Irwin Toy* test for infringement of the section 2(b) guarantee of freedom of expression is subject to extensive independent investigation.

---

[36] It is noteworthy that the example the Court so carefully constructs is of *political* expression. The court keeps returning instinctively to such cases as the paradigm examples.

[37] *R v Keegstra et al* (1990) 61 CCC (3d) 1, at 24.

The next case, *Slaight*,[38] the case of the fired radio station advertising sales-man, contains no new theoretical argument, and is a foretaste of how freedom of expression cases will proceed under the Court's commercial expression doc-trine. There is no discussion of whether the adjudicator's order infringes the radio station's section 2(b) freedom of expression; the topic is solely whether the order is justified under section 1. Dickson CJC makes a number of references to the principles of political morality underlying the Charter, but these are brought to bear only on the issue of whether the infringement passes the *Oakes* test for a valid limitation of a Charter right or freedom.

The Court then decided *Edmonton Journal*.[39] This case, if one wanted to cat-egorize it U.S.-style, would be a case of freedom of the press, not freedom of commercial expression. It concerned provisions of the Alberta Judicature Act, which limited the publication of information arising out of court proceedings in matrimonial disputes. The newspaper successfully challenged the provisions of the Act as an unjustified limitation on its freedom of expression. The case is important here for the principles of the 'methodology of Charter application', which Wilson J lays down in her opinion. These have become adopted by the Court as correct principles of interpretation. Note again that, as far as concerns cases involving section 2(b), these are principles to be applied at the stage of sec-tion 1 analysis, not at the stage of determining whether there is an infringement of section 2(b). Whether that is so follows essentially from whether the restricted activity is expression that conveys a meaning.

Wilson J distinguishes (at 581 ff) between an 'abstract' and a 'contextual' approach to the application of the Charter. She illustrates what she means by the 'abstract' approach through reference to Cory J's opinion in the instant case. He alludes to the historically fundamental role of freedom of expression in the development of Canada's political, social, and educational institutions, and the seriousness of restricting the free exchange of ideas in a democratic society. Wilson J's concerns about the value of such an abstract approach are that there is too great a gap between such grand ideals and the details of a given particular case. In the instant case, she points out, the value of privacy to the litigants in a matrimonial dispute has to be balanced against the value to the public of an open court process. La Forest J, she says, also takes an abstract approach, appealing to the same background values as Cory J. But whereas the latter judges that the value of an open court process must prevail, the former judges that the value of privacy must prevail. The abstract approach, she believes, too easily yields contradictory conclusions. She favours a focus on the specific real-izations of relevant values in the specific context of a given piece of litigation. She claims:

---

[38] *Slaight Communications Inc (Operating as Q107 FM Radio) v Davidson* (1989) 59 DLR (4th) 416.
[39] *Edmonton Journal v Attorney-General for Alberta et al* (1989) 64 DLR (4th) 577.

One virtue of the contextual approach, it seems to me, is that it recognizes that a particular right or freedom may have a different value depending on the context. It may be, for example, that freedom of expression has greater value in a political context than it does in the context of disclosure of the details of a matrimonial dispute. The contextual approach attempts to bring into sharp relief the aspect of the right or freedom, which is truly at stake in the case, as well as the relevant aspects of any value in competition with it. It seems to be more sensitive to the reality of the dilemma posed by the particular facts and therefore more conducive to finding a fair and just compromise between the two competing values under s.1.

It is my view that a right or freedom may have different meanings in different contexts. . . . I believe that the importance of the right or freedom must be assessed in context rather than in the abstract and that its purpose must be ascertained in context. [at 583–4]

While the approach seems to embody the flexibility inherent in a discipline in which equity is a central virtue, we shall see that the approach is not without problems of its own.

After *Edmonton Journal*, freedom of commercial expression returned to the forefront when the Court took its own view of the issue of solicitation and section 195.1(1)(c) (now section 213(1)(c)) of the Criminal Code.[40] Again, no opinion in the case contests that the impugned section constitutes an infringement of the section 2(b) guarantee of freedom of expression. Lamer J (as he then was) gives the fullest discussion. He identifies the section as aimed at 'restricting commercial expression in perhaps its purest form' (at 114). Solicitation is simply the communication of information concerning the availability of a service and the cost of that service. To restrict solicitation is to restrict an expression conveying a meaning just because of its meaning. Just such restrictions the guarantee of freedom of expression is designed to rule out. Lamer J goes further still. He identifies (at 110) twenty-six other sections of the Criminal Code 'whose *actus reus* may consist either in whole or in part of speech or other form of expression', together with numerous aspects of criminal procedure. All of these provisions, he suggests, would count as infringements of the section 2(b) guarantee of freedom of expression. Criminalization, he says, is not a test of whether the activity is protected by section 2(b) (at 111).

Lower courts have not been enthusiastic about taking up Lamer J's invitation to find sections of the Criminal Code to be violations of section 2(b). Refusals will be found in this Chapter 4.4 below. Sections which have been held to be violations are section 175(1)(a)(i), swearing in a public place;[41] section 300, defamatory libel;[42] section 462.1, 462.2 defining 'literature for illicit drug use' and making the knowing trade in such literature an offence;[43] section 486.1 giving a

---

[40] *Reference re ss. 193 and 195.1(1)(c) of the Criminal Code (Man)* (1990) 56 CCC (3d) 65; the Prostitution Reference case.

[41] *R v Lawrence* (1992) 74 CCC (3d) 495 (Alta QB), *affirmed* (1993) 81 CCC (3d) 159 (Alta CA).

[42] *R v Stevens* (1995) 96 CCC (3d) 258 (Man CA), after two lower court decisions not only holding the section to be a violation, but also not to be justified under s.1; *R v Lucas* (1996) 104 CCC (3d) 550 (Sask CA).

[43] *Iorfida v MacIntyre* (1994) 93 CCC (3d) 395 (Ont Ct Gen Div).

discretionary power to trial judges to exclude the public, including the press, from a courtroom.[44] Sections 175(1)(a)(i), 300, and 486.1 were held to be justified violations under section 1. The Supreme Court itself has considered sections of the Criminal Code in *Keegstra* (section 319(2), wilfully promoting hatred), *Butler*,[45] *Zundel*,[46] and, by implication, *Langer*[47] and *Sharpe*.[48] None of these cases, with the possible exception of section 462.2, has to do with *commercial* expression. They are mentioned here as illustrations of the application of the Court's methodology only. All were considered infringements of section 2(b); only section 181 was held not to be justified under section 1.

In *Rocket*,[49] the Court spends little time on concluding that, since professional advertising has meaning, it is protected expression under section 2(b) (at 77). The Court also again urges the superiority of its 'contextual approach' over the 'categories' approach of the U.S. Supreme Court:

While the Canadian approach does not apply special tests to restrictions on commercial expression, our method of analysis does permit a sensitive, case-oriented approach to the determination of their constitutionality. Placing the conflicting values in their factual and social context when performing the s.1 analysis permits the courts to have regard to special features of the expression in question. . . . [alluding to the above quotation from Wilson J in *Edmonton Journal*] [N]ot all expression is equally worthy of protection. Nor are all infringements of free expression equally serious. [at 78, per McLachlin J (as she then was)]

The Court acknowledges that the commercial character of advertising may be of constitutional significance, but at the stage of section 1 analysis (at 75). The Court holds the restrictions not justified under section 1.

To sum up: the elements of the Court's methodology concerning the section 2(b) guarantee of freedom of expression are now in place. 'Expression' in section 2(b) is to be given an extremely broad interpretation, so that anything with a meaning counts as 'expression'. The purpose or effect of the impugned governmental activity must be to restrict expression so construed. The kind of considerations of background political morality which led lower courts to limit the scope of section 2(b) now come in either as relevant to the determination of effect or, in the vast majority of cases, as bearing on section 1 analysis, as components of the *Oakes* test. That test itself is to be applied, not on the basis of abstract generalizations of value, but on the basis of a contextual consideration of the particular instant case. 'Commercial expression' may serve as a convenient label for a subset of the set of cases of freedom of expression, but

---

[44] *Canadian Broadcasting Corp. v New Brunswick (Attorney-General)* (1996) 110 CCC (3d) 193.

[45] *R v Butler* (1992) 89 DLR (4th) 449, s.163, restricting obscenity.

[46] *R v Zundel* (1992) 75 CCC (3d) 449, s.181, spreading false news.

[47] *Ontario (Attorney-General) v Langer* (1995) 97 CCC (3d) 290 (Ont CA), leave to appeal to Supreme Court of Canada refused (1995) 100 CCC (3d) vi, s.163, child pornography.

[48] *R v Sharpe* [2001] 1 SCR 45, s.163.1, child pornography.

[49] *Royal College of Dental Surgeons of Ontario et al v Rocket et al* [Indexed as Rocket v Royal College of Dental Surgeons of Ontario] (1990) 71 DLR (4th) 68.

it does not denote a special category of expression with special rules for that category.

4 BUT NOT ALL EXPRESSION IS 'EXPRESSION'

The Supreme Court decided no further commercial expression cases until *RJR-MacDonald*, the tobacco advertising case,[50] discussed in detail in Chapter 4.5 below. A few cases were decided in lower courts. Shortly after *Irwin Toy* in 1989, the British Columbia Court of Appeal decided its own dentists' advertising case of *Griffin*.[51] The trial judge had declared restrictions on professional advertising to be outside the scope of section 2(b). The Court of Appeal acknowledged that, after *Irwin Toy*, this judgment must be incorrect (at 655). All the same, by a majority decision the court ruled that the impugned regulations were justified under section 1. Other subsequent lower court decisions which would count as decisions concerning commercial expression are *Pinehouse*,[52] *Cabaret Sex Appeal*,[53] *388923 Alberta*,[54] *Lapointe*,[55] and *Ratelle*.[56] In the first- and last-mentioned, the infringement was upheld under section 1; in the remaining four cases it was not.

Common sense prevailed, mostly in the lower courts, over the Supreme Court's capacious characterization of 'expression' within the meaning of section 2(b). The Supreme Court itself in *Walker*[57] rejected the claim of a certified general accountant that the Prince Edward Island Public Accounting and Auditing Act limiting the right to practise as an accountant to chartered accountants was an infringement of a section 2(b) guarantee of freedom of commercial expression. The Court was doubtful that the practice of accountancy was an expressive act. It also ruled that, even if the reporting functions of public accounting and auditing were activities conveying a meaning, the Act did not restrict anyone from performing these activities, but the capacity in which a person could perform them. Two lower court cases involved activities that clearly

---

[50] *RJR-MacDonald Inc v Attorney-General of Canada; Imperial Tobacco Ltd v Attorney-General of Canada* [Indexed as RJR-MacDonald Inc v Canada (Attorney-General)] (1995) 127 DLR (4th) 1.

[51] *Re Griffin and College of Dental Surgeons of British Columbia* [Indexed as Griffin v College of Dental Surgeons of British Columbia] (1989) 64 DLR (4th) 652 (BC CA).

[52] *R v Pinehouse Plaza Pharmacy Ltd* (1991) 62 CCC (3d) 321 (Sask CA), planning by-law prohibiting advertising by exterior signage.

[53] *Montreal (City) v Cabaret Sex Appeal Inc* (1994) 120 DLR (4th) 535 (Que CA), city by-law prohibiting display of image representing human body outside erotic establishments.

[54] *R v 388923 Alberta Ltd* (1995) 174 AR 292 (Alta CA), city by-law prohibiting portable signs on private property.

[55] *Lapointe c Ordre des denturologistes du Québec* (1994) 66 QAC 311 (Que CA), professional advertising restrictions.

[56] *R v Ratelle* (1994) 92 CCC (3d) 176 (Que CA), leave to appeal to Supreme Court of Canada refused (1995) 94 CCC (3d) vii, paragraph of Bankruptcy and Insolvency Act prohibiting canvassing for assignments under the Act.

[57] *Walker v Prince Edward Island* (1995) 124 DLR (4th) 127.

'conveyed a meaning' but were held nonetheless not to involve infringements of section 2(b). In *Cheema*,[58] a municipal noise-control by-law was held not to impinge on the section 2(b) guarantee because its purpose was to protect citizens from excessive noise, not to restrict expression. In *Baig*,[59] legislation preventing unregistered persons from holding themselves out as medical practitioners or psychologists was held not to violate section 2(b), as no-one can have a right to misrepresent their professional qualifications. In two cases, the activity of selling, which typically involves the conveying of a meaning and is even for many commentators the paradigm of commercial expression, was held not to be within the scope of section 2(b).[60] In *Rosen*, the court also rejected the plaintiff's claim that the prohibition on the sale of tobacco to minors forced them to give assent to the government's policy concerning the sale of tobacco. In *Chabot*,[61] the village of Ferland, Saskatchewan, passed resolutions which resulted in the village making rental payments on a copying machine owned by Chabot's business when he was mayor of Ferland. Chabot did not disclose his pecuniary interest in the outcome of the resolution, contrary to law,[62] and was disqualified from continuing as mayor. Chabot argued that his freedom of commercial expression under section 2(b) was violated; the court roundly rejected the hypothesis that the disclosure requirement represented compelled expression within the scope of section 2(b).

All of these cases amount to claiming that, contrary to the Supreme Court's official doctrine, there are cases of expressions with a meaning that do in fact fall outside the scope of section 2(b). In other cases, the court's ruling that the activity in question did not infringe section 2(b) turns on a failure to find an expressive dimension in what is *prima facie* simply behaviour. Unlike the trial court, the appeal court in *Edible Oil* was not impressed by the claim that the choice of colour for margarine was an expressive activity.[63] In two lap-dancing cases, which, since it is the commercial establishment which is charged rather than the performers, might be held to be cases of commercial expression, the activity in question was held to be simply physical and not to convey a meaning.[64]

The Supreme Court's approach to the meaning of 'expression' in section 2(b) can be faulted on two grounds: a failure to respect the doctrinal structure of the

---

[58] *Cheema v Ross* (1991) 82 DLR (4th) 213 (BC CA).

[59] *R v Baig* (1992) 78 CCC (3d) 260 (BC CA).

[60] *R v Sharma* (1991) 62 CCC (3d) (147) (Ont CA), prohibition on selling on a sidewalk; *Rosen v Ontario (Attorney-General)* (1996) 131 DLR (4th) 708 (Ont CA), leave to appeal to Supreme Court of Canada refused (1996) 137 DLR (4th) vii, prohibition on selling tobacco in a pharmacy.

[61] *Chabot v Brisebois* [1988] 3 WWR 669 (Sask CA).

[62] Urban Municipalities Act, S.S. 1984-84, c. U-11, s.33.

[63] *Re Institute of Edible Oil Foods et al and the Queen* [Indexed as Institute of Edible Oil Foods v Ontario] (1989) 64 DLR (4th) 380 (Ont CA), leave to appeal to Supreme Court of Canada refused (1990) 74 OR (2d) x. Since leave to appeal was refused, presumably the Supreme Court was no more impressed.

[64] *Ontario Adult Entertainment Bar Association v Metropolitan Toronto (Municipality)* (1995) 101 CCC (3d) 491 (Ont Div Ct); *R v Ludacka* (1996) 105 CCC (3d) 565 (Ont CA).

Charter itself and a failure to make sense of freedom of expression. I will discuss these criticisms below, after considering one further case.

5 RJR-MACDONALD V CANADA

I have left until now for separate mention the high-profile litigation in the 1990s concerning the federal Tobacco Products Control Act,[65] and the attempt (in the end successful) by the tobacco manufacturers to have the sections of the Act regulating tobacco advertising declared unconstitutional on freedom of expression grounds. The litigation is a cautionary tale for the Supreme Court of Canada's approach to freedom of commercial expression.

At trial, the government argued that the very threat to health posed by the consumption of tobacco excluded tobacco advertising from the scope of section 2(b).[66] The trial judge, Chabot J, had no difficulty after the definition of 'expression' in *Irwin Toy* in concluding that tobacco advertising was within the coverage of the section 2(b) guarantee of freedom of commercial expression. In his section 1 analysis, the judge had no doubt that 'the Act as now drafted . . . in fact constitutes a form of censorship and social engineering which is incompatible with the very essence of a free and democratic society' (at 503). He found the connection proposed by the government between health protection and tobacco advertising to be 'tenuous and speculative' (at 512). In his summing up, the judge was no more open-minded: 'the type of social engineering described above constitutes an extremely serious impairment of the principles inherent in a free and democratic society which is disproportionate to the objective of the Act' (at 517). He therefore invalidated the whole Act.

By the time the Court of Appeal hearing came about in 1993,[67] the Attorney-General for the Crown conceded that the Act was an infringement of section 2(b) of the Charter. The only issue to be litigated, therefore, was whether the infringement could be justified under section 1 and the *Oakes* test. This time, the government won: the court deemed the Act indeed to be a reasonable limitation of the section 2(b) freedom.

And so inevitably on to the Supreme Court. Again, it was conceded by the Attorney-General (Canada) that there was an infringement of the section 2(b) guarantee of freedom of commercial expression. The only issues litigated were under section 1. Section 7 of the Act, prohibiting the free distribution of samples of the product, was upheld. Sections 4–6 and 8–9, which contained the provisions regulating tobacco advertising, were struck down as not justified limitations

---

[65] S.C. 1988, c.20.

[66] *Re RJR-MacDonald Inc and Attorney-General of Canada; Re Imperial Tobacco Ltd v Attorney-General of Canada* (1991) 82 DLR (4th) 449 (Que Sup Ct), at 479–80.

[67] *Re RJR-MacDonald Inc and Attorney-General of Canada; Re Imperial Tobacco Ltd and Attorney-General of Canada* [Indexed as RJR-MacDonald Inc v Canada (Attorney-General)] (1993) 102 DLR (4th) 289 (Que CA).

under section 1. The holding in the case was complex. Seven different opinions were written, and there were different levels of assent to different propositions concerning the constitutionality of different provisions of the Act. At the heart of the decision was no more than a five to four split on whether the Act passed muster after section 1 analysis. I concentrate here only on the importance of the case for the theoretical issues, which are the concern of this book.

In my view, the case serves well to shed doubt on three central aspects of the Supreme Court of Canada's approach to freedom of commercial expression— the 'contextual approach' to adjudication under the Charter, the capacious approach to the interpretation of 'expression' in section 2(b), and the claimed distinction between the approach of the Supreme Court of Canada and the U.S. Supreme Court to freedom of commercial expression.

The contextual approach. There are two objections that might be raised against the contextual approach. The first has to do with a misapprehension that the Court seems to have about the problem-solving capacities of the approach. As I indicated (this Chapter 4.4), Wilson J's repudiation of the 'abstract approach' in *Edmonton Journal* turned on her perception that the same abstract premise could lead to contradictory concrete results. *RJR-MacDonald* shows that the contextual approach fares no better by this criterion. The 'contextual approach' was previously glorified by McLachlin J (as she then was) in *Rocket* at 78, and La Forest J, the dissenting judge in *RJR-MacDonald*, quotes her eloquence in his opinion at 53–4. He does so in the course of arguing that the 'contextual approach' leads to upholding the Act. McLachlin J herself wants to strike down the relevant sections of the Act. So what is her response to this use of her own ideas? It amounts to nothing more than, 'There are contexts and contexts, and when I said "contextual", I didn't mean "contextual"' (cf. 90–1). The net effect of La Forest J's contextual approach in *RJR-MacDonald* is deference to the legislature. McLachlin J objects to the degree of *de facto* deference which La Forest J's holding implies. But she does not, and cannot, argue that his holding is wrong as a matter of principle. She can argue only that she sees the context, and the degree of deference to the legislature appropriate for that context, differently from the way that he does. That way of phrasing the disagreement is all that the contextual approach allows. The use of the contextual approach, therefore, does not eliminate the possibility of contradictory readings of the same evidence. Moreover, in its eschewal of principle, it will not help to build up a body of serious and coherent jurisprudence on constitutional questions.

The second objection concerns the contextual approach in relation to the structure of the Canadian Charter itself. The issues here are deep ones having to do with the internal architecture of the Charter. It was well remarked in the early days of the Charter that:

It cannot be correct that the substantive rights and freedoms should be given their most expansive meaning on the ground that all control is supposed to lie in s.1, while, at the same time, s.1 is to be construed stringently because it is overriding an infringement of a substantive right or freedom.[68]

Currently, however, the Supreme Court errs in the opposite direction. There is much written about the need to be flexible and contextual in carrying out the balancing called for by section 1. But section 2(b) is also being given the most expansive meaning possible. So there is no control of jurisprudential or constitutional principle anywhere in the Court's approach to freedom of expression. If the thought behind the design of the Charter is that section 1 has a different role to play in constitutional adjudication from the other sections, then interpreting a section such as section 2(b) so broadly that little falls outside its scope makes such a different role impossible. In this way, the contextual approach in cases of freedom of expression, including freedom of commercial expression, subverts the inherent design of the Charter. Arguably, it also subverts the political morality behind the notion of judicial review. As Hogg has eloquently argued,[69] a broad interpretation of a right or freedom, combined with an approach which looks contextually at differences between instances of the putative exercise of the right or freedom, leads inevitably to a low standard of justification under section 1. The result would be that judicial review would become even more pervasive, even more policy-laden, and even more unpredictable than it is now. Such an outcome would be regrettable.

The capacious interpretation of 'expression'. Ironically, the best argument to be made against the contextual approach was made by McLachlin J herself while a member of the British Columbia Court of Appeal. In *Andrews*,[70] she considered the exactly analogous issue in relation to the meaning of the term 'equality' in section 15 of the Charter, the section that guarantees equality before the law and the right to the equal protection and benefit of the law without discrimination. She explicitly rejected (at 606) the proposition that 'any discrimination [sc. any making of a distinction between two seemingly similar cases] is sufficient to establish discrimination under s.15 at which point the analysis moves to s.1' (at 605). Such an approach, she said, would 'trivialize the fundamental rights guaranteed by the Charter' (at 606); would deprive the phrase 'without discrimination' of content (ibid); and would lead to all sorts of 'manifestly desirable legal distinctions' being required to 'run the gauntlet of s.1' (at 607). McIntyre J for the Supreme Court accepted this point while otherwise departing from her judgment.[71] It does not appear to have occurred to McLachlin J and those who think like her on the Supreme Court that the current approach to section 2(b) and the notion of 'expression' mimics faithfully the approach so robustly repudiated as regards section 15 in *Andrews*. The discussion of cases above, especially those to do with challenges to requirements of

---

[68] *Re Cromer and BC Teachers' Federation* (1986) 29 DLR (4th) 641 (BC CA), at 652.
[69] *Constitutional Law*, 33-19–33.21.
[70] *Re Andrews and Law Society of British Columbia et al* (1986) 27 DLR (4th) 600 (BC CA).
[71] *Law Society of British Columbia et al v Andrews et al* 56 DLR (4th) 1 (1989), at 10.

the Criminal Code, indicates many 'manifestly desirable legal' provisions which, as a result of the capacious approach to section 2(b), become justiciable, with all the public and private expense that is involved, followed by the inevitable endorsement of the provision after section 1 analysis.[72]

Freedom of commercial expression north and south of the border. As noted (this Chapter 4.4), the Supreme Court of Canada refused to recognize a specific category of 'commercial expression' analogous to the U.S. Supreme Court's use of 'commercial speech'. This refusal was allied to the adoption of the contextual approach to Charter adjudication. But it can be questioned whether this dissociation from the approach of the U.S. Supreme Court has in fact led to any substantive doctrinal differences as regards cases identifiable as instances of commercial expression.

In the U.S., the identification of an expression as falling within the category of 'commercial speech' triggers a lower standard of review for the government to meet to justify the speech regulation, lower than for political, artistic, or scientific speech, for example. U.S. court decisions on commercial speech teem with the metaphor of 'core' and 'periphery'. Political speech is the very heart or 'core' form of speech protected by the constitutional value of freedom of speech. The values served by commercial speech are not core constitutional values. In the freedom of expression decisions of the Supreme Court of Canada, the same metaphor has been deployed. In the Prostitution Reference case, Dickson CJC denied that communications regarding a transaction of sex for money 'lie at, or even near' the core of the guarantee of freedom of expression' (at 74). In *Keegstra*, he speaks of 'the tenuous link between communications covered by s.319(2) [the section prohibiting hate propaganda] and other values at the core of the free expression guarantee' (at 51). In *Butler*, Sopinka J found that pornography 'does not stand on equal footing with other kinds of expression which directly engage the "core" of the freedom of expression values' (at 482). LeBel JA of the Quebec Court of Appeal quite rightly sums all this up by saying that 'the Supreme Court jurisprudence has tended to distinguish between so-called core values and those lying on the periphery' (*RJR-MacDonald* (1993) at 320). The metaphor is also central to La Forest J's statement of his dissenting opinion in the Supreme Court's hearing of *RJR-MacDonald* (at 53–5).

It might be pointed out that all these justices draw internal authority for the use of the metaphor from the opinions of Wilson J in *Edmonton Journal* and McLachlin J in *Rocket* (1990), both of whom are careful to deny that they are creating categories of expression. But they entertain explicitly the thought that not all cases of expression are of equal value. McLachlin J both in *Rocket* (1990) (at 75, 79) and in *RJR-MacDonald* (1995) (at 102) implies that commercial expression is of lower value than paradigm forms of expression. In the same case, Iacobucci J says the same (at 107), and three judges concur with La Forest

⁷² See also for similar criticism Janet L. Hiebert, *Charter Conflicts: What Is Parliament's Role?* (Montreal and Kingston: McGill-Queens University Press, 2002), 74–6.

J's opinion containing its uncompromising adherence to the same evaluation (at 55). If, as is the case, a certain range of cases of expression are regularly assigned a high value in section 1 balancing, and another range of cases are regularly assigned a lower value, then do we not have *de facto* a 'core' and a 'periphery', with commercial expression somewhere out towards the periphery?[73]

Moreover, although the U.S. Supreme Court has had a commercial speech doctrine for a lot longer than the Supreme Court of Canada has been acknowledging freedom of commercial expression, there is a considerable overlap in the kind of case decided and manner of deciding. Both Courts have struck down numerous state and provincial restrictions on professional advertising. Both Courts have invalidated legislation controlling the advertising of, respectively, alcohol and tobacco. To the *Irwin Toy* ready deference to the legislature concerning advertising to children there corresponds a similar deference to speech regulations, which in part protect children. (The U.S. Supreme Court denied *certiorari* in *Anheuser-Busch* (alcohol advertising) and *Penn Advertising* (cigarette advertising):[74] the Fourth Circuit court in each case highlighted the need for 'special solicitude in the First Amendment balance' towards children (*Anheuser-Busch*, at 329).) It may be the case that the U.S. Supreme Court's 'categories' approach 'giv[es] rise to difficult definitional problems';[75] I alluded to the issue in Chapter 1.3 above. But self-consciously discarding principle in favour of contextual balancing seems only to reproduce the substance of those very problems in a different guise.

6 Recent developments

The Supreme Court of Canada has considered the issue of freedom of commercial expression only once since *RJR-MacDonald*, in *Guignard*.[76] Guignard owned several properties in the city of Saint-Hyacinthe, Quebec. He became incensed at treatment he received from his insurance company after a loss at one of these buildings. 'He placed a sign on another of his buildings that eloquently expressed his dissatisfaction' (paragraph 3), and was charged under the city's by-law forbidding advertising signs on buildings outside areas zoned for industrial

---

[73] These spatial metaphors are here, as in most instances of their use to refer to conceptual 'geography', slippery. See William Van Alstyne, 'A Graphic Review of the Free Speech Clause', *California Law Review* 70 (1982): 107–50. For the slipperiness of spatial metaphors in analytical jurisprudence generally, see Roger A. Shiner, *Norm and Nature: The Movements of Legal Thought*, Clarendon Law Series (Oxford: Clarendon Press, 1992), 316–21.

[74] *Penn Advertising Inc v Mayor of Baltimore* 63 F 3d 1318 (USCA 4th Cir), *vacated and remanded* 116 SCt 2575 (1996), *modified* 101 F 3d 332 (USCA 4th Cir), *certiorari denied* 117 SCt 1569 (1997); *Anheuser-Busch Inc v Schmoke* 63 F 3d 1305 (1995) (USCA 4th Cir), *vacated and remanded* 116 SCt 1821 (1996), *modified* 101 F 3d 325 (USCA 4th Cir), *certiorari denied* 117 SCt 1569 (1997). The remands were in order to reassess the decisions in the light of the U.S. Supreme Court's holding in *44 Liquormart: 44 Liquormart Inc v Rhode Island* 116 SCt 1495 (1996), see Chapter 3.5 above.

[75] The Supreme Court of Canada in *Ford* at 610.

[76] *R v Guignard* 2002 SCC 14, file 27704.

use. The Supreme Court reaffirmed its commitment to freedom of commercial expression on familiar grounds: 'The need for [commercial] expression derives from the very nature of our economic system, which is based on the existence of a free market . . . commercial enterprises have a constitutional right to engage in activities to inform and promote, by advertising' (paragraphs 21, 23). The Court also acknowledged that 'consumers also have freedom of expression. This sometimes takes the form of "counter-advertising" to criticize a product or make negative comments about the services supplied' (paragraph 23). The Court then invalidated the relevant aspects of the by-law.

Note, however, these comments by the Court:

'Counter-advertising' is not merely a reaction to commercial speech, and is not a form of expression derived from commercial speech. Rather, it is a form of the expression of opinion that has an important effect on the social and economic life of a society. It is a right not only of consumers, but also of citizens. . . . Signs, in various forms, are thus a public, accessible and effective form of expressive activity for anyone who cannot undertake media campaigns. . . . This infringement impacts especially on the freedom of expression of a person who does not have access to substantial financial resources. [paragraphs 24–26]

The Court clearly assimilates the expression of Guignard's which it wants to protect to political expression, the protection of which is unproblematic, and it does so in the style of Dickson CJC's concern that the *Charter* 'does not simply become an instrument of better situated individuals to roll back legislation which has as its object the improvement of the condition of less advantaged persons'.[77] However defensible the decision in *Guignard*, it hardly stands for the 'constitutional right' of 'commercial enterprises' to 'engage in activities to inform and promote, by advertising'.

The other development to be noted is in relation to the (doubtless) continuing saga of tobacco advertising. The decision in *RJR-MacDonald* in fact afforded less comfort to the tobacco manufacturers than at first sight appeared.[78] It was not long before the federal government introduced a portfolio of new restrictions on tobacco advertising, the Tobacco Act,[79] designed to succeed where the Tobacco Products Control Act failed, in passing constitutional muster. The tobacco manufacturers took their time before challenging the new Act in Court, but they duly did. The decision in the Quebec Superior Court was handed down as this book was being completed.[80] The manufacturers lost on virtually every point, in particular in relation to freedom of commercial expression. The federal government and a vast array of intervenors assembled huge stockpiles of reports and data to make sure that no talk of 'tenuous and speculative' (cf. this Chapter

---

[77] *R v Edwards Books and Art Ltd* (1986) 35 DLR (4th) 1.

[78] Cf. Roger A. Shiner, 'The Silent Majority Speaks: *RJR-MacDonald Inc v Canada*', *Constitutional Forum* 7, no. 1 (1995): 8–15.

[79] S.C. 1997, c.13.

[80] *JTI MacDonald Corporation et al c La procureure générale du Canada* 500-05-031299-975 (2002) (Que Sup Ct).

4.5 above) connections between tobacco consumption and health problems, and between tobacco advertising and health problems, arose on this occasion. Denis J's general stance towards the tobacco manufacturers is altogether different from the deference shown by Chabot J in the *RJR-MacDonald* Superior Court hearing: 'la cigarette est un produit nocif qui n'apporte aucun bénéfice à la personne humaine' (paragraph 281). As for any supposed right of freedom of expression belonging to the manufacturers, 'ce serait parodie de justice que d'accorder la même protection constitutionnelle à la liberté de presse et à la liberté de vanter les vertus d'une cigarette ultra-légère' (paragraph 283). 'La liberté d'expression prévue à la Charte est un concept plus grand et plus généreux que ce que plaident les cigarettiers' (paragraph 464). Doubtless we have not heard the last on the Tobacco Act from the tobacco manufacturers. But the foundation laid by Denis J's immensely thorough 190-page decision is altogether different from the flimsy argumentation and fiery rhetoric of Chabot J twelve years before. The tobacco companies have also begun a challenge to comparable provincial legislation in Saskatchewan.[81] They have lost the first round, relating to the assertion of provincial jurisdiction,[82] although leave has been granted to take this setback to the Court of Appeal.[83]

7 CONCLUSION

As in the U.S., freedom of commercial expression is now well established in Canada. But the Supreme Court of Canada has provided no more of a substantial basis for the commercial expression doctrine, either historical or conceptual, than we saw in the case of the U.S. Supreme Court. The Court began with language rights and Dickson CJC's concern in *Slaight* (at 423) for 'remedy[ing] the unequal balance of power . . . between an employer and employee', and 'with the protection of a particularly vulnerable group'. It ends with defending 'the right of tobacco corporations to advertise the only legal product sold in Canada which, when used precisely as directed, harms and often kills those who use it',[84] and a ringing endorsement of 'constitutional right' of 'commercial enterprises' to 'engage in activities to inform and promote, by advertising' (*Guignard*, paragraph 23). I acknowledge again that there are still many theoretical questions to be studied and answered before a critical stance towards freedom of commercial expression can be shown to be justified. Parts II and III of this book take on that task. But those questions cannot be properly appreciated without a sense of the institutional history that has given rise to them, and in particular without a sense of how consistently those questions are not being addressed in the case law.

---

[81] The Tobacco Control Act, S.S. 2001, c. T-14.1.
[82] *Rothmans, Benson & Hedges Inc v Saskatchewan* 2002 SKQB 382 (Sask QB).
[83] 2002 SKCA 119 Docket 624 (Sask CA).   [84] La Forest J in *RJR-MacDonald*, at 72.

5

Commercial Expression in Europe

The remaining legal orders within which there is formal legal protection for freedom of commercial expression under the rubric of protection for human rights or rights of political morality, and which will be familiar to most readers of this book, are those of the Member States of the Council of Europe and of the European Union. Neil MacCormick has recently argued that in Europe one finds a legal ordering of a unique and distinctive kind, posing fundamental questions for traditional ideas of nationhood and sovereignty.[1] There is therefore perhaps some risk in speaking collectively of constitutional protection for freedom of commercial expression in Europe, in the sense that there is not only one legal order, nor do the legal orders that there are have 'constitutions' in the sense that in those orders some document bears the relation to the order that the U.S. Constitution does to the U.S. legal order, or the Canadian Charter of Rights and Freedoms does to the Canadian legal order. The discourse in Europe in fact is more often one of human rights than of constitutional rights. But the risk must be taken, in order to bring out the commonalities of doctrine which are the focus of this research.

The European Union consists of a specific number of Member States, primarily located in Western Europe, who have signed specific treaties of union, most recently the Treaty of Amsterdam (1997). The Union has various bodies with legislative or quasi-legislative powers, and the scope of this legislation is focussed primarily on creating and maintaining a common economic market between the Member States. The European Union was originally conceived of as an economic union, one once familiarly referred to as 'the Common Market'. Only relatively recently have broader and deeper integrationist visions come to take a prominent place in European political and cultural discussion. The Union has a central court, the European Court of Justice, for the settlement of litigation arising out of the interpretation and application of legislation promulgated by the Union's law-making agencies.

The Council of Europe is a different body, with virtually all the countries of Europe now as members. The European Convention for the Protection of Human Rights and Fundamental Freedoms (the European Convention on Human Rights, for short) is a legal document of the Council of Europe. The Convention entered into force in 1953. Its formal status is simply that of any other convention or treaty under international law by which a group of nation states have consented to be bound, in this case the Member States of the Council

[1] Neil MacCormick, *Questioning Sovereignty: Law, State and Practical Reason* (Oxford: Clarendon Press, 1999).

of Europe. The European Court of Human Rights, set up in 1959, is responsible for adjudicating on issues raised under the Convention. The Court functions as a level of court from which to seek legal redress above that of the supreme tribunal within a Member State. Applications may be made for relief under the Convention when and only when avenues have been exhausted for obtaining the desired relief under national law. The Court was reorganized in 1998 as the sole body with jurisdiction to hear cases under the Convention, the reorganization being a simplification of what was previously a complex and multi-body procedure.[2]

Some case law has developed concerning the status of commercial expression in a context of rights protection, and we will consider that case law in this Chapter. The case law develops in two ways, under the European Convention on Human Rights as interpreted and applied by the European Court of Human Rights, and under European Union law generally as interpreted and applied by the European Court of Justice. I will examine these in turn. I will begin with the European Court of Human Rights, as the case law there is older.

1 COMMERCIAL EXPRESSION IN THE EUROPEAN COURT OF HUMAN RIGHTS

The part of the European Convention on Human Rights relevant to freedom of expression is Article 10. It reads as follows:

1. Everyone has the right to freedom of expression. This right shall include freedom to hold opinions and to receive and impart information and ideas without interference by public authority and regardless of frontiers. This Article shall not prevent States from requiring the licensing of broadcasting, television or cinema enterprises.

2. The exercise of these freedoms, since it carries with it duties and responsibilities, may be subject to such formalities, conditions, restrictions or penalties as are prescribed by law and are necessary in a democratic society, in the interests of national security, or crime, for the protection of health or morals, for the protection of the reputation or rights of others, for preventing the disclosure of information received in confidence, or for maintaining the authority and impartiality of the judiciary.

The parallel with the *Canadian Charter of Rights and Freedoms* is clear, in that paragraph 2 of the Article contemplates the possibility of the Court ruling that restrictions of freedom of expression may be upheld nonetheless as valid. The cases reveal that the main operative phrases in paragraph 2 have been the reference to 'duties and responsibilities', the list in the last half of the legitimate goals for a restriction, and the phrase 'necessary in a democratic society'. This phrase was interpreted in *Sunday Times*[3] as a burden on the respondent state to show:

---

[2] See Colin Turpin, *British Government and the Constitution: Text, Cases and Materials* (3rd edn., Law in Context, London: Butterworths, 1995), 533–7, complete with flow chart.

[3] *Sunday Times v UK* Ser A 30 (1979) (ECtHR).

whether the interference complained of corresponded to a pressing social need, whether
it was proportionate to the legitimate aim pursued, whether the reasons given by the
national authorities to justify it are relevant and sufficient. [at paragraph 62]

The wording of paragraph 1 of Article 10 is more explicit and overtly generous than either section 2(b) of the Canadian *Charter* or the First Amendment of
the U.S. Constitution. It is not surprising therefore that 'there appears to be no
expression which is not protected at all by paragraph 1 of Article 10 because of
its [sc. the expression's] content'.[4] The Court has said that gratuitously offensive remarks about the religious opinions of others 'do not contribute to any
form of public debate capable of furthering progress in human affairs',[5] but it
nonetheless regarded the expression as within paragraph 1. In *Autronic*,[6] the
government argued that, because the content of the programme was irrelevant
to the company's purpose (it wished to arrange to receive a signal at a trade fair
from a communications satellite purely in order to demonstrate home satellite
dishes which it was marketing), the restriction on the receipt of the signal did
not come within Article 10. The Court rejected this argument, ruling that Article
10 protects the mode of transmission or reception as much as the content of a
communication.

Given such a broad interpretation of paragraph 1 of Article 10, all cases fall
to be decided under paragraph 2. There are not even the steps of examining the
purpose and effect of the infringing government action, steps which, as we saw
in the previous chapter, can play some role in Canadian adjudication despite a
similarly broad interpretation of the meaning of 'expression' in *Charter* section
2(b) (see Chapter 4.1 above). Moreover, the Court, again like Canada, has not
adopted any particular discrete category of 'commercial expression'. The discovery of how the Court treats 'commercial expression' is a matter of inferring
from the cases patterns of response to patterns of fact situations. As in both
Canada and the U.S., the fact that commercial or economic interests are heavily
involved in the case will not suffice to show that the case is 'commercial expression'.

The European Commission on Human Rights, which until the 1998 reorganization functioned as a preliminary filter on applications for relief, recognized
commercial expression as being within Article 10 in 1979, although it said that
the level of protection given to commercial expression under the Article 'must
be less than that accorded to the expression of "political" ideas in the broadest
sense', the safeguarding of the latter being the main purpose of the Convention.[7]
In 1985, in *Barthold*,[8] the Court rejected a claim by Germany that the case concerned commercial expression, in order to assert a greater right to regulate it.

---

[4] D.J. Harris, M. O'Boyle, and C. Warbrick, *Law of the European Convention on Human Rights*
(London: Butterworths, 1995), 373.
[5] *Otto-Preminger-Institut v Austria* Ser A 298 (1994), para. 49.
[6] *Autronic AG v Switzerland* Ser A 178 (1983).
[7] *X and Church of Scientology v Sweden* 16 DR 68 (1979), at 73.
[8] *Barthold v Germany* Ser A 90 (1985).

Barthold ran the only emergency veterinary clinic in Hamburg. He was interviewed by a local newspaper, and in the interview deplored this state of affairs as well as indicating that his clinic was open for business. Other veterinarians in Hamburg instigated an action against him for advertising in conflict with Germany's Unfair Competition Act as applied to professional advertising. The Court ruled that Barthold's remarks were public discussion of a matter of general interest, and that his rights under Article 10 had been violated.[9]

The first, and still controlling,[10] case of commercial expression proper was *Markt Intern*,[11] another case concerning the German Unfair Competition Act. Markt Intern, a company publishing consumer magazines, published in an information bulletin the dissatisfaction of a consumer who had been unable to get a promised reimbursement from a mail-order firm, and invited readers to submit other information on the practices of the firm. It was restrained from further publication of these statements under the Act. The government's position was that Article 10 did not extend to expression directed solely at furthering the business interests of the expresser, as here. The Commission ruled that, even if purely promotional expression could be more severely restricted, the expression in this case did not fall within that category, and found for the applicant. The Court ruled, first, that even though the bulletin article in question 'conveyed information of a commercial nature', all the same 'such information cannot be excluded from the scope of Article 10(1) which does not apply solely to certain types of information or ideas or forms of expression' (at paragraph 26). The Court cites for this latter conclusion *Müller*,[12] a case of an art exhibition closed for being obscene. The Court thus produces its own variant on the invalid argument we saw above in *Virginia Board*.[13] It simply does not follow from the fact that the right of freedom of expression cannot legitimately be interpreted to exclude sexually explicit art that it has to be interpreted as also not excluding commercial expression.

Nonetheless, having stated that commercial expression is within the coverage of Article 10, the Court went on to rule following its analysis of the standards of review in Article 10(2), on the deciding vote of the President after a tie, that there had been no breach of Article 10:

---

[9] 'Its application [sc. of the Unfair Competition Act] risks discouraging members of the liberal professions from contributing to public debate on topics affecting the life of the community if even there is the slightest likelihood of their utterances being treated as entailing, to some degree, an advertising effect. By the same token, application of a criterion such as this is liable to hamper the press in the performance of its task of purveyor of information and public watchdog' (at para. 47).

[10] 'Controlling', in the sense that it is still referred to: see *Hertel v Switzerland* (59/1997/843/1049) (1998), discussed below, at para. 47. There is no formal system of precedent in European law: cf. T.C. Hartley, *The Foundations of European Community Law* (3rd edn., Oxford: Clarendon Press, 1994), 83.

[11] *Markt Intern Verlag v Germany* Ser A 195 (1989) (ECtHR).

[12] *Müller and Others v Switzerland*, Ser A, no 133 (1988).

[13] *Virginia State Board of Pharmacy et al v Virginia Citizens Consumer Council Inc et al* 425 US 748 (1976); see Chapter 2.4 above.

It is obvious that opinions may differ as to whether the [German] Federal Court's reaction was appropriate or whether the statements made in the specific case by *Markt Intern* should be permitted or tolerated. However, the European Court of Human Rights should not substitute its own evaluation for that of the national courts in the instant case, where those courts on reasonable grounds, had considered the restrictions to be necessary. [at paragraph 37]

In repudiating such deference to the Member State, the dissenters appealed to the importance of free dissemination of information and ideas in order to ensure the openness of business activities, and to the value of the kind of criticism at issue here in consumer protection:

Only in rare cases can censorship or prohibition of publication be accepted . . . This is particularly true in relation to commercial advertising or questions of economic or commercial policy . . . The protection of the interests of users and consumers in the face of dominant positions depends on the freedom to publish even the harshest criticisms of products.[14]

It is noteworthy that, in contrast to the U.S. Supreme Court in *Virginia Board*, the dissent accepts that the need for the flow of commercial information to be 'clean as well as free' may imply the regulation of truthful information—by, for example, disclosure requirements—as well as of false or misleading information.[15]

Such subsequent commercial expression cases as there have been have followed this pattern. In *Colman*[16] and *Coca*,[17] cases in which promotion by professionals fell foul of restrictions on professional advertising, there was held to be no violation of Article 10. The Commission's report in *Coca* emphasized the value to the citizen of the information in the advertisement, and held that Article 10 had been violated. The Court, however, while acknowledging this point, also reiterated that even truthful information might have to be restricted 'owing to the special circumstances of particular business activities and professions' (at paragraph 51). The Court found that in the case of lawyer advertising (the issue in *Coca*), such circumstances did exist, and found no violation of Article 10.

In *Stambuk*,[18] on the other hand, the reasoning followed the pattern of *Barthold*. Stambuk, an ophthalmologist, was interviewed and photographed for a newspaper article about a new technique in laser surgery he offered. The relevant Rules of Professional Conduct prohibited co-operation with the press to the extent that publications had an advertising character, indicated name, and showed a photograph, although the presentation of pure information was acceptable. The Stuttgart Disciplinary Appeals Court accepted that Stambuk had tolerated an article of an advertising character, and that for reasons of

---

[14] From the opinion of Judge Pettiti; there was also a joint dissent of seven judges, and two more individual dissents.

[15] I will return to this issue in Chapters 10 (10.5, 10.8) and 13 (13.3–4) below.

[16] *Colman v UK* Ser A 258–D (1993); case settled after Commission report.

[17] *Casado Coca v Spain* Ser A 285–A (1994) (ECtHR).

[18] *Stambuk v Germany* (37928/97) (2002) (ECtHR).

maintenance of professional standards, the disciplinary ban outweighed his right to freedom of expression. The Court reversed, saying that the article in question was sufficiently non-commercial for Stambuk's rights and the import-ance of the press to outweigh the restriction on advertising.

The Court struggled with the same 'is it or isn't it commercial?' issue in *Jacubowski*.[19] The case is yet another involving Germany's Unfair Competition Act. Jacubowski was fired by the press agency for which he worked, and it issued a press release questioning his competence. He in turn sent out to a large number of journalists who had received the release a letter enclosing a number of newspaper articles critical of his former employer and soliciting the business of these journalists for himself as an independent press agency. He was enjoined from making any further mailings under the Act. The Court accepted that the case did involve commercial expression, and again ruled there was no violation of Article 10.

Hertel is another case resulting from the broad sweep of an Unfair Competition Act, in this case Switzerland's. Hertel, an independent research sci-entist, published in a lay journal an account of research he and a collaborator had done into the effects on human beings of food prepared in microwave ovens; the effects were claimed to be highly toxic. The article seemed in itself to present the research results in a relatively straightforward way, although doubts were raised about their scientific worth. However, the editor of the journal pre-sented the paper with lurid titling and cover art, and an equally lurid editorial likening microwave ovens to the death chambers at Dachau. The Swiss Association of Manufacturers and Suppliers of Household Electrical Appliances prosecuted Hertel under the Act. The Berne Commercial Court brushed aside concerns raised in the District Court (at paragraphs 17 and 22) that no issue of commercial competition was raised. In their view, any piece of writing which had 'the mere potential aptitude to affect competition' implicated the Act (at paragraph 22), and that would certainly include Hertel's piece. The Swiss Federal Court likewise found against Hertel. The Court ruled that there was clearly an interference with Hertel's Article 10(1) right of freedom of expression (at paragraph 31), and even that the Act properly extended to Hertel's article (at paragraph 36). The Court, however, distinguished Hertel's case from *Markt Intern* and *Jacubowski*:

The Swiss authorities thus had some margin of appreciation to decide whether there was a 'pressing social need' to impose the injunction in question on the applicant. Such a mar-gin of appreciation is particularly essential in commercial matters, especially in an area as complex and fluctuating as that of unfair competition. . . . It is however necessary to reduce the extent of the margin of appreciation when what is at stake is not a given indi-vidual's purely 'commercial' statements, but his participation in a debate affecting the general interest, for example, over public health. . . . In that respect, the present case is substantially different from the Markt Intern and Jacubowski cases cited above.

[19] *Jacubowski v Germany* Ser A 291–A (1994) (ECtHR).

The Court then rejected the prosecution of Hertel as 'necessary in a democratic society' and found there had been a violation of Article 10.

There was an ironic twist to these issues in *VGT*.[20] VGT is an association devoted to activism in favour of animal rights. It prepared a film 'commercial' (the point of the scare-quotes will emerge shortly), showing the dire condition of animals raised for food, as a counterweight to television advertising by the beef industry. Sole responsibility for arranging for television advertising in Switzerland was in the hands of the Commercial Television Company, which refused to run the film. Its refusal was based on what it determined to be the 'clear political character' of VGT's film (paragraph 11), in the light of the prohibition in section 18 of the Swiss Federal Radio and Television Act of religious and political advertising. This provision of the Act was aimed at preventing economically powerful interests from biassing elections. VGT sought (paragraph 50) to have its film deemed to be commercial advertising in order to escape the reach of section 18, even at the cost of the standard for review of the ban on the film being more deferential to government (paragraph 69). The Court, however, was having none of this crafty move: 'In the Court's opinion the commercial indubitably fell outside the regular commercial context in the sense of inciting the public to purchase a particular product. Rather, . . . the commercial reflected controversial opinions pertaining to modern society in general and also lying at the heart of various political debates' (paragraph 57). But the Court came through in the end and denied that the standard of 'necessary in a democratic society' had been met (paragraph 79). VGT's Article 10 rights were indeed violated.

2   COMMERCIAL EXPRESSION IN THE EUROPEAN COURT OF JUSTICE

I turn now to consider the role, such as it is, of freedom of commercial expression in the jurisprudence of the European Court of Justice, the Court which adjudicates within the legal framework of the European Union and whose working material is the Union's laws and regulations. The concern of the European Court of Justice is with the degree and mode of reflection of human rights values in those laws and regulations and their administration,[21] whereas the European Court of Human Rights is concerned with the degree and mode of reflection of human rights values in the laws and regulations of the Member States. Until very recently, the development of a jurisprudence of human rights within the Union was in the hands of the Court itself. The Court developed the principle that:

The Union shall respect fundamental rights, as guaranteed by the European Convention

---

[20] *Verein gegen Tierfabriken v Switzerland* (24699/94) (2001) (ECtHR).

[21] For the history of this concern see Hartley, *The Foundations of European Community Law*, 139–49.

for the Protection of Human Rights and Fundamental Freedoms signed in Rome on 4 November 1950 and as they result from the constitutional traditions common to the Member States, as general principles of Community law.

That principle was eventually incorporated into the Maastricht Treaty of European Union in 1992, as Article F.2, from which the above quotation is taken. In late 2000 the EU Charter of Fundamental Rights was proclaimed, which takes the formal articulation of human rights in European law a stage further. But the Charter is not at the present time legally binding, and its future development, status, and substantive content are matters for continuing academic and political discussion.[22]

The European Court of Justice is still predominantly concerned with monitoring the operation of a common economic market within the Union, and especially with potential barriers to the free movement of goods and services, and for that matter of citizens, within the Union. Nonetheless, given the adherence proclaimed above to the values embodied in the European Convention on Human Rights, it would not be unreasonable to expect that, in the context of a focus on economic matters, issues of freedom of commercial expression would arise for adjudication. In reality, any such expectation is largely unfulfilled. Despite a rich mother lode of cases before the Court, and equally rich jurisprudence developed by the Court, addressing issues of trade mark protection and violation, and product-labelling restrictions in and by Member States, and in contrast to the case law in Canada and the U.S., no suggestion arises in these cases that the value of freedom of expression bears on their resolution. The issues are treated simply in terms of potential restraints on trade and the European law relating to such restraints. There have been three exceptions.

The first, and most important for the analytical and normative purposes of the present book, is the legal challenge to Directive 98/43/EC of the European Parliament and of the Council, issued on 6 July 1998, on the approximation of the laws, regulations, and administrative provisions of the Member States relating to the advertising and sponsorship of tobacco products.[23] The Directive comprised a number of required constraints on the advertising of tobacco products and permissible sponsorship of such products, of a kind which are familiar in the present-day social context of government attempts to reduce consumption of such products. Germany sought to have the Directive annulled: the United Kingdom, taking advantage of the reference facilities offered by the Court, sought an opinion on the validity under European law of measures it pro-

---

[22] Cf. e.g. Sandra Fredman, Christopher McCrudden, and Mark Freedland, 'An E.U. Charter of Fundamental Rights', [2000] *Public Law*: 178–86; Françoise Tulkens, 'Towards a Greater Normative Coherence in Europe: The Implications of the Draft Charter of Fundamental Rights of the European Union', *Human Rights Law Journal* 21 (2000): 329–32; J.H.H. Weiler, 'A Constitution for Europe? Some Hard Choices', *Journal of Common Market Studies* 40 (2002): 563–80.

[23] *Germany v Parliament and Council*, Case C–376/98 (Advocate General's opinion 15 June 2000; judgment 5 October 2000); *R v Secretary of State for Health et al, ex parte Imperial Tobacco Ltd et al*, Case C–74/99 (Advocate General's opinion 15 June 2000; judgment 5 October 2000).

posed to take to implement the Directive, such measures having been challenged by the tobacco manufacturers in the national courts. The Advocate General in his advisory opinion to the Court considered both challenges together, as they raised similar legal issues.

The challenges to the Directive raised seven different possible grounds for its annulment. The two that are relevant here are the ground on which the case was actually decided—the lack of a proper legal basis for the Directive—and a violation of the principle of freedom of expression, that being an authoritative principle of European law for the reasons given above. The idea of a proper legal basis is, briefly, this. The European Council and the Parliament, as legal bodies under international law, must be construed as having only the powers which have been delegated to them by the Member States. Among those powers is the power to 'approximate' the different legal provisions of Member States—to harmonize them, in effect—but only to fulfil specified purposes, in particular and especially to maintain the free market in goods and services. The Council and the Parliament, to put it simply, do not have free powers to govern Europe as they see fit. That would be incompatible with the continuing sovereignty of the Member States. The Council and the Parliament in proclaiming the Directive at issue here claimed that they were in fact acting *intra vires*, acting to maintain the free market.

Advocate General Fennelly, in a thorough analysis, roundly rejected these claims (paragraphs 82–120). In his view, the tightness of the restrictions proposed made no sense as an attempt to maintain a free market. The Court's subsequent decision tracked his analysis. The challenge by Germany was upheld and the Directive annulled. In view of the annulment, the request by the U.K. for an opinion on its own implementing legislation was declared moot. The Advocate General spent some time assessing the compatibility of the Directive with the right of freedom of expression, as the advisory nature of his opinion required him to do. If the Court in formulating its final judgment had not accepted his opinion that the Directive should be annulled for lack of proper legal basis, other considerations raised by Germany and the tobacco manufacturers would become relevant to the final decision. In the event, since the Court did accept his reasoning for annulment on the ground of lack of legal basis, the issue of compatibility with a right of freedom of expression was not addressed in the judgment.

The Advocate General notes (at paragraph 153) that 'the case-law of the European Court of Human Rights indicates that all forms of expression merit protection by virtue of Article 10(1) of the Convention. This includes what is commonly known as commercial expression.' He concludes then (at paragraph 154 in full; the footnote reference is to *Handyside*[24] and the commentary on the value of freedom of expression in that case) that:

Commercial expression should also be protected in Community law. Commercial

---

[24] *Handyside v UK* Ser A 24 (1976) (ECtHR).

expression does not contribute in the same way as political, journalistic, literary or artistic expression do, in a liberal democratic society, to the achievement of social goods such as, for example, the enhancement of democratic debate and accountability or the questioning of current orthodoxies with a view to furthering tolerance or change. However, in my view, personal rights are recognized as being fundamental in character, not merely because of their instrumental, social functions, but also because they are necessary for the autonomy, dignity and personal development of individuals.[184]

Thus, individuals' freedom to promote commercial activities derives not only from their right to engage in economic activities and the general commitment, in the Community context, to a market economy based upon free competition, but also from their inherent entitlement as human beings freely to express and receive views on *any* topic, including the merits of the goods or services which they market or purchase.

The Advocate General then turns to the other scale of the balance: 'it is clear that the exercise of freedom of expression, like that of other rights and freedoms, may be subject to proportionate restrictions in order to secure the enjoyment of rights by others or the achievement of certain objectives in the common good' (at paragraph 155 of his Opinion). He underlines the legitimacy of public health as just such an objective (it is specifically mentioned in Article 10(2) of the European Convention on Human Rights), and the obvious implication of the marketing and consumption of tobacco products in the attainment of such an objective (paragraphs 156–157). Then he (correctly) notes that the European Court of Human Rights has distinguished between political expression and commercial expression in terms of the burden a state has to meet to justify restriction of the right of freedom of expression. 'Political expression itself serves certain extremely important social interests; beyond its role in promoting economic activity, in respect of which the legislator properly enjoys considerable discretion to impose public-interest restrictions, commercial speech does not normally perform a wider social function of the same significance' (at paragraph 158; footnote omitted). He continues (at paragraph 159), 'I would advocate, therefore, that a similar approach be adopted in the Community legal order.' After some discussion of the issue of evidentiary requirements as regards the impact of consumption of tobacco products on health and of the evidence presented (at paragraphs 160–162), he concludes that 'the Community legislator had reasonable grounds to believe that the comprehensive prohibition of tobacco promotion would result in a significant reduction in consumption levels and would, thus, contribute to the protection of public health' (at paragraph 163), and that, despite the ban on tobacco advertising being 'nearly total', the requirement that the restrictions be 'no more burdensome than necessary' had been met. He concluded further (at paragraphs 165–175) that the restrictions proposed were proportionate to the significant potential gain in public health. He drew the line, however, at the ban on so-called diversification products— T-shirts, caps, key chains, and the like with tobacco manufacturers' logos or slogans. No evidence was presented as to the efficacy of a ban on these to attain the goal of public health. 'In so far as the application of such a brand or mark to a product also constitutes an exercise of freedom of commercial expression, I conclude that Article 3(3)(a) of the Advertising Directive has not been shown to be a justified restriction on that freedom and should be annulled' (at paragraph 176). In sum, with the exception of the one Article noted, Directive 98/43 would, in the opinion of the Advocate General, pass legal muster as far as concerned its compatibility with the right of freedom of commercial expression.

There are aspects to applaud in the Advocate General's discussion of freedom of commercial expression, and one matter about which to express concern. He distinguishes properly between political expression, as the main focus of the right of freedom of expression, and commercial expression. He properly emphasizes the significance of the economic context, that the freedom is freedom of *commercial* expression. It is true that, like the Supreme Court of Canada and the U.S. Supreme Court, he positions the role of the context as being to lower the burden on the restricting government to justify the restriction: how far that is a satisfactory response I shall address later (see Chapter 13.1 and 13.3 below). He properly reminds us not only of the legitimate role of governments in the regulation of the economic market but also of the weight of that role, and considers restrictions on advertising to be an aspect of such regulation. He has little patience with supposed evidentiary problems about the relation between tobacco products and public health, and between the advertising of tobacco products and their consumption. In this respect, his opinion is in marked contrast to that of the Supreme Court of Canada in *RJR-MacDonald*,[25] although in all fairness to the latter Court it was more than somewhat sandbagged by the trial judge (cf. Chapter 4.5 above).

The reason for concern can be seen in paragraph 154 of the opinion, quoted above. The Advocate General adduces the standard grounds within liberal political morality for the high value given to freedom of expression—that 'they are necessary for the autonomy, dignity and personal development of individuals'. The *Handyside* case concerned the publication *The Little Red Schoolbook*, a book recommending an uninhibited approach to sexuality for persons in their teens, and which was subject to prosecution on grounds of obscenity in the U.K. Such a prosecution, and its compatibility with Article 10, indeed presents sharply issues of the 'autonomy, dignity and personal development of individuals'. 'Political, journalistic, literary or artistic expression', to quote again from paragraph 154, are the prime domains of freedom of expression, and in those domains the value of freedom of expression brings the noted developmental rewards. But it is a long step from there (exactly how long it is the goal of this study to demonstrate) to the thought that a business corporation—a tobacco manufacturer, for example—is an 'individual' possessing a right of freedom of expression, even of commercial expression, such that its possession of that right

[25] *RJR-MacDonald Inc v Attorney-General of Canada; Imperial Tobacco Ltd v Attorney-General of Canada* [Indexed as: RJR-MacDonald Inc v Canada (Attorney-General)] (1995) 127 DLR (4th) 1.

is grounded in a manner comparable to the familiar rights of 'political, journalistic, literary or artistic expression'. The Advocate General is too easily led, like many other courts and commentators, from the value to participants in the economic market of freedom to engage in economic activities (including, certainly, advertising their goods for sale) to the idea that freedom of trade and freedom of expression are freedoms of a piece with one another. As I shall argue below (Chapter 9), and as La Forest J's dissent in *RJR-MacDonald* also pointed out (see Chapter 4.5), business corporations are not 'individuals' of the appropriate kind, such that their 'autonomy, dignity and personal development' are matters for legal protection. The Advocate General's opinion buys into the increasingly dominant idiom of business corporations as possessors of rights of freedom of commercial expression *in propria persona*. Legally, that is now so. But whether it should be, or could be, so as a matter of political morality is a different question, one which it is the goal of this book to explore, and one the proper answer to which the dominant idiom obscures rather than illuminates.

The European Parliament and Council issued a second Directive, 2001/37/EC, proclaimed on 5 June 2001, in relation to tobacco products, on the approximation of the laws, regulations, and administrative provisions of the Member States concerning the manufacture, presentation, and sale of tobacco products. The regulations mainly concerned limits on maximum tar, nicotine, and carbon monoxide yields, but also contained labelling requirements in the form of mandatory health warnings, and reporting requirements of the products' contents both to the government and to the public. This Directive also was challenged by the tobacco manufacturers, and found its way to the European Court of Justice as a request again by the U.K. government for a ruling on the Directive in the light of its forthcoming legislation to implement the Directive.[26] The main thrust of the challenge to the Directive was again the lack of a proper legal basis. However, this time, presenting as it did a different set of issues and regulations, the Directive survived. This time, despite the precedent in *RJR-MacDonald* of mandatory health warnings and other labelling restrictions being deemed to raise issues of freedom of commercial expression, no mention of Article 10 and freedom of expression appears in the Advocate General's opinion; the tobacco manufacturers did not raise freedom of expression as a possible ground for annulment of the Directive. Presumably, the message contained in Advocate General Fennelly's opinion in the challenge to Directive 98/43 was heard, that this road led nowhere.

Sandwiched in between the two tobacco cases was another case where freedom of expression was raised, *Gourmet*.[27] Gourmet International Products are the publishers of *Gourmet*, a food and drink magazine. Sweden's tight regulatory regime on the availability of alcohol involves in part restrictions on the

---

[26] *R v Secretary of State for Health, ex parte British American Tobacco (Investments) Ltd*, Case C–491/01 (Advocate General's opinion 10 September 2002; judgment 10 December 2002).

[27] *Konsumentombudsmannen v Gourmet International Products Aktiebolag*, Case C–405/98 (Advocate General's opinion 14 December 2000; judgment 8 March 2001).

advertising of alcohol, including a ban on advertising spirits, wines, or strong beers in periodicals and magazines. Just such advertisements were published in a supplement to an issue of *Gourmet* magazine. The Swedish Consumer Ombudsman applied for an injunction to prevent the publication of these advertisements. Gourmet International challenged the injunction as inconsistent with the European Union's trade rules concerning the import of goods and the free movement of (here, publishing) services. The Swedish National Court referred the issue to the European Court of Justice for a ruling. The Court ruled that the Swedish restrictions were compatible with the trade regulations in question, but only so long as no measures were available to protect public health against the harmful effects of alcohol having less effect on intra-Community trade. Again, the Court tracked the analysis of Advocate General Jacobs in his opinion as regards the substance of its decision. In his opinion, however, the Advocate General also briefly addressed the issue of Article 10 of the European Convention on Human Rights and its effect on these restrictions on the advertising of alcoholic beverages. As he acknowledges (paragraph 73), the issue was not raised in argument, and he does not offer a formal analysis. He does, though, state that 'the existence of any encroachment on advertisers' fundamental right to freedom of expression . . . can only mean that the incompatibility with Article 59 of the EC Treaty must be viewed with particular seriousness' (paragraph 74). With respect, this sentiment repeats the error identified above in Advocate General Fennelly's opinion in the challenge to the first tobacco directive. 'Fundamental rights' belong to natural persons, human beings, not to business corporations. It may be that 'the incompatibility with Article 59 of the EC Treaty must be viewed with particular seriousness', but, if so, it will not be because of any 'advertisers' fundamental right to freedom of expression'.

3 CONCLUSION

A quick look at the bottom line of European decision-making on freedom of commercial expression reveals a motley—on the face of it, sometimes a breach of Article 10 is held justifiable, sometimes it is not. In fact, though, there is a clear pattern to the decisions. When the Court, whether the European Court of Human Rights or the European Court of Justice,[28] is convinced that the expression concerned is purely commercial—in the memorable words of the *VGT* decision, a matter of 'inciting the public to purchase a particular product'—the court has invariably upheld the restriction on advertising as justified under Article 10 (*Markt Intern, Colman, Casa Coca, Jacubowski, Germany*). On the

---

[28] I must enter the important qualification that, in the case of the European Court of Justice, I have been and will be talking about opinions of Advocates-General, not of the Court itself. I do not know of any systematic survey on whether the Advocates-General are more or less deferential to governments than the Court itself. There is certainly too little material to found such a study for freedom of expression in particular.

other hand, where the court has deemed the expression concerned to be as much political as commercial, or even essentially political—quoting *VGT* again, 'reflect[ing] controversial opinions pertaining to modern society in general and also lying at the heart of various political debates—the court has protected the right of freedom of expression from government encroachment: *Barthold, Stambuk, Hertel, VGT*. The European Courts commendably have not shown the kind of willingness to tinker, enthusiasm for tinkering even, with government restrictions on advertising displayed by courts in Canada and the United States. The courts are not willing to buy the idea that any expression with a commercial dimension is 'commercial expression'. When they do identify a case of commercial expression, they are, so far at least, very unwilling to topple the judgments of the courts and legislatures of Member States.

It is important to put this apparent willingness to defer to governments into perspective. It has been argued in recent studies comparing the European Court of Human Rights with its counterparts in Washington and Ottawa with respect to freedom of expression of various kinds[29] that a more 'community-oriented' conception of freedom of expression is emerging in Europe, as compared both with the U.S. and with Canada. The argument looks at the final verdict in Article 10 cases, and how often that defers to national governments as putative guardians of the interests of their communities as opposed to the interest of individual citizens. Along the same lines, the decision of the Supreme Court of Canada in *RJR-MacDonald* has been taken as a worrisome precedent for what might happen when tobacco manufacturers get their hands on a right to freedom of expression in Europe.[30] Arguably, in some areas of freedom of expression, hate speech and literature especially, there is a difference between each of all three of Canada, Europe, and the United States. Moreover, there is no doubt that a fundamental individualist hostility to government regulation of any kind plays a role in the development of the commercial expression doctrine in the United States. But the position taken by the two European Courts on freedom of commercial expression has roots, I believe, which are much more institutional than romantically communitarian.

I have not discussed so far a concept central to adjudication by European Courts, and which is dispositive, in the Courts' mind, of cases like those mentioned. This is the concept of a 'margin of appreciation' which the Courts have

[29] See the symposium consisting of Eric Barendt, 'Freedom of Speech in an Era of Mass Communication', Christopher McCrudden, 'Freedom of Speech and Racial Equality', and Paul Mahoney, 'Emergence of a European Conception of Freedom of Speech', all in P. Birks (ed.), *Pressing Problems in the Law*, i (Oxford: Oxford University Press, 1995), at 109–16, 125–48, and 149–55.

[30] See Christopher McCrudden, 'The Impact on Freedom of Speech', in *The Impact of the Human Rights Bill on English Law*, edited by Basil S. Markesinis, The Clifford Chance Lectures Vol. III (Oxford: Oxford University Press, 1998), 85–7, 95–7. For greater optimism on this matter see Eric Barendt, 'The Importation of United States Free Speech Jurisprudence?' and Ian Loveland, 'Introduction: Should We Take Lessons from America?' both in Ian Loveland (ed.), *A Special Relationship? American Influences on Public Law in the UK* (Oxford: Clarendon Press, 1995), at 224–6 and 18–25.

to allow the governments of Member States in the assessment of a limitation on a Convention right or freedom in the context of interest-balancing such as that contemplated by paragraph 2 of Article 10.[31]

The doctrine of a margin of appreciation was first enunciated in *Handyside*:

By reason of their direct and continuous contact with the vital forces of their countries, state authorities are in principle in a better position than the international judge to give an opinion on the exact content of those requirements[32] as well as on the 'necessity' of a 'restriction' or 'penalty' intended to meet them . . .

Nevertheless, Article 10(2) does not give the contracting states an unlimited power of appreciation. The Court, which . . . is responsible for ensuring the observance of those states' engagements, is empowered to give the final ruling on whether a 'restriction' or 'penalty' is reconcilable with freedom of expression as protected by Article 10. The domestic margin of appreciation thus goes hand in hand with a European supervision. [at 48–9]

The doctrine has become an essential element in the Courts' handling of their powers of judicial review in relation to legislative and administrative activity by Member States.

Clearly, the deference to government evident in the Courts' handling of freedom of commercial expression is a function of the doctrine of a 'margin of appreciation'. The assertion in *Markt Intern* that 'the European Court of Human Rights should not substitute its own evaluation for that of the national courts in the instant case' is an application. In the same case, the Court averred that 'a margin of appreciation appears essential in commercial matters, in particular in an area as complex and fluctuating as that of unfair competition' (paragraph 33; repeated in *Jacubowski*, paragraph 26, *Coca*, paragraph 50). In *Coca* (ibid.) the Court extended the principle to regulation of advertising. The Court asserted that 'the country's courts are in a better position than an international court to determine how, at a given time, the right balance can be struck between the various interests involved' (at paragraph 55).

To those who see the European Convention on Human Rights as the defender of individual rights against oppressive governments, such deference to national governments appears problematic.[33] One can certainly imagine that, were the Supreme Court of Canada or the U.S. Supreme Court similarly to defer almost automatically to their respective federal, provincial, and state governments,

---

[31] As Peter Hogg points out, Peter W. Hogg, *Constitutional Law of Canada* (Loose-leaf edn., Toronto: Carswell, 2002), 35–34, n. 160, the term 'margin of appreciation' is a 'mechanical' translation into English of the French expression, *'une marge d'appréciation'*. Hogg suggests 'measure of discretion' as a clearer term in English. However, by now the 'mechanical' translation is too deep-rooted and well understood.

[32] Sc. 'of morals': see the text of Art 10(2) at the beginning of this section.

[33] Compare the hailing in Anthony Lester and David Pannick, 'Advertising and Freedom of Expression in Europe', *Public Law* [1985]: 349–52, of Art 10 as a device for the striking down of repressive control of advertising with the disappointed and critical tone ten years later of David Pannick, 'Article 10 of the European Convention on Human Rights', in P. Birks (ed.), *Pressing Problems in the Law*, i (Oxford: Oxford University Press, 1995), 117–23.

there would indeed be loud talk of failure to accept responsibility and to take charters and bills of rights seriously. But arguably the case of the European Courts is different. Article 1 of the Convention explicitly gives to contracting states (which, by virtue of contracting, give their assent to it) the primary responsibility for securing protection for Convention rights and freedoms.[34] Moreover, the European Union, as noted already, is not a federation in the sense of Canada or the United States. That is, it is not a case of a group of entities (provinces or states) sharing power with a central federal government, but with the federal government being for fundamental purposes paramount. The contractors to the Convention are autonomous nation states, and retain their independence as nation states despite their recognition in specific ways of the authority of the Court. Thus the Court cannot but weight the judgments of governments in the balance differently from the manner in which the Supreme Court of Canada or the U.S. Supreme Court weights governmental interests. As Paul Mahoney has put it:

There is a legitimate area of action conferred on the national authorities and a legitimate area of review conferred on the Commission and the Court, in other words a shared responsibility for enforcement [of the Convention], with the Court having the ultimate power of decision. The doctrine of the margin of appreciation is the natural product of that distribution of powers; it serves to delineate the dividing line.[35]

There are two points to be made about the proposed distinctively communitarian approach to freedom of expression in Europe. In the first place, the proposal, at least as far as freedom of commercial expression is concerned, is comparing the incommensurable, for the reasons just given. The final results in cases before European courts are heavily influenced by the doctrine of the margin of appreciation. But deference to an autonomous national government in Europe is not the same as deference to a parliament in Canada or a congress in the U.S. While the margin of appreciation means that substantively different results may well be reached in Europe as opposed to Canada or the U.S., the reason is not necessarily one having to do with respect for a substantively different range of values of political morality, more 'communitarian' values as opposed to individualist values. It is rather the result of the unique systemic context in which the Court operates.

In the second place, perhaps in the case of regulation of broadcasting, analysed by Barendt ('Freedom of speech in an era of mass communication'), there may be truth to the claim of more community-oriented results. The effect of applying the margin of appreciation in these cases has often been to support national governments in their attempts to keep commercial broadcasting companies from dominating the airwaves and to maintain some measure of equality

[34] The Article reads: 'The High Contracting Parties shall secure to everyone within their jurisdiction the rights and freedoms defined in Section I of this Convention'.
[35] Paul Mahoney, 'Judicial Activism and Judicial Self-Restraint in the European Court of Human Rights: Two Sides of the Same Coin', *Human Rights Law Journal* 11 (1990): 81.

of viewpoint in political and social debate. While domination of broadcasting by purely commercial organizations is not as far advanced in Canada as in the U.S., Europe is different again. Likewise, the case of racial expression and hate propaganda focussed on by McCrudden ('Freedom of speech and racial equality') supports the claim of European distinctiveness. The Supreme Court of Canada in *Keegstra*[36] applied a community-oriented test to uphold the restriction on hate propaganda, whereas in the U.S. there is no such thing as 'group libel'.[37] Where the existing national law is more along the lines of Canada's, the margin of appreciation will produce a more community-oriented result. But that is serendipitous from the point of view of the Court's procedure. It is an artefact of the pre-existing content of the national law to which deference is made. The outcome of the Court's respect for the margin of appreciation in the case of commercial expression is not a community within which many voices flourish; it is a tightly regulated 'market-place of commercial ideas' in which individual voices are silenced. But with freedom of *commercial* expression, that is only to be expected, and arguably to be justified.

[36] *R v Keegstra et al* (1990) 61 CCC (3d) 1.

[37] See John E. Nowak and Ronald D. Rotunda, *Constitutional Law* (6th edn., St. Paul, Minn.: West Group, 2000), 1171. Although *Beauharnais v Illinois* 343 US 250 (1952) upheld a state law making it a crime to libel a class of citizens, 'the dissenting views in *Beauharnais* were a precursor to the future position of the Court . . . While the Court has never explicitly overruled *Beauharnais*, it should be impossible to reach its results under the modern cases' (Novak and Rotunda, above). See also *Collin and National Socialist Party v Smith* 578 F 2d 1197 (1978) (FCA 7th Cir), *certiorari denied* 439 US 916 (1978); *RAV v City of St Paul* 112 SCt 2538 (1992).

6

Conclusion

The above summary of the decided cases in the area of commercial expression has been lengthy. There are two reasons for this. The first has to do with the nature of jurisprudential argument itself. Philosophers in general have a tendency to imagine that philosophical argument proceeds, or at least aims to proceed, downwards from unquestionable first principles by means of unquestionable rules of inference to unquestionable conclusions. This is fantasy; the reality is vastly more untidy and inconclusive. I certainly am not pretending in this book to prove in this fantastic way the unsoundness of the commercial expression doctrine. Rather, the aim is two-fold: to create some sense of the doctrine's unusual character in relation to issues of constitutional rights with which we are familiar, especially rights of freedom of expression, and to show how weak are the arguments used by supporters of the doctrine. The former of these projects is more informal and intuitive than the latter. To it a survey of the cases is indispensable: the aim of the survey is to create a sense in the large of what the doctrine is and how it has been interpreted and applied by courts. My purpose, though, is subversive, not supportive; I want the survey to reveal the intuitive oddness of the doctrine, rather than its intuitive soundness. I want the case-by-case argument to show why the doctrine is wrong, not why it is right.

The matter of the argumentation in the cases is different. Here, the ground is more familiar, and harder. We need to take the array of arguments for the commercial expression doctrine that emerge from the cases and assess their cogency. In one sense, this is not so hard to do. As I will shortly show, there is a clear pattern to the arguments in the cases, wherever they may be found. Courts outside the United States have largely followed that jurisdiction in the reasoning deployed to support the commercial expression doctrine, because (I assume) it seemed to them to be right and proper reasoning, and not because they were bound to follow it by some formal rule of authoritative precedent. In another sense, however, the project of assessing the cogency of these arguments is both hard and deep. Supreme Court jurists, their staffs, and academic theorists are not foolish people. Many statements made in the course of the arguments for the commercial expression doctrine are perfectly true and reasonable statements taken in themselves. But argumentation requires that statements be linked together in logically appropriate ways if the truth of the conclusion—the commercial expression doctrine—is to be derived from the truth of the premises. Though the cases present the arguments for the commercial expression doctrine as if they were obvious and straightforward, in fact they are not obvious and straightforward, as I hope even the *ad hoc* comments in Chapters 2–5 above have indicated. The arguments make many tacit assumptions—assumptions about the nature of rights, about what it is to defend a jurisprudential thesis, about the nature of constitutional rights, and about the appropriate way to argue for constitutional rights. If the commercial expression doctrine is to be properly deconstructed, as this study proposes, these underlying assumptions and their controversial and unsatisfactory character must be elucidated and exposed. Such an elucidation is the work of the next two Parts of this book. It remains now to build the bridge between this chapter and its successors by describing in a structured form the arguments for the commercial expression doctrine that the survey of the cases reveals.

Essentially, eight different theses are advanced about commercial expression/speech in the original case, the U.S. Supreme Court case of *Virginia Board*:[1]

(a) Commercial speech cannot be wholly outside the protection of the First Amendment (at 761–2).
(b) The purely economic interest of the speaker of commercial speech is a constitutionally legitimate interest (at 762–3).
(c) The consumer's interest in commercial speech may be keener by far than his interest in political speech (at 763–4).
(d) Society also has an interest in the free flow of commercial information, because some commercial messages deal with matters of public interest (at 764–5).
(e) Society has an interest in the free flow of commercial information because it leads to the proper allocation of resources in a free market system (at 765).
(f) For the government to decide which information it is proper for citizens to receive is unacceptable paternalism (at 770).
(g) The government may legitimately ensure that the flow of commercial information is clean as well as free—false or misleading speech may be regulated (at 771–2).
(h) There are commonsense differences between commercial speech and other speech, which differences imply that commercial speech may receive a lower level of constitutional protection (at 771–2).

I will comment on each of these points in turn.

(a) After the chronologically next U.S. case, *Linmark Associates*, this claim is no longer made. The Court no longer feels it has to justify granting constitutional protection to commercial speech at all. Rather, the focus of the opinions is on the details of the commercial speech doctrine, especially the level of protection and how speech is to deserve it, together with some attention to exactly what qualifies as commercial speech. The point surfaces briefly again twice in Canada, with due acknowledgment to *Virginia Board*. It appears in *Klein and Dvorak*, as the first case heard at the provincial Court of Appeal level in Canada

---

[1] All cases referred to in this section are discussed in the survey above; citations will not be repeated here. The Table of Cases may also be consulted.

(at 510). It appears as part of Henry J's dissent, since the majority holds that commercial expression is outside Charter protection. It appears again in *Ford* (at 610), the first Supreme Court of Canada case in which constitutional protection for commercial expression is at all an issue, although in the end the case was not decided on pure commercial expression grounds. In Canada, too, the Supreme Court after this case does not think that the possible exclusion of commercial expression from constitutional protection is a live issue. In Europe, also, no attention is paid to the possibility that commercial expression might be 'wholly outside the protection' of Article 10. After *Markt Intern*, whose unsatisfactory comment we have already discussed (Chapter 5.1 above), the matter is never addressed. The European Court of Justice has not ruled on the matter, although Advocate General Fennelly in the first Tobacco Directive case said he thought the European Court of Human Rights precedent should be followed.

(b) The claim that the purely economic interest of the speaker is a constitutionally legitimate interest is mentioned in passing in *Central Hudson* (at 561). It is pressed more vigorously in *Wileman* in the U.S. (at 2143) and *Klein and Dvorak* in Canada (at 501). In each of these cases, however, the point is pressed by the dissent when the majority has voted to uphold the expression-restricting regulation. Acknowledgment of the relevance of the speaker's economic interest was mentioned in *Virginia Board* (at 761) primarily to argue that such an interest did not disqualify a speaker from constitutional protection. As I explained at length in discussing *Virginia Board* (Chapter 2.6 above), this point about there being no exclusory role for the interest is quite proper. Its force as a supportive reason for the commercial expression doctrine is weak, and the move straight from the propriety of the absence of exclusory role to the supportive force is wholly illegitimate.

(c) What one might term the 'keener by far' argument turns up sporadically in later U.S. cases—*Linmark* (at 92), *Bates* (at 364), and the dissent in *Friedman* (at 22), but then not again until *Coors* (at 1589). It appears most recently in the dissent in *Wileman* (at 2141), and in *Western States* (at 8). As I indicated above in my discussion of *Virginia Board* (Chapter 2.4), it is difficult to parse the 'keener by far' argument as stated in that case to have much argumentative cogency. The argument, however, becomes transformed in the form it takes in Canadian decisions. In *Ford* (at 618) the Supreme Court declares that 'commercial expression . . . plays a significant role in enabling individuals to make informed economic choices, an important aspect of individual self-fulfilment and personal autonomy.' This passage is quoted *verbatim* in *Rocket* (at 74), and the point made in somewhat different terms in *RJR-MacDonald*: 'Smoking is a legal activity yet consumers are deprived of an important means of learning about product availability *to suit their preferences*' (at 99, my emphasis). The original 'keener by far' argument in *Virginia Board* did not give any reason why such a keener interest should be of constitutional significance. The Supreme Court of Canada's expansion of the argument fills the gap. In relating the possession of commercial information to 'individual fulfilment and autonomy', the

Court is fitting it into the traditional scheme of justification for freedom of expression—the instrumental value of freedom of expression for the fostering of autonomy. Individual self-fulfilment and autonomy do not figure in arguments in Europe for freedom of commercial expression.

(d) The claim that there is a societal interest in the free flow of commercial information because some commercial messages deal with matters of public interest appears again in *Friedman* (at 8) and then not again until the recent case of *GNOBA* (at 1930). The reasons for this absence are not hard to find. In the majority of cases, the idea that the advertisement embodies a public interest message is preposterous. Moreover, the U.S. Supreme Court in fact speedily made it clear that the commercial speech doctrine meant constitutional protection for purely commercial speech. *Primus* showed that speech which, even if it did no more than propose a commercial transaction, had a public interest component to it, would be treated for purposes of constitutional review as political, rather than commercial, speech, an approach articulated to the full in *Bolger* and foreshadowed by *Bigelow*. In Canada, the argument was briefly tried by the Ontario Court of Appeal in *Rocket*: 'Governments and public-spirited organizations may wish, by means of commercial messages, to warn the community of the dangers of polluting the air and water by the use or misuse of certain products' (at 664). It does not reappear. *Guignard* applies the argument to what the court there calls 'counter-advertising'. In several European decisions, the public interest aspect of what are arguably advertisements is taken seriously, but with the result that the expression is thought of more as political than as commercial.

(e) The thought that commercial expression is of value to society may, however, be expressed differently, as it was in *Virginia Board* at 765. Free enterprise societies need the economic market to operate efficiently. For the economic market to operate efficiently, market participants must have information. Commercial expression provides information. This claimed societal interest in the free flow of commercial information becomes the main argument for freedom of commercial expression in the U.S., in Canada, and in Europe. It is mentioned explicitly in virtually all of the decided commercial expression cases, whether by the majority in overturning a restriction on commercial expression, or by the dissent in arguing that an upheld restriction should have been overturned.

(f) The condemnation of the advertising restrictions in *Virginia Board* as 'paternalistic' also struck a chord heard to be harmonious. Anti-paternalistic rhetoric, in varying degrees of colour, appears in roughly half of the cases decided in the U.S. Supreme Court, up to and including the most recent case, *Western States* (at 16). The thought is that there is something both morally and constitutionally intolerable in the government deciding for the citizen which consumer information it is proper for the citizen to have. The argument does not appear in Canada or in Europe, thus providing some support for the cliché that these cultures lack the fundamental cultural mistrust of government, which is so influential in the U.S.

(g) *Virginia Board*'s apt image of the flow of commercial information need-ing to be clean as well as free, and its implication that false or misleading speech does not merit constitutional protection, is repeated in the six cases immediately following *Virginia Board*, but only once again thereafter (*Edenfield* at 1799). It rightly becomes established that constitutional protection for commercial expression applied only to truthful information about a legal product or service. This qualification is easy to understand, in the light of the emphasis placed on the informational function of commercial expression. False or misleading expression provides no, or scant, information, and it is hardly the task of the law to promote illegal activities.

(h) *Virginia Board* talks (at 771–2) of 'commonsense differences' between commercial speech and other forms of speech protected under the First Amendment; commercial speech is more objective and more hardy. The Court suggests that these differences may justify a lower level of protection for com-mercial speech than for other speech. It was not slow to take up its own invita-tion. The differences were emphasized again in *Ohralik*, the first case after *Virginia Board* in which a restriction on commercial speech was upheld. The lower level of protection was formalized and operationalized in the four-part test stated in *Central Hudson*, and has been followed by the court since. The Supreme Court of Canada has rejected anything as mechanical as the *Central Hudson* test for identifying commercial expression, which merits constitutional protection. Nonetheless, it has made it clear that not all expression will have an equal status under section 2(b) of the Charter: 'It is . . . destructive of free expres-sion values, as well as the other values which underlie a free and democratic society, to treat all expression as equally crucial to those principles at the core of s.2(b).'[2] This scale of values shows itself in the application of the *Oakes* test in section 1 analysis, in terms of how readily the Court will find there to be a government interest which is 'pressing and substantial', and how readily it will find the limitation on expression to be proportionate to that purpose. Analogously, the European Court of Human Rights displays its rating of com-mercial expression in how readily it finds a margin of appreciation owed to the government regulation at issue.

Those, then, are the arguments by which courts have defended the commer-cial expression doctrine. Academic commentators, while supplementing the rea-soning in this way or that in particular cases, have added little to the stock of general reasons for the doctrine. My aim in the following chapters is to provide a principled critique of these arguments, with the aim of showing on how flimsy a jurisprudential base the doctrine rests. Argument (a), the 'not wholly outside' argument, will be further considered in Chapter 8. This argument depends cru-cially on regarding as salient the mere fact that commercial speech is speech. I show in Chapter 8 how unhelpful is such reliance. Argument (b), the constitu-tional legitimacy of the economic interest, along with (e), the role of the free

---

[2] *R v Keegstra* (1990) 61 CCC (3d) 1, at 47, per Dickson CJC.

flow of commercial information in an efficient allocation of resources, will be considered in Chapters 13 and 14. My aim there will be to question the role in constitutional reasoning of economic values, including the economic value of information, and to reject the possibility of a general 'public good' argument for freedom of commercial expression. Argument (c), in its strongest form as presented by the Supreme Court of Canada, that freedom of commercial expression is linked to self-fulfilment and autonomy, will be discussed in Chapters 9–12, as will Argument (f), the anti-paternalism argument. These arguments will be criticized in four stages. First, in Chapter 9, I shall show that corporations cannot hold *in propria persona* any right resulting from self-fulfilment and autonomy as values. If they are to have such a right in law, its moral ground must be some right of a natural person. The most obvious candidate is the hearer. In Chapter 10, therefore, I discuss generally the notion of hearers' rights, and show that such importance as the idea has cannot be transferred over to the case of commercial expression. In Chapter 11, I question the assumption of the 'keener by far' argument that freedom of commercial expression promotes individual self-realization, self-fulfilment, and autonomy. Finally, in Chapter 12, I show that the anti-paternalism argument is unsound. Some issues concerning the role of Argument (g), the exclusion of false or misleading expression/speech, have been considered in Chapter 3.2 above. Argument (d), as I have indicated just above, to the extent that it has been relied on by courts does not advance the cause of the commercial expression doctrine. I will not address it further except incidentally. As for Argument (h), the fundamental thesis of this work is that the commercial expression doctrine is unsound. If that is so, it does not matter what level of constitutional protection is in fact given to commercial expression. Argument (h) therefore will not receive further consideration either. If commercial expression deserves no constitutional protection at all, then *a fortiori* it does not deserve a level of protection lower than that of other forms of expression. My view is that the differences between commercial expression and traditionally protected forms of expression are sufficient to show that commercial expression should not be protected at all, not that it should be protected albeit at a lower level.

PART II
THEORETICAL INTERLUDE

7

The Conceptual Background

Part I of this book has been devoted to a survey of the case law in different jurisdictions. The survey has shown how some level of constitutional protection has been afforded to freedom of commercial expression—that is, how the U.S., Canada, and Europe have developed a commercial expression doctrine. The longer-term purpose of this survey was two-fold—to make clear the kind of case and the kind of jurisprudential issues at stake in this book, and to present some preliminary considerations concerning the fragile theoretical justification for the commercial expression doctrine. The remainder of this book is devoted to defending its primary normative claim, the claim that the commercial expression doctrine has no sound theoretical foundation in political morality.

That claim, of course, is a large claim. It is not surprising, therefore, that the steps to be taken to justify the claim will need to be careful, and they will need to be many. It is equally not surprising that the programme of justifying the claim presumes a certain conceptual background. The purpose of this chapter is to lay out that assumed conceptual background. Since the chief project of this book overall is the application of such a background, the independent justification of the background will not receive a lot of attention. I make no apology for this limitation. One way to justify a conceptual background is to show how powerful it can be in its application to theoretical problems. On the other hand, I recognize that it is the right of any reader to refuse to accept the framework being here proposed, and to deny therefore any credibility to the succeeding argument. I do not believe myself that a philosophical writer has to justify everything before he or she can justify anything, or even, for that matter, that it would make sense to propose such a requirement. I act here on that belief.

There are two large areas of clarification which will be charted in this chapter. The first concerns terminology used in constitutional opinions and commentaries. We need to consider further the terms 'expression' and 'speech' as they occur in the phrases 'commercial expression' and 'commercial speech'; and we need to elucidate and clarify the pair of terms 'cover' and 'protect'. I will consider the latter point immediately, in the early part of this Chapter. The matter of the meaning of 'expression' and 'speech' is fundamentally important to this study, both methodologically and substantively. I will consider it last, in this Chapter 7.4, as the point will be expanded upon and applied in the remaining chapters of the book.

The second area where the conceptual background requires clarification concerns a number of issues having to do with the concept of a 'right'. Colloquially, freedom of expression is typically listed among basic human rights; the phrase 'right of freedom of expression' often occurs in judicial opinions and academic commentaries. The Canadian *Charter of Rights and Freedoms*, on the other hand, distinguishes rights from freedoms. The variety of different senses of the term 'right' must be distinguished, and the interrelations between the different senses carefully charted. In particular, we need to be clear about freedom of expression as a fundamental value in political morality, and freedom of expression as a constitutional right in a particular institutionalized normative system (this Chapter 7.2). I shall also present a taxonomy of rights developed by Meir Dan-Cohen, involving the distinction between (in his terminology) autonomy rights and utility rights, and between original rights and derivative rights (this Chapter 7.3).[1] As I will show in Chapters 9–13, many of the more intuitively plausible arguments in favour of the commercial expression doctrine crucially depend on blurring, or even ignoring, these distinctions.

1 COVERAGE AND PROTECTION

One important conceptual distinction most relevant to the present project is Frederick Schauer's.[2] This is the distinction between 'coverage' and 'protection' in relation to constitutionally guaranteed rights. To state what is covered by a constitutional provision is to state what actions, etc., come within its scope, what actions raise or implicate the issues embodied in the constitutional provision. To state what is protected is to state what actions, for example, one may appeal to the courts to enable one to perform or what restrictions one may appeal to the courts to lift as a final holding in a case.

This distinction is conveniently institutionalized in the Canadian *Charter of Rights and Freedoms* in the relation of section 1 to section 2 of the *Charter*, and in Article 10 of the European Convention on Human Rights in the relation between sections 1 and 2 of the Article. Section 2 of the *Charter* defines the fundamental freedoms (see Chapter 4.1 above). Section 1 states conditions under which a limitation on a fundamental freedom may be justified. Section 2(b) simply states that the section covers any actions that constitute the exercise of freedom of expression. That is to say, the section, as interpreted by the courts, states the scope of the freedom specified. If an activity—say, the publication of advertising for a tobacco product—comes within the scope of the section, then it is *covered* by the section. Whether such publication is in law constitutionally protected, however, depends on the outcome of section 1 analysis. One will not know for any specific action whether it will indeed receive constitutional protection—that is to say, whether any government regulation restricting such

[1] Meir Dan-Cohen, *Rights, Persons and Organizations: A Legal Theory for Bureaucratic Society* (Berkeley and Los Angeles, Cal.: University of California Press, 1986), Chapter 4.

[2] Frederick Schauer, *Free Speech: A Philosophical Enquiry* (Cambridge: Cambridge University Press, 1982), 89–92.

action will be struck down—until the court has considered whether or not the restriction on that action is demonstrably justified in a free and democratic society. If the limitation fails to be justified under section 1, then the activity is not merely covered but also *protected*.

The value of this conceptual distinction can be seen from the Supreme Court of Canada's Prostitution Reference case.[3] Lamer J (as he then was) argues (at 108–11) that section 2(b) should be interpreted so as to have the widest possible scope and a very narrow set of exclusions, with the consequence that the vast majority of putative restrictions on freedom of expression will be justified, if at all, under section 1 analysis. He therefore makes remarks such as: 'I am of the view that s.2(b) of the Charter *protects* all content of expression irrespective of the meaning or message sought to be conveyed'; '[w]hile the guarantee of free expression *protects* all content, all forms are not, however, similarly *protected*' (at 108: my emphasis). He summarizes his discussion thus: 'All content of expression is *protected* while the set of forms that will not receive *protection* is narrow and includes direct attacks by violent means on the physical liberty and integrity of another person' (at 112: my emphasis). He thus concludes that the speech at issue in the case, the speech of a prostitute soliciting, is expression 'protected' by section 2(b). However, when he turns to section 1 analysis, Lamer J is in no doubt at all that section 195.1(1)(c) of the Criminal Code of Canada constitutes a reasonable limit on freedom of expression within the meaning of section 1 of the *Charter*. Now, there is a real conceptual oddity to declaring solicitation for commercial sex, for example, 'protected' by the *Charter*, but also that the government can legitimately restrict such expression by making it criminal. In the proposed terminology, this oddity disappears. Solicitation is *covered* by the *Charter* through section 2(b) in that it is not regarded as an expression which raises no constitutional issues at all. Yet the *Charter* does not protect it, because restriction of it is a limit justifiable by section 1 analysis.

In the case of the First Amendment, it is crucial to make the conceptual distinction clearly and deliberately, because there is no institutional representation of the distinction. As we saw in Chapter 3.2, in the four-part test for assessing legislative limitations on commercial speech developed by the U.S. Supreme Court in *Central Hudson*,[4] the speech under examination is determined to be 'commercial speech' before the four-part test comes into play. The test corresponds quite closely to the Supreme Court of Canada's test for whether a limitation of a *Charter* right or freedom is justified under section 1 (see Chapter 4.1 above). The coverage/protection distinction may be applied as follows. The determination that the restricted speech is 'commercial' is the determination of whether the speech is 'covered' by the First Amendment. The question whether the government regulation passes the four-part test answers the question whether the speech is 'protected' by the First Amendment.

[3] *Reference re ss. 193 and 195.1(1)(c) of the Criminal Code (Man)* (1990) 56 CCC (3d) 65.
[4] *Central Hudson Gas & Electric Corporation v Public Service Commission of New York* 447 US 557 (1980).

Consider this pair of passages from *Virginia Board*:

Speech does not lose its First Amendment protection because money is spent to project it. . . . Speech is likewise protected even though it is carried in a form, which is 'sold' for profit, and even though it may involve a solicitation to purchase or otherwise pay or contribute money. If there is a form of commercial speech that lacks all First Amendment protection, it must be distinguished by its content. [at 761]

We of course do not hold that commercial speech can never be regulated in any way. Some forms of commercial speech regulation are surely permissible. . . . There is no claim, for example, that the prohibition on prescription drug advertising is a mere time, place and manner restriction. Restrictions of that kind have been approved. Untruthful speech, commercial or otherwise, has never been protected for its own sake. [at 770–1]

The issue before the Court, as I noted in the analysis of the decision in Chapter 2.6 above, is the then controlling rule in *Chrestensen*,[5] which automatically excluded commercial speech from the scope of the First Amendment just because it was *commercial*. Issues of scope are issues of coverage. But the Court all the way through uses the language of 'protection'. The first quotation conflates the thought that speech being commercial does not exclude it from the scope of the First Amendment with the thought that speech being commercial does not necessarily imply that the final decision in the case—the protection decision, if you like—must go against the speech. As far as the second quotation is concerned, the Court's ruling is that untruthful commercial speech is outside the scope of the First Amendment—that is, is not covered by it, and not that the untruthful character of some speech weighs heavily against it in the final decision concerning protection.

In this book, I am primarily concerned with the issue, framed in Canadian terms, whether commercial expression should be covered by section 2(b). I shall often talk of 'protection', because, clearly, if constitutional coverage is to amount to anything worthwhile, most of the actions, for example, covered must also be protected. But I am not here much concerned with what conclusions the Supreme Court of Canada has reached about the actual protection of various cases of commercial expression through its section 1 analysis; I am concerned only with their reasons for thinking that commercial expression is covered by section 2(b) of the *Charter*—that is to say, their reasons for thinking that commercial expression as understood above is an activity which implicates the reasons a society has for having a provision like section 2(b) in its constitution.

Apart from a general preference for precision over imprecision, I have a particular reason here for highlighting the distinction between coverage and protection. This book is an essay in the theoretical foundations of the commercial expression doctrine. The issue of what a constitutional provision ought to cover is clearly an issue of jurisprudential theory, in this case normative jurisprudential theory. The issue of what a constitutional provision ought to protect, on the

    [5] *Valentine v Chrestensen* 316 US 52 (1942).

other hand, carries us beyond issues of, for example, the notion of freedom of expression as such into issues where that value or interest is balanced against other values or interests, issues of politics as well as of political morality, of policy and practicality, of ideology and culture. This book is not especially concerned with those issues, though the occasional *ad hoc* comment will intrude. The coverage/protection distinction is needed in order to demarcate properly the scope of this book, as well as to understand aright judicial opinions and arguments that form the book's raw material.

2 NATURAL, MORAL, AND INSTITUTIONAL RIGHTS

The focus of this book is on the commercial expression doctrine, the doctrine that commercial expression (commercial advertising, for example) deserves the same, or sufficiently similar, constitutional protection as any other form of constitutionally protected expression or speech. A human activity or status which has constitutional protection is typically referred to as a constitutional *right*. The term 'right', however, is systematically ambiguous. This book is not the place to develop a theory of rights, and indeed I try here as far as possible to present an argument which leaves open some of the contested questions about rights within normative theorizing. Nonetheless the multiple meanings of 'right' require that I make some formal statement as to the meanings deployed in this book. I will do that now, although I shall not pretend that I have a full theory of rights either conceptually or politically unassailable. There are two different taxonomies of rights, which are significant for the arguments of this book. I will explain them in this Chapter 7.2–3.

The results of decisions in cases involving section 2(b) of the Canadian *Charter* or the First Amendment are often colloquially described in terms of 'rights'. Thus the outcome of *Ford* is said to be that shops in the province of Quebec do have the constitutional right to have advertising signs in the English language. *44 Liquormart*[6] is said to show that liquor stores in Rhode Island do have the right to show product prices in their advertising. But what exactly is it that is being shown by these decisions? Is it that for liquor stores to show prices in their advertising or Quebec shops to display advertisements in English is the right thing from the point of view of morality? Is it that liquor stores and Quebec shops have a natural, or basic human, right to show prices or to use English? It is entirely possible to accept that the form of words above in terms of 'constitutional right' makes perfectly good sense, while having some doubt whether the forms of words in terms of moral or natural rights make sense. So these notions are distinct, and need to be distinguished.

In the most general sense, a 'right' represents a normative reason of some considerable weight. As Wayne Sumner has put it, 'rights function normatively as

---

[6] *44 Liquormart Inc v Rhode Island* 116 SCt 1495 (1996).

relatively insistent or peremptory moral considerations'.[7] Rights are, in Ronald Dworkin's famous image, 'trumps' in the game of political or moral argument and struggle.[8] They are one example of what Joseph Raz has called 'exclusionary reasons', reasons which function to exclude, rather than outweigh, competing reasons.[9] A right not to be imprisoned without due process of law intuitively counts as indeed a right. The right to fondle one's own beard intuitively does not, unless some special scenario is laid out to make the action an instance of something appropriately weighty. Subsequent specifications here of the notion of a right should be seen as applications of this general notion.

The notion of a 'natural right' will play little role in this book. The term belongs to an ancient, and honourable, tradition in political and moral theory, a tradition that roots moral value in human nature as the theory conceives it. Such a concept carries with it much in the way of philosophical, and sometimes theological, presupposition about the essential unity and permanency of human nature, and about the capacity of human reason to ascertain such a nature and the truths about morality that it subtends. Whatever may be the merits of such a view, it is clear that the view represents one interpretation of one aspect of the more fundamental concept of 'moral right'. One could express the core content of 'natural right' independently of the presuppositions of natural law theory by speaking of 'human rights', those rights that one has simply by virtue of being human. It is still the expression of a moral point of view to state that there are such rights, and to give an inventory of them. I hazard the judgement that, at least where individual human beings are concerned, the right to speak one's native language is a strong candidate for a 'natural' or 'human' right. The attempts by the Canadian federal government to prevent aboriginal children in their care from using their native languages, or by the Spanish government to suppress the use of the Catalonian language, have been moral nadirs in the history of those countries. I am a good deal more sceptical, unsurprisingly, about whether there is a 'natural' or 'human' right for liquor stores to display prices in their advertising.

The notion of a 'moral right' will play a somewhat greater role in this book, although not usually specifically by name. In its most straightforward sense, a moral right is a right acknowledged by a system of morality or of moral value. A moral system does not have to be 'right-based'—that is, to make the notion of a right its fundamental concept. Moral systems may be based on duty, happiness, rational self-interest, well-being, or on a variety of other notions, or be irreducibly pluralistic in their basic values. The root idea of a moral right is

---

[7] L.W. Sumner, *The Moral Foundation of Rights* (Oxford: Clarendon Press, 1987), 12.

[8] Ronald M. Dworkin, *Taking Rights Seriously* (2nd edn., Cambridge, Mass.: Harvard University Press, 1978), xi.

[9] Joseph Raz, *Practical Reason and Norms* (London: Hutchinson, 1975), Chapter 1.2. There is a considerable literature on the acceptability of Raz's view: for a discussion of the view and of some of the perceived difficulties see Roger A. Shiner, *Norm and Nature: The Movements of Legal Thought*, Clarendon Law Series (Oxford: Clarendon Press, 1992), Chapters 1.2, 2.1, and 3.

this—that there is sufficient justification within the moral system for the appropriate 'relatively insistent or peremptory moral consideration'. Thus Sumner is properly able to defend in *Moral Foundation* the seemingly counter-intuitive thesis (given the popularity of the idea in contemporary moral philosophy that utility and rights are essentially incompatible) that the best theory of rights is utilitarian.

Freedom of expression is regarded by many different kinds of moral system as being such a privileged consideration. It is held by many right-based systems to be a basic manifestation of personal autonomy, or a fundamental precondition for the exercise of such autonomy. It is held by utilitarian or consequentialist systems to be the cause of much human happiness and flourishing, or an essential precondition for the same. Sometimes the argument focusses on the direct benefit to the individual of freedom of expression. Sometimes the argument is more indirect—that freedom of expression is essential to a healthy civil society, and such a society is the cause of much human happiness and flourishing or an essential pre-condition for the same. For such a range of reasons, a large number of moral systems hold individuals to possess a moral right to enjoy freedom of expression.

The concern of this book with the moral right to freedom of expression in general is more covert than overt. That right forms the background to the book; it is not the foreground. The foreground is, in a narrow sense to be specified, the putative moral right to freedom of *commercial* expression. As I indicated in Chapter 1, my starting-point is the assumption that the value of freedom of expression is related to three human activities—the search for truth, enlightened political decision-making, and individual self-realization. These are assumed to be morally desirable activities, whether in themselves or for their consequences. A putative moral right to freedom of commercial expression figures in this book only as a matter of the similarities and differences in the way in which freedom of commercial expression is related to those same activities. The moral question is whether freedom of commercial expression promotes those values that freedom of expression in general promotes; if so, how, and if not, then why not.

The third kind of right distinguished in this section is that of an institutional right. We arrive at the idea of an institutional right as follows. Norms, or standards of behaviour, are of many kinds—maxims of manners and etiquette: 'It is polite to turn off your cell-phone during the performance'; statements of moral duties: 'Thou shalt not kill'; principles of successful horticulture: 'Newly planted trees should be watered in twice a week'; rules of sports and games: 'The penalty for playing into a water hazard is stroke and distance'; valid rules of logical inference: 'P and (if P then Q) implies Q'; and so on. Norms also form groups—the Ten Commandments, a manual of gardening techniques, a logic primer all contain groups of norms. Some groups of norms are interlocking and so form systems. The rules of bridge, for example, presuppose each other; the game succeeds as the game it is only if all the rules are observed. The axioms and rules of inference of a logical system unite all the theorems of the system. Some groups of norms exist only as the products of an institution—the constitution and rules for a social club are adopted by that club, can be changed only by that club, and are applied or enforced by that club in the context of its activities. These two features of forming a system and being institutionalized may be combined, so that a group of norms may be said to form an *institutionalized normative system*.[10]

The typical legal system—the Canadian legal system, for example—is a paradigm case of an institutionalized normative system. A norm counts as *a law*, and not some other kind of norm, in part because it emerges from a specific kind of institution—a governing legislature or a court deciding a case.[11] Laws are thus institutionalized norms. Laws and legal institutions presuppose or outrank each other—administrative tribunals are established by legislatures; constitutional courts can invalidate legislation; law-making by a provincial legislature presupposes a constitution giving it law-making powers. Laws also have common origins in specific agencies—parliaments, courts, certain positions, and offices. Laws therefore form systems. A legal system is therefore an institutionalized normative system.

This special character of institutionalized normative systems yields the concept of an institutional right. Just as a right in general is a moral consideration with a certain kind of privileged position within a moral system, so an institutional right will be a normative consideration with a privileged position within an institutionalized normative system. A legal right will be a consideration with a privileged, or protected, position within a legal system. Individuals can come to possess legal rights by different means. Property rights may be acquired by signing contracts, by inheritance, by donation, and so forth. Legal rights, as examples of institutional rights, may also be granted by that specific kind of legal document known as a constitution, and especially by a charter or bill of rights. These rights are examples of constitutional rights.

Legal rights in general, and constitutional rights in particular, are importantly different from moral rights because of their institutional character, despite their frequently having similar content. A shop unquestionably has the legal right to prosecute for theft under section 322 of the Canadian Criminal Code a desperate and impoverished parent who shoplifts medical supplies for a sick child. Whether the shop has the moral right to do so is much more debatable. Some will hold that the parent has the moral right to take what is needed, even if the parent does not have the legal right. In the city of Edmonton, as I once found out the hard way, one has no legal right to reverse into an angle parking space, although morality would likely permit such an act.

---

[10] The detailed analysis of institutionalized normative systems, including legal systems, is more complicated than this brief account here indicates. See Raz, *Practical Reason and Norms*, 123–48.

[11] The matter of the sources of law is, of course, a large topic. See Roger A. Shiner, *Legal Institutions and the Sources of Law*, vol. III of Enrico Pattaro, Gerald J. Postema, and Peter Stein (eds.), *A Treatise of Legal Philosophy and General Jurisprudence* (Dordrecht: Kluwer Academic Publishers, 2003).

The intuitive difference between moral and legal rights is clearest when the two normative systems differ in the content of their norms on the same point. But in many cases law and morality do not normatively diverge. Both forbid a similar range of acts of violence against the person, for example. A promise to build a fence and a contract to build a fence would both be held to imply that the promisor/contractor should build the fence. But it remains true that, to take the case in point in this book, freedom of expression as a moral right and freedom of expression as a legal right are quite different. Freedom of expression is a moral right, if it is (and it is), because in some preferred moral system there is sufficient justification for morally privileging freedom of expression. Freedom of expression is a legal right, if it is, because the legal system has institutionalized a privileged position for freedom of expression within its system of norms. This position need not be the result of a constitution, although it is so in the U.S. and Canada. It could be a matter of the applicability in some given jurisdiction of an array of non-constitutional statutes or common law rules amounting when taken as a whole, to a significant degree of protection for acts of expression.[12]

When it comes to the kind of fundamental right which is typically the content of a formal charter or bill of rights, the common content between law and morality is typically striking. A charter or bill of rights gives a privileged position to certain moral values by defining constitutional rights and freedoms. But the distinctness between constitutional rights and moral rights is still there. The institutional history of the interpretation of the constitution by the supreme tribunal in a jurisdiction, or by lower courts when the supreme tribunal has not spoken, defines the nature and scope of the institutional rights in that jurisdiction. That nature and scope are not defined by the nature and scope of the analogous moral rights, whether or not they bear the same name. So the nature and scope of the constitutional right to freedom of expression in Canada is, putting the matter crudely, what the Canadian legal system, and especially the Supreme Court of Canada, says it is, and the deliverances of the Court may or may not overlap in content with the deliverances of morality.

This distinctness of moral right and constitutional right goes along with a further difference. The question whether there should be a moral right of a given kind and the question whether there is a moral right of a given kind amount pretty much to the same question. This question is a matter of whether a preferred system of morality implies a privileged normative position of the requisite sort. In the case of constitutional rights, the matter is altogether different. In the first place, the question whether there *should be* a constitutional right of a given kind is not at all the same as the question whether there *is* a constitutional right of a given kind. The latter is a matter of the institutional history within the

---

[12] That was how freedom of expression was (or was insufficiently) protected in the U.K. before the passing of the Human Rights Act in 1998. For an assessment of the level of protection see John Gardner, 'Freedom of Expression', in Christopher McCrudden and Gerard Chambers (eds.), *Individual Rights and the Law in Britain* (Oxford: Clarendon Press, 1994), 209–38.

appropriate legal system. The former is a question whether there is a sufficient justification for giving a privileged institutional position to the relevant activity or status. Moreover, while in the case of constitutional rights this justification is regularly in part moral—the reasons for the activity or status meriting constitutional protection are a function of the moral worth of the activity or status—the justification is not wholly moral. Even in the case where a morally worthy activity or status is at issue, there may still be different kinds of reasons for not granting it constitutional protection. These arguments also may be moral—the activity or status is, though morally worthy, not morally worthy enough to receive such a high level of privilege as constitutional protection. Or the arguments may be historical—it would be a severe divergence from institutional history to extend constitutional protection to such an activity or status. Or the arguments may be formal—it is not of the essence of constitutionality to extend constitutional protection to such an activity or status. Or the arguments may be practical or political—to extend constitutional protection to such an activity or status would pose too many problems of defining the scope of the protection, or of operationalizing the protection within a legal framework.

How would all this apply to freedom of commercial expression as a candidate constitutional value? First, there is a distinction between the question whether commercial expression is a morally worthy activity in its own right and the question whether it should receive constitutional protection. The question of the soundness of the commercial expression doctrine, that is, is not the question whether commercial expression is a morally worthy activity. It is important to realize that the prime concern of this book is not with the latter question, not with the question of the moral status of commercial expression as such. The focus is on the range of arguments that ask specifically whether there is a justification for the constitutional protection of freedom of commercial expression. Should freedom of commercial expression be constitutionally protected? Should there be an institutional right, a constitutional right, to freedom of commercial expression? That in fact, and to what degree, there currently is such an institutional right in the three jurisdictions studied is evident from Part I. In those chapters, we saw courts giving a variety of reasons for extending constitutional protection to freedom of commercial expression, for acknowledging freedom of commercial expression to be an institutional right within the institution of those legal systems. It is those reasons which this book analyses and criticizes as normative, but not (beyond comments already made in Part I) as institutional, reasons.

3 Autonomy, utility, and rights

I presented in the previous section the distinction between natural or human rights, moral rights, and institutional (primarily, in our case, legal and, of those, primarily constitutional) rights. In this section, I will consider a different taxonomy, based on the normative ground for the protected normative position which the right represents. I am going to speak as though it is a taxonomy of rights, although it is properly a taxonomy of grounds for rights.

The taxonomy is Meir Dan-Cohen's.[13] Dan-Cohen argues that there are two paradigms in the law for the justification of legal decisions—the paradigm of social utility and the paradigm of individual autonomy.[14] Each paradigm is a candidate for the justification of the acknowledgment of constitutional rights. An autonomy right, or AR, is a legal right, a legally protected normative position, which is, or claims to be, justified by arguments drawn from the paradigm of autonomy. A utility right, or UR, is a legal right, a legally protected normative position, which is, or claims to be, justified by arguments drawn from the paradigm of social utility. For example, the constitutionally guaranteed presumption of innocence embodied in section 11(d) of the Canadian *Charter* is an autonomy right. The typical justification in background political morality for such a right turns on the need to promote autonomy by protecting autonomous choices. The so-called exclusionary rule in the law of torts, the rule which confines recovery for purely economic loss to very few specific cases, gives an immunity to most defendants. The rule is defended on grounds of social utility, chiefly the fear of the 'liability in an indeterminate amount for an indeterminate time to an indeterminate class', in Cardozo J's famous phrase,[15] that would occur in the absence of such a rule, and on the perception that economic loss occurs mostly in the business world where mechanisms other than tort liability are easily available to control potential loss. The resultant immunity for potential tortfeasors is therefore an example of a right justified by arguments from utility, a utility right. I shall speak straightforwardly of 'autonomy right' and 'utility right', even though what I will at times be referring to is a candidate such right for which, in my view, the justification is inadequate.

Dan-Cohen also valuably distinguishes original rights, or ORs, and derivative rights, or DRs. ORs, original rights, are rights A has out of a normative concern for the welfare (in a broad sense) of A. DRs, or derivative rights, are rights A has out of a normative concern for the welfare (in an equally broad sense) of another, B.[16] A's possession of a DR means that A may validly and even successfully rest a legal claim on a right without himself or herself having that right—A may rely on B's right, as in subrogation in insurance litigation, or invoke B's right, as in guardianship cases. Consider also *Big M Drug Mart*.[17]

[13] Dan-Cohen, *Rights, Persons and Organizations*, Chapter 4.
[14] It would of course be a substantial project in itself to determine whether he is right about this. I am not going to pursue that project. I am going to assume that he is right enough about it for the purposes of this book. As will be clear from subsequent chapters, all the important justifications for the commercial expression doctrine fall into one of these two categories, and that is all that we require for this book.
[15] *Ultramares Corp v Touche* 174 NE 441 (1931) (NY CA), at 179. See also Bruce Feldthusen, *Economic Negligence* (4th edn., Toronto: Carswell, 2000), Chapter 5.
[16] Dan-Cohen, *Rights, Persons*, 58.
[17] *R v Big M Drug Mart Ltd* (1985) 18 DLR (4th) 321.

This case concerned the Lord's Day Act, legislation prohibiting shops from opening on Sundays. The Supreme Court of Canada ruled that the Act interfered with the freedom of religion of non-Christians, and invalidated the Act. Thus the fine imposed on the drug store was lifted, even though the drug store itself possessed no freedom of religion.

In the case of an original right, OR, the justification is one-track: it simply has to be shown that the paradigm appealed to justifies the right. In the case of derivative rights, DRs, the justification is two-track. Not only does the original right from which the derived right is derived have to be justified. Also, it has to be shown that the two parties—the A and the B in some given case—are related in such a way that the derivation of B's right from A's right is itself justified.

The two classifications of rights cut across each other. A legal right may thus in terms of this taxonomy be one of four kinds—original autonomy right (OAR), derived autonomy right (DAR), original utility right (OUR), derived utility right (DUR).[18] It will be investigated in later chapters what is the effect on arguments for the commercial expression doctrine of making these important distinctions. The typical piece of actual argumentation in judicial opinions for the commercial expression doctrine is a mud-puddle of arguments within the paradigm of autonomy and arguments within the paradigm of utility. The arguments need to be distinguished, since they have different shapes and raise different issues. In Chapter 9, we will consider, and reject, the case for freedom of commercial expression as an OAR for corporations. In Chapters 10, 11, and 12 we will consider, and reject, the case for freedom of commercial expression as a DAR for corporations; it will turn out that both the tracks of justification for such a derived right lead to insurmountable obstacles. In Chapters 13 and 14, we will consider, and reject, the case for freedom of commercial expression as a UR for corporations.

4 PRINCIPLED FREEDOM OF EXPRESSION

Anyone who travels a main urban road is familiar with portable signboards containing advertising. They are usually about six feet high, eight feet wide, with a garish yellow background (for visibility), on which are placed several rows of black capital letters, with the message the advertiser wishes the passing motorist to read. The City of Edmonton's Land Use Bylaw section 814.1 (paragraph 9) established certain 'major commercial corridors' adjacent to busy roads, and bans the erection of such portable signs in these corridor areas without a permit to do so. A company whose business it was to lease such signs placed some within the 'corridors' without obtaining a permit, and was duly convicted under

---

[18] Note that Dan-Cohen himself suggests that the distinction between OUR and DUR may be more apparent than real: Dan-Cohen, *Rights, Persons and Organizations*, 79–82; I will allude to the matter in Chapter 9.5 below.

the by-law. The company appealed, claiming that the by-law contravened the guarantee of freedom of expression in section 2(b) of the *Charter*.[19] The case found its way to the Alberta Court of Appeal, which categorically asserted:

The bylaw sections in question expressly forbid expression or communication of ideas, both in form and in substance. So the breach of the *Charter* is direct, deliberate, and central. [at 293]

That's it. That is all the argument that the Court provides for the claim that the activity of placing a portable advertising sign beside a roadway is expression within the scope of constitutional protection for freedom of expression in Canada. It communicates an idea, so it is a candidate for constitutional protection.[20] My main aim now is to show that this approach—it's expression, so it's a candidate for constitutional protection—is far too quick a way with some deeply important normative issues.

It is very important to be clear about the direction in which any argument defending or attacking the commercial expression doctrine has to flow. The term 'expression' or 'speech' to denote a kind of behaviour covered by constitutional provisions such as section 2(b) of the Canadian *Charter*, the First Amendment to the U.S. Constitution, or Article 10 of the European Convention on Human Rights is a *term of art*. This can be easily shown. There are many instances of 'expression' which are not regarded as the kind of expression which may be subsumed under a constitutional provision to protect freedom of expression—cases of fraudulent expression, of price-fixing by a cartel, for example, and the Supreme Court in *Irwin Toy*[21] says the same of violent expression (at 607). There are many examples of expressive behaviour which are properly held to be subsumable and are not linguistic—silent political protest marches, wearing a certain garment, burning a flag, and so forth.

It therefore does not follow merely from the fact that some piece of behaviour, linguistic or no, is 'expression' or 'speech' in some plain extra-legal sense that it is in law a candidate for constitutional protection under section 2(b) of the Canadian *Charter*, the First Amendment to the U.S. Constitution, or Article 10 of the European Convention on Human Rights. The term 'expression' in section 2(b) of the *Charter* or Article 10 of the Convention, and the term 'speech' in the First Amendment, are *theory-laden*: they are not the philosophically innocent terms of pre-analytic discourse.[22] Consequently, the argument that some behaviour is within the scope of some constitutional protection must be

---

[19] *R v 388923 Alberta Ltd* (1995) 174 AR 292 (Alta CA).

[20] In all fairness to the Alberta court, the approach of the Supreme Court of Canada to the interpretation of s.2(b) licenses such taciturnity. See Chapter 4.3 above. Any implicit criticism of the Alberta court here is also implicit criticism of the Supreme Court of Canada.

[21] *Attorney-General of Quebec v Irwin Toy Ltd* [Indexed as Irwin Toy Ltd v Quebec (Attorney-General)] (1989) 58 DLR (4th) 577.

[22] For more on the importance to legal theory of the distinction between pre-analytic and theoretical concepts see Shiner, *Norm and Nature*, 5–9; Shiner, *Legal Institutions and the Sources of Law*, Chapter 8.

'top-down' or, to use Schauer's apt term, 'architectural'.[23] The same is therefore true of any argument within political morality to the effect that a certain kind of expression should be subsumed under provisions for constitutional protection. The commercial expression doctrine is such an argument. It therefore also is 'theory-laden', and must be supported by 'top-down' argumentation. As Schauer puts it:

In this sense 'speech' is a functional term. It must be defined by the purpose of a deep theory of freedom of speech, and not by anything the word 'speech' might mean in ordinary talk. We must remember that 'free speech' is defined not by what it is, but by what it does.[24]

Schauer's point is a general one, whatever the kind of speech or expression at issue. But the point is particularly sharp for commercial expression simply because commercial expression is in part a matter of economics. Economic activity as a human activity cannot be carried out without the use of speech; that is a transcendental point, given that humans are language-users. Yet at first sight the right of governments to regulate the economy through statutory or other regimes is unquestioned. Commercial expression pits a form of behaviour, which is paradigmatically non-regulable—expression—against one which is paradigmatically regulable—commercial activity. Initial intuitions clearly divide. Ever since *Virginia Board*[25] and *Irwin Toy*, the Supreme Courts of Canada and the U.S. have claimed that the economic character of commercial expression or speech is less fundamental from the point of view of constitutional jurisprudence than its character as expression or speech. Commentators have not always agreed. Strauss writes:

Commercial speech has no especial importance to the political process. . . . The First Amendment does not protect commercial activity generally. And there is little about commercial *speech* that distinguishes it from other commercial activity.[26]

Taken merely as intuitions, neither one has precedence over the other. A theory is needed to defend either one. The particular approaches that the respective Supreme Courts have chosen to take are not forced on them by the very con-

[23] Frederick Schauer, *Free Speech*, 3–14, 103–6; Frederick F. Schauer, 'Commercial Speech and the Architecture of the First Amendment', *University of Cincinnati Law Review* 56 (1988): 1181–203. See also Frederick F. Schauer, 'Speech and "Speech"—Obscenity and "Obscenity": An Exercise in the Interpretation of Constitutional Language', *Georgetown Law Journal* 67 (1979): 899–933, esp. 902–19; Frederick F. Schauer, 'Must Speech Be Special?', *Northwestern University Law Review* 78 (1983): 1284–306.

[24] *Free Speech*, 91.

[25] *Virginia State Board of Pharmacy et al v Virginia Citizens Consumer Council Inc et al* 425 US 748 (1976).

[26] David A. Strauss, 'Constitutional Protection for Commercial Speech: Some Lessons from the American Experience', *Canadian Journal of Business Law* 17 (1990): 45–54. See also Thomas H. Jackson and John Calvin Jeffries Jr., 'Commercial Speech: Economic Due Process and the First Amendment', *Virginia Law Review* 65 (1979): 1–41; Lillian BeVier, 'The First Amendment and Political Speech: An Inquiry Into the Substance and Limits of Principle', *Stanford Law Review* 30 (1978): 299–358.

cepts of speech or expression themselves. The approach is a political choice, and it needs a justification by a theory in political morality.

As freedom of expression or speech is normally interpreted in normative political theory, the weight of the commitment to freedom of expression is shown by the fact that expression is considered to be in principle worthy of special protection even though it causes harm,[27] and even though granting it special protection interferes with the promotion of positive good. It is difficult to deny that hostile racial epithets either directed at members of the target group or placed where such members will inevitably see them cause emotional reactions painful enough to be called 'harms'. Relatively few people would regard the presence of hate propaganda and associated manifestations as more of a positive good than their absence. Yet attempts to promote the positive good of the absence of hate propaganda by legislation specifying penalties for spraying swastikas, preventing the accused from offering the defence of truth in Holocaust denial propaganda, creating an offence of possession of hate literature for distribution, and so forth will be highly controversial in the light of a commitment to freedom of expression.

Hate propaganda has proved to be a paradigm site for claims of constitutional protection on freedom of expression grounds. That is sufficient to show that constitutional protection for freedom of expression needs to be justified by reference to its own independent justifying principle. If freedom of expression caused no harm it would not need special justification. If freedom of expression automatically yielded to the promotion of positive good, it would not need special justification. But neither of those conditions is satisfied. One would suppose, other things being equal, that if an action caused harm it should be restricted. In the case of expression or speech, other things are not equal. It is no answer to the question why they are not equal to reply: expression is expression; speech is speech.

An analogous argument may be made in a further case. Commentators and judges often speak of a person's 'free expression interests'/'free speech interests', or 'section 2(b) interests'/'First Amendment interests', both in general and with respect to some specific context or kind of context. What do these phrases mean? It cannot be that they refer simply to an interest people have in being able to express themselves or to speak. The bank robber demanding money with menaces has no 'free expression interest' in being able to say, 'Hand over the cash or I'll kill you', though the robber does have an interest in being able to utter those words. Neither does the company executive have a 'free expression interest' in saying the things that amount to the harassment of an employee. The kind of expression or form of expression which yields a 'free expression

---

[27] See for a detailed discussion of the implausibility of the famous adage about sticks, stones, and words: Frederick Schauer, 'The Phenomenology of Speech and Harm', *Ethics* 103 (1993): 635–53; Susan J. Brison, 'Speech, Harm and the Mind-Body Problem in First Amendment Jurisprudence', *Legal Theory* 4 (1998): 39–61.

interest' is determined, not by the mere fact that what occurs is 'expression' in some ordinary sense of that term, but by the purpose or function of the promotion of freedom of expression, or of constitutional protection for freedom of expression according to some sound theory of that purpose or function.

As I noted above (Chapter 4.3–4), the Supreme Court of Canada has not taken this approach. For it, anything which has a meaning counts as 'expression' of the kind alluded to by section 2(b) of the *Charter*, and thus within that section's scope or coverage. In *Irwin Toy*, the Court even suggests that parking a car might count as a case of expression, if done as a protest of an unfair parking policy.[28] But the Court's reasoning displays its own shortcomings. The Court tells an elaborate story to explain why an act which otherwise is extremely unlikely to constitute expression in a sense which calls up free expression interests in fact does so. The message of the story, however, is exactly the same, whether we are considering parking a car or uttering a syntactically well-formed sentence with a sense and reference in a natural language. The context of the utterance, together with a theory of why certain contexts give value to utterances, is what makes the case one of 'expression' in the sense in which freedom of expression is a value. We are familiar with the way in which contexts of political protest of unfair treatment create free expression interests. So we see that parking a car counts as expression in the technical sense, which implies free expression interests. It is true that, human life being what it is, the case where the utterance of a piece of language occurs in a context which creates free expression interests is a great deal more frequent than the case where parking a car does so. So it is easy to be seduced into thinking that it is the mere utterance that creates the interests. But that would be a mistake.

The validity of the fundamental methodological insight by Schauer, which I have elaborated here, is crucial to the position developed in this book. My argument depends centrally on making out four theses. The first is between an ordinary, everyday, pre-analytic sense of 'expression' or 'speech', and a technical, jurisprudential sense as found in constitutions, typically in charters or bills of rights. The second thesis is that there is no automatic step from the applicability of the ordinary language term to the applicability of the technical, constitutional term. The third thesis is that a theory of freedom of expression or freedom of speech is needed to underwrite the proper interpretation from the point of view of political morality of any technical, constitutional occurrence of the term. The fourth is the claim that the theory most consistent with the traditions of liberal democracy is the theory that the values which underlie freedom of expression or freedom of speech are the familiar trinity of the search for truth, democratic self-government, and individual self-fulfilment. The chief implication I draw from the fourth thesis is that freedom of commercial expression is not justified by such a theory. It is the task of Chapters 9 to 14 to expand upon

---

[28] At 607. Fortunately for the Court, some time after that a person did indeed drive a jeep up the steps of the Parliament in Ottawa and leave it there as a political protest.

and justify that claimed implication. In the current section, I have given some indication of the meaning of the first three theses, and how they might be defended. But more needs to be said. I will therefore in the next chapter, Chapter 8, illustrate and defend further the idea that expression or speech in the idea of freedom of expression or freedom of speech is a technical and theory-laden term, and that arguments for the commercial expression doctrine regularly ignore this constraint.

8

The Importance of Theory Determined

In the previous chapter, I distinguished 'expression' or 'speech' in an ordinary sense from 'expression' or 'speech' in a special sense covered by a principle of freedom of expression or of speech. I also argued that the determination of whether an instance of the ordinary sense is an instance of such a special sense is a matter of top-down argumentation. I believe that theorists and courts have thought commercial expression or speech to be covered by a principle of freedom of expression or freedom of speech in large part because commercial expression/speech is in the ordinary sense 'expression/speech'. And so, of course, it is. This undoubted fact, however, is not enough to get the commercial expression doctrine off the ground. I have accepted that the primary values underlying a principle of freedom of expression or speech are the search for truth, democratic self-government, and individual autonomy and self-fulfilment. To claim the importance of commercial expression (and thus the disvalue of regulating it), however, appeal is typically made to values like economic efficiency and consumer choice. Those values are unrelated to the primary justifying values sketched above. Now, the standard arguments for the commercial expression doctrine that I reviewed at the end of Chapter 6 above do seem to their sponsors in fact to promote the traditional values. I will be arguing in Chapters 9 to 14 that such an impression is false. First, though, in this chapter, I will pursue further the theme of the importance of theory. I will defend my claim that the commercial expression doctrine rests on an illicit move from the premise that commercial expression or speech is expression or speech in the ordinary sense to the conclusion that commercial expression or speech comes within the coverage of the right of freedom of expression.

I shall do so by working through three examples of purely commercial contexts that have been the subject of energetic debate recently. The examples are chosen for a reason. Each of them represents an issue that for a long time the courts did not see as subject to the commercial speech doctrine. Commentators, on the other hand, have urged the applicability of the doctrine to the issues, and in some cases courts have now fallen into line. The three examples are those of tortious interference with contractual relations, the promotion of off-label uses of drugs, and the right of publicity. In the case of the first two examples, I will show that in each instance the argument for the relevance of freedom of commercial expression rests on either the simple assumption that expression/speech in the ordinary sense is involved, or on values which are far removed from the traditional foundational values detailed above. In the case of the right of publicity, we will see that the commercial character of the expression at issue is legitimately to be considered in analysing the relation between the right and the value of freedom of expression. However, I shall show that the distinct role of commercial expression in the analysis of the right of publicity is fully explained by the traditional grounds for freedom of expression assumed in this book. The right of publicity thus provides an illustrative contrast to the other two cases.

1 TORTIOUS INTERFERENCE WITH CONTRACTUAL RELATIONS

Some torts do not involve the use of language, or do so only incidentally: false imprisonment is an example. Other torts essentially involve the use of language: negligent mis-statement is an example. Also in the latter category is the tort of interference with contractual relations. This tort imposes liability on the interferor for intentionally and improperly inducing a party to break a contract. The foundational case historically is that of *Lumley v Gye*.[1] Johanna Wagner, niece of the famous Richard and in her day an operatic soprano just as famous, signed a contract to perform at Lumley's theatre in London. Gye, owner of a rival theatre, offered her more money to sing at his theatre, whereupon she broke her contract with Lumley. Lumley sued Gye *inter alia* on the ground that it was a tort to entice someone to break a contract, and the Court of Queen's Bench agreed. In the succinct words of Erle J:

He who procures the non-delivery of goods according to contract may inflict an injury, the same as he who procures the abstraction of goods after delivery; and both ought on the same ground to be made responsible. [at 756]

Perhaps the most spectacular modern case is the one in which Texaco, knowing that Getty Oil had agreed sell out to Pennzoil for US$110 a share, offered US$125 a share plus indemnification of the damages for breach of the contract with Pennzoil.[2] The final award was for US$8.53 billion, plus accumulated interest, though the case was ultimately settled for US$3 billion.

As the tort of inducing breach of contract stands in major common-law jurisdictions, the interferor (the party which induces the breach) will be found liable even if the party did no more than offer truthful information without coercion, aware that such information might induce a breach of contract—Gye's saying to Wagner, essentially, 'I will pay you more to sing in my theatre than Lumley is going to pay you to sing in his theatre'. The party that acts on the information and breaches is not liable in tort, though clearly liable in contract.

---

[1] *Lumley v Gye* 118 (1853) 2 E&B 216; 118 ER 749.
[2] *Texaco Inc v Pennzoil Co* 729 SW 2d 768 (1987) (Tex CA 1st Dist), *certiorari denied* 485 US 994 (1988).

Two theorists, David Anderson[3] and Robert Tucker,[4] have recently argued that tort law thus unduly burdens speech, in violation (in the case of the U.S.) of the First Amendment's constitutional protection of truthful commercial speech. These articles raise two distinct questions. The first is whether, even if it is true that the tort of inducing breach of contract as it stands is incompatible with the constitutional protection accorded to speech by the First Amendment, is the constitutionalization of this part of tort law the best institutional remedy? Tucker does not address this issue at all, while Anderson presents a cogent argument that the problem is best addressed at the level of state action to reform the law of tort.[5] This question is an issue of practical institutional design that I shall not consider here. The second question is the important one for our purposes— whether, and in what sense, Anderson and Tucker are right to say that the tort of inducing breach of contract burdens speech in a constitutionally impermissible way.

There is no doubt that in a narrowly legal sense, as far as concerns constitutional law in the U.S., there is a good case to be made out for the proposition that it is incompatible with the constitutional protection accorded to speech by the First Amendment to make into an actionable tort the communication of truthful information for the purpose of non-coercively persuading a party to breach a contract. After all, 'I will pay you more to do X than B is going to pay you to do X' is sufficiently close to 'I will sell you X product at Y price' to fall within the category of commercial speech, supposing one to be concerned to delineate such a category.

Of the two arguments for the incompatibility of the tort with constitutional protection for commercial speech, Anderson's is to be preferred. Tucker simply inventories a large range of cases, and flatly concludes that

as a matter of federal constitutional law, an actor cannot be subject to tort liability for communicating truthful information to another that leads the other to discontinue or refuse to enter into a contract.[6]

He lists four conditions on this immunity, including that the giving of the information 'does not impinge on some state interest of the highest order' (ibid.). He does not give enough weight to the fact that most of the cases he mentions as grounding for his claim involve considerations that detract from the

---

[3] David A. Anderson, 'Torts, Speech and Contracts', *Texas Law Review* 75 (1997): 1499–538. See also his analysis of the *Pennzoil* case in David A. Anderson, 'An Errant Tort', *Review of Litigation* 9 (1990): 409–40, although in that article Anderson does not deal with potential First Amendment implications of the tort.

[4] Robert L. Tucker, ' "And the Truth Shall Make You Free": Truth as a First Amendment Defense in Tortious Interference with Contract Cases', *Hastings Constitutional Law Quarterly* 23 (1997): 709–39.

[5] See 'Torts, Speech and Contracts', at 1532–8.

[6] Tucker, 'Truth', 739. Cf. also Dan D. Dobbs, 'Tortious Interference with Contractual Relationships', *Arkansas Law Review* 34 (1980): 361: 'insofar as tort liability is imposed for the communications of facts, opinions or arguments, that liability is simply inconsistent with the law's long commitment to freedom of speech'.

'purely commercial' aspect of a case like *Lumley* or *Pennzoil*. They concern information being provided, or withheld, by print and other news media; boycotts or protests with arguably a political motivation; literary works; and so forth. This heterogeneity seems to open Tucker to the familiar charge of question-begging if he seeks to base a theory about purely commercial speech on such cases. It does not follow from the fact that some case of, for example, political speech has a commercial element and deserves constitutional protection that therefore commercial speech deserves protection. The reason the hypothesized speech deserves protection is that it is political, not that it is commercial. Other commentators are no better than Tucker. Dobbs likewise bases much of his analysis on the dubious status of the tort of 'alienation of affections', which would apply metaphorically, but not legally, to commercial cases. Gary Wexler also concentrates on cases where the tort is used to restrict 'fully protected speech'.[7]

Anderson by contrast analyses the tort in a pure commercial form at some length and with considerable subtlety, in the light of the four-part test established by the U.S. Supreme Court in *Central Hudson*[8] and later cases. He argues that even on the most legislation-friendly interpretation of the test, speech aimed at inducing breach of contract by persuasion through the provision of truthful information fails to merit restriction. Wexler also considers at length the arguments in favour of the tort and rebuts them, though with only slight reference to the *Central Hudson* test. I am concerned here with the unsoundness of arguments that proceed simply from the fact that an action involves speech in the ordinary sense to the conclusion that it implicates free expression issues. I will work towards that goal by first laying aside the fact that tortious interference with contractual relations involves speech, and considering the case that Anderson and Wexler build against the tort in itself. Then we will consider what, if anything, is added to this case by introducing supposedly constitutional aspects.

Between Anderson and Wexler, there are five arguments made against the tort in the case where the interference involves simply the giving of truthful information, what Anderson calls 'persuasion cases' (at 1502). Three of these arguments are rebuttals of claims made by supporters of the tort, and two are freestanding arguments.[9] Here are the arguments.

(i)   Supporters of the tort claim that it is essential for commercial stability. Wexler argues that commerce needs, not the maximization of contracts made, but their optimization (at 301). Anderson points to the fact that

---

[7] Gary D. Wexler, 'Intentional Interference with Contract: Market Efficiency and Individual Liberty Considerations', *Connecticut Law Review* 27 (1994): 279–328.

[8] *Central Hudson Gas & Electric Corporation v Public Service Commission of New York* 447 US 557 (1980). See Chapter 3.2 above for a detailed discussion of the case.

[9] Since the reform of tort law is not the focus of this book, the arguments will simply be sketched here. Readers interested in tort reform should consult the original articles.

courts seem now to accept the notion of 'efficient breach', the doctrine that, if economic efficiency is promoted by a contract being breached, the contract should not be legally enforced. It seems a very short step to accepting that inducers of efficient breaches should not be legally penalized (at 1518–19). He points out, moreover, that the tort arises in only a small number of breach of contract cases, so it would be hard to claim the very function of contract law turns on the (non-)existence of the tort (at 1522).

(ii) The tort is said to involve the wrong of harm to property. Against this, Wexler argues, first, that it is controversial whether a contractual interest is in fact a property interest (at 303). Secondly, he argues that, even if it is currently recognized to be one, legal rights should not be reified or given metaphysical status. They are as the courts or legislatures determine them to be, and the courts or legislatures can change their minds.

(iii) The tort is said in fact to promote economic efficiency. Both Anderson and Wexler strenuously dispute this claim. Anderson discusses the issue in some technical detail (at 1626–9), and Wexler argues the structural point that the tort is designed to protect the individual competitor in the market, the interferee, not the market generally. The tort protects the normative position of the interferee, whether one calls that position a right or not, and such a norm or cluster of norms has an exclusionary force against first-order considerations of economic efficiency.[10]

(iv) Both Anderson (at 1529) and Wexler (at 319) argue that, as the law stands, the tort is defined far too vaguely and thus engenders too much legal uncertainty.

(v) Both Anderson and Wexler argue that, even if there is a need to have a special mechanism for deterring breaches of contract, many mechanisms are possible other than allowing the invasion of the law of contract by the tort of inducing breach of contract. Anderson also refers to an essay by Mark Gergen in which he shows how many ways there are to protect contract and other bodies of law from encroachment by the interference tort, all dealing with what Gergen calls 'internal doctrinal restrictions' on the tort; constitutional law is not mentioned.[11]

Though the merits of the issue are, as I have said, not my concern, the argument against allowing so-called persuasion cases into the tort of interference with contractual relations seems a strong one. Notice, on the other hand, that none of the arguments mentioned focus on the fact that, in order to commit the tort, one must use language. None of the arguments even *presuppose* that, in order to commit the tort, one must use language. The arguments are of a quite general shape that would comprehend equally well putatively tortious acts of a

[10] For norms as exclusionary reasons see Joseph Raz, *Practical Reason and Norms* (London: Hutchinson, 1975), 35–48.
[11] Mark P. Gergen, 'Tortious Interference: How It Is Engulfing Commercial Law, Why This Is Not Entirely Bad, and a Prudential Response', *Arizona Law Review* 38 (1996): 1219–29.

wholly non-linguistic kind. (iv) presupposes that the definition of the tort takes place in language—but that is a totally trivial involvement of language. It is true that the tort does have to be committed via the use of language, but that is legally, though not of course empirically, an entirely contingent feature of the tort.

So whence comes the idea that constitutional issues of great moment are at stake here, in particular issues relating to freedom of speech? Simply from this contingent fact that empirically the tort is committed via the use of language, and nothing else. It is clear that, in the absence of any prior institutional commitment to extending constitutional protection to commercial speech, there is no intuitive reason to regard tortious interference with contractual relations as raising constitutional issues at all.

In all fairness to him, Anderson, as opposed to his *confrères*, is well aware of the tangential nature of the involvement of speech. He notes the failure of application of traditional First Amendment arguments to the tort (at 1505). Moreover, he argues at some length that, if the case against the tort is to be followed up, it is best done through state action to change the law of tort, rather than court action to apply the First Amendment (at 1532–8). In the passage where he considers whether the tort in persuasion cases would pass the *Central Hudson* test for commercial speech (at 1520–5), the reasons he gives for thinking that the tort fails the third and fourth parts of the test are these. If there is a state interest in discouraging breach of contract, the tort advances it indirectly, rather than directly, as would changes in the law of contract itself. Since very few breaches of contract involve a third party, the tort advances the interest only minimally. The hard evidence to support the claim of advancing an interest required by *Edenfield*[12] will be difficult to find. Since remedies can be found within the law of contract without reference to third parties, it is not even clear that the tort forms a reasonable fit with the problem it is meant to solve.

The point to notice about Anderson's constitutional argument is that it takes the form it does only because the U.S. Supreme Court has decided to extend First Amendment coverage to commercial speech, and in *Central Hudson* laid down a four-part interest-balancing test. The points made against the tort would (or would not) be valid anyway as putative policy reasons for not retaining it. The arguments could be made pretty much as they stand, without the constitutional language, to a legislative committee holding hearings on tort law reform. That would not be true for the standard argument as to why a political protest should not be suppressed, a scientific article published, or an art exhibition closed. The protest probably is also expression or speech in the ordinary sense, though protests can be silent. The article undoubtedly is expression or speech in the ordinary sense. The exhibition may be; some installations contain written words or spoken words. A given case of expression or speech in the theoretical sense may or may not, therefore, be empirically also expression or speech in the

---

[12] *Edenfield v Fane* 113 SCt 1792 (1993). See Chapter 3.4 above.

ordinary sense. In these cases, what is legally constitutive of the entitlement to constitutional protection is the fact that they are 'expression' or 'speech' in the theoretical sense, that subtended by principles of freedom of expression. There is no background argument in Anderson's, Wexler's, or Tucker's essays as to why commercial speech, and *a fortiori* the speech involved in inducing breach of contract, should be eligible to receive constitutional protection. There is only the premise that here we have a case of speech. Anderson does quote passages from *44 Liquormart*[13] and *Virginia Board*[13a] which talk about the importance of the 'free dissemination of information about commercial choices in a market economy' (*44 Liquormart*, at 1517), and 'proper allocation of resources in a free enterprise system' (*Virginia Board*, at 765), and he remarks that the recipient's interest in learning that someone is willing to offer a better deal, in the words of *Virginia Board* (at 763) 'may be as keen, if not keener by far, than his interest in the day's most urgent political debate'. I have however argued for the question-begging nature of these comments in my discussion of these cases in Chapters 2.4 and 3.5 above.

2 Promotion of off-label uses of pharmaceutical drugs

The U.S. federal Food and Drug Administration (FDA) has extensive regulatory powers over the nutrition and pharmaceutical industries, in order to protect the health of the nation's citizens. These powers include the approval of pharmaceutical drugs and nutritional products both on prescription and over the counter, and control over the content and format of labelling and of promotional activities by pharmaceutical drug and nutritional product manufacturers. A variety of statutes and regulatory guidelines exist to spell out the precise character of these powers. The FDA's original base-line position was that all these different regulations have a common nature and purpose—they have to do with the regulation of drugs and medical devices;[14] the manufacture and sale of such things is a purely economic activity, the regulation of which is constitutionally unproblematic; the long-term goal is simply the protection of public health.

The pharmaceutical drug and nutritional products manufacturers themselves and their supporters in the legal profession and academy, however, have seen in the development by the U.S. Supreme Court of a commercial speech doctrine an opportunity to challenge many aspects of FDA regulation of the industry on constitutional grounds. After all, the labelling and promotion of a product take place through the use of language. The use of language is speech, and the First Amendment places constitutional limitations on the regulation of speech. *Coors* is the first commercial speech case that acknowledges product labelling to be

[13] *44 Liquormart, Inc v Rhode Island* 116 SCt 1495 (1996).
[13a] *Virginia State Board of Pharmacy et al v Virginia Citizens Consumer Council Inc et al* 425 US 748 (1976)
[14] Cf. 62 *Federal Register* 64,076 (1997).

'commercial speech' for constitutional purposes.[15] Pharmaceutical industry supporters were not slow to seize on the opportunity provided by this decision to belabour the FDA.[16] I use here the term 'opportunity' advisedly, since I intend to argue here that the use of the First Amendment in this context is a matter of what has been well termed 'opportunism'[17] or 'imperialism'.[18] No manufacturing industry likes government regulation, and deep-pocketed manufacturers will use litigation as much as lobbying to forward the goals if the opportunity arises. Business is business. But it remains to be seen whether business is freedom of expression.

Many different aspects of FDA regulation of the pharmaceutical and nutritional industries have been thought to raise freedom of speech issues. In the case of the latter, the FDA was largely successful until *Pearson*.[19] In that case, the court ruled that commercial free speech principles required the FDA to permit marketing of nutritional products with disclaimers as to the veracity of the health claims made, rather than first requiring that the health claims be substantiated before marketing can be undertaken. Critics of the decision fear a deleterious effect on public health.[20]

I focus here on the pharmaceutical industry, specifically on the control of promotion of so-called 'off-label' uses of prescription drugs, and on only two aspects of that. The FDA regularly approves drugs for specific uses to be reflected in the drug's labelling. For FDA purposes, the 'labelling' is not simply any material on the packaging itself. The labelling also includes all material accompanying a product, such as a leaflet in the package, and even supplementary or explicative information from the manufacturer whether or not it actually accompanies the drug.[21] Subsequent research may show that some given drug is valuable in treating a different problem from that for which it has been approved, or that a different dosage level or method of administration, or administration to a different patient population, from that which has been approved may be also effective. A use of the drug for such purposes, in the absence of FDA approval for the new use, is called an 'off-label' use.

[15] *Rubin v Coors Brewing Company* 115 SCt 1585 (1995).

[16] Lars Noah and Barbara A. Noah, 'Liberating Commercial Speech: Product Labeling Controls and the First Amendment', *Florida Law Review* 47 (1995): 63–112.

[17] Frederick Schauer, 'First Amendment Opportunism', in Lee C. Bollinger and Geoffrey R. Stone (eds.), *Eternally Vigilant: Free Speech in the Modern Era* (Chicago, Ill.: University of Chicago Press, 2002), 175–97 (commercial speech is discussed at 177–80).

[18] Daniel J.H. Greenwood, 'First Amendment Imperialism', *Utah Law Review* (1999): 659–72 (the incursion of the First Amendment into economic regulation is discussed at 659–61); Paul D. Carrington, 'Our Imperial First Amendment', *University of Richmond Law Review* 34 (2001): 1167–211 (commercial speech is discussed at 1188–92, and health product advertising specifically at 1190–1).

[19] *Pearson v Shalala* 172 F 3d 72 (1999) (USCA DC Cir).

[20] David C. Vladeck, 'Devaluing Truth: Unverified Health Claims in the Aftermath of *Pearson v Shalala*', *Food and Drug Law Journal* 54 (1999): passim; Margaret Gilhooley, 'Constitutionalizing Food and Drug Law', *Tulane Law Review* 74 (2000): 848–62.

[21] *Kordel v United States* 335 US 345 (1948).

It is beyond the authority of the FDA to control whether physicians actually prescribe drugs for off-label use. Evidence suggests that off-label use is common and accepted within the health-care profession. The FDA, however, until a few years ago interpreted its mandate to protect health to entail strict regulation of the advertising and promotion of off-label uses of prescription drugs. In particular, the FDA tightly restricted the distribution of reprints of scientific journal articles describing the results of research on off-label uses, so-called 'enduring materials'. The restrictions were aimed at ensuring that the main focus of the material was the FDA-approved use, and that the material was at arm's length from any interested manufacturer.[22] The FDA also tightly regulated scientific or educational programmes, such as information seminars, which were supported by a pharmaceutical manufacturer, especially those where off-label uses of the drug were discussed. The regulations were aimed at securing the independent and non-promotional character of any such programme.[23]

The FDA substantively defended these regulations on two grounds. First, the regulations would lower the risk of harm occurring to patients as a result of physicians being unduly influenced by misleading printed statements, or misleading presentations at such promotional activities. Secondly, the regulations would preserve the integrity of the drug approval process: without such regulations it would be only too easy for pharmaceutical manufacturers to procrastinate and so avoid having to seek FDA approval for the off-label uses.[24] Constitutionally, as noted above, the FDA took the view that it was regulating economic activity, not speech.[25]

The constitutional pressure from the commercial speech doctrine, however, was intense. In the Final Guidance, the agency added the defence that, alternatively, if the regulations are constitutionally speech, then they are commercial speech, and the regulations satisfy the standards for restriction on commercial speech.[26] Then began a saga of litigation to defend the agency's view from constitutional criticism. The charge was led by the Washington Legal Foundation, a public interest group representing a group of physicians who claimed that their First Amendment right to hear any information the drug manufacturers wished to pass on to them was violated by the Final Guidance regulations. The first round went to the physicians; even though the promotional activities were commercial speech, not scientific speech, they failed the *Central Hudson* test.[27] In the interim, Congress had passed the Food and Drug Administration Modernization Act 1997, which came into force in 1998. Some sections concerned mechanisms for using reprints to promote off-label uses of drugs,[28]

---

[22] Advertising and Promotion: Guidances, 61 *Federal Register* 52,800 (1996).

[23] Final Guidance on Industry-Supported Scientific and Educational Activities, 62 *Federal Register* 64,074 (1997).

[24] Final Guidance, 64,075–8.   [25] Final Guidance, 64,076–8.

[26] Final Guidance, 64,078–82.

[27] *Washington Legal Foundation v Friedman* 13 F Supp 2d 51 (1998) (USDC DC).

[28] 21 U.S.C. §360aaa(b).

regulations that were weaker than those in the Final Guidance regulations. They were still too much for the industry and for the D.C. District Court, and they too were invalidated.[29] The FDA appealed the decision, but by the time the hearing took place the agency had taken on board the political realities. As the Court put it:

The stage . . . appeared set for us to consider a difficult constitutional question of considerable practical importance. However, . . . the dispute between the parties has disappeared before our eyes.[30]

The FDA announced that its regulations concerning manufacturer promotion of off-label uses of drugs were to be construed, not as mandatory restrictions on speech, but as a 'safe harbor' (ibid.). Breach of the regulations was not in itself to be considered a breach of the law; rather, the fact of such a breach, if proven, would be taken into account as evidence in any hearing of a charge of misbranding or diverging from a declared intended use. Following the regulations would constitute a 'safe harbour' from any such charge. For its part, the WLF then withdrew its constitutional objections to the regulations, and the Court declined to rule on any hypothetical question whether the regulations even on that interpretation were unconstitutional.

The WLF's concession has not impressed the most zealous of the pharmaceutical industry's supporters among legal commentators.[31] My concern here, however, is with the FDA's implicit concession that, if regarded as directly restricting speech, the regulations fall foul of the First Amendment. From the point of view of jurisprudential theory, as opposed to *realpolitik*, this concession is to be regretted. I hope to show that the agency would have good reason on its side if it had taken the high road and stuck all the way through this litigation solely to the claim that what is being regulated is not constitutionally 'speech'.

Opponents of the FDA regulations, of which there are many (and of defenders few), bring forward a sizeable number of arguments. The following list is intended to be illustrative, not exhaustive.[32]

(i)   Off-label *use* of prescription drugs is already extensive, and fully accepted not only by the medical profession, but also by the FDA itself. Such use is in fact beneficial, as patients receive even life-saving treatment that they would otherwise not receive.

---

[29] *Washington Legal Foundation v Henney* 56 F Supp 2d 81 (1999) (USDC DC).

[30] *Washington Legal Foundation v Henney* 202 F 3d 331 (2000) (USCA DC Cir), at 335.

[31] Lars Noah, 'What's Wrong with "Constitutionalizing Food and Drug Law"?', *Tulane Law Review* 75 (2000): 137–48. Noah characterizes the FDA 'safe harbour' story as 'fanciful' (at 146), and chastises the Court for going along with the Agency's attempt to 'dodge the issue' (at 148) of whether the regulations unconstitutionally restrict speech.

[32] The literature is considerable. For a thorough and clear analysis of the whole issue see Steven R. Salbu, 'Off-Label Use, Prescription, and Marketing of FDA-Approved Drugs: An Assessment of Legislative and Regulatory Policy', *Florida Law Review* 51 (1999): 181–227.

(ii) The risk of harm occurring from greater off-label use of prescription drugs as a result of educational and promotional programmes by pharmaceutical manufacturers is very small. Physicians are professionals who are well able to assess the value and truthfulness of claims made in enduring materials and in promotional seminars.

(iii) Relaxation of the regulations would encourage innovation in the industry. Manufacturers have no incentive to pursue research into off-label uses, if each new such use cannot be promoted, and so provide return on research investment, until full FDA approval has been obtained.

(iv) There are plenty of economic incentives without the regulatory restrictions for pharmaceutical drug manufacturers in any case to seek FDA approval for new off-label uses of drugs. There is the possibility of products liability litigation, and in some jurisdictions even malpractice litigation. Insurance carriers are also leery of reimbursement for off-label uses.

(v) The restrictions on the distribution of enduring materials and on promotional or educational activities are illogical:

(a) The restrictions affect only the manufacturer of the pharmaceutical product. Not only does the FDA permit, it even encourages, the publication or dissemination of scientific information in educational or informational programmes by sources other than the manufacturer.

(b) The FDA endorses the creation of medical affairs departments by pharmaceutical drug manufacturers. Such departments are typically staffed by physicians, and send out copies of studies, reprints of articles, and so forth—exactly the kind of 'enduring materials' that are regulated. The FDA permits these activities by physicians who are employed by the drug manufacturers, yet tightly regulates those same activities by independent physicians.

(c) The FDA in fact permits off-label promotion, as long as the manufacturer plans ultimately to make a supplementary filing for formal approval of the new use. Such activity is expressly promotional, and engaged in by the manufacturer. Yet non-promotional activity relating to off-label uses engaged in by persons independent of the manufacturer is tightly regulated.

(vi) Even if the U.S. Supreme Court had not developed its commercial speech doctrine, and commercial speech was not eligible for constitutional protection, still the FDA regulations under scrutiny deserve to be invalidated on constitutional grounds. The First Amendment fully protects scientific and educational speech. The 'enduring materials' and the presentations by physicians and scientists at educational seminars are such speech, and so merit full protection under the First Amendment. They do not propose a commercial transaction; they are not product labelling or advertising. 'The belief that the very same scientific claims automatically lose their full level of constitutional protection when made by a product manufacturer in a commercial advertisement needs some logical basis, in terms of free speech theory, for the drawing of such a strict dichotomy. It is doubtful, however, that such a basis may be found.'[33]

(vii) The FDA regulations are regulatory overkill. 'Under the *Guidance*, it would be impermissible for a pharmaceutical manufacturer to set up and fund a program on a particular off-label topic, *even if* the manufacturer's sponsorship is fully disclosed and every bit of information provided is perfectly true, free of safety concerns, and exceptionally valuable.'[34] It is not difficult to devise alternative regulatory schemes which are less restrictive, employing such methods as disclosure requirements relating to manufacturer influence, involvement, and sponsorship; requirements of truth, balance, and non-misleadingness in presentations, especially as regards the off-label, and so unapproved, character of the drug uses presented; and analogously for the distribution of enduring materials.

As in the previous subsection concerning tortious interference with contractual relations, with the exception of argument (vi) which I will address shortly, the striking point is that none of the arguments says anything about the special character of distribution of enduring materials and the holding of promotional and educational programmes, as *speech*. (i)–(iii) are concerned with the causal consequences of certain activities, and debate the accuracy of the FDA's assessment of those consequences. (iv) debates the accuracy of the FDA's assessment of the rationality of pharmaceutical drug manufacturers' economic decision-making. (v) points to logical tensions within the structure of the FDA regulations themselves. (vii) engages in the time-honoured pursuit of second-guessing the legislature on what regulatory schemes it might or might not be best to enact. It is true that scientific reprints and product information leaflets, and anything else that makes up 'enduring materials', are written in a natural language. It is also true that language will be used many, many times during educational and promotional programmes. But those are not the features of such materials and programmes on which the above arguments are focussed.

Moreover, it is relevant to note that the commentators who are the sources for the arguments listed fall into two distinct groups. Some present the arguments in a constitutional context. That is, they present their arguments by way of assessing whether the FDA regulations under discussion will pass the *Central Hudson* test for commercial speech. Others do not refer to constitutional issues at all; they focus simply on the arguments as public policy arguments. Yet the substantive content of the arguments of each group is not essentially any

[33] Martin H. Redish, 'Product Health Claims and the First Amendment: Scientific Expression and the Twilight Zone of Commercial Speech', *Vanderbilt Law Review* 43 (1990): 1444. See also Glenn C. Smith, 'Avoiding Awkward Alchemy—In the Off-Label Drug Context and Beyond: Fully-Protected Independent Research Should Not Transmogrify Into Mere Commercial Speech Just Because Product Manufacturers Distribute It', *Wake Forest Law Review* 34 (1999): 963–1055.

[34] I. Scott Bass, Paul E. Kalb, and Bradford A. Berenson, 'Off-Label Promotion: Is FDA's Final Guidance on Industry-Supported Scientific and Educational Programs Enforceable?', *Food and Drug Law Journal* 53 (1998): 204; their emphasis.

different in the constitutional from the non-constitutional context. This fact strongly supports the thesis of this chapter, that the constitutionalization of these issues is opportunistic, and an artifact of the U.S. Supreme Court's commercial speech doctrine. It is not something that flows from the character of what is being regulated according to some background theory about the value of freedom of speech. Exactly the same arguments could be made to criticize the regulations on pure grounds of public policy even if the commercial speech doctrine had not been developed, and, as illustrated, they are in fact so made.

Lars Noah, even, who is one of the strongest promoters of de-regulation for the pharmaceutical industry, fully documents courts requiring company sales representatives to convey precautionary information about prescription medications to physicians.[35] He does this without constitutional objection, and indeed any objection. Yet such a requirement, if pharmaceutical company utterances were 'speech' in the constitutional sense, would be compelled speech, in apparent violation of the First Amendment. The naturalness with which we understand without comment the appropriateness of the courts' action shows how inappropriate it is to regard all speech as 'speech'. As Salbu notes, in an institutional context where constitutional protection has been extended to commercial speech, the arguments against the FDA can be cast in terms of the value of free speech.[36] In such a context, it might well be true that 'unless one adds the First Amendment to the calculus, agencies will often prefer regulatory alternatives that receive speech because of their relative ease of implementation and greater political palatability'.[37] But ease of implementation and political palatability are, other things being equal, good-making features for a regulatory policy. The implication in this comment that things are not equal, and that the FDA are doing something other than that which they ought to do, question-beggingly assumes, but does not independently prove, the applicability of the value of free speech to assessment of the policy.

Argument (vi), too, as noted, is independent of the commercial speech doctrine. It is an argument that presupposes a valid theory of freedom of speech—primarily relating the dissemination of scientific information to the free speech value of the search for truth. However, I take up Redish's challenge (see (vi) above) to explain the differential treatment of seemingly the same 'speech'. The argument is unsound because it involves the conflation of two distinct possible meanings of 'speech'. To show this, I need to make a brief excursus into philosophy of language.

The Oxford philosopher J.L. Austin argued that there was a systematic distinction between the *force* of an utterance and its *sense and reference*.[38] In the

---

[35] Lars Noah, 'Constraints on the Off-Label Uses of Prescription Drug Products', *Journal of Products and Toxics Liability* 16 (1994): 152.

[36] Salbu, 'Off-Label Use, Prescription, and Marketing', 199.

[37] Noah, 'What's Wrong', 143.

[38] J.L. Austin, *How To Do Things With Words* (2nd edn., edited by J.O. Urmson and Marina Sbisà, Cambridge, Mass.: Harvard University Press, 1975), 98 ff.

utterance, 'There's a bull right behind you!', said by A to B, the force of the utterance is that it is a warning; its sense and reference have to do with the syntax of the sentence in question and the semantics of the various terms. Austin also introduced further technical terminology—the notions of 'locution' and 'locutionary act', 'illocution' and 'illocutionary act'. A locution is a vocable with a sense and a reference in a language—'There's a bull right behind you!', for example—and a locutionary act the act of uttering such a vocable with that sense and reference, as A does in uttering just those words. The illocutionary act is the act performed in uttering such a vocable with a given force. A's saying those words to B is a warning to B about the bull.[39] Finally, Austin emphasizes that the distinction between a locutionary and illocutionary act is conceptual; the former cannot be performed independently. 'To perform a locutionary act is in general . . . eo ipso to perform an *illocutionary* act'.[40]

Given this set of precise, technical concepts, it is easy to see that the term 'speech' is ambiguous, as between a *locution* and an *illocutionary act*. When the aide hands the politician 'her speech' after the coffee is poured, in so far as the reference is to more than a set of inscriptions on numbered sheets of paper—or to a laptop containing an electronic representation of such inscriptions— 'speech' refers to a set of words—a vocable—with a sense and reference in a language. When the politician says afterwards, 'In my speech, I let them know in no uncertain terms exactly where we stand', she is thinking of her speech as a (set of) illocutionary acts performed after dinner.

The question now arises: what is it that the value of freedom of speech is designed to foster and promote? Is it locutions, or is it illocutionary acts? The most plausible answer is the latter. The value of freedom of speech does not protect pieces of language as such. Rather, it protects (some of) the things human beings do in using language. It is not the poem as a piece of language, or the political pamphlet as a piece of language, that is potentially protected. The poet is protected, or the pamphleteer, in publishing the poem or displaying the poster.[41]

Let us return now to the case of the reprint of the scientific article about (let's say) success with a particular off-label use of a given pharmaceutical drug. The manufacturer obtains hundreds of copies of the reprint, and mails them out to a mailing-list of physicians. The reason the level of constitutional protection changes[42] for the very same 'speech' from the writing of the article by the scient-

---

[39] It also informs B about the whereabouts of the bull. One given locutionary act may amount to more than one illocutionary act.

[40] *HDTW* 98, Austin's emphasis. It is not clear what the exceptions are to this general rule. Certainly, there seem none that affects the discussion here.

[41] For arguments that free speech has to do with illocutionary acts, see Jennifer Hornsby and Rae Langton, 'Free Speech and Illocution', *Legal Theory* 4 (1998): 21–37. I myself presented a version of the argument many years ago: see Roger A. Shiner, 'Freedom of Speech-Acts', *Philosophy and Rhetoric* 3 (1970): 40–50.

[42] I am speaking here for the sake of argument within the institutional realities of current U.S. Supreme Court First Amendment jurisprudence.

ist(s) to the distribution of the article by the pharmaceutical drug manufacturer should be clear. The article considered just as a set of sentences, or vocables, in a language is 'speech' in the sense of 'locution' only. But locutions are not candidates for constitutional protection; persons performing speech-acts, specifically illocutionary acts, are candidates. The scientist is performing the illocutionary act of informing; the manufacturer is performing the illocutionary act of promoting or advertising. That is true, even though the sentences uttered are exactly the same in each case. It does not follow from the fact that the First Amendment protects informing that it also protects promoting or advertising. That the very same words may be used to perform advertising as well as informing does not change this fact.

The point may be further refined. In the recent Supreme Court of Canada commercial expression case of *RJR-MacDonald*,[43] one issue concerned the mandatory health warnings on tobacco products called for by the Tobacco Products Control Act.[44] The tobacco manufacturers claimed that this requirement was compelled expression, and as such a violation of their freedom of expression. La Forest J, who wrote the main opinion for the dissent, argued that mandatory unattributed health warnings on packs of cigarettes do not constitute a breach of the tobacco manufacturers' section 2(b) right of freedom of expression (at 83). La Forest J accepts the principle, well established in free expression jurisprudence, that to be required to say something one does not wish to say is as much an interference with freedom of expression as to be prevented from saying something one does wish to say. All the same, he says, he does not accept that the argument is relevant here. His reason is that one cannot reasonably infer merely from the appearance of certain words on a cigarette packet that they are an expression of opinion by the manufacturer of the cigarettes. As he goes on to argue, government warnings on dangerous products are a fact of contemporary life. No-one regards the skull and crossbones on a bottle of poisonous liquid as an expression of opinion by the manufacturer of the liquid. So why is not the same true for warnings on tobacco products?

If this line of argument concerning mandatory health warnings is cogent, it seems to undermine the idea that freedom of expression protects speech-acts, and not merely 'speech' in the sense of a set of words in a language. It would also have enormous ramifications for the coherence of the Supreme Court of Canada's approach to the interpretation of section 2(b). The Court has deemed that anything with meaning is covered by section 2(b). But if that is true, then the unattributed health warnings certainly have a meaning, and under the Court's usual approach there would be no question about their being covered by section 2(b). So the implication of La Forest J's argument is that not every-

---

[43] *RJR-MacDonald Inc v Attorney-General of Canada; Imperial Tobacco Ltd v Attorney-General of Canada* [Indexed as RJR-MacDonald Inc v Canada (Attorney-General)] (1995) 127 DLR (4th) 1; see Chapter 4.5 above.
[44] SC 1988, c. 20; s.11.

thing with a meaning is expression within the scope of section 2(b). That thought goes right against the existing drift of the Court's thinking. It is of course compatible with the position defended in this book.

There are indications, however, that La Forest J may not be thinking anything so revolutionary. He may rather be thinking that unattributed health warnings are not covered by section 2(b), not because they are not 'expression' at all within the meaning of section 2(b), but because they are expression, but *no-one's* expression. Such a thought needs some care. Consider other cases in which the Court has accepted that required expression is an infringement of freedom of expression. In *Slaight*,[45] a company was required by a labour arbitrator to write a letter of reference a certain way. In *Moore*,[46] a forced retraction after a libel suit was similarly deemed an infringement. In each of these cases, only the guileless suppose that the company or the newspaper is really sincere in such expressions. The requirement to publish is justified for reasons of fairness and justice that do not need the expression to be sincere. If the unattributed health warnings are supposedly different, as La Forest J suggests, why are they different?

Perhaps the thought is that, unlike words in a signed letter or in a newspaper with a masthead, the warnings hang in space as words of a language without a speaker, as the skull and crossbones symbol hangs without a painter. Now, we can in fact think of linguistic expressions that we understand in that way as having a sense and reference merely in themselves as expressions in a language. Consider the case of the American feminist artist Jenny Holtzer. Her art consists of apt sentiments of one kind or another displayed in different ways in public places. To run across a Holtzer piece without knowing anything about the artist is to run across an expression of opinion that seems indeed to be disembodied. You know (or at least you think you do) that it is someone's opinion; but you do not know whose, and you understand, laugh at, or object to the sentiments expressed regardless. In 1982 'FATHERS OFTEN USE TOO MUCH FORCE' appeared on a public billboard in Times Square.[47] It would not necessarily be assumed that the owner of the billboard or any other assignable entity is expressing the sentiments. Nor would one assume that 'RAISE BOYS AND GIRLS THE SAME WAY', installed in 1987 at Candlestick Park in San Francisco,[48] was an opinion expressed by the Giants or the 49ers or the city of San Francisco or anyone else. Contrast the case of a slogan on a T-shirt: that we take, and rightly, to be an expression of opinion by the wearer of the T-shirt.

Do parallels like these make plausible the claim that unattributed health warnings are no-one's expression, but are candidates for constitutional protection anyway? Moreover, U.S. courts, at least, have not found it odd for linguis-

---

[45] *Slaight Communications Inc (Operating as Q107 FM Radio) v Davidson* (1989) 59 DLR (4th) 416.
[46] *Moore v Canadian Newspapers Co Ltd et al* (1989) 60 DLR (4th) 113 (OHC).
[47] Sponsored by the Public Art Fund.
[48] Sponsored by Artspace, San Francisco.

tic objects themselves to be defendants in free expression cases where there are difficulties in arraigning actual persons.[49] There is no precedent for the idea that it has to be established whose expression it is before something can count as an expression within the scope of section 2(b) or the First Amendment.

In fact, we need more conceptual distinctions. In the context of understanding how works of art may be 'expressions', aesthetician Francis Sparshott distinguishes three ways in which works of art may have 'designs', by which he means 'all those aspects of a performance [in a sense that would cover paintings and novels, e.g., as well as dances and playings of sonatas] that constitute it a single aesthetic object'.[50] These aspects may be of three kinds—messages, expressions, and patterns. He writes:

To construe a design as a message is to take it as comprising properties given it by someone for someone else to take note of. To construe [a design] as an expression is to take it as comprising properties that reflect agency in some integral way but are not directed to conveying anything to anyone else. To construe [a design] as a pattern is to prescind from any considerations about agent or public and attend to the intrinsic properties it has . . . as though it would be a matter of indifference whether it was a natural or an artificial object if it were not taken as a manifestation of skill. [ibid., 155]

In this terminology, the mistake made by argument (vi) above (to return to freedom of commercial speech and the advertising of off-label uses of drugs) is to take a scientific article, for example, as a 'pattern'. 'Pattern' is analogous to 'locution' in J.L. Austin's terminology. But the characterization of 'message' and 'expression' gives us a way of understanding how to take cases like the Holtzer artworks or the celebrated twelve 200-foot reels. We are not required to see them as 'no-one's expression'. We see that as 'comprising properties that reflect agency in some integral way', but we do not know whose agency. If you like, there can be such things as disembodied illocutionary acts. Unattributed health warnings and the like do not constitute counter-examples to the thesis that freedom of speech has to do with speech-acts or illocutionary acts. They can, depending on context, be taken as 'messages' or 'expressions' in Sparshott's sense, a sense that presupposes agency without requiring it to be clear whose agency. Thus, even in the case where a scientific reprint about an off-label use of a pharmaceutical drug arrives on a physician's desk anonymously in a plain brown wrapper, we are not forced to conclude that what is a candidate for constitutional protection is just that reprint. The forwarding of the reprint by the manufacturer is still a different illocutionary act from the writing of it by the scientists, even though the agency of the manufacturer is not revealed. 'Messages' and 'expressions' display agency in themselves.

---

[49] Cf. e.g., *United States v One Book Called 'Ulysses'* 5 F Supp 182 (1933) (SDNY), *affirmed* 72 F 2d 705 (1934) (USCA 2nd Cir); *United States v Twelve 200' Reels of Super 8mm Film* 413 US 123 (1973).

[50] Francis Sparshott, *The Theory of the Arts* (Princeton, NJ: Princeton University Press, 1982), 154.

In short (for this has been a long discussion), argument (vi) fails because it depends on a false conflation of 'speech' in the sense of 'locution' and 'speech' in the sense of an illocutionary act or speech-act of some sort. That remains true, even if the authorship of or agency behind the 'speeches' in question is not revealed, as it is not in the case of mandatory health warnings on tobacco products. Argument (vi) presupposes a theory of freedom of speech all right, but it does not show what its supporters wish it to show. The remaining arguments (i)–(v) and (vii) are general arguments of public policy, of a legislative rather than a constitutional kind, to do with the proper regulation of the health-care industry. There is no ground for seeing the issue of the regulation of promotion of off-label uses of pharmaceutical drugs as a freedom of speech issue, other than that the promotion involves 'speech' in a non-technical sense. But that is not a sufficient ground.

3 THE RIGHT OF PUBLICITY

The right of publicity is a cause of action in tort in the United States.[51] It has historical connections and family resemblances to copyright and the right of privacy, but is not identical to either. The tort is committed when someone appropriates a celebrity's identity without authorization for that person's commercial advantage, with harm to the celebrity as a result. Relief may be in the form of an injunction against such a use, damages, or both. The right of publicity is different from the right of privacy, in that typically the celebrity does not object to the resultant publicity as such, but only to the fact that it was unauthorized and uncompensated. The right is different from copyright, in that the appropriation may be of something in which the celebrity does not hold copyright—a distinctive, raspy voice, for example.[52]

Different justifications are offered for the right among commentators and courts. The one most frequently given, perhaps, analogizes the right to a property right. The celebrity—an actor, for example—achieves by his or her own hard work and labour an identity of sufficient stature to be worth appropriating. He or she is therefore entitled to the rewards of that labour. The unauthorized appropriator is taking what does not belong to him or her—namely, those rewards. Other justifications are: the prevention of consumer deception (that is, when consumers falsely believe a celebrity endorses a product); decreased incentives for creative activity, and thus a diminished expressive 'commons'; unjust enrichment, when advertisers 'free ride' on celebrities' fame. One or more of these justifications may be found together depending on the facts of the case in hand.

The right of publicity achieved formal judicial recognition first in *Haelan Laboratories*.[53] A baseball player had granted to Haelan the exclusive use of his

---

[51] No comparable tort cause of action exists in Canada or the U.K. Tort is a matter of state law in the U.S., and so variations between jurisdictions in the exact profile of the tort occur. I ignore these complications here.

[52] *Waits v Frito-Lay* 978 F 2d 1093 (1992) (USCA 9th Cir).

[53] *Haelan Laboratories Inc v Topps Chewing Gum Inc* 202 F 2d 966 (1953) (USCA 2nd Cir).

photograph in its advertising. Topps produced a baseball card bearing the photograph of the player without the consent of Haelan. The Second Circuit court recognized these facts as providing an enforceable right, the right of publicity. For two decades or so, the right was restricted to appropriation of the 'name or likeness' of a person, where 'likeness' meant specifically visual likeness. This conception of the right has been aptly labelled the 'no frills' right of publicity, since it makes for easy decision-making on the part of courts.[54] The 'no frills' approach is still that found in most statutory definitions of the right. However, in *Eastwood*,[55] the California common law right of publicity was explicitly recognized, which laid the foundation for further development of the right by judicial decision-making. Courts subsequently began to realize that there were other potential aspects or indicia of a person's identity equally subject to appropriation, and equally deserving of protection through the right of publicity. During the roughly twenty years following *Haelan*, a racing car,[56] performances,[57] nicknames,[58] catchphrases,[59] use of a look-alike,[60] use of a sound-alike,[61] characters portrayed,[62] all have been the subject of right of publicity litigation in which the celebrity was successful in his or her suit.

The case, however, which created consternation concerning the right of publicity was *White*.[63] The plaintiff was Vanna White, hostess of the popular television game show 'Wheel of Fortune'. The Ninth Circuit in this decision extended the right of publicity considerably beyond that implicit in the list above. Both at the original hearing and at the rehearing, the majority decision in the plaintiff's favour received vigorous dissent. Much of the debate, both subsequently in the ivory tower and at the time on the bench, concerned the bearing of the majority decision on freedom of speech. This discussion and its implications are the focus here.

To give the facts of the case, I quote from the majority opinion:

The dispute in this case arose out of a series of advertisements prepared for Samsung by Deutsch [their advertising agency and co-defendant]. Each of the advertisements . . . depicted a current item from popular culture and a Samsung electronic product. Each

---

[54] Arlen W. Langvardt, 'The Troubling Implications of a Right of Publicity "Wheel" Spun Out of Control', *Kansas Law Review* 45 (1997): 329–452.

[55] *Eastwood v Superior Court* 198 Cal R 342 (1983) (Cal CA).

[56] *Motschenbacher v RJ Reynolds Tobacco Co* 498 F 2d 821 (1974) (USCA 9th Cir).

[57] *Zacchini v Scripps-Howard Broadcasting Co* 433 US 562 (1977). Zacchini made his living as a 'human cannonball'. A television station owned by the defendant showed the whole of Zacchini's act on a newscast, against the latter's express wishes. The case is the first and so far only time the Supreme Court has considered substantively the right of publicity.

[58] *Hirsch v SC Johnson and Son Inc* 280 NW 2d 129 (1979) (Wis Sup Ct).

[59] *Carson v Here's Johnny Portable Toilets Inc* 698 F 2d 831 (1983) (USCA 6th Cir).

[60] *Onassis v Christian Dior-New York Inc* 472 NYS 2d 254 (1984) (NY Sup Ct), *affirmed without opinion* 488 NYS 2d 943 (1985) (NY App Div).

[61] *Midler v Ford Motor Company* 849 F 2d 460 (1988) (9th Cir); *Waits* above.

[62] *McFarland v Miller* 14 F 3d 912 (1994) (USCA 3rd Cir).

[63] *White v Samsung Electronics America Inc et al* 971 F 2d 1395 (1992), *rehearing denied and suggestion for rehearing en banc rejected* 989 F 2d 1512 (1993) (USCA 9th Cir), *certiorari denied* 113 SCt 2443 (1993).

was set in the twenty-first century and conveyed the message that the Samsung product would still be in use by that time. . . . The advertisement that prompted the current dispute was for Samsung videocassette recorders. The ad depicted a robot, dressed in a wig, gown and jewelry that Deutsch consciously selected to resemble White's hair and dress. The robot was posed next to a game board that is instantly recognizable as the Wheel of Fortune game show set, in a stance for which White is famous. The caption of the ad read: 'Longest-running game show. 2012 A.D.' [at 1396]

White sued Samsung and Deutsch for the unauthorized use of her identity under three heads—the right of publicity as defined in the California Civil Code §3344, the California common law right of publicity, and §43(a) of the Lanham Act.[64] The court of first instance granted summary judgment in favour of the defendants on all three counts. The Ninth Circuit on appeal agreed as far as concerns the statutory ground, as the section was narrowly worded in terms of 'name or likeness' only. But the majority held that the other claims should not have been summarily denied and remanded the case for trial. The majority reasoned that in principle the common law right of publicity did extend as far as a fact situation like that before it, and that a jury should decide the issue.

There is no doubt that the majority's reasoning is thin. They hold that White raised a genuine issue of likelihood of consumer deception, even though they acknowledge that no-one could confuse the robot with Vanna White herself.[65] They also have no difficulty in seeing Vanna White's blonde hair, gown, jewellery, and stance as unique distinguishing characteristics of her analogous to 'name or likeness', sound, nickname, and so forth, and thus sufficient to underwrite a right of publicity claim by her. As the dissent cogently argues,[66] there is a two-fold error here. Blonde hair, a gown, jewellery, and even a stance are not unique to Vanna White, even in the way that 'Here's Johnny' is unique to Johnny Carson. Moreover, what makes the robot instantly recognizable as evoking Vanna White is not any of the above features alone, but the fact that the robot is standing by the instantly recognizable Wheel of Fortune game-show set. But that set is not a feature of Vanna White. To loosen the connection to a celebrity necessary to underwrite a right of publicity to this degree indeed raises the spectre of 'Arnold Schwarzenegger [suing] body builders who are compensated for appearing in public' (Alarcon J dissenting, at 1407), or 'George Lucas [wanting] to keep Strategic Defense Initiative fans from calling it "Star Wars"' (Kozinski J dissenting, at 1512).

However, what really annoys the dissent, and makes the case relevant to my argument in this chapter, is the fact that the majority reject out of hand the claim

---

[64] 15 USC §1125(a). The Act regulates trade marks and associated business practices, and §43(a) grants relief for false or misleading representations creating the likelihood of consumer confusion. I do not consider this cause of action here.

[65] For the curious, I note that Kozinski J appends to his dissent a picture of Vanna White and the advertisement at issue. Even at the low graphic production values of the *Federal Reporter*, the difference is clear.

[66] Alarcon J at 1404–5; Kozinski J at 1515.

that the Samsung advertisement is a permissible parody, and otherwise ignore any bearing on the case of issues of freedom of speech (at 1401).[67] The reason the court gives is simply that the advertisement's 'primary message' is 'buy Samsung VCRs' (ibid.), a purely commercial message. But the status of the advertisement as an instance of paradigm 'commercial speech' is essentially beside the point. That is, we do not need to presuppose the commercial speech doctrine in order to see why the Ninth Circuit majority's approach to freedom of speech in *White* is unsatisfactory.

The tort defines what is objectionable as the attainment of a 'commercial advantage'. But the notion of 'commercial advantage' is too blunt an instrument to capture what is at stake here. Courts realize that a 'newsworthiness' exception to the right is appropriate. Unauthorized use of someone's identity in, say, a magazine or newspaper article is regarded as a legitimate use. However, it is so regarded even if the point of the article is to make a profit for the magazine or newspaper, and the use of the celebrity's identity materially contributes to that anticipated profit. To that degree, it is accepted that First Amendment issues relating to the freedom of the press specifically must circumscribe the right. But why not then also principles of freedom of speech in general?

If recent cases are a guide, the tide of judicial opinion is swinging back against the celebrity claiming the right. In *Cardtoons*,[68] the Tenth Circuit fully protected under the First Amendment readily identifiable caricatures of baseball players, as constituting social commentary. Los Angeles Magazine published an article in which stills from sixteen different films were digitally altered into displays of contemporary fashion, including one showing Dustin Hoffman dressed as a woman in *Tootsie*. Hoffman's permission was not sought, and he sued on grounds, *inter alia*, of violation of his statutory and common law rights of publicity. The Ninth Circuit overturned the lower court decision in Hoffman's favour.[69] Rich Rush, a sports artist, produced and marketed a 'limited edition' print of the golfer Tiger Woods playing in the Masters tournament, without Woods' permission. Woods' licensing agent sued Rush and his publishing company for violation of Woods' right of publicity. The Sixth Circuit has rejected the claim.[70]

The message from both of these cases is that, whatever 'commercial advantage' means in the definition of the right of publicity, it cannot mean simply that a profit was made from the claimed violation of the right. Profit-making—commercial advantage—can coexist with meriting constitutional protection under

---

[67] Langvardt, 'Troubling Implications', at 358–60, plausibly argues that the Supreme Court case of *Zacchini* casts a long shadow here. The Supreme Court there was also dismissive of First Amendment (i.e., freedom of speech) concerns. Normally, a television newscast would be classified as 'non-commercial', and granted full First Amendment protection. The Court did not explain why showing all of Zacchini's 15-second act, as opposed, say, to only the first 14 seconds, should take the newscast out from under the protection of the First Amendment.

[68] *Cardtoons LC v Major League Baseball Players' Assn* 95 F 3d 959 (1996) (USCA 10th Cir).

[69] *Hoffman v Capital Cities/ABC et al* 255 F 3d 1180 (2001) (USCA 9th Cir).

[70] *ETW Corp v Jireh Publishing Inc* 2003 FED App 0207P (USCA 6th Cir).

the First Amendment. Both Rush and *Los Angeles Magazine* were able to argue that their impugned expression was the kind of artistic expression it is the purpose of the First Amendment to protect. It seems unlikely, for example, that Andy Warhol would have been held to violate Marilyn Monroe's right of publicity in his famous series of representations of her face.[71] To have withheld protection, then, from Rush or *Los Angeles Magazine* would have had the courts drawing some very dubious lines between 'genuine art' deserving protection and 'low-grade kitsch' (or some such distinction) not deserving protection.[72]

Kozinski J in his *White* dissent locates the right of publicity in the general area of intellectual property law (at 1516), especially the area of copyright law. As he argues (ibid.), there are well-established limitations in that area on the right of an individual to command exclusive use of the products of the intellect. The two chief ones are these. First, there is the notion of a 'fair use' by one person of what is nonetheless some other person's intellectual property. Secondly, there is the distinction between an idea as such and a given expression of an idea. A given expression can be copyrighted, but the idea itself being expressed cannot be. Intellectual property law, Kozinski J says, 'balances what's set aside for the owner [of intellectual property] and what's left in the public domain for the rest of us' (ibid.). The reason we want to protect the owner is to encourage and reward creativity. That may be because we want to maximize the number of *loci* of happiness and satisfaction in the world, or because we regard such creativity as producing fruits for all of us to enjoy and thereby flourish. Freedom of speech is essential to creating an environment to promote such flourishing. So in the name of freedom of speech, we limit the rights of the owners of intellectual property to keep exclusive control.

Kozinski J's problem with the right of publicity as extended by the *White* majority is that it is not subject to these limitations that safeguard the interests of 'the rest of us'. As he suggests (at 1516–17), it is not difficult to show how these limitations would play themselves out in *White*. It is easy to argue that the idea of a game show hostess is given one expression by the real Vanna White (or the show's director, at least), and another by Samsung and Deutsch in the robot advertisement. Vanna White, or rather Merv Griffin Enterprises, the owners of the copyright in 'Wheel of Fortune', cannot assert copyright over the very idea of a game show hostess, but only in some given expression of that idea.

The issue over the 'fair use' exception to copyright is trickier, but crucial to my argument. §107 of the Copyright Act mentions four factors:

(1) the purpose and character of the work, including whether such use is of a commercial nature or is for non-profit educational purposes;
(2) the nature of the copyrighted work;

---

[71] *Comedy III Productions Inc v Gary Saderup Inc* 21 P 3d 797 (2001) (Cal SC), at 811.

[72] Cf. Diane Zimmerman, 'Fitting Publicity Rights Into Intellectual Property and Free Speech Theory: Sam, You Made the Pants Too Long!', *Journal of Art and Entertainment Law* 10 (2000): 301.

(3) the amount and substantiality of the portion used in relation to the copyrighted work as a whole; and

(4) the effect of the use upon the potential market for or value of the copyrighted work.

I focus here only on the first factor. In a recent case on copyright and parody,[73] though one subsequent to *White*, the Supreme Court made it clear that what was characterized as a 'commercial parody' may in principle constitute a 'fair use' of a copyrighted work. The defendants recorded and sold a quarter of a million copies of a version of a song in which the plaintiff held copyright. The defendants claimed that their version was a parody and so legitimate as a 'fair use'. The defendants' version was not an advertisement, but was recorded and sold by them in order to make money. It is different from the parody in *Falwell*.[74] This parody is classified as a 'non-commercial' expression, since it appeared by way of fully protected 'editorial' comment by the magazine.

It is clear that the Court does not conceive the first factor as a 'bright line' test, but as one that involves a continuum of cases. The Court in *Campbell* made these two comments: that 'the more transformative a new work, the less will be the significance of other factors, like commercialism, that may weigh against a finding of fair use' (at 1171), and that 'the use, for example, of a copyrighted work to advertise a product, even in a parody, will be entitled to less indulgence under the first factor of the fair use enquiry, than the sale of a parody for its own sake' (at 1174). I hazard no opinion on whether the robot advertisement in *White* would receive protection as a 'fair use' if a qualifying test such as the above were applied to it. That is not the point. The point is that the Court in *Campbell* has devised an entirely sensible way of handling the commercial dimension of expressions impugned under the Copyright Act, within the context of wanting to protect free speech values.

Freedom of speech is concerned with the promotion of creative expression (among other things, of course) for the general benefit as much as for the benefit of the creator. The most rational way to achieve the benefit to all is to require a measure of creativity in the work which is to be protected as a fair use, even if that work is 'commercial' in the sense that it is 'sold for its own sake', and even if it is used 'to advertise a product'. Such an analytical framework can be applied as well to the right of publicity as to the case of copyright. The right of publicity explicitly concerns what are in some sense commercial expressions, but this feature does not entail removing the right from the scope of traditional arguments for freedom of speech or freedom of expression.

Moreover, the right of publicity comes within the scope of freedom of speech, not simply because the vehicle for intruding on the right is speech or expression

---

[73] *Campbell v Acuff-Rose Music Inc* 114 SCt 1164 (1994).

[74] *Hustler Magazine Inc v Falwell* 485 US 46 (1988). Falwell was a well-known television evangelist represented by the magazine in a mock advertisement as a drunkard who fornicated with his mother. It is ironic that such a mordant and offensive parody receives full constitutional protection, while the whimsical and gentle wit of the robot hostess received none from the Ninth Circuit.

in the ordinary sense. It comes within the scope of freedom of speech because freedom of speech as a value is there to foster certain societal benefits, and the right of publicity raises issues of how to achieve those benefits in certain cases of conflict. Theories of freedom of expression have to be, and are, appealed to in order to resolve these conflicts.

Of course, since *White* was decided subsequent to *Virginia Board* and *Central Hudson*, the Samsung advertisement for institutional reasons could be taken to count as 'commercial speech', and within the institution of U.S. First Amendment law may have its desert for constitutional protection assessed by the *Central Hudson* test. The Ninth Circuit majority did not make such an assessment, and was criticized for this omission by Kozinski J in his dissent (at 1520). But a commercial speech doctrine is not needed in order to examine and debate the extent of any failure on the part of the *White* majority to respect fully the implications of freedom of speech as a constitutional value. In fact, a commercial speech doctrine in the form developed by the Supreme Court may even hinder such an examination. It has been plausibly argued that the *Central Hudson* test will not do justice to the legitimate First Amendment rights of a defendant like Samsung in *White*.[75]

The right of publicity in the appropriate fact situation pits celebrities against commercial advertisers, in the context of genuine conflict between the right a celebrity has over the use of indicia of his or her identity and the supposed expressive interests of the advertisers. But we do not need a commercial speech doctrine or commercial expression doctrine to resolve, or even to understand, the conflict. The advertisers may be speaking or expressing in some ordinary sense, but that is not what secures the relevance of constitutional issues of freedom of speech or expression. That relevance is secured by the fact that well-understood free speech theory supports in the appropriate cases the claims of the commercial advertisers to constitutional protection for their advertisements.

The contrast between two different possible arguments should be clear. One is: 'The robot ad is speech, so it deserves constitutional protection'. The other is: 'The robot ad, though commercial, is a new and transformative expression of societal benefit, and so it deserves constitutional protection'. Both those statements are in themselves oversimplifications, of course. But they serve to illustrate the difference which concerns me here—the difference between the 'bottom-up' argument for constitutional protection which begins with the dull fact of something being speech, and the 'top-down' argument of jurisprudential theory which establishes principles of free speech and derives from them a conclusion about constitutional protection. My claim is that only the latter kind of argument has relevance and value. Here, in the case of the right of publicity, the top-down argument shows how speech which might seem to qualify as

---

[75] Stephen R. Barnett, 'The Right of Publicity Versus Free Speech in Advertising: Some Counter-Points to Professor McCarthy', *Hastings Communications and Entertainment Law Journal* 18 (1996): 604.

'commercial speech' can merit constitutional protection by serving traditional free speech values while having its commerciality taken into account. The top-down argument also shows how the kind of speech that is the subject of the commercial speech doctrine must fall outside the scope of the traditional values underlying freedom of speech. If it did not, it would be protectable in terms of those values. We do not need a commercial speech doctrine to deal with these cases where the right of publicity conflicts with the First Amendment. We need only the traditional values of the First Amendment. The right of publicity cases are in this way significantly different from the two previous examples I have discussed, where no such 'top-down' argument is available. The appeal in the case of tortious interference and marketing of off-label uses can only be to the idea that these are cases of speech and deserve protection as such. But that is not what the value of freedom of speech stands for.

4 CONCLUSION

My aim in this chapter has been to defend, not merely the value, but the necessity of theory in debates about the proper scope of constitutional protection for forms of what is in a plain, ordinary sense 'expression' or 'speech'. So-called commercial expression or commercial speech faces the demands of theory especially sharply, since there are powerful intuitions against including it within such scope. Commercial expression has to do primarily with economic matters, and not with the search for truth, self-realization, and self-expression, and robust political debate. Rodney Smolla has claimed that to ask of commercial speech that it *earns* its way into constitutional protection turns classic First Amendment thinking upside-down. The theoretical question, Smolla says, should be what, if anything, *disqualifies* commercial speech?[76] But what he means here by 'classic First Amendment thinking' seems to be the idea that all speech in the ordinary sense of 'speech' deserves constitutional protection unless shown otherwise. But neither the First Amendment nor in general the right of freedom of expression/speech has ever stood for any such thing. I have tried to show in this chapter that such an approach to the issue of commercial expression is a mistake. The theoretical questions indeed must be taken seriously, but examination of them must begin with normative principles, not with facts about instances of terms in ordinary language. The commercial expression doctrine needs a foundation in theory, and that advertisements, for example, are a form of 'expression' does not provide such a foundation. Nor, as I hope to show in the remainder of this book, do the foundational normative principles of freedom of expression.

---

[76] Rodney A. Smolla, 'Information, Imagery and the First Amendment: A Case for Expansive Protection of Commercial Speech', *Texas Law Review* 71 (1993): 779–80.

PART III
THE ARGUMENTS ASSESSED

9

Original Autonomy Rights

As I have noted a number of times already, there are two very powerful antecedent intuitions from normative political morality against constitutional protection for commercial expression—first, freedom of expression has to do with political, scientific, or artistic expression, and not with offering products for sale: secondly, the primary bearers of the right of freedom of expression are natural persons, but corporations, the prime beneficiaries of freedom of commercial expression, are not natural persons. Thus baldly stated, these intuitions are at best conclusions without supporting argument, and, to many, controversial if not plainly false conclusions. It is the aim of this chapter and its successors to try to provide theoretical support for these intuitions and demonstrate their soundness. If the latter can be demonstrated, then important consequences follow for the commercial expression doctrine. It cannot be that the doctrine will have been shown to be false, for the following reason. I have argued that any doctrine of freedom of expression must be defended 'top-down'—that is, by derivation from sound theoretical principles. It does not follow from the fact that a given doctrine cannot be derived from one set of principles that therefore it can be derived from none. Yet only if the given doctrine can be derived from none can it be cogently claimed to be false. Freedom of commercial expression, however, has seen by its supporters as part of the mainstream of liberal democratic thought. The aim of my argument here is to deny that this is so—or rather, perhaps more modestly, to make clear the size of the distortion of liberal democratic thought that occurs when the commercial expression doctrine is embraced.

Freedom of expression as part of background political morality is thought of as a moral right, and in the constitutional context is thought of as a constitutional right. In Chapter 7, I made a number of distinctions between different kinds of right and different kinds of justifications for the acknowledgment of rights. This analysis of rights forms an essential part of the theoretical background embedded in any normative defence of freedom of expression, and so of freedom of commercial expression. The normative consequences of the analysis of rights must now be explored. They will be explored for their bearing on the two intuitions against the commercial expression doctrine with which this chapter began.

I shall consider first the claim that freedom of commercial expression is an original autonomy right, in the sense of that term identified in Chapter 7 above—that is, a right, a protected normative position some person possesses in some given circumstances, such that possession of it in the given circumstances

is normatively justified for reasons of autonomy. That is rather an elaborate formulation, but the elaboration is needed for reasons of precision. Already we see,
however, just in that formulation, where the focus is going to be in the case of
freedom of commercial expression. I wrote of a protected normative position
possessed by some *person*. Consider the claim that corporate advertising, for
example, or corporate labelling practices merit constitutional protection on
freedom of expression grounds, because the expressing corporation has an original autonomy right to freedom of commercial expression. Such a claim may
immediately be countered by the claim that original autonomy rights accrue
only to natural persons, and a corporation is not a natural person. I shall argue
that this counterclaim is justified. But the issues are complex, and merit full discussion.

1 AUTONOMY AS A VALUE

The roots of autonomy as a value are political. *Autonomia*—creating and living
under one's own (*autos*) laws (*nomos*)—was a condition much valued by the
city-states of fifth- and fourth-century classical Greece. Self-governance as a
moral value in a general sense became prominent in the eighteenth century.[1]
However, the specific interpretation of autonomy as the central value of morality was different. 'Kant invented the conception of morality as autonomy.'[2]
Autonomy in this Large-K Kantian sense connotes an extra-causal freedom
through which we can, and are duty-bound to, impose on ourselves the moral
law. The content of the moral law includes a deep commitment to acknowledging the autonomy of others. In contemporary moral and political philosophy
autonomy connotes a much wider and looser set of notions, but still is deeply
connected to the ideas of self-governance and freedom, and of respect by any
one for these characteristics of others.

Joel Feinberg distinguishes four connected notions of autonomy—as capacity, condition, ideal, and right.[3] Autonomy as a *capacity* connotes the ability to
govern oneself—to make and to live by one's own choices. What exactly that
latter phrase means is subject to further interpretation. In one well-known formulation, autonomy 'is a second-order capacity of persons to reflect critically
upon their first-order preferences, desires, wishes, and so forth, and the capacity
to accept or attempt to change these in the light of higher-order preferences'.[4]
Such a formulation captures well the intuition that a person who is either at the
mercy of his or her own desires or unknowingly subject to the will of another is

---

[1] J.B. Schneewind, *The Invention of Autonomy: A History of Modern Moral Philosophy* (New
York: Cambridge University Press, 1998), Part III.
[2] Ibid., 3. The sentence constitutes the dramatic beginning to this work.
[3] Joel Feinberg, *Harm to Self*, vol. III of *The Moral Limits of the Criminal Law* (New York:
Oxford University Press, 1986), Chapter 18.
[4] Gerald Dworkin, 'Autonomy', in Robert E. Goodin and Philip Pettit (eds.), *The Blackwell
Companion to Contemporary Political Philosophy* (Oxford: Blackwell Publishers Ltd., 1993), 360.

not autonomous. But it is broad enough to admit a life of subservience with which a person identifies, and such a life is not obviously autonomous.[5] Joseph Raz argues that autonomy construed as a capacity requires not merely the ability to evaluate information and choose between options, but also the ability to adopt personal projects, develop relationships, and accept commitments to causes, to be creators of their own moral world.[6] Such a 'thicker' formulation does not seem open to the objection just noted, but it clearly has built into it many normative commitments about the nature of the good life, to which others may object. However, the purpose of this paragraph is not to provide a tight definition of autonomy as a capacity, but simply to remind the reader of the general content of the concept being sketched.

Autonomy as a *condition* connotes simply that some given person who possesses the capacity for autonomy is exercising it. Persons who possess the capacity may nonetheless be prevented from exercising it, usually by coercion of one kind or another. Raz, for example, claims that autonomy requires certain external conditions for its successful exercise—an appropriate range of options between to choose, and enough goods not to have to struggle always to maintain the minimum conditions of a worthwhile life.[7] He notes that one person may invade another's autonomy by reducing the quality or quantity of the options available to that other person (ibid.). Such a view, however, is too perfectionist for the more libertarian kind of liberal, who requires for the exercise of autonomy simply that one's choices are made by reason and are not unfree.[8] Again, I am not aiming to settle such issues here, but simply to indicate the general shape of the concept.

Autonomy as an *ideal* requires the construction out of some notion of autonomy as a capacity and its exercise the concept of a virtuous condition of persons, at the attainment of which persons should aim. Feinberg, with some plausibility, suggests that the basic notion of autonomy is so complex, with some of its strands not necessarily good in the first place, that construction of such ideal will be fraught with difficulty.[9] Again, we can here simply note the complexity, and continue.

Autonomy as a *right*, finally, takes the possession and exercise of autonomy as a protected normative position. That is to say, some value(s) or other imply that there should be, in the moral or the legal realm, special rules—exclusionary rules—which, first, exclude from the balance of reasons some reason against some given action, and, secondly, do so on the ground of protecting or promoting the

---

[5] Cf. John Christman, 'Constructing the Inner Citadel: Recent Work on the Concept of Autonomy', *Ethics* 99 (1988): 113.

[6] Joseph Raz, *The Morality of Freedom* (Oxford: Clarendon Press, 1986), 154.

[7] Raz, *Morality of Freedom*, 154–7. Cf. also Feinberg, *Harm to Self*, 31.

[8] Loren E. Lomasky, *Persons, Rights, and the Moral Community* (New York: Oxford University Press, 1987), 42–3. The term 'unfree' clearly is subject to interpretation in a characterization such as this.

[9] Feinberg, *Harm to Self*, 44–7.

autonomy of some person(s).[10] The character of the value in question depends on how autonomy is conceived as a value itself. Autonomy can be conceived of as the quintessential expression of what it is to be human, as an intrinsic value in itself. Such a conception regularly results in demands for acknowledgement of equality, dignity, and respect. Secondly, autonomy can be conceived of as an essential constitutive element of human happiness and flourishing, whose constitutive role requires special acknowledgment despite its role being instrumental. Thirdly, autonomy may be conceived of as one of the most important means to the end of human happiness and flourishing, and again as requiring special acknowledgment because of the importance of this instrumental role. As usual, it is not the purpose of this section to select one of these possibilities over another, but rather to issue a reminder of what the possibilities are. We will find versions of all of them in subsequent discussion.

2 AUTONOMY AND FREEDOM OF EXPRESSION

Traditionally, freedom of expression has been thought to deserve special treatment for two reasons. The first is its connection with democratic self-government. Democracy would seem to be a meaningless idea if the government were to have complete control of the time, place, and manner of political expression by citizens. The second is its goal in the attainment of truth. As Mill put it, if an opinion is silenced then,

if the opinion is right, [we] are deprived of the opportunity of exchanging error for truth: if wrong, [we] lose, what is almost as great a benefit, the clearer and livelier impression of truth, produced by its collision with error.[11]

In the mid-twentieth century, a third reason for valuing freedom of expression became current, in both academic writing and judicial opinions: the value of personal autonomy and self-fulfilment, especially in the U.S. The person generally credited with advancing this value is Thomas Emerson, first in an early article,[12] and definitively in his later book.[13] Emerson asserted the proper end of Man to be the realization of his character and potentialities as a human being, and that to cut off expression was to place Man under the arbitrary control of others.[14] Edward White has suggested that Emerson's positioning of the self-fulfilment value at the top of the hierarchy of First Amendment values paradoxically arose out of the emphasis in the 1950s and 1960s on democratic

---

[10] For the notion of exclusionary reason see Joseph Raz, *Practical Reason and Norms* (London: Hutchinson, 1975), 35–48.

[11] John Stuart Mill, *Essential Works of John Stuart Mill* (ed. and intro Max Lerner, New York: Bantam Books, 1961), 269.

[12] Thomas I. Emerson, 'Toward a General Theory of the First Amendment', *Yale Law Journal* 72 (1963): 877–956.

[13] Thomas I. Emerson, *The System of Freedom of Expression* (New York: Random House, 1970).

[14] Ibid., 6.

self-government.[15] Democratic self-government values the individual participant in a democracy. Once the individual is the locus of value, it is a short step
from valuing the individual's self-expression in democratic government to valuing the individual's self-expression in all its possible forms. Once postulated,
autonomy and self-expression became prominent freedom of expression values,
especially so (as we shall see anon) in the defence of the commercial expression
doctrine.

Different kinds of argument link freedom of expression with autonomy and
connected values like self-realization, self-expression, and self-fulfilment. The
standard argument is that freedom of expression is protective of the conditions
for autonomy and self-realization.[16] That is, a person in order to attain autonomy and self-realization requires space in which to make choices, and options
between which choices can be made. Freedom of expression creates and maintains such a space. The argument appears in different forms. The first values
autonomy only as instrumental to political self-governance:

Freedom of speech . . . amounts to a protection of autonomy—law places a shield around
the speaker. . . . The underlying purpose [is cast] in social or political terms: The purpose
of free speech is . . . the preservation of democracy. . . . Autonomy is protected . . . as a
means or instrument of collective self-determination.[17]

Two further versions make autonomy and self-realization the ends, but interpret freedom of expression itself narrowly or broadly. The argument may allude
to the role of political discourse, or more generally to refer to any discourse or
communicative process. The narrow variant stays close to the traditional picture of freedom of expression as relating to political self-governance. As Edwin
Baker puts it, 'respect for people's autonomy requires a right to meaningful
participation in the processes that formulate the values through which people
define themselves'.[18] Baker emphasizes political processes, but such a limitation
is not needed. The wider variant emphasizes the role of participation in public
discourse and communication of whatever kind in the promotion of autonomy
and self-realization.[19] Another version of the argument takes freedom of expression as not instrumental to autonomy, but constitutive of it: expression is valued for its own sake, seen as an aspect of individual autonomy, which is
essential to personal growth and self-realization.[20] Freedom of expression is

---

[15] G. Edward White, 'The First Amendment Comes of Age: The Emergence of Free Speech in
Twentieth-Century America', *Michigan Law Review* 95 (1996): 354 ff.

[16] Ronald K.L. Collins and David M. Stover, 'Commerce and Communication', *Texas Law
Review* 71 (1993): 733.

[17] Owen Fiss, *Liberalism Divided: Freedom of Speech and the Many Uses of State Power*
(Boulder, Colo.: Westview Press, 1996), 13; see also 37.

[18] C. Edwin Baker, *Human Liberty and Freedom of Speech* (New York: Oxford University Press,
1989), 205.

[19] Richard Moon, *The Constitutional Protection of Freedom of Expression* (Toronto: University
of Toronto Press, 2000), 19–21, 24–6.

[20] Robert J. Sharpe, 'Commercial Expression and the Charter', *University of Toronto Law
Journal* 37 (1987): 232.

constitutive (partly) of autonomy, and autonomy is the instrument to self-realization and self-fulfilment.

The general idea of freedom of expression construed as an original autonomy right amounts then to this. The value of autonomy, whether political or individual, is especially fostered by freedom of expression. This distinctive role of freedom of expression in fostering autonomy justifies there being special exclusionary rules which, first, exclude from the balance of reasons some (or even all) reasons against interference with freedom of expression, and, secondly, do so on the grounds of protecting or promoting the autonomy of some person(s).

3 Freedom of Commercial Expression as an Original Autonomy Right

The above remarks about autonomy and freedom of expression indicate the strength of the case for construing freedom of expression in many of its forms as an original autonomy right. As long as the person protected by the right is a natural person, deserving of equal treatment and respect, whose happiness and flourishing are of paramount value, whose right of political participation and self-government is normatively secure, then there is no doubt that freedom of expression can have the status of an original autonomy right. The question now to be considered is the plausibility of construing as an original autonomy right freedom of *commercial* expression as a special case of freedom of expression.

The immediate difficulty, of course, is the obvious one. If freedom of expression is thought[21] primarily to protect the normative position of those who express, or speak, then the typical expresser in the case of commercial expression is a corporation, and not a natural person. Yet values such as dignity, equality, respect, happiness, flourishing are primarily values for natural persons, not for artificial persons such as corporations. La Forest J in his dissent in the *RJR-MacDonald* case[22] puts the matter well. The majority opinion had treated the Court's decision in *Ford*[23] as authority for *Charter* protection of commercial expression. *Ford*, however, dealt with language rights.[24] La Forest rejects the parallel. The *Ford* court quoted with approval its own remarks in the *Manitoba Language Rights* case, that 'the importance of language rights is grounded in the essential role that language plays in human existence, development and dignity'.[25] La Forest pungently comments: 'In my view, it cannot be

---

[21] I am aware of the size of this 'if'. The role of hearers and listeners in the justification of a right to freedom of expression, especially of commercial expression, will be discussed at length below in Chapter 10.

[22] *RJR-MacDonald Inc v Attorney-General of Canada; Imperial Tobacco Ltd v Attorney-General of Canada* [Indexed as RJR-MacDonald Inc v Canada (Attorney-General)] (1995) 127 DLR (4th) 1.

[23] *Attorney-General of Quebec v La Chaussure Brown's Inc et al* [Indexed as Ford v Quebec (Attorney-General)] (1988) 54 DLR (4th) 577.

[24] See the analysis in Chapter 4.3 above.

[25] *Reference re Language Rights under the Manitoba Act, 1870* (1985) 19 DLR (4th) 1, at 19.

seriously argued that the "dignity" of the three large corporations whose rights are infringed in these cases [the tobacco manufacturers] is in any way comparable to that of minority group members dealt with in *Ford*' (at 82). The Ontario Court of Appeal expressed much the same sentiments. In *Edible Oil*,[26] they rejected the argument that the requirement of the Ontario Oleomargarine Act that margarine be coloured differently from butter was an infringement of the section 2(b) freedom of commercial expression of the margarine manufacturer. The Court asserted that:

it is difficult to see how the freedom of expression asked for in this case furthers the purposes for the guarantee of the freedom as suggested by the Supreme Court of Canada . . . [references omitted], i.e., the search for truth, a contribution to the formulation of beliefs or to the effective operation of democratic institutions, or the fulfilment of individual autonomy or of self-validation. [at 381]

Commentators have agreed: Sharpe acknowledges that 'few will contend that the autonomy interest of the speaker is at stake in the case of commercial expression'.[27] The sentiment is repeated by Machina,[28] Hutchinson,[29] and Dan-Cohen.[30]

The preceding point may seem obvious and, in fact, as we shall see in the next chapters, most defences of the commercial expression doctrine by both courts and commentators do not appeal to an original autonomy right of an expresser corporation. Nonetheless, it is hard to construe a very recent case in the U.S. Court of Appeal as anything other than a tacit assumption of a corporate autonomy right. Moreover, arguments can be made that the corporate form is misleading, and that, when a corporation expresses itself, natural persons are really doing the expressing and thus deserve whatever protection for their expression their own original autonomy rights would give them. Thus the matter deserves further exploration, and I shall deal with these issues in order.

The case I have in mind is *US West*.[31] It concerns the use made by telecommunications carriers of so-called 'customer proprietary network information' (CPNI) for marketing purposes. Telecommunications carriers keep extensive databases concerning the use made by their customers of their services. Whenever we make a telephone call using the services of a telecommunications carrier, the database is automatically updated to reveal over time the patterns of such things as typical time of day the phone is used, typical number called, and

---

[26] *Re Institute of Edible Oil Foods et al and the Queen* [Indexed as Institute of Edible Oil Foods v Ontario] (1989) 64 DLR (4th) 380 (Ont CA); leave to appeal to Supreme Court of Canada refused (1990) 74 OR (2d) x.

[27] Sharpe, 'Commercial Expression and the Charter', 236.

[28] Kenton F. Machina, 'Freedom of Expression in Commerce', *Law and Philosophy* 3 (1994): 387–8.

[29] Allan C. Hutchinson, 'Money Talk: Against Constitutionalizing (Commercial) Speech', *Canadian Business Law Journal* 17 (1990): 21.

[30] Meir Dan-Cohen, 'Freedoms of Collective Speech: A Theory of Protected Communications by Organizations, Communities and the State', *California Law Review* 79 (1991): 1245.

[31] *US West Inc v FCC* 182 F (3d) 1224 (1999) (USCA 10th Cir).

so on; and of course the database will include other such information as equipment used, tariff subscribed to, and so forth. We naturally think that what we say in any given phone call is no business of the telecommunications carrier; we would regard it as a gross intrusion of privacy for the carrier routinely to listen in and record our calls. Arguably, it is no more the company's business whom we call or when we call them either, although on the other hand CPNI clearly has value to the carrier, and we would not be able to make such calls in the first place without the carrier's equipment.

With full CPNI at its disposal, the carrier is well placed to market to customers different kinds of rate plans, different kinds of equipment, and so forth, to the betterment of its own economic position. FCC regulations postulated the division of a telecommunications company into three service categories, local, long-distance, and cellular, and regulated the transfer of CPNI between these categories. It has been suggested that U.S. West were also intending to sell CPNI to other companies willing to pay for the information. Sale of transaction-generated information of that kind is now widespread in innumerable industries, and would raise more severe issues of both privacy and autonomy-based expression rights than the intra-company transfers discussed here. However, the fact is that the case report does not mention for-profit sales of CPNI outside U.S. West. It discusses only intra-company transfers of information, and the decision is based on those.[32]

The privacy aspects of CPNI were given weight to both in the original legislation[33] and in subsequent regulations of the Federal Communications Commission to interpret further these privacy requirements. The Act generally speaking requires that the telecommunications carrier obtain customer approval for use of CPNI, but without specifying what would count as obtaining approval. The carriers sought clarification, and the FCC decided to require the so-called 'opt-in' approach. That is to say, the carriers were required to obtain prior express approval from any given customer before making use of CPNI for purposes of marketing to that customer, as opposed to, say, an 'opt-out' approach under which use of CPNI for marketing purposes is the default and customers must explicitly inform the carrier that they do not wish CPNI used.

In the case in point, U.S. West, with a number of other carriers on board as *amici curiae*, challenged the FCC ruling as a restriction on its commercial speech in violation of the First Amendment. The ruling, U.S. West claimed, restricted its ability to engage in commercial speech with customers (at 1230). The Court agreed, and invalidated the regulation (at 1239). There are several issues at stake in the case as well as freedom of commercial expression—how, and how weight-

---

[32] Dana Grantham Lennox, 'Hello, Is Anybody Home? Deregulation, Discombobulation, and the Decision in *U.S. West v FCC*', *Georgia Law Review* 34 (2000): 1649, 1652.

[33] 47 U.S.C. s. 222, Telecommunications Act of 1996, section entitled 'Privacy of customer information'. There are many technical details to the fact situation in this case, which my summary here does not reveal. See 1228–30, II—Background, of the case report.

ily, privacy interests bear on the decisions, satisfaction of the appropriate standard for judicial review of agency action, whether the court was illicitly substituting its own views for those of the legislature. There is ample reason to
criticize the majority decision on each of those grounds.[34] However, my concern
is with the acceptance by the Court of US West's claim that *its* freedom of speech
was violated.

The only natural persons affected by the FCC's choice of an 'opt-in' requirement over an 'opt-out' requirement are those who would not wish to be the target of CPNI-based marketing. They benefit from opting in, rather than opting
out, being the base-line. One can see why US West wanted to have the 'opt in'
option invalidated. According to figures before the Court (at 1239), a pilot study
conducted by US West showed that only 28 per cent of persons called agreed to
their CPNI being used for intra-company transfers to assist marketing. 33 per
cent specifically denied permission, and 39 per cent either hung up or asked not
to be called again. Thus the standard hearer-based argument for freedom of
commercial expression is not applicable here; there is no issue of a person being
deprived of a chance of hearing something he or she wishes to hear.

In holding for US West, and agreeing that its freedom to speak commercially
is violated, the Court in fact treats US West like any individual speaker whose
opportunity to speak is taken away by the government. In theory, the Court
could have treated the case as one where the prime directive was the maximally
free flow of information, independently of any hearers' interest or expresser's
autonomy right. But in fact no such argument was mentioned.[35] The Court talks
of the need to respect 'important civil liberties' (at 1228). While the Court
acknowledges that the free expression rights of either speaker or hearer may
ground constitutional protection, nothing more is heard of the rights of hearers,
and justly so. Such an approach interprets freedom of expression as an original
autonomy right. The Court wholly approved of US West's view of itself as having the same entitlement to outrage at being prevented from speaking as any
silenced politician, any scientist forbidden to publish research, any artist the
exhibition of whose work is cancelled. US West, though, is a large corporation,
and not entitled to any original autonomy rights.[36]

US West would thus fit well with a pattern arguably discernible in First
Amendment decisions more generally. Edwin Baker has recently concluded
from an examination of decisions relating to broadcast media that there is under
way 'a subtle and undefended reconceptualization of the First Amendment . . .

---

[34] Julie Tuan, 'U.S. West, Inc. v FCC', *Berkeley Technology Law Journal* 15 (2000): passim;
Lennox, 'Discombobulation', passim.

[35] Moreover, it is in any case not clear how strong such pure 'free flow' arguments are: see
Chapter 13 below.

[36] In the same vein, Martin Redish argues that a requirement for tobacco advertising to be only
in so-called 'tombstone' form (simple black-and-white plain text) would 'interfere with a speaker's
choice of method of expression', in violation of the First Amendment (Martin H. Redish, 'Tobacco
Advertising and the First Amendment', *Iowa Law Review* 81 (1996): 626). He entirely ignores the
question whether a tobacco manufacturer is a 'speaker' of the morally relevant kind.

media enterprises [are being treated] as rights bearers in their own behalf'.[37] 'Earlier cases,' he urges, 'treated media entities instrumentally in terms of serving a democratic society's need for non-governmentally created or approved information and vision' (ibid.), but that seems no longer to be the underlying norm. Baker alludes to cases striking down on First Amendment grounds FCC prohibitions on telecommunications companies also owning cable systems in the geographic area of their operation,[38] and cases striking down restrictions on concentration of cable system ownership and 'must-carry' rules for cable systems, again on First Amendment grounds.[39] The First Amendment grounds in all these cases amount to an acknowledgment that media corporations have in themselves forms of speakers' free expression rights which can prevail over the public interest in the availability of information.

One should also consider in the context of supposed corporate original autonomy rights of free expression cases of compelled expression or speech. It is well established, and rightly so, in both *Charter* section 2(b) and First Amendment jurisprudence that 'there is certainly some difference between compelled speech and compelled silence, but in the context of protected speech, the difference is without constitutional significance, for the First Amendment guarantees "freedom of speech," a term necessarily comprising the decision of both what to say and what not to say'.[40] But why? The underlying reason is that to compel a person to express what he or she does not wish to express is an intrusion into, and even a repudiation of, that person's autonomy—'in a free society one's beliefs should be shaped by his mind and his conscience rather than coerced by the State'.[41] How meaningful is it, however, to think of a corporation as a being with a conscience, of the kind that freedom of expression protects? Recent case law in the U.S. has been discussed in Chapter 3 above.[42] Here I will say something about the struggles of the Supreme Court of Canada with this issue.

The *National Bank* case concerned a labour dispute in which the Canada Labour Relations Board found against the bank. As part of the remedy, the Board ordered the bank to set up a trust fund, and also to write to every employee announcing the creation of the trust fund; the Board moreover specified the wording of this letter, and prohibited the bank from modifying the

---

[37] C. Edwin Baker, 'Media Concentration: Giving Up on Democracy', *Florida Law Review* 54 (2002): 854.

[38] *Chesapeake & Potomac Tel Co v US* 42 F 3d 181 (1994) (USCA 4th Cir), *vacated* 516 (US) 415 (1996); *US West Inc v United States* 48 F 3d 1092 (1994) (USCA 9th Cir), *vacated* 516 US 1155 (1996). The decisions were vacated, not on the merits, but in order to determine mootness.

[39] *Comcast Cablevision v Broward County* 124 F Supp 2d 685 (2000) (USDC SD Fla); *Times Warner Entertainment Co v FCC* 240 F 3d 1126 (2001) (USCA DC Cir).

[40] *Riley et al v National Federation of the Blind of North Carolina Inc et al* 487 US 781 (1988), at 796–7; *Re National Bank of Canada and Retail Clerks' International Union* (1984) 9 DLR (4th) 10, at 31.

[41] *Abood v Detroit Board of Education* 431 US 209 (1977), at 234–5.

[42] See comments on *Glickman v Wileman Brothers and Elliott Inc et al* 117 SCt 2130 (1997), *United States v United Foods Inc* 121 SCt 2334 (2001), discussed in Chapter 3.6. above.

specified text even by a single word. The bank challenged this order on the ground, *inter alia*, that it was an infringement of the bank's freedom of expression. The Court relied heavily on a perception that the letter could be taken to attribute to the bank approval of the Board's decision and of the applicable regulatory framework, and thus to attribute to the bank a political opinion. For this reason, the order was referred to as 'totalitarian and as such alien to the tradition of free nations like Canada' (at 31, per Beetz J). The same issue came up again a few years later in *Slaight*,[43] another labour case. Slaight had fired Davidson, a salesman, and a labour arbitrator had found the dismissal wrongful. As part of the remedy, Slaight was required to write a letter of reference for Davidson in a specified form, and to respond to requests from other prospective employers for information about Davidson by and only by sending that letter. The Court again found this to be an interference with the company's freedom of expression, even though it distinguished the case from *National Bank* on the ground that the letter in question detailed facts about Davidson's satisfactorily meeting his sales quotas. Beetz J likened the arbitrator's order to the Inquisition's suppression of Galileo's scientific theories (at 431), a piece of extraordinary rhetoric which, it must be said, his colleagues did not endorse, although they did approve of his milder, but still strong, condemnation of the Board's decision in *National Bank*. In the event, the arbitrator's order was upheld by the Court as a justified limitation on freedom of expression under section 1 of the *Charter*.[44]

There is no doubt that the Supreme Court of Canada in these cases treats a corporation in the same way that it would treat a person—as an autonomous being whose mind and conscience should be shaped by it and not by the State. But the National Bank of Canada and Slaight Communications Inc are not Galileo, and neither is U.S. West Inc.

There are other constitutional rights that seem to be original autonomy rights meaningfully possessed only by natural persons. Were the idea to become established that corporations have the same original free expression autonomy rights as natural persons, freedom of expression would be far out of line with courts' treatment of corporations with respect to those other rights. Consider, for example, the position of corporations under other provisions of the Canadian *Charter*. Section 7 of the *Charter* declares:

Everyone has the right to life, liberty and security of the person and the right not to be deprived thereof except in accordance with the principles of fundamental justice.

Unsurprisingly, the question arose whether 'everyone' in this section included corporations. In *Irwin Toy*,[45] the Supreme Court of Canada decided that it did not:

---

[43] *Slaight Communications Inc (Operating as Q107 FM Radio) v Davidson* (1989) 59 DLR (4th) 416.

[44] For the interplay between s.1 and the remainder of the *Charter*, see Chapter 4.1 above.

[45] *Attorney-General of Quebec v Irwin Toy Ltd* [Indexed as Irwin Toy Ltd v Quebec (Attorney-General)] (1989) 58 DLR (4th) 577.

It appears to us that this section was intended to confer protection on a singularly human level. A plain, common sense reading of the phrase 'Everyone has the right to life, liberty and security of the person' serves to underline the human element involved; only human beings can enjoy these rights. 'Everyone' then, must be read in the light of the rest of the section and defined so as to exclude corporations and other artificial entities incapable of enjoying life, liberty or security of the person, and include only human beings. [at 633]

The same reasoning was applied in *Amway*[46] to deny that 'everyone' in sections 11(c)[47] and 13[48] includes corporations: the sections were 'intended to protect the individual against the affront to dignity and privacy inherent in a practice which enables the prosecution to force the person charged to supply the evidence out of his or her own mouth' (at 40). Section 15 on equality rights uses the term 'individual' instead of 'everyone',[49] and it is clear from the legislative history that the change was intended by Parliament to make it clear that the section applied to natural persons only.[50] Courts, however, are not bound by legislative history. To this point, the Supreme Court has chosen not to confront the issue. Lower courts are divided. The Federal Court of Appeal has excluded corporations from section 15,[51] even in the case of a non-profit corporation.[52] The Ontario Court of Appeal has done so even in the case of a quasi-criminal, regulatory offence.[53] Only the Alberta Court of Appeal has granted limited standing to bring constitutional challenge under section 15, in *Cabre*,[54] a case of which more shortly.

In the case of sections 8 to 14 of the *Charter*, the sections that grant various procedural rights in connection with the criminal justice system, Canadian courts have distinguished with some care between rights that meaningfully apply to corporations and rights that do not. The sections typically begin with 'everyone', or 'any person', and such broad formulations in principle include corporations. Some examples of inapplicability to corporations are obvious. The section 9 right against arbitrary imprisonment does not apply, since corporations cannot be imprisoned. The section 11(c) right not to be compelled as a

---

[46] *R v Amway Corp* (1989) 1 SCR 21.

[47] 'Any person charged with an offence has the right . . . not to be compelled to be a witness in proceedings against that person in respect of the offence.'

[48] 'A witness who testifies in any proceedings has the right not to have any incriminating evidence so given used to incriminate that witness in any other proceedings, except in a prosecution for perjury or for the giving of contradictory evidence.'

[49] 'Every individual is equal before and under the law and has the right to the equal protection and equal benefit of the law without discrimination . . .'. The text continues with a specification of clearly illegal discriminations and a subsection permitting so-called reverse discrimination.

[50] Dale Gibson, *The Law of the Charter: Equality Rights* (Toronto: Carswell, 1990), 53–5.

[51] *Canada (Attorney-General) v Central Cartage Co* (1990) 2 FC 641 (FCA); leave to appeal to Supreme Court of Canada refused (1991) 33 CPR (3d) v.

[52] *National Anti-Poverty Organization v Canada (Attorney-General)* (1990) 60 DLR (4th) 712 (FCA); leave to appeal to Supreme Court of Canada refused (1989) 105 NR 160.

[53] *R v Paul Magder Furs* (1989) 49 CCC 3d 267 (Ont CA); leave to appeal to Supreme Court of Canada refused (1989) 51 CCC 3d vii.

[54] *Cabre Exploration v Arndt* (1988) 51 DLR (4th) 451 (Alta CA), additional reasons at (1988) 55 DLR (4th) 480, leave to appeal to Supreme Court of Canada refused (1989) 93 AR 239.

witness in one's own trial has no application to corporations. Employees, who are natural persons, can be compelled to give evidence, because any employee can be so compelled. But only employees of a corporation, and not the corporation itself, can actually give evidence (*R v Amway*). The section 11(e) right against unreasonable denial of bail does not apply, because corporations cannot need the right.

Analogously, in the United States, in *White*[55] the Court definitively ruled that the constitutional privilege against self-incrimination is restricted 'to natural individuals acting in their own private capacity' (at 700). The case concerned a labour union president pleading the privilege in the face of a request to produce union documents. Even though the Court acknowledged the variety of possible organizations, and the unique character of the business corporation (at 697), and stated that it was only deciding the facts of this case concerning officers of a union (at 698), the reasoning employed is general in scope. The Court states that the privilege 'grows out of the high sentiment and regard of our jurisprudence for conducting criminal trials and investigatory proceedings upon a plane of dignity, humanity and impartiality' (ibid.). Being designed to protect individuals, 'it cannot be utilized by or on behalf of any organization, such as a corporation' (at 699). The Court did consider the application of the Fifth Amendment privilege against self-incrimination to corporations in an earlier case.[56] However, the reasoning relied on different grounds—that the privilege was designed for the protection of the individual concerned, not for the protection of third parties, and *a fortiori* not for the protection of a corporation of which the individual was an officer (at 69–70); 'the question whether a corporation is a "person" within the meaning of this amendment really does not arise' (at 70). Later, although the Court says that 'there is a clear distinction in this particular between an individual and a corporation' (at 75), the reason the Court gives is the old-fashioned reason that the corporation is a 'creature of the state' (at 74–5), and thus that the state must have the power 'to investigate its contracts and find out whether it [the corporation] has exceeded its powers. The reasoning in *White* represents a more profound analysis.

In other cases, where there is not the same kind of essential inappropriateness to applying the right to corporations, Canadian courts have nonetheless differentiated between the application of the right to natural persons and to corporations. Section 11(b) grants a right to be tried within a reasonable time, which seems as applicable to a corporation as to a natural person. However, in *CIP*,[57] the Court distinguished between the purposes of the section 11(b) guarantee. Two of them, having to do with the minimization of pre-trial detention and anxiety, had no application to corporations. However, the Court held that the third purpose, preserving the ability to make a full answer and defence to the charges, did have application, as it clearly does. Nonetheless, the Court limited

---

[55] *United States v White* 322 US 694 (1944).   [56] *Hale v Henkel* 201 US 43 (1906).
[57] *R v CIP Inc* (1992) 71 CCC (3d) 129.

the applicability severely in its ruling. In the controlling case on section 11(b) with regard to defendants who are natural persons,[58] the Court spoke of a 'general, and in the case of very long delays an often virtually irrebuttable presumption of prejudice to the accused resulting from the passage of time' (at 484). In *CIP*, the Court ruled that a corporation may not rely on this presumption, but must demonstrate prejudice to its fair trial interest to the court (at 144). The Court bases this conclusion largely on the impossibility of a corporation being affected psychologically by trial delays in the way that a natural person can (ibid.).

Contrast here section 8, the section guaranteeing security against unreasonable search and seizure. The guarantee is given to 'everyone', including corporations. In the earliest *Charter* case on section 8, the trial judge held that corporations were as much as natural persons capable of enjoying the benefit of security against unreasonable search,[59] and neither the Alberta Court of Appeal[60] nor the Supreme Court of Canada[61] contested this conclusion. On the other hand, the Court has ruled that an order to produce business documents is a 'seizure' within the meaning of section 8, but that such an order is less intrusive of privacy than a search of the premises, and as such is to be judged by a lower standard of unreasonableness.[62] In the case of activities under a scheme of governmental regulation, courts at all levels have consistently ruled that here supervision is only to be expected, and the requirement of reasonableness is easily met.

The situation is similar in the U.S. with respect to corporations under the Fourth Amendment, which protects against unreasonable searches and seizures. In *Biswell*,[63] the Court declared that 'in the context of a regulatory inspection system of business premises that is carefully limited in time, place and scope, the legality of the search depends not on consent but on the authority of a valid statute. . . . If the law is to be properly enforced and inspection made effective, inspections without warrant must be deemed reasonable official conduct under the Fourth Amendment' (at 316). Here both Courts take into account differences in the actual situation of corporations and natural persons, without making any tacit appeal to such fundamental characteristics of natural persons as their psychology.

It is clear from the case opinions themselves that, when *Charter* protection is straightforwardly extended to corporations in sections 8–14, it is not out of any desire to attribute personhood to corporations. Rather, the underlying appeal is to the integrity of the justice system itself. Trials, especially criminal trials, who-

---

[58] *R v Askov* (1990) 59 CCC (3d) 449.
[59] *Hunter v Southam Inc* (1982) 68 CCC (2d) 356 (Alta QB), at 364.
[60] *Hunter v Southam Inc* (1983) 3 CCC (3d) 497 (Alta CA).
[61] *Hunter v Southam Inc* (1984) 14 CCC (3d) 97.
[62] *Thomson Newspapers Ltd v Canada (Director of Investigation and Research, Restrictive Trade Practices Commission)* (1990) 67 DLR (4th) 161.
[63] *United States v Biswell* 406 US 311 (1972).

ever or whatever the defendant, must be seen to be fair and just. As the Court remarked in *CIP*, 'the right to a fair trial is fundamental to our adversarial system. Parliament has seen fit to accord that right constitutional protection, I can find no principled reason for not extending that protection to *all* accused.'[64] Section 11(d), for example, of the *Charter* constitutionally guarantees the common-law right to a presumption of innocence. In *Wholesale Travel*,[65] this guarantee was ruled to cover quasi-criminal regulatory offences as well as true criminal offences, and thus clearly brought corporations within the coverage of the guarantee. Granted, the Court also decided on a narrow five to four split that the legislation in question, section 37.3(2) of the Competition Act,[66] constituted a justified limitation of the section 11(d) right. In reaching this conclusion, the Court balanced the societal interest behind the presumption against the patent societal interest in successful enforcement of regulatory schemes, and in this case at least the latter interest prevailed. In the U.S., the Double Jeopardy Clause of the Fifth Amendment was unhesitatingly applied to corporate defendants in *Martin Linen*,[67] with the reasoning appealing to the general principles of criminal justice lying behind the Clause (at 574–5).

This paramountcy of the general societal interest in the fairness of the justice system explains what might otherwise seem a strange decision, that in *Big M Drug*[68] to grant the drug store company standing to challenge the Lord's Day Act,[69] on the ground that the Act was a violation of the *Charter* guarantee of freedom of religion in section 2(a). The Attorney-General for Alberta argued, reasonably enough, that 'freedom of religion is a personal freedom and that a corporation, being a statutory creation, cannot be said to have a conscience or hold a religious belief' (at 335). The Court, however, would have none of this:

Any accused, whether corporate or individual, may defend a criminal charge by arguing that the law under which the charge is brought is unconstitutional. . . . Whether a corporation can enjoy or exercise freedom of religion is therefore irrelevant. The respondent [the drug store company] is arguing that the legislation is constitutionally invalid because it impairs freedom of religion—if the law impairs freedom of religion it does not matter whether the company can possess religious belief. . . . It is the nature of the law, not the status of the accused, that is in issue. [at 336–7]

The Court did distinguish between requesting a remedy under section 24(1) of the *Charter* on the ground that one's own *Charter* rights have been violated,[70] and benefiting from a declaration under section 52(1) that a given law is unconstitutional.[71] The drug store company is not entitled to a section 24(1) remedy,

[64] At 139, per Stevenson J; his italics.

[65] *R v Wholesale Travel Group Inc* (1991) 84 DLR (4th) 161.   [66] R.S.C. 1970, c. C-23.

[67] *United States v Martin Linen Supply Co et al* 430 US 564 (1977).

[68] *R v Big M Drug Mart Ltd* (1985) 18 DLR (4th) 321.   [69] R.S.C. 1970, c. L-13.

[70] 'Anyone whose rights or freedoms, as guaranteed by this Charter, have been infringed or denied may apply to a court of competent jurisdiction to obtain such remedy as the court considers appropriate and just in the circumstances.'

[71] 'The Constitution of Canada is the supreme law of Canada, and any law that is inconsistent with the provisions of the Constitution is, to the extent of the inconsistency, of no force or effect.'

because it cannot enjoy freedom of religion. But it may benefit from the striking down of an unconstitutional law. The Court's thought is that it is to the great benefit of all of us to live in a regime where all laws are consistent with the Constitution, which includes the *Charter*. Thus standing to challenge laws as being inconsistent with the Constitution should not be idly limited.

Once this broad principle of standing became valid, it was subsequently applied with respect to other sections of the *Charter* where corporations had been rejected as bearers of the right or freedom in question. In *Cabre*, the Alberta Court of Appeal allowed a corporation to raise the issue of the compatibility of section 26(9) of the Surface Rights Act[72] with section 15 of the *Charter*, the equality section, even though a corporation could not enjoy the right defined in the section. In *Wholesale Travel*, a corporation was allowed to impugn sections 36 and 37(3) of the Competition Act making a regulatory offence of misleading advertising. The Supreme Court of Canada determined that procedurally the Act imposed on the accused an onus of proof of innocence, in violation not only of section 11(d) of the *Charter* (see above), but also of the section 7 guarantee of 'life, liberty and security of the person'. The provisions of the Act in question apply as well to individual natural persons as to corporations. Therefore, even though corporations cannot in their own right receive the section 7 guarantee (see above), they do have standing to assert the unconstitutionality of a piece of legislation which would affect the constitutional rights of others and benefit, if so ruled, from its invalidation.

The implication of all of these cases is clear. In the vast majority of cases, courts simply do not recognize corporations as possessors of original autonomy rights. In cases where they appear to be recognizing such rights, they are in fact granting to corporations a normative status protected in law for wider reasons of social justice. If freedom of commercial expression is to be thought of as an original autonomy right, then one of two alternatives must follow. Either a constitutional guarantee of freedom of commercial expression is a unique case of a grant to a corporation of an original autonomy right, and is therefore a grant that poses to courts severe questions of doctrinal coherence. Or the guarantee is defensible on the kind of wider grounds alluded to above. We shall explore this latter possibility at some length in the next three chapters. But before then there is some unfinished business on the topic of corporations and original autonomy rights.

4 THE PERSONHOOD OF CORPORATIONS

The central difficulty in the assignments of original autonomy rights to corporations lies in the fact that such rights are essentially the privilege of natural persons, and corporations are not in themselves natural persons. Or at least they

---

[72] S.A. 1983, c. S-27.1.

are seemingly not natural persons. They are certainly legal persons—that is, at law, in circumstances where they do function as legal actors and patients, with the same range of rights, liberties, powers, immunities, and their jural correlatives as natural persons, the law treats them analytically in the same way as it treats natural persons.[73] But their being legal persons is of no significance for the present discussion. Our concern here is with the possible justification in political morality for the fact that in the jurisdictions under review courts have awarded constitutional protection to commercial expression by corporations. Corporations are legal persons with a legal right to commercial expression given constitutional protection. Should they be, as a matter of political morality?

The so-called 'legal fiction' theory of the corporation stops at this point in the search for justification. According to the theory, a corporation is, in Marshall CJ's famous words, 'an artificial being, invisible, intangible, and existing only in contemplation of law'.[74] This artificiality was held by Marshall CJ in this case, and by many others for some time afterwards, as a reason for strictly limiting the legal rights of the corporation. In the late nineteenth century, however, corporations had become much larger, and a more powerful and important economic presence.[75] They still faced regulation, but on the *a posteriori* ground of unacceptable consequences of their activities, rather than the *a priori* ground of corporate status. The thought that corporate status in itself justified regulation transmuted from the legal fiction theory into what became known as the 'regulatory theory'.[76] In the present day, however, the most economically prominent corporations are huge multi-national conglomerates, while incorporation itself has become open to anyone merely by filing a form available from stationers and paying a fee at the appropriate government office. The empirical basis for the regulatory theory has lost all plausibility: 'the fact that corporations are brought into existence by a perfunctory state filing does not justify a "state creation" view any more than does the role of obtaining a birth certificate indicate state creation of a child'.[77] This is not to say that the conclusion of the theory is false, but only that it cannot be held to follow merely from the status of the corporation as corporation. Corporate status in facts poses, rather than settles, the question of when and where government regulation of corporate activity is justified.

Corporations clearly bear some relation to natural persons, in that natural persons create them, invest in them, manage them, work for them, are harmed and benefited by them, analyse them, etc. It is therefore not surprising

---

[73] It may not treat them the same way practically; but major issues about social equity in access to justice lie well beyond the scope of this book.

[74] *Dartmouth College v Woodward* 17 US (4 Wheat) 518 (1819), at 636.

[75] Gregory A. Mark, 'The Personification of the Corporation in American Law', *University of Chicago Law Review* 54 (1987): 1441–55.

[76] See Henry N. Butler and Larry E. Ribstein, *The Corporation and the Constitution* (Washington, DC: AEI Press, 1995), 1 ff. The theory has also been called the 'concession theory' by Dan-Cohen; Meir Dan-Cohen, *Rights, Persons and Organizations: A Legal Theory for Bureaucratic Society* (Berkeley and Los Angeles, Cal.: University of California Press, 1986), 200.

[77] Butler and Ribstein, *Corporation and Constitution*, 20.

that theorists have argued that corporations bear to natural persons the kind of relationship which implies that corporations should be regarded by society and the law as having in principle exactly the same range of rights as natural persons, including rights classifiable as original autonomy rights. Several strategies have been employed to defend such a claim, and I will review them here. I shall argue shortly that none is successful. But first it is important to be clear about the logic of such claims in relation to the ontology of collective entities such as corporations.

The most plausible way of attributing personhood to a corporation in virtue of its having persons as constitutive elements intuitively seems to be a reductionist one—a corporation is reducible without remainder to the individual persons out of which it is constituted. But a moment's reflection will show that such a reductionist view cannot be correct. Minimally, a conglomeration[78] of persons can be no more than a 'mereological sum'.[79] The mereological sum of a set of entities is that entity which overlaps with every part of every entity in the set and with nothing else. The gold that is constituted simply out of a pile of gold bricks is a mereological sum. A conglomeration of persons can constitute simply a mereological sum of those persons: all the persons alive in Kelowna, British Columbia, at 1.45pm on 9 August 2002 whose surnames begin with S constitute a mereological sum. Corporations are a long way from being mere mereological sums of persons.

Nor are corporations merely what Copp calls 'aggregates' of persons.[80] Aggregates—all the people on Gyro Beach in Kelowna on the afternoon of 9 August 2002[81]—persist over time and change membership. This aggregate need not have a common or even a similar purpose (some may be there to sell ice-cream, some to watch for swimmers in difficulty; not all need be holidaying in the sunshine), though aggregates may (a group of political protestors). Although, as Copp rightly emphasizes,[82] we are dealing with differences of degree and not of kind, organizations such as the business corporation differ from aggregates (let alone from mereological sums) in being more coherently structured and more or less formally structured. All these elements—persistence over time, possible lack of common or even similar purpose, some amount of formal and coherent structure—combine to defeat any straightforward reduction of a corporation to its constitutive persons. We need an account of the structural unity of a corporation that embodies the relation of the corporation to its constituent persons in a way that does justice to the collective and inde-

---

[78] This term is intended to be totally non-theoretical and neutral. Other terms which might denote the same kind of entity do have theoretical commitments, as will emerge.

[79] See David Copp, 'What Collectives Are: Agency, Individualism and Legal Theory', *Dialogue* 23 (1984): 252. The notion goes back to Henry S. Leonard and Nelson Goodman, 'The Calculus of Individuals and Its Uses', *Journal of Symbolic Logic* 5 (1940): 45–55, at 47.

[80] Copp, 'What Collectives Are', 252–4.

[81] Regretfully, being a member of the first conglomeration mentioned is not a sufficient condition for membership of the second.

[82] Copp, 'What Collectives Are', 257.

pendent character of the corporation while preserving the individual natural personhood of the constituents and the theoretical advantages flowing therefrom. This will turn out to be a need impossible to fulfil.

1 French's CID Theory

Among philosophers, at least, the most well-known theory to justify attributing personhood to corporations based on their relation to natural persons as their constituents is that defended by Peter French. French claims that 'corporations can be full-fledged moral persons and have whatever privileges, rights, and duties as are, in the normal course of affairs, accorded to moral persons'.[83] French relies on arguing that corporations are genuinely agents, with moral personhood flowing from this agency. In order to demonstrate this agency, French relies on what he calls a corporation's internal decision structure, or CID for short. CID structures, he says (at 212) have 'an organizational or responsibility flow chart that delineates stations and levels within the corporate power structure, and a corporate decision recognition rule'. 'When operative and properly activated, the CID Structure accomplishes a subordination and synthesis of the intentions and acts of various biological persons into a corporate decision' (ibid.). 'The CID Structure licenses the descriptive transformation of events, seen under another aspect as the acts of biological persons . . . , into corporate acts, by exposing the corporate character of those events' (ibid.).

Elsewhere, in work done in collaboration with Guangwei Ouyang, I have criticized (and even, we think, refuted) French's argument.[84] I offer a summary of our argument here. The root difficulty with French's theory of corporate moral personhood lies in the form of agency that he attributes to corporations, namely, what he calls 'Davidsonian agency' (at 211: call it 'D-agency' for short).[85] On this notion, a person is an agent of an event if, and only if, there is a description of what he did that makes true a sentence that says he did it intentionally. Such an account may also be called a semantic account of agency as a reflection of its emphasis on the truth conditions of sentences. French's story about CID structures may then be understood as an account of the semantics of corporate agency; it provides a way of describing happenings within a corporation that make it true that the corporation did things intentionally. Just so far, there is nothing wrong with French's line of thought. The story about CID structures *does* provide a way of making true sentences that say that a corporation did something intentionally. In such a guise its competitors are other theories of collective action as applied to corporations. In fact, in the latter part of the

---

[83] Peter A. French, 'The Corporation as a Moral Person', *American Philosophical Quarterly* 16 (1979): 207.

[84] Guangwei Ouyang and Roger A. Shiner, 'Organizations and Agency', *Legal Theory* 1 (1995): 283–310.

[85] Donald Davidson, 'Agency', in Donald Davidson, *Essays on Actions and Events* (New York: Oxford University Press, 1980), 43–61.

article mentioned, Ouyang and I spend some time suggesting our own semantic account of corporate agency.[86] The burden of our case against French is that D-agency is not a robust enough notion of agency to support by itself attributions of moral personhood.

As Davidson himself acknowledges, D-agency is a weak notion of agency.[87] That is, deployment of it yields as genuine cases of agency a much wider range of cases than the paradigm of intentional action as illustrated by cases like case 1 below.[88] Consider the following three examples (they are based on Davidson's original ones):[89]

1. Don intended to spill coffee and he did just that.
2. Don spilled the coffee without knowing that it was a cup of coffee. He thought it was a cup of tea.
3. Don's hand was jiggled by someone, and he (Don) spilled the coffee.

Case 1 is an unproblematic case of agency, and equally unproblematically in case 3 Don is not the agent of the coffee being spilt. D-agency is weak enough to permit Don to be the agent of spilling the coffee in Case 2. Clearly, though, it is too weak to be a sufficient condition of moral personhood, meaning by that the kind of 'person' that natural persons undoubtedly are. The fact that D-agency can very plausibly be attributed to corporations of course makes it an attractive candidate for a theory of corporate agency. The plausibility arises, though, precisely from the fact that D-agency is a form of agency without metaphysical presuppositions. But if it is, then it is powerless as a device to justify attributing to corporations a quality such as moral personhood that has metaphysical presuppositions. It does not follow from the fact that, in the examples, Don is a moral person and in Case 2 has D-agency that D-agency implies moral personhood.

2 Partnerships and Contracts

There are two other closely connected theories of the corporation to be considered, theories which have emerged from economic and legal theory rather than from the philosopher's abstract concerns with personhood. These are the theory of the corporation as a kind of partnership and the theory of the corporation as a nexus of contracts. These theories all the same will turn out to have underlying philosophical commitments open to criticism. I will consider them in turn.

The partnership theory does not make the false claim that a corporation is literally a legal partnership. Rather, it claims that it should be considered no different from a partnership for the purposes of assessing its rights and liberties, immunities and powers. The value of the partnership analogy is clear. Imagine two persons each practising independently as chartered accountants. They

---

[86] Ouyang and Shiner, 'Organizations and Agency', 299–310.   [87] Davidson, 'Agency', 47.
[88] The concept in criminal law of 'basic' or 'general', as opposed to 'specific', intent is similarly a weak notion.
[89] Davidson, 'Agency', 45.

become friends, and decide that there would be savings and benefits of various kinds if they combined their operations into one. So they create a partnership. So far, so good. Whether the partners when operating singly were operating as sole proprietors or as incorporated professionals, arguably little or nothing has changed as far as their individual rights are concerned except for any changes voluntarily made as part of the partnership agreement. The argument then, as offered by Robert Hessen,[90] is that by some inductive procedure the preservation of individual rights that occurs with the move from one person to a partnership of two is maintained as more and more persons are added, up to and including the complexities of the modern corporation.

Hessen's argument is important, and tempting to many people.[91] If sound, it would certainly underwrite the idea that a corporation possesses all the original autonomy rights of the individuals of which it is seemingly constituted. I say 'seemingly', because I shall argue shortly that it is easy to represent mistakenly the relation between the corporation and the multiplicity of natural persons who have roles in and relationships with that corporation. I shall show, however, that Hessen's inductive argument is not sound.

In his story about the hypothetical development of a firm from a two-person partnership to a large corporation, Hessen acknowledges full well that differentiation of function appears—that formal separation between investor-owner and management that is the prime mark of a corporation as opposed to a partnership. He argues, however, that such a transformation comes about by voluntary contractual agreements between individual rights-holders; these agreements are of precisely the same kind conceptually as those which led to the creation of the first two-person partnership, and the transition to a many-person partnership with agency powers restricted to a minority of partners. He considers also the case of a limited partnership, which he refers to as the 'the genetic link between a partnership and a corporation, because it establishes a new status—the investor who plays no role in management'.[92] Limited partnerships and corporations both are required to file their creations with the government. Hessen explains this apparent concession to the state-creature theory by treating the filing as evidence of an implied contract between shareholders and creditors concerning the way that the partnership or corporation's debts will be handled.

Mark notes that the partnership theory appeared in the 1880s as a response to the fiction theory.[93] The force of the theory is clear. If a corporation is essentially a partnership writ large, then it is hard to conceive of it as a creature of the state as opposed to a creature of the individuals who joined forces to form it. But Mark also refers to the partnership theory as a 'radical disaggregation' of the

[90] Robert Hessen, *In Defense of the Corporation* (Stanford, Cal.: Hoover Institute Press, 1979), 43–5.

[91] Cf. Martin Redish, *Money Talks: Speech, Economic Power, and the Values of Democracy* (New York: New York University Press, 2001), 78–9.

[92] Hessen, *In Defense*, 44.   [93] Mark, 'Personification of the Corporation', 1457–8.

corporation,[94] and it is not hard to see why. Take my accountants, Leversedge Hepburn of Edmonton. It is a partnership of two people, Daniel Leversedge and Suzanne Hepburn. But when I first became their client, the firm was Rusnell Leversedge, a partnership of Carl Rusnell and Daniel Leversedge; Suzanne Hepburn first came into the firm not as a partner. But Carl retired and Suzanne became a partner. The firm, of course, is not just the partners; they are supported by a staff of secretaries and accounting technicians. Moreover, a couple of months ago the firm became absorbed into a larger firm, and no longer exists as Leversedge Hepburn but only as part of Peterson Walker of Edmonton. Such a series of events is the norm in the vast majority of business corporations. All the same, such happenings make quite implausible the partnership theory. A partnership is not simply a mereological sum, in the sense elucidated above of the individuals in the partnership. Partnership is a legal status, with legal consequences; it is not simply a continuing exchange of gratuitous promises. Partnerships thus do not eliminate the state entirely. They presuppose a network of facilitating laws, in H.L.A. Hart's sense. 'Such laws', Hart writes, 'do not impose duties or obligations. Instead, they provide individuals with *facilities* for realizing their wishes, by conferring legal powers upon them to create, by certain specified procedures and subject to certain conditions, structures of rights and duties within the coercive framework of the law.'[95]

Once the complexities of a large modern corporation are reached, it becomes absurd to suggest that the internal relations between the parts can be modelled on those of the creation of a two-person partnership. The absurdity is as much empirical as anything—just look at General Motors: does it look like a partnership of individual right-holders each of whom has consented, whether explicitly or implicitly, even to those aspects of the life of the corporation which concern such individuals directly, let alone to every aspect? Consider the so-called stakeholder theory of the corporation. The theory regards as essential to the corporation any group with a material enough relationship to the corporation to affect or be affected by the corporation's objectives;[96] employees, customers, competitors, governments and non-governmental organizations, suppliers, media, and local communities—even the environment[97]—might all qualify as stakeholders, in addition to shareholders. My point is not the correctness of stakeholder theory as an analytical tool. It is rather to reveal the essential social embeddedness of a modern corporation, which embeddedness makes it implausible on the face to think of the corporation as a partnership writ large. It is true that stakeholder theory as practised is primarily used as a basis for attributing

---

[94] Mark, 'Personification of the Corporation', 1457.

[95] H.L.A. Hart, *The Concept of Law* (2nd edn., by Penelope A. Bulloch and Joseph Raz, Oxford: Clarendon Press, 1994), 29–30.

[96] R. Edward Freeman, *Strategic Management: A Stakeholder Approach* (Boston, Mass.: Pitman Publishing, 1984), 24–6.

[97] R. Edward Freeman, Jessica Pierce, and Richard Dodd, *Environmentalism and the New Logic of Business: How Firms Can Be Profitable and Leave Our Children a Living Planet* (New York: Oxford University Press, 2000), 54–5.

to corporations a politico-moral obligation to give weight to the needs and interests of parties other than shareholders and management. Partnership theory is just as much used as a basis for attributing to corporations a politico-moral obligation to give weight to the needs and interests of only shareholders and management.[98] The proprieties of corporate social responsibility, however, cannot be considered here.

This social embeddedness of corporations, and in particular the embeddedness in a network of facilitating legal rules, has its conceptually important aspect. Hessen's defence of the partnership theory evinces much confusion on this point. He claims that:

Every organization, regardless of its legal form or features, consists only of individuals. A group or an association is only a concept, a mental construct, used to classify different types of relationships between individuals. Whether the concept is a marriage, a partnership, . . . or a corporation, one fact remains constant: the concept denotes the relationship between individuals and has no referent apart from it. . . . If a census-taker were to enumerate three individuals—two real (husband and wife) and one fictitious legal entity (the couple or the marriage)—the error would be obvious. Yet the same error goes unrecognized when the subject is corporations. The term corporation actually means a group of individuals who engage in a particular type of contractual relationship with each other. Designating their relationship as a corporation is a 'mere labour-saving device'.[99]

It is true that a marriage is not a third entity in addition to the husband and wife. It is also true that a marriage 'consists of' (in the vast majority of cases!) two people standing in certain relationships with each other. But it is not true that the term marriage merely 'classifies' these relationships, or that there is nothing to the meaning of the term beyond the fact that it denotes (which it does) a certain relationship. That relationship cannot be understood to be what it is without understanding the embeddedness of the marriage relationship in a network of facilitating laws which give it status. That these laws may have their origins in statute, the common law, or sheer human custom does not affect the truth of my claim. The same applies to the term corporation. Recall here the late Gilbert Ryle's notorious metaphysically-challenged tourist in Oxford, who claimed he could see the college buildings, the libraries, the playing-fields, the museums, the scientific departments, and administrative offices, but could not see the University. The university, Ryle said, is not another collateral institution, but involves the way in which all that the tourist has seen is organized.[100]

---

[98] Cf. Hessen, *In Defense*, 42. David Millon has recently suggested that the whole debate over corporate personhood is driven by these politico-moral considerations: see David Millon, 'The Ambiguous Significance of Corporate Personhood', *Stanford Agora: An On-Line Journal of Legal Perspectives* 2, no. 1 (2001): 39–58. My discussion in this section clearly presumes that, while Millon may be correct about motivation, he need not be about logic.

[99] Hessen, *In Defense*, 41–2. The emphasis is Hessen's, and he is quoting from F.W. Maitland, 'Introduction', in Otto van Gierke, *Political Theories of the Middle Ages* (Cambridge: Cambridge University Press, 1900), xxiv.

[100] Gilbert Ryle, *The Concept of Mind* (London: Hutchinson, 1949), 17–18.

Ryle labelled the tourist's mistake a 'category mistake'—a university is simply not the kind of thing that exists as an item to be seen or as a conglomeration of denoted buildings. A university is essentially embedded in a social context, as is a marriage, as is a corporation, and, as in the case of a marriage and a corporation, no small part of that context is legal.

Hessen claims that 'the rights of any organization or association are the rights it derives from the individuals who create and sustain it' (at 41). On the face of it, this claim is simply false, at least as applied to any modern corporation, whether small and numbered or huge and multi-national. Rights are protected normative positions within some background normative scheme; legal rights presuppose a legal system as the relevant normative scheme. Even if one is thinking, as Hessen likely is, of pure natural rights, still a normative scheme is presumed which subtends the protected positions. If one wanted to be charitable to the 'legal fiction' theory, one could even find fault with Hessen's denigration of the theory as a multiplier of unneeded entities. For the 'fiction' part of the theory surely evinces a realization that Hessen is right to deny that there is any extra entity that may be seen and denoted. The 'legal' part may be seen as an appropriate acknowledgment of the role played in displaying the essence of a corporation by background facilitating laws.

Hessen does concede that there is as much reason to say that a partnership is state-created as to say that a corporation is (at 40). But he treats this as a *reductio ad absurdum* of the view of corporations as creatures of the state. He has a point. Those who form a formal partnership are taking advantage of state-created facilitating laws to do so, and one may think of those who form a corporation similarly. But the lesson of the parallel is not the one Hessen draws, that in both partnerships and corporations the partnership or corporation has all and only those rights which the individuals in it had before they voluntarily created it. Rather, the lesson is that the rights of the partnership as much as the rights of the corporation depend on a prior legal or quasi-legal scheme (whether a statutory, judicial-customary, or person-customary scheme) to subtend those rights as protected normative positions.

Here is a further corollary of the position I am defending. Hessen notes that every partner is presumed to possess the powers and incur the obligations of a sole proprietor, and that in fact the early name for partnership was co-proprietorship (at 37). Sole proprietorship, in fact, is an embedded status as much as partnership or corporate status. Adam and Eve were not sole proprietors of the Garden of Eden for more theoretically interesting reasons than that God had the power to throw them out.[101] I am myself, as a matter of fact, the sole proprietor of a small publishing business. Nonetheless, the business has legal powers that I, as simply the individual Roger Shiner considered independ-

---

[101] For some discussion of the relevance to legal theory of such pristine conditions see Roger A. Shiner, *Norm and Nature: The Movements of Legal Thought*, Clarendon Law Series (Oxford: Clarendon Press, 1992), 311–21.

ently of this sole proprietorship, do not have—to deduct certain legitimate business expenses, for example, prior to the determination of taxable income.[102] The publishing business does not have all and only those rights that I as the individual who created it have; it has all and only those rights that the legal system gives it. Courts seem to have well recognized this in the context of freedom of expression as a legal right. The formal title of the important Canadian legal case of *Ford* (see Chapter 4.3 above) is '*Attorney-General of Quebec v La Chaussure Brown's Inc et al*'.[103] Among the '*al*', and after whom the case is regularly indexed, is Valerie Ford, sole proprietor of Les Lainages du Petit Mouton Enr. The other respondent businesses are corporations. The Court treats all respondents absolutely equally. There is not even the slightest whiff of a suggestion that Valerie Ford's wool shop has different rights from the other businesses because they are corporations and it is a sole proprietorship. Likewise, it seems from the U.S. Supreme Court case report in *PruneYard*[104] that, in one of the classic shopping-centre leafleting cases in the U.S., the PruneYard shopping centre is a sole proprietorship of one Fred Sahadi. The Court clearly rejects any attempt to construe the shopping centre as having First Amendment rights of expression comparable to, and so capable of being balanced against, the freedom of expression possessed by the persons who wished to distribute leaflets in the shopping centre. Both Courts are correct in this approach. Neither corporations nor partnerships nor sole proprietorships are natural persons, even though they may in whole or in part, and in some sense of the term, 'consist of' natural persons. They do not, because they cannot, have the original autonomy rights of natural persons.

The pattern before the European Court of Human Rights is somewhat different. In cases where seemingly genuine expressive rights are at issue in an apparently commercial context, the Court has resolved the matter by counting the expression as more political than commercial, rather than by denying the right to a corporate entity, albeit one comprised by a person in business for himself. In *Barthold*,[105] an individual veterinarian deploring the availability of any clinic on an emergency basis except his own was held to be contributing to a public debate. *Jakubowski*,[106] an individual journalist, published criticism of his former employer and announced his availability for employment; again this expression was said not to be primarily 'commercial'. Hertel, a research scientist who published an article critical of the safety record of household appliances,[107] and

---

[102] Edwin Baker even suggests this distinction could be used to institutionalize the difference between personal and corporate speech: C. Edwin Baker, 'Realizing Self-Realization: Corporate Political Expenditures and Redish's "The Value of Free Speech"', *University of Pennsylvania Law Review* 130 (1982): 654–5.

[103] *Attorney-General of Quebec v La Chaussure Brown's Inc et al* [Indexed as Ford v Quebec (Attorney-General)] (1988) 54 DLR (4th) 577; see 583–4.

[104] *PruneYard Shopping Center v Robins* 447 US 74 (1980), at 77.

[105] *Barthold v Germany* Ser A 90 (1985) (ECtHR).

[106] *Jacubowski v Germany* Ser A 291–A (1994) (ECtHR).

[107] *Hertel v Switzerland* (59/1997/843/1049) (1998) (ECtHR).

Stambuk, an ophthalmologist describing in a newspaper interview a surgical technique he pioneered,[108] were both held to be offering legitimate non-commercial expression. These cases are discussed in more detail in Chapter 5 above. It could truly be said that even so the Court does not face the issue of whether corporations, even of one person, can be properly entitled to freedom of political expression, but that issue is not up for discussion in this book.

Let me give the second-last word in this section to Hessen. He puts the challenge to his opponent thus: when precisely did the enterprise cease to be an aggregate of individuals who possess rights and become transformed into an entity which has no rights? (at 45) I am not here claiming that corporations possess no rights, but only that they do not possess original autonomy rights as do persons. I can point to such a moment—when the partnership was first created. Even the two-person partnership already differs from a gratuitous mutual agreement between me and my neighbour to water each other's plants while one is on vacation. It has a structure and a context, and it has the enabling support of a framework of facilitating laws. In fact, as I have argued, even the tacit assumption that a sole proprietorship is simply a bundle of natural rights is a mistake. Partnership theory cannot make a corporation into a bearer of original autonomy rights.

No more can the *contract theory*, the theory that represents a corporation as a 'nexus of contracts' among participants in the corporation. The corporation is seen as 'the market writ small, a web of ongoing contracts (explicit or implicit) between various real persons'.[109] The origins of the contract theory are in the discipline of economics. The firm is construed as a device for the efficient handling of transaction costs and agency costs. Maximizing individuals contract to form firms in order to minimize transaction and agency costs that they would otherwise be faced with as individual actors in the market.

There is no doubt that as a way for economists to model corporate activity in the market, and for legal theorists to elucidate the body of corporate law, the contractual theory of the corporation has proved a powerful tool. But success as an economic model does not entail success as a descriptive model. As much as the partnership theory, the contractual theory 'de-reifies'[110] the corporation. Allen rightly characterizes it as a 'nominalist' theory of the corporation;[111] there are many realities of a corporation's relations, both relations between groups internal to the corporation and relations with outsiders, that the contractual theory cannot adequately explain. Allen mentions those between long-term stockholders and management receiving excessive compensation or management proposing a 'poison pill', and employees working diligently to meet production goals (ibid.).

---

[108] *Stambuk v Germany* (37928/97) (2002) (ECtHR).

[109] William T. Allen, 'Contracts and Communities in Corporation Law', *Washington & Lee Law Review* 50 (1993): 1400. See also Henry N. Butler, 'The Contractual Theory of the Corporation', *George Mason University Law Review* 11 (1989): 99–123; Butler and Ribstein, *Corporation and Constitution*, 27.

[110] Millon, 'Ambiguous Significance', 53.   [111] Allen, 'Contracts and Communities', 1401.

There is in fact a deep internal tension with both the partnership theory and the contractual theory of the corporation. Whether one thinks of the corporation as a partnership writ large, or as the market writ small, both theoretical tendencies are fundamentally opposed to what it is that drives theorists to think of corporations as persons, even though they are supposed to be arguments to save the corporation as a legitimate bearer of original autonomy rights. Let us follow the lead again of Allen's 'realist' approach to corporations.[112] Actual bargains, explicit or implicit, provide an incomplete account of the social order found in organizations. The idioms of institutional culture and values, institutional goals, institutional learning, capacity to plan and co-ordinate, possession and execution of intentions, and, in the context of the commercial expression doctrine, the capacity to speak or express—all of these constitute natural ways of speaking about corporations. All of them involve some assimilation of the corporation to the individual natural person. Such social-psychological processes are simply not visible to the 'nexus of contracts' theory, except as dogmatic speculations. The disaggregating, or de-reifying, force of the partnership and contractual theories drives thought away from the unity of the corporation. The drive to see a corporation as itself a person is centrifugal; the drive to see it as a partnership or a nexus of contracts is centripetal. What inclines one to see a corporation as in itself a rights-holder is exactly opposed to these two latter attempts to justify the corporation as rights-holder by virtue of its reducibility to constituent individuals.

5 CONCLUSION

The topic of this chapter has been the plausibility of construing corporations as possessors of what I have called original autonomy rights—that is, rights held in virtue of the possession of autonomy. I spent some time clarifying the notion of autonomy and its role in elucidating freedom of expression as a value. I argued that the values associated with autonomy are values for natural persons; it makes little sense to see them as values for corporations. I showed that by and large courts have explicitly or implicitly acknowledged this discrepancy, with the possible exception of the recent *US West* case (see this Chapter 9.3 above). The acknowledgment is especially strong in the case of constitutionally protected original autonomy rights, where courts have been very reluctant to grant such rights to corporations, and in fact do so only when protection of some autonomy right of natural persons is the ultimate goal. I then turned to consider various arguments for treating corporations as appropriately related to natural persons, so that they may in themselves be cast as bearers of original autonomy rights. I argued that all these attempts fail.

[112] Ibid., 1401–2.

It is important to recall, however, that one avenue was left unexplored. The discussion of the Canadian case of *Big M Drug Mart* forms a model for arguments according to which corporations justifiably are granted constitutional protection for expressive activities on instrumental grounds—on the ground, that is to say, that values important to individuals will be fostered. Such constitutional rights as ascribed to corporations will be derived rights, not original rights. In fact, many of the defences of the commercial expression doctrine deemed most plausible have this derivative character. No assessment of the commercial expression doctrine can be complete without a thorough exploration of the issues raised by the attribution to corporations of a derivative autonomy right to freedom of expression.

It is to that task that I now turn in Chapters 10–12. However, one topic remains to be mentioned in this chapter, for completeness. In the taxonomy of rights in Chapter 7 above, I distinguished between autonomy rights and utility rights—rights possessed for reasons of autonomy and rights possessed for reasons of utility. I also distinguished original rights and derived rights. In this chapter, I have been discussing freedom of expression as an original autonomy right of corporations, and I have raised a number of objections to any such idea. Formal symmetry seems to require that the next topic addressed be the corporation as potential possessor of original utility rights. Inspection of the Table of Contents, however, will have revealed scant reference to such an idea. I want to end this chapter with a brief explanation of this omission, before turning to the idea of corporate derived rights.

The omission arises because the distinction between original utility right and derived utility right cannot have the significance of the distinction between original autonomy right and derived autonomy right. A utility right is a protected normative position that an entity has, according to some scheme of values, just in case its being so protected maximizes utility.[113] (By using 'maximize', I do not mean to settle the debate among versions of contemporary utilitarianism as to the correct function over utility—maximizing or satisficing—or over whether the concern should be with aggregate or average utility. The points made here are cogent, or not, independently of the outcome of those debates.) If an isomorphism between the two named original rights holds, then one might think that only persons have original utility rights. The individual's happiness, seemingly, is what gives that individual an original utility right, and organizations cannot be 'happy' in that sense. Meir Dan-Cohen argues, however, that this individualism is misleading. In classical maximizing utilitarianism, a given person's increased happiness is not valuable as such, but valuable because of its contribution to overall social welfare. It is a familiar criticism of classical maximizing utilitarianism that it 'does not take seriously the distinction between persons'.[114] In that case, the original utility rights themselves of a person have a

---

[113] L.W. Sumner, *The Moral Foundation of Rights* (Oxford: Clarendon Press, 1987), passim.
[114] John Rawls, *A Theory of Justice* (Cambridge, Mass.: Harvard University Press, 1971), 27.

derivative quality to them. The status therefore of organizations within the paradigm of utility 'is not essentially different from that of individuals'.[115] In short, for Dan-Cohen, 'there is nothing in the paradigm of utility that would necessarily, as a matter of principle, limit the range of rights given to organizations and prevent the law from assigning to them utility rights that are coextensive with, or indeed even broader than, those given to individuals'.[116]

The corollary of this disappearance of a salient distinction between persons and corporations is that the distinction between original and derived utility rights is unimportant. Let me explain. Autonomy to a large extent[117] is conceived of as having value in itself, not instrumentally. The distinction between original autonomy rights and derived autonomy rights is normatively significant, because original autonomy rights reflect this intrinsic value in the justification for the protected normative status they imply. That is not so for derived autonomy rights. The justification for the protected normative status they imply is in terms of instrumental, not intrinsic, value. Moreover, for reasons given at the beginning of this chapter, only natural persons can be the locus of the value of autonomy, and so only natural persons can be the possessors of original autonomy rights. So the distinction between the two kinds of autonomy right has a point to it, and a structure. Under utilitarianism, on the other hand, the status of both persons and corporations is the same—*loci* of whatever qualities are necessary to be instrumental to utility. The distinction between original and derived utility right could at best be a function of position in an instrumental chain leading to utility. But the possession or not of any given position in any given chain will be contingent. Such contingencies may be of great practical importance, but cannot be of systematic importance.

It is of course extremely important to consider proposed justifications for the commercial expression doctrine that are based on assigning to corporations what amount to utility rights. The 'free flow of commercial information' is a goal with social utility, and courts and commentators have relied upon justifications of freedom of commercial expression appealing to this utility heavily. That specific task, though, is deferred to Chapter 13 below.

---

[115] Dan-Cohen, *Rights, Persons and Organizations*, 81.   [116] Ibid., 82.
[117] See here the discussion in this Chapter 9.1 above.

10

Hearers' Rights

The purpose of this and the next two chapters is to explore proposed justifications for the commercial expression doctrine based on the idea that the corporation whose expression is regulated or restricted has a derived autonomy right of some kind to constitutional protection for its commercial expression or speech. This derived right will be a protected normative position that is justified by a valid derivation from someone else's original autonomy right. The preceding formulation is abstract, but even so sets one of the constraints that the commercial expression doctrine must meet. The concrete questions that need answering are these. First, is there a satisfactory account available of the derivation relation? In general, can we make sense of the idea of a hearers' right to receive information? Are appropriate models for that right available? Does the position of the consumer as potential recipient of commercial expression fit these models? This group of questions I will consider in the present chapter. Secondly, is there an appropriate holder available of the original autonomy right? Is the value of autonomy indeed sufficiently promoted in the case of the hearer of commercial expression? I will consider these questions in Chapter 11. Finally, is there any justification for the claim that regulation of commercial expression necessarily involves an unacceptable—unacceptable because autonomy-restricting—form of paternalism? I will consider this question in Chapter 12. I will show by the end of that chapter that the key questions have not been answered in a way sufficient to justify the commercial expression doctrine, if and in so far as it has to rely on a derived autonomy right to constitutional protection for commercial expression or speech. The argument of these chapters is important, because, as I showed in Chapter 6, many of the most frequently adduced arguments for the commercial expression doctrine do appeal to hearers' autonomy as the ground for freedom of commercial expression. Deconstructing these arguments is an essential part of deconstructing the commercial expression doctrine.

1 THE DERIVATION OF AUTONOMY RIGHTS

Consider again the claim of the Supreme Court of Canada in *Ford*[1] that that commercial expression plays a significant role in enabling individuals to make informed economic choices, an important aspect of individual self-fulfilment

---

[1] *Attorney-General of Quebec v La Chaussure Brown's Inc et al* [Indexed as Ford v Quebec (Attorney-General)] (1988) 54 DLR (4th) 577, at 618.

and personal autonomy. The litigant whose expression is rendered free by the grant to it of constitutional protection is the corporation doing the expressing, typically advertising. How does a corporation, attribution of autonomy to which makes no sense, become the beneficiary of constitutional protection that is based on reasons of autonomy? The *Ford* claim shows the train of thought. The individual whose autonomy provides the reason for constitutional protection is the consumer who hears or sees the corporate expression—the advertisement—in question. Crudely: I see an advertisement for a new brand of beer. I try it, and it's great. There's more pleasure in my life; I feel better about myself, and my life gets more on track. Or I see an advertisement for a new kind of retirement investment instrument, and move my savings over. The investment does really well. I have many more choices now available for me as to when to retire than I did before. My autonomy is increased; I am less dependent on rules laid down by my employer. Or (closer to the facts of *Virginia Board*) I am a diabetic, say, dependent on regular injections of insulin and associated supplies. Once pharmacies can advertise the prices of prescription drugs, I can readily find out where the cheapest drugs and supplies are to be found, so that this necessary expense takes up less of my disposable income. I have more choices now on how to spend my time and my money. My autonomy is improved.

The question here is not, which of two worlds otherwise equal in all respects is the better—the one in which I have more autonomy or the one in which I have less autonomy? The answer to that question is obvious. The question is, how does my right to maximal autonomy, all things being equal, turn into a constitutionally protected normative position for a piece of corporate advertising? One answer is the instrumental one—because the advertising is the cause of my improved autonomy as its effect. That answer in itself is much too weak. For not everything that improves autonomy merits constitutional protection; a high-tech mountain bike would improve my autonomy by giving me more recreational choices, but I have no constitutional right to a high-tech mountain bike. And not all commercial expression *in point of empirical fact* improves autonomy, not even all truthful commercial expression about legal products. Arguably, tobacco products make people tobacco addicts; junk and fast food makes people obese. Advertising for unapproved off-label uses of pharmaceutical drugs may lead to people taking drugs that actually damage or destroy their health. Consumers (in the so-called West, at least) already have all the autonomy they could need to choose a brand of toothpaste; the advertising of a new brand may evoke interest, but does not improve autonomy. In short, if improvements in my autonomy are to ground constitutional protection for commercial expression, several argumentative demands must be met. It has to be shown that the particular fashion in which my autonomy is improved is something to which I have a right; that this right is, or may be significantly fostered by, a freedom of expression right; and that somehow the way to protect this freedom of expression right is to grant constitutional protection to commercial expression.

The general form of a derived right is that B has some right based on a right of A. As Dan-Cohen puts it, 'in order for an organization to have a DAR [derived autonomy right], it must have the protection of some OAR [original autonomy right] as a goal, and the DAR must be thought conducive to the pursuit of that goal.'[2] In the case of freedom of expression, the thought is that free expression promotes the autonomy of the expresser.

The most obvious and familiar case of a derived autonomy right stems from the principal–agent relation. Agency is 'the fiduciary relation which results from the manifestation of consent by one person to another that the other shall act on his behalf and subject to his control, and consent by the other so to act.'[3] The agent is legally considered to represent the principal in a way that affects the principal's legal position. The agent, within the terms of the relevant agreement, has the same legal rights as the principal. It is clear that agency so understood is of no help in modelling the derivation of a corporate expresser's right to freedom of commercial expression from some original autonomy right of an individual. Agency depends on formal agreement to underwrite the derivation of powers, and there are no such agreements between individuals and corporate expressers.

There are some well understood paradigms for a DAR to freedom of expression based on the idea that A's freedom to express, and so autonomy, is promoted by granting a freedom of expression right to B. A journalists' association may invoke the right to freedom of expression of one of its members. The organization here plays a purely procedural role.[4] A university, or a university staff association, may have a DAR to academic freedom in the name of protecting the OAR to academic freedom of its staff.[5] There are decided cases in the area of freedom of expression that are like this. In civil rights era cases in the U.S., the National Association for the Advancement of Colored People (NAACP) won two important decisions, receiving protection under the First Amendment despite its corporate status. The Supreme Court had ruled in 1886 in *Santa Clara*[6] that corporations were 'persons' for purposes of the due process and equal protection clauses of the Fourteenth Amendment, but denied that corporations were 'citizens' for purposes of the privileges and immunities clause. The Court then ruled in 1938 in *Hague*[7] that, while an ordinance forbidding the distribution of printed matter and the holding of public meetings violated the rights of individual union members to freedom of speech and of association, the CIO, as a corporation, could claim no such rights. Nonetheless, in 1958, the Court

---

[2] Meir Dan-Cohen, *Rights, Persons and Organizations: A Legal Theory for Bureaucratic Society* (Berkeley and Los Angeles, Cal.: University of California Press, 1986), 74.

[3] U.S. Restatement, Second, Agency sec. 1.   [4] See Dan-Cohen, note 2 above, at 62.

[5] But caution must still be exercised: 'The multiplicity of organizational goals, the phenomenon of goal displacement, as well as organizational tendencies toward self-aggrandizement, all complicate the task of maintaining full correspondence between an organization's DAR and its underlying individual autonomy right' (Dan-Cohen, 77). I ignore these complications here.

[6] *Santa Clara County v Southern Pacific Railroad* 116 US 394 (1886).

[7] *Hague, Mayor, et al v Committee for Industrial Organization et al* 307 US 496 (1939).

ruled in *NAACP v Alabama*[8] that the NAACP had standing to assert the personal rights of its members under the Fourteenth Amendment to carry out lawful activities, and thus that it was constitutionally protected from having to hand over its membership lists. In 1963 in *NAACP v Button*,[9] the NAACP benefited from a ruling that 'although petitioner is a corporation, it may assert its right and that of its members and lawyers to associate for the purpose of assisting persons who seek legal redress for infringement of their constitutionally guaranteed rights'. This case was an important precedent in the Supreme Court's decision to protect solicitation by American Civil Liberties Union lawyer Edna Primus of clients who might have been illegally sterilized.[10]

Another plausible source of derived autonomy rights in the context of freedom of expression is cases concerning unions and picketing. Individual union members may express themselves in banners they carry, slogans and insults they shout, position statements they enunciate. But the union may do all these things too on their behalf, and on the face of it is just as much expressing an opinion. Canadian courts have held that union picketing can be expression within the coverage of section 2(b) of the *Charter*. The issue is complicated, in that in many cases the relevant law is common law governing relations between private parties. But in *Dolphin Delivery*[11] McIntyre J claimed as an *obiter dictum* that picketing would in theory be expression within the scope of section 2(b) of the Charter. In *Vancouver Courthouse*,[12] an injunction against picketing the courthouse summarily issues by the Chief Justice of B.C. was held to be government action enough to invoke the *Charter*, although the injunction was upheld after section 1 analysis. Full statutory basis for a restriction on picketing was not challenged until *KMart*[13] and the restriction there was invalidated. Most recently, in *Pepsi-Cola*,[14] the Supreme Court ruled that the common law in this area must be developed in accordance with *Charter* values, to give much weight to freedom of expression. The Court invalidated the restrictions on picketing.

Both of these kinds of cases turn on issues very different in substance from commercial expression—the political aspirations of African-Americans in the U.S., and the desire of workers to form protective associations. Commercial advertising is only contingently advertising to form an association; most cases are nothing of the kind, but the advertising of a product or service with a view to financial gain for the advertiser. One may stretch language and represent the

---

[8] *National Association for the Advancement of Colored People v Alabama ex rel Patterson, Attorney-General* 357 US 449 (1958).

[9] *National Association for the Advancement of Colored People v Button, Attorney-General of Virginia et al* 371 US 415 (1963).

[10] *In re Primus* 436 US 412 (1978), at 421–6; the disciplining of Ms Primus by the Supreme Court of South Carolina was overturned.

[11] *Retail, Wholesale and Department Store Union, Local 580 et al v Dolphin Delivery Ltd* (1986) 33 DLR (4th) 174.

[12] *British Columbia Government Employees Union v British Columbia* [1988] 2 SCR 214.

[13] *United Fabric and Clothing Workers, Local 1518 v KMart Canada Ltd* [1999] 2 SCR 1083.

[14] *Retail, Wholesale and Department Store Union, Local 558 et al v Pepsi-Cola Canada Beverages (West) Ltd* 2002 SCC 8.

advertisee who then purchases the product or service as 'forming an association' with the advertiser 'for their mutual benefit'. But the distance between the cases survives such a stretch.

A third sort of case where DARs are arguably involved is in relation to freedom of information. An individual may have the right to know what is being said about him or her in some repository of personal information, say, in an employment file, or in the database of a credit-reporting company. Citizens may also have some more diffuse 'right to know' concerning matters of political relevance; such a 'right to know' plays a strong rhetorical role in attempts by news media to break bans on reporting of litigation. It is at least plausible to suppose, first, that such rights are original autonomy rights, and, secondly, that such rights may transfer over to an investigative journalist, although the weaker any explicit principal/agent-type relation, the weaker the derived right. I shall consider in more detail shortly what sense can be made of a 'right to know' in the context of justifications for the commercial expression doctrine. I shall just note now that, again, we seem to be dealing with a different kind of issue. Reporting or broadcasting bans typically implicate freedom of the press, as a derived right possessed by the press notwithstanding its corporate and profit-making character, the right deriving from the role of the press in the promotion of democratic self-government. The charms and attractions of the latest DVD player that a consumer might be seeking to discover are not private and personal information like a job performance report or a credit rating. The typical corporate advertiser, in fact, usually wants to make product information available to consumers whether they wish to have it or not, as opposed to the government or the employer, who surrenders such information only because so required by law, and not always then.

The attractiveness of 'right to know' cases for the support of the commercial expression doctrine is easy to see. 'Right to know' cases involve the idea of a right to *receive* information, as hearer or listener. As Burt Neuborne has rightly noted, in commercial expression cases it seems to be that a speaker who in itself has no speaker's right to freedom of expression 'borrows' the right to hear possessed by a hearer.[15] We have seen in the decided cases that there is much emphasis on the supposed right of hearers to have the information suppressed by the impugned governmental regulation, and that this right to hear is a freedom of expression right. Neuborne talks of the corporate speaker 'borrowing' the hearer's freedom of expression right. 'Borrowing' is, of course, a metaphor, though a vivid and potentially accurate one. But appropriating what belongs to another is under certain circumstances not 'borrowing', but stealing. The appropriation has to be rightful or justified. In the case of the agency relation, there are clear safeguards to ensure that the transfer of legal power from principal to agent is consensual. While sharedness of associative purpose cannot be

---

[15] Burt Neuborne, 'The First Amendment and Government Regulation of Capital Markets', *Brooklyn Law Review* 55 (1989): 26.

parsed into an exact network of consensual agreements, still the element of voluntary association is strong. Considerations such as these cannot underwrite the metaphor of 'borrowing' in the commercial expression context. The metaphor of 'borrowing' highlights the relationship between advertiser and advertisee that needs to be explained, but it does not itself provide an explanation.

'Borrowing' carries connotations of legitimacy. We need to investigate what it is about the relationship between advertiser and advertisee that constitutes that relationship so as to justify the commercial expression doctrine, so as to justify the granting of constitutional protection to the expression *of the advertiser*. To begin with, we need to be satisfied that the advertisee—the hearer or listener—really has an original autonomy right to hear or listen, such that this right is available to be 'borrowed' under specifiable circumstances by the corporate advertiser. That the hearer or listener does have such a right is taken for granted by both the ivory tower and the bench in writing about commercial expression. I want now to spend some time examining the concept of hearers' or listeners' rights. I will show that in fact the idea of such rights construed as original autonomy rights is in fact of little avail to supporters of the commercial expression doctrine.

2 THE UNNECESSARY DUPLICATION PRINCIPLE

Traditionally, we think of the bearer of the right to freedom of expression or speech as the person who has something to express or say, and who is prevented from doing so by government action of some kind. The root idea of an expresser's constitutional right to freedom of expression is this: the legal system will acknowledge the claim of an expresser to be free from governmental restriction in expressing something. The root idea of a hearer's constitutional right to freedom of expression, then, is that the legal system will acknowledge the claim of a hearer to be free from governmental restriction in hearing something. As the commercial expression doctrine presents the matter, when the government prevents citizens from receiving information—information about drug prices or the hours of opening of a dentist's surgery, for example—the government impermissibly prevents citizens from hearing something that they have a right to hear. Citizens have a right to be told that a given pharmacy is selling drugs at a lower price than others in the neighbourhood, or that the local dentist's hours of opening are 8 am to 3 pm. The shop or the dentist wishes to provide this information, but they are prevented from doing so by government regulation, in these cases regulations forbidding professional advertising. The regulation is struck down, not on the ground that the shop or dentist have in themselves an expresser's freedom of expression right to give out the information, but on the ground that citizens have a *hearers'* freedom of expression right to hear or receive the information.

Speakers' rights have a long history. The foundational hero in the U.S. is John Paul Zenger, who published a weekly newspaper in New York in the 1730s aimed at arousing opposition to the new colonial governor William Cosby. He achieved an acquittal in the face of undoubted guilt under black-letter law by pleading a natural right to criticize government. Hearers' rights are a good deal more recent; they did not appear in the case law until the early 1960s.[16] As William Lee points out (ibid.), the U.S. Supreme Court has done little to articulate a formal basis for hearers' rights, and the Supreme Court of Canada is no different. I hope to show that this lack is not coincidental, as it is difficult to construct a plausible theory. There are several attractive intuitions that seem to show the need for a doctrine of hearers' rights, but the implications of these intuitions will turn out to be elusive and evanescent. It is never a simple task to show the shallowness of attraction, and so this discussion of hearers' rights will not be brief.

First, I shall argue that any robust doctrine of hearers' rights must be constrained by what I shall call the Unnecessary Duplication Principle. Hearers' rights will be robust enough to bear the weight that the commercial expression doctrine puts upon them only if the hearers' rights to which the commercial expression doctrine appeals fall outside the scope of this principle. Since I will argue eventually that no commercial expression cases do fall outside the scope of this principle, let me therefore explain, and try to motivate, the principle.

Let us assume for the sake of argument that there is available a sound normative theory of freedom of expression in general. I call this an 'assumption', not because I do not believe there is any such theory, but because it would be too big a project here to state and defend such a theory. Plausibly, this sound normative theory will not say that freedom of expression is absolute, but that, though restrictions on expression are mostly not justified, sometimes they are. The theory will specify the conditions when restrictions are justified and what it is for those conditions to be satisfied. Such a theory will include as a part a theory of expressers' rights, that is, of those occasions on which restrictions on expression or speech are not justified for reasons having to do with the effect of the restriction on the expresser or speaker, or the further and wider consequences of that effect.

The Unnecessary Duplication Principle says that hearers' rights are of no normative value if all they do is justify the invalidation of a restriction on freedom of expression, the invalidation of which would in any case be justified by expressers' rights. In short, the Unnecessary Duplication Principle says that hearers' rights cut no normative ice when they duplicate expressers' rights.

In the context of the commercial expression doctrine, the reason for the Unnecessary Duplication Principle is obvious. *Ex hypothesi*, the corporate expresser has in itself no expresser's rights. The corporate expresser has to 'borrow' a freedom of expression right from the hearer. For that 'borrowing' to be a possible ground for the commercial expression doctrine, hearers must possess

[16] William E. Lee, 'The Supreme Court and the Right to Receive Expression', *Supreme Court Review* 7 (1987): 303 ff.

their freedom of expression right in itself, and not as the obverse of a right fundamentally possessed by an expresser.

Strictly, my argument here requires only that the Unnecessary Duplication Principle apply in the context of the commercial expression doctrine. I am inclined to think that the Principle is of general applicability, though I shall not claim to demonstrate that here. One motivation for a broader application of the Unnecessary Duplication Principle, at least within legal systems, is that legal systems abhor unlimited extensions of liability,[17] and unwarranted extensions of standing to bring litigation. If an expresser already has valid standing to challenge a regulation, it is unnecessary duplication to allow also a hearer to bring exactly the same challenge.

It might be felt that the tort analogy is inappropriate for a constitutional right such as the guarantee of freedom of expression. Presumably, sound political morality requires the coverage of constitutional rights to be as wide as possible. That is why, in the Canadian *Charter*, for example, the sections defining the rights and freedoms begin with phrases like 'Everyone . . .', 'Anyone . . .', 'Every citizen . . .'. The intent behind the Unnecessary Duplication Principle, however, is not to impose a limitation of such a kind on the coverage of the constitutional guarantee of freedom of expression. The intent is simply to avoid unnecessary duplication. Here's an example. Arguably, I have the right to stand on my soapbox and defend the New Democratic Party (NDP) in a provincial or federal election. But suppose that Kelowna City Council passes a by-law making it illegal to speak in public in defence of the NDP. A sound theory of expressers' rights would say that this by-law should be invalidated. What is added by arguing that, for your part, you have a hearers' right to hear me defending the NDP, and that this hearers' right is violated by the by-law? Nothing. The traditional expressers' right gives all the justification needed to invalidate the by-law. Suppose, on the other hand, a sound theory of expressers' rights does not justify invalidating some given restriction because it labels the case as one where restriction on expression is justified—wantonly shouting 'Fire!' in a crowded theatre, or whatever is one's favourite case. If a sound theory of hearers' rights would also not justify invalidating the restriction, then, as before, the Unnecessary Duplication Principle applies. A hearers' right which is justified when and only when an expresser's right is justified, or unjustified when and only when an expresser's right is unjustified, unnecessarily duplicates expressers' rights and adds nothing.

It might seem as though the state of affairs described in the last sentence does not in fact obtain. There could be many cases where, *pace* the Unnecessary Duplication Principle, a hearers' right is justified when no expresser's right is justified, and presumably, then, such cases may form the foundation of a robust

---

[17] In Cardozo J's famous words, liability should not be extended 'in an indeterminate amount for an indeterminate time to an indeterminate class': *Ultramares Corp v Touche* 174 NE 441 (1931) (NY CA), at 444.

doctrine of hearers' rights. Of course there are such cases; I will consider them shortly. But my claim is that their significance is much constrained; any doctrine of hearers' rights that results from them is quite narrow and limited in scope, and certainly insufficient to support the weight placed on hearers' rights by the commercial expression doctrine.

3 THE BARREN MARKETPLACE OF IDEAS

In *Lamont*, a case of which more anon, Brennan J memorably remarked: 'It would be a barren marketplace of ideas that had only sellers and no buyers.'[18] It is not hard to unpack this image to produce an argument that seems to promote the value of hearers' rights—call it the 'barren marketplace' argument. The 'barren marketplace' argument urges that the freedom to speak is not merely a freedom to project sounds into the ether, sounds that constitute well-formed sentences in a language. The argument certainly calls attention to the importance of the audience to meaningful freedom of expression. But it is not obvious that this importance underwrites a notion of hearers' rights.

Consider the following scenarios. *Scenario (1)*: in a certain country, the government is frightened of the growing power and influence of the leader of the opposition party, one Oppol. But the government also, conscious of the potential effect of human rights abuses on its international standing, does not wish to prohibit Oppol outright from giving speeches. So it allows Oppol to hire the main football stadium for a rally and give his speech. It does, on the other hand, prohibit all citizens from attending the rally and hearing Oppol. On this scenario, we have little hesitation in saying that the government's respect for the value of freedom of expression is negligible. But also we have little hesitation in explaining why we think that in terms of the rights of Oppol as speaker. It is Oppol's freedom of expression right that is being marginalized, even though the restriction is being placed on the freedom of his potential audience.

Here are two further variations. *Scenario (2)*: the government permits Oppol to give his speech in a public arena, and it lifts the formal restriction on citizens attending. But the arena in which the government permits Oppol to speak is in an extremely remote and inaccessible part of the country, and attendance can be expected to be minimal. Most courts and most normative theories of freedom of expression acknowledge the validity of time, place, or manner restrictions on expression, provided *inter alia* that satisfactory alternative modes of expression are available. It is doubtful whether the restriction on Oppol's expression in this scenario satisfies such a necessary condition for validity. The focus, though, is still on Oppol's expression as the target of restriction, even though those wishing to hear him are also frustrated.

---

[18] *Lamont v Postmaster General of the United States* 381 US 301 (1965), at 308.

Scenario (3): in this scenario, the government modifies its stance to the point where it allows Oppol to give any speech he likes in any forum anywhere, even the large football stadium in the capital. Moreover, there is no blanket prohibition on citizens attending Oppol's rallies. However, members of Oppol's own political party are prohibited from attending the rallies and hearing the speeches. In this case, we begin to see the outline of a hearers' right. The best we could make of a supposed infringement of Oppol's freedom of expression as speaker is that he is not being allowed to choose his audience. It is not clear, though, that freedom of expression as a value subtends a right to choose one's audience. Arguably, the freedom of Oppol's party colleagues is being restricted, the freedom to *hear* a person who is free to speak and whom they wish to hear. We feel intuitively sure that in Scenario (3) the government has violated *someone's* freedom of expression, and, since Oppol's own speaking is *ex hypothesi* not restricted in itself, the most tempting candidate for a violated right of freedom of expression seems to be the right to hear on the part of those prevented from hearing.

I referred to Scenario (3) as containing the outline of a hearers' right to freedom of expression. The outline needs filling in. It seems to be possible now to go in several different directions, to fill in the outline with substantive hearers' rights, and in fact courts have done just that. I will examine these alternatives in the next five sections. It is important to be clear about exactly what kind of hearers' right can be found in the institutional history, because of the way that the U.S. Supreme Court sought to rely on precedent in *Virginia Board*.[19] The Court there raised the question 'whether, even assuming that First Amendment protection attaches to the flow of drug price information, it is a protection enjoyed by the appellees [a Virginia resident and two non-profit organizations] as recipients of the information, and not solely, if at all, by the advertisers themselves who seek to disseminate that information' (at 756). The Court then states that it is 'clear from the decided cases' (ibid.) that constitutional protection of communication extends to the recipient as well as the source. The Court then listed as precedents nine cases, and tacitly offered these cases as establishing a general hearers' or listeners' right to receive messages or information. In fact, those cases do no such thing. The Court grievously misrepresents institutional history.

4 THE EARLY CASES

The very first case in which some notion of a hearers' rights, or a right to receive expression, appears is *Martin*.[20] *Martin* casts a long shadow over subsequent

---

[19] *Virginia State Board of Pharmacy et al v Virginia Citizens Consumer Council Inc et al* 425 US 748 (1976).
[20] *Martin v City of Struthers* 319 US 141 (1943).

First Amendment cases in the U.S. The Court's comment that the First
Amendment 'necessarily protects the right to receive [literature]' (at 142) is frequently quoted as one of the institutional sources for constitutional protection
of speakers' expression. It is therefore worth noting just how far short the
Court's reasoning in *Martin* in fact falls of actually justifying any normative
position that might be called 'a right to receive information'.

In the first place, the Court does not explain how the implication that a right
to receive information follows necessarily from a right to distribute can be substantiated. Given the degree to which the Court also talks about the position of
the householder, the Court presumably has in mind some precursor to the 'barren marketplace' argument from *Lamont*, that a right to distribute literature
would not make any sense if the recipient could be constitutionally prevented
from receiving literature. That point can be conceded. The question that
remains, however, is how we are to understand the constitutional immunity that
a prospective recipient has against being prevented from receiving. I shall show
that the supposedly unitary *Martin* right to receive can be resolved into two
quite distinct rights: one is a householder right of privacy and so not a right to
receive at all, while the other is an illusory 'right to receive' which is no more
than the obverse of a speaker's right to express.

A statute in the city of Struthers, Ohio, prohibited 'any person distributing
handbills, circulars or other advertisements from ringing the door bell, sound-
ing the door knocker, or otherwise summoning the inmate or inmates of any residence to the door for the purpose of receiving such handbills, circulars or other
advertisements they or any person with them may be distributing' (*Martin*, at
142). Martin, a Jehovah's Witness, was engaged in door-to-door canvassing,
knocking on doors delivering leaflets advertising a religious meeting. She was
fined $10.00 for violating the ordinance, and challenged the ordinance as an
unconstitutional restriction on her freedom of speech. The Court invalidated
the ordinance on those grounds. However, the Court also went to great pains to
make clear that, in striking down the ordinance and thus acknowledging door-
to-door canvassing to be a protected form of expression, it was not giving to
canvassers a right to 'summon the inmate or inmates of any residence to the
door for the purpose of receiving such handbills'. The Court limited the infir-
mity of the ordinance to its prohibiting canvassers from entering residential
property at all. The Court contemplated that householders could display signs
indicating that they were unwilling to be disturbed by canvassers, and municipalities could prohibit canvassers from actually knocking on doors in defiance
of such signs (cf. 147–9).

The Court in fact saw itself, and correctly so, as engaged in a delicate balancing exercise, weighing the First Amendment right of canvassers against the
right of householders to be free from unwanted intrusions into their home: 'We
are faced in the instant case with the necessity of weighing the conflicting interests of the appellant in the civil rights she claims, as well as the right of the individual householder to determine whether he is willing to receive her message,

against the interest of the community which by this ordinance offers to protect the interests of all of its citizens, whether particular citizens want that protection or not' (at 143). The rhetoric of privacy is pervasive in majority opinion, concurring opinions, and dissenting opinion alike: 'Constant callers . . . may lessen the peaceful enjoyment of a home' (at 144), 'a man's home is his castle' (at 150), 'homes are sanctuaries from intrusions upon privacy' (at 153), 'the annoyance of being called to [the] door to receive printed matter' (at 156), and so on. It is clear beyond doubt that the comment about freedom of speech 'necessarily protect[ing] the right to receive' literature at 143 is an ill-considered throwaway.

The sense in which a 'right to receive' is protected by *Martin* is just this: a canvasser has a First Amendment speakers' right to enter residential property with the intention of summoning the householder to the door; the householder has a privacy right to indicate by means of a sign, or simply by a refusal to answer, that he or she does not wish to be summoned. We are talking about what the Court properly characterizes as a 'right of the individual householder to determine whether he is willing to receive [a canvasser's] message' (at 143). That right is a right of privacy, not a right to receive expression. The sense in which there is a 'right to receive' is that the householder has the option to determine whether to receive a message. The householder would not have that option, if the possibility of delivering the message were foreclosed, as it was by the impugned ordinance. But the reason the householder does have the option to receive the message is that the speaker has the right to deliver it; the ordinance is invalidated for violating that speakers' right. The seeming 'right to receive' is simply the right to speak seen from a different perspective. *Martin* is cited in the commercial expression context as standing for the kind of 'right to receive' which recipients of expression may assert in their own right, when the presence of an expresser with freedom of expression is problematic (cf. *Virginia Board*, at 757). But *Martin* does not establish such a freestanding 'right to receive' at all; the 'right to receive' it establishes is parasitic on a speaker's freedom of expression. *Martin* does not show that hearers have an independent original autonomy right which commercial expressers who lack any such right may 'borrow'.

The next case in which some notion of a right to receive appears, the *Lamont* case, seems impossible to explain without validating the concept of hearers' rights. The case involved a challenge to a restriction on expression brought by the late Corliss Lamont of the Columbia University Philosophy Department. According to U.S. Post Office regulations then in force, any publication that the Post Office identified as 'communist political propaganda' was subject to procedural restrictions. The P.O. detained the mail, and notified the addressee of its arrival. The addressee had to return the notification card and specifically request delivery of the item. Lamont challenged these procedural hurdles as an interference with his freedom of expression under the First Amendment of the U.S. Constitution . The government's counter-argument was that the expressers in question, the senders of the mail, were foreign governments which had no constitutional right to freedom of expression. The Court accepted Lamont's submission and invalidated the regulations. This case involved no interference with any expressers' rights, since there were no expressers with rights in the case. The Unnecessary Duplication Principle is therefore not breached by the holding in favour of Lamont.

This case, however, concerns a very specific fact situation, one that does nonetheless reoccur. In *Mandel*,[21] Ernest Mandel, a Belgian academic and Marxist theoretician, was invited to give a number of lectures at universities in the U.S., but was denied a visa by the U.S. immigration authorities. The denial of a visa was appealed all the way to the U.S. Supreme Court, where it was upheld as being within the exercise of the regulatory discretion of the Attorney-General. The constitutional ground for the appeal could not be any First Amendment right of Mandel to express his views to U.S. audiences: it could be only a supposed First Amendment right of his audiences to hear him. The Court in fact acknowledged the existence of such rights (at 762–5), although it also explicitly refused to balance them against the Attorney-General's power to refuse entry visas to aliens, regarding that power as paramount. Another, and very recent, case presents a very similar situation.[22] The El Paso Housing Authority had regulations that allowed residents of its developments to canvass door to door, but not non-residents. Vasquez, a non-resident candidate for political office, and De La O, a resident elector, challenged these regulations as violating the First Amendment. The trial court found for the authority, and only De La O chose to appeal the ruling. Thus, for the hearing in the Court of Appeal, there were no speakers but only would-be hearers. The appeal had to be based on a supposed right of De La O to receive oral and written presentations from political candidates or their representatives. The court determined that the impugned regulations were indeed an unreasonable restriction on De La O's First Amendment right to receive political information. Interestingly, the court appealed to *Martin* as precedent for its decision, but not *Lamont*. It is obvious that, had Vasquez joined the appeal, the case could have been decided on the basis of his rights as a political speaker alone; the court need not have reached any potential rights of De La O as hearer. But Vasquez did not join the appeal, and the trial decision deserved to be appealed.

These decisions seems normatively satisfying largely because they concern political literature and political canvassing, forms of expression which have been traditionally at the core of freedom of expression. It seems hard to find in *Lamont* and *Vasquez* any theoretical principles that would underwrite a general recognition of hearers' rights. Rather, the two cases suggest that, if the notion of hearers' rights is to have any value at all, its value will be found only in narrow circumstances such as those of these cases. The cases stand at least for the thought that, where political expression is at issue and the expressers have in themselves no right of expression of a relevant kind, and a government restricts

[21] *Kleindienst v Mandel* 408 US 753 (1972).
[22] *Vasquez et al v Housing Authority of the City of El Paso* Docket 00-50702, decided November 5th, 2001 (USCA 5th Cir).

the availability of political expression to its citizens, a citizen who wishes to receive the expression in question may *ceteris paribus* successfully challenge the restriction. This thought does not imply that generally hearers have freedom of expression rights comparable to those of speakers, and still less that hearers have a right to receive commercial information, which right can be 'borrowed' by corporate expressers.

The third case, *Stanley*,[23] is very different. Stanley was convicted under a statute that prohibited the possession of obscene material. Striking down the statute, the Court boldly observed that the 'right to receive information and ideas, regardless of their social worth, [is] fundamental to our free society' (at 564). The Court, moreover, refers to the right as 'now well established' (ibid.), even though, as Lee points out,[24] only *Lamont* of the three cases to which the Court appeals in fact has anything to do with the idea of a right to receive information. *Martin*, as I have shown, really has to do with the expressers' right to canvass door to door and deliver religious leaflets and a householder's right of privacy. *Griswold*[25] famously is an important plank in the framework for a constitutional right of privacy, concerning as it does a Connecticut statute prohibiting the use of contraceptives.

The *Stanley* court all the same could read the fine print. The Court in *Martin* in fact does declare that freedom of speech 'embraces the right to distribute literature, and necessarily protects the right to receive it' (at 143; citations omitted). The Court in *Griswold* includes 'the right to receive' in the long list of more specific rights implied by the overall freedom of speech and press contained in the First Amendment. Soon after *Stanley* was decided, it became clear that the obscenity industry could read the fine print too, and lower courts followed them. As one trial judge put it, 'if a person has the right to receive and possess this material, then someone must have the right to deliver it to him'.[26] *Reidel* was one of four cases in quick succession testing various restrictions on the acquisition or importation of obscenity, in all of which the importer appealed to a supposed right to receive.[27] The Court had to repeat time and time again that it did not mean what it said, that *Stanley* was all about (as indeed it was, bar the throw-away lines discussed here) the freedom to possess the expressive material of one's choice in one's own home, and the error of government attempts to invade the home and the mind. It seems possible that the U.S. Supreme Court considered *Stanley* as clarified by its successor cases to stand only for the proposition that there is no right under the First Amendment to receive *obscenity*. In both *Pico*[28] and *Virginia Board* (at 757), the Court lists *Stanley* among the precedents for the

---

[23] *Stanley v Georgia* 394 US 557 (1969).   [24] Lee, 'Right to Receive Expression', 311 n 45.
[25] *Griswold v Connecticut* 381 US 479 (1965).
[26] Quoted in *United States v Reidel* 402 US 351 (1971), at 355.
[27] *United States v Thirty-seven Photographs* 402 US 363 (1971); *United States v Twelve 200' Reels of Super 8mm Film* 413 US 123 (1973); *United States v Orito* 413 US 139 (1973).
[28] *Board of Education, Island Trees Union Free School District No. 26, et al v Pico, by his next friend Pico, et al* 457 US 853 (1982), at 867. I discuss this case in more detail in this Chapter 10.5.

form of the right to receive information that it acknowledges in those cases. But even on this construal of the fact situation in *Stanley*, there is no plausible way of extrapolating to a general right to receive from a 'no-right' to receive obscenity, any more than there is from the specific rights for which *Lamont* or *Martin* may be held to stand.

In short, in terms of its institutional history, the notion of a general hearers' right to receive expression is off to a very shaky start. The cases to which later courts have appealed as grounds for the right are not such at all. Let us see whether the right fares any better conceptually.

5 FREEDOM OF INFORMATION AND THE LIKE

Another obvious kind of case from which it seems plausible to try to develop a substantive doctrine of hearers' rights are cases where a speaker does not wish to speak, but a hearer wishes to hear. The speaker's expression is not being restricted by government; it is simply being withheld by the speaker in question. The speaker very often in fact is also the government, but that is a contingent feature. If the hearer has a *right* to hear, however, then the speaker cannot remain silent: the speaker has a duty to respond.

It is not hard to pick out cases that conform to such a pattern. One example is the typical piece of freedom of information legislation, which imposes on governments under specified circumstances a positive obligation to provide to citizens information of a given kind—typically, confidential information about oneself, and public information about the workings of government.[29] Similarly, in the law of contract, there is one clear example of a strong right to have information and of a correlative duty to provide it—namely, in so-called contracts *uberrimae fidei*, 'of the utmost good faith'. Familiar examples of these are insurance contracts, where the insuree has a duty to the insurer to disclose all information relevant to forming the contract of insurance and the insurer a claim-right to expect such disclosure, and contracts involving fiduciary relationships, such as those between broker and client. If I am applying for life insurance, the prospective insurer has a right to know about my state of health and I have a duty to provide such information.

Such claim-rights create correlative duties in some party to provide the information. Such duties are formally, and in the cases mentioned justifiably, restrictions on the government's or the insuree's freedom to express as it wishes. Consequently, it is hard to see how hearers' rights in freedom of expression can fit this model. Unlike the situation in *Lamont*, in these examples there are speakers whose freedom of expression is overridden in favour of the supposed right

---

[29] The former cases can also be treated as though personal information is proprietary; like any other piece of property, it cannot be taken or used without consent. The merits of this suggestion need not be considered here.

of the hearer to hear.[30] The examples also suggest that there is something perverse about commercial expression cases where a government regulation requires disclosure of information and the corporate expresser challenges the regulation. From the government's perspective, the consumer has a right to have such information and the corporation no right to withhold it. There is no 'right not to have the information' that belongs to the consumer and which the corporate expresser may 'borrow' to justify its silence. Such cases cannot even be treated as cases where the right of the consumer to have the information is balanced against the freedom of expression right of the corporate expresser to remain silent, for there is no such freedom of expression right.

A different kind of case where there is talk about a right to receive information is illustrated by two Canadian cases in which there is much rhetoric about hearers and the right to know, or to have access to information. Cory J, speaking for the Supreme Court of Canada, in *Edmonton Journal*,[31] urged that freedom of expression protects listeners as well as speakers. The case concerned a (successful, in fact) challenge brought by the *Edmonton Journal* newspaper to sections of the Alberta Judicature Act[32] that limited the extent to which matrimonial proceedings could be reported. While it may be true that, in order to appreciate the value of newspapers in a democratic society, one needs to realize that they are *read*, an interpretation of freedom of expression such that it protected only the expresser newspaper would be quite sufficient to justify the decision. In this case, the reference to hearers' rights adds an unnecessary duplication of rights. One should note, moreover,[33] that public access to the courts, first-hand or second-hand through media reports, additionally serves the distinct value—distinct, that is, from the value of freedom of expression—of justice being seen to be done; any residual importance to be found in hearers' rights in cases such as *Edmonton Journal* is easily explained by reference to this value and not by the value of freedom of expression.

The *IFAW* case concerned regulations relating to the annual winter seal hunt on the ice floes off Canada's east coast.[34] The regulations banned aircraft altogether from the seal hunt area, and forbade any approach within half a nautical mile by sea without a permit. The appellants IFAW had been repeatedly denied a permit, and chose to challenge the regulations as an interference with their freedom of expression. MacGuigan J for the Court reasserted the trial judge's view that 'freedom of expression must include freedom of access to all information pertinent to the ideas or beliefs sought to be expressed' (at 467), and found that indeed there was a breach of the *Charter* section 2(b) guarantee of freedom

[30] There is of course a large literature on the topic of the government as a participant in the so-called expressive marketplace of ideas. I am treating the government as a *bona fide* expresser for the purposes of the present discussion. Nothing turns here on whether I am *sub specie aeternitate* correct in this treatment.

[31] *Edmonton Journal v Attorney-General for Alberta et al* (1989) 64 DLR (4th) 577.

[32] Judicature Act R.S.A. 1980, c. J-1.   [33] As indeed does Cory J, at 608–9.

[34] *International Fund for Animal Welfare Inc et al v The Queen et al* (1988) 45 CCC (3d) 457 (FCA).

of expression. Such an approach, if taken at face value, extends to private persons the right of access often extended to the media and only the media. But the acknowledgment of such a right of access in the case of the media is very much a function of the public role played by free news media in a democratic society. It is a huge step to grant to private persons pursuing their own research agendas a similar potentially unlimited right of access to information. In fact, IFAW, during the time it was able to reach the hunt, used the opportunity to transport members of the media. It seems likely that IFAW was conceived of as having a media-like role, despite the trial judge (quoted at 466) rejecting the claim that it *was* media. Moreover, as in *Lamont*, there is more than a little validity to the suspicion that the government really was using the regulations in question to hinder the expression of political points of view with which the government disagreed. Governmental restrictions on political expression are perhaps the most condemned of all restrictions by the value of freedom of expression. Courts therefore will bend over backwards to invalidate such restrictions, garnering rationales where they may. It does not follow that the rationales will in fact cohere in themselves and truly ground substantial constitutional rights.

However unpromising it might seem, the idea of a right of access to information possessed by private persons was in fact taken seriously by the U.S. Supreme Court in *Pico*. This case concerned the removal by a school board of certain books deemed unsuitable from a school library, and a challenge that this violated their freedom of expression by some of the students in the school. The case was decided narrowly (by five to four) in favour of the students. Brennan J in the main plurality opinion offered two theories to justify his judgment (at 867). The first theory was that 'the right to receive ideas follows ineluctably from the *sender's* First Amendment right to send them,' a candidate general justification for hearers' rights that would fall foul of the Unnecessary Duplication Principle.[35] The second theory, somewhat like the court's argument in *IFAW*, was that the right to receive ideas is valuable and deserves protection, because it is a 'necessary predicate to the *recipient's* meaningful exercise of his own rights of speech, press, and political freedom.'

There is some apparent plausibility to the latter argument. As I noted above (this Chapter 10.3), the 'barren marketplace' argument implies that a government that allowed an expresser to express all the expresser wants but ensured that no-one would hear would surely be in violation of freedom of expression. But my question again is, how does one get from this plausibility to hearers' rights of freedom of expression? In the supposed hypothetical case, the most obvious explanation is that the *expresser's* rights are being violated. Consider the *IFAW* case again. If anyone is being denied 'a necessary predicate to [its] meaningful exercise of [its] own rights of speech, press, and political freedom',

---

[35] The argument also has no relevance in the instant case. As both Burger CJ (at 888) and Rehnquist J (as he then was; at 912) observed in dissent, there can be no reciprocal right to receive expression in a place where no speaker has the right to speak. No author has a right to have his or her books in a school library.

it is most plausibly the IFAW itself and its officer co-appellants, Brian Davies and Stephen Best. It seems unnatural to present the case as one in which my or your rights, as potential hearers of what IFAW has to say, are the persons whose rights are violated.

On the other hand, suppose we take as dispositive one particular element of the fact-situation in *Pico*, namely, that there are no operative rights of expressers, because no publisher has a right to have its publications in a library. Then to grant hearers a freedom of expression right to *any* 'necessary predicate to the *recipient's* meaningful exercise of his own rights of speech, press, and political freedom' surely goes too far. As Burger CJ's dissent in *Pico* pointed out (at 888), that would create large-scale affirmative duties on the part of government to provide information of all kinds, not merely the restricted kind of information which freedom of information legislation creates a duty to provide. As a minimum, huge increases in public library acquisition budgets would have to be funded. That public library acquisition budgets and Defence Department budgets should trade magnitudes is, of course, on many grounds an attractive scenario. But that attractiveness is not the point. The point is that the consequence of recognizing such a 'right to receive information' would unleash enormous government intervention in the marketplace of ideas, when the aim is to restrict such intervention.

Pico could be interpreted narrowly and negatively as standing for a hearers' right only that the stock of information presently received in some context not be reduced. It is not that students have a right that books be added to the library, but only a right that those already there not be removed. So understood, though, *Pico* would not underwrite the vast majority of supposed hearers' rights cases, which concern impugned restrictions on receiving information that the hearer does not presently have. The best way to understand *Pico* is in terms of it being conceived as a matter of political expression, an interpretation which, when made, tends to lead courts to latch on to any doctrine seemingly available to keep governments under control. School Boards have a not wholly undeserved reputation for playing politics with the matter of acquisitions for school libraries, and the U.S. Supreme Court was likely to be squeamish about ruling in favour of the Board in the circumstances of this case.

Let me sum up this discussion. Courts appear to turn to the notion of a right to hear, or to receive information, in cases where they sense an infringement of a constitutional guarantee of freedom of expression, but it is not possible to claim that the freedom of the speaker is being infringed because the speaker in question is exercising freedom by not speaking. However, it is not plausible, or even possible, to develop from this range of cases a substantive doctrine of general hearers' rights to freedom of expression, or to support the commercial expression doctrine by finding a hearers' right that a corporate expresser may 'borrow'. In the case of freedom of information legislation, a duty is imposed on the speaker to speak, which is in conflict with that speaker's supposed freedom of expression. In the case of that journalists' favourite, the 'public's right to know', the strongest theoretical ground for freedom of expression is the freedom of the press or media themselves, not in fact any right of the public to receive information. To assert in these cases a hearers' right to receive information falls foul of the Unnecessary Duplication Principle, since the freedom of the press is sufficient to explain the supposed right to know. The idea of a general right to have access to any desired information is, despite the majority in *Pico*, too far-reaching to have any credibility. Whatever force there is to the conclusion that the reluctance of the speaker in these cases to speak ought to be overridden, that force cannot normatively depend on a substantive doctrine of hearers' rights.

6 PRISONERS' RIGHTS

The complex issue of prisoners' rights under the First Amendment has brought some appeal to the notion of hearers' rights or rights to receive expression. Part of the relevant background legal framework is the following. The U.S. Supreme Court has noted that 'prison walls do not form a barrier separating prison inmates from the protection of the Constitution',[36] but also, bearing in mind that 'the problems of prisons in America are complex and intractable, and . . . courts are ill equipped to deal with the increasingly urgent problems of prison administration and reform',[37] the standard of constitutional review is low: regulations are 'valid if [they are] reasonably related to legitimate penological interests'.[38]

Rights to receive have been appealed to in two ways. Both concern the regulation of what would be in the ordinary sense 'expression'—regulation of prisoners' correspondence, and regulation of reading-matter available to prisoners. Regulation of correspondence is regularly seen as justified for reasons relating to prison security. In general, there are three classes of exception based on the strength of constitutional rights—communication with members of the legal profession, with members of the press, and with immediate family. The first-named has to do with rights relating to access to justice; the second with freedom of the press. The third case concerns us here. In *Procunier*, the challenge was brought on freedom of expression grounds to mail censorship regulations of the California Department of Corrections, regulations that gave very broad powers of censorship to prison authorities. The Court ruled that, even under the relatively undemanding standard of review appropriate to prison regulations, such broad powers could not stand. The Court's reasoning, however, is unusual:

---

[36] *Turner v Safley* 482 US 78 (1987), at 84.
[37] *Procunier v Martinez* 416 US 396 (1974), at 404–5.
[38] *Turner*, at 89; the Court specified a four-part test for such reasonableness at 89–90.

In determining the proper standard of review for prison restrictions on inmate corre-spondence, we have no occasion to consider the extent to which an individual's right to free speech survives incarceration, for a narrower basis of decision is at hand. In the case of direct personal correspondence between inmates and those who have a particularized interest in communicating with them, mail censorship implicates more than the right of prisoners. Communication by letter is not accomplished by the act of writing words on paper. Rather, it is effected only when the addressee reads the letter. Both parties to the correspondence have an interest in securing that result, and censorship of the commun-ication between them necessarily impinges on the interest of each. Whatever the status of a prisoner's claim to uncensored correspondence with an outsider, it is plain that the lat-ter's interest is grounded in the First Amendment's guarantee of freedom of speech. And this does not depend on whether the non-prisoner correspondent is the author or intended recipient of a particular letter, for the addressee as well as the sender of direct personal correspondence derives from the First and Fourteenth Amendments a protec-tion against unjustified governmental interference with the intended communication. [at 408–9]

The Court cites here *Lamont* and *Martin*, but then it also goes on to say:

We do not deal here with difficult questions of the so-called 'right to hear' and third-party standing but with a particular means of communication in which the interests of both parties are inextricably meshed. The wife of a prison inmate who is not permitted to read all that her husband wanted to say to her has suffered an abridgment of her inter-est in communicating with him as plain as that which results from censorship of her let-ter to him. In either event, censorship of prisoner mail works a consequential restriction on the First and Fourteenth Amendments rights of those who are not prisoners. Accordingly, we reject any attempt to justify censorship of inmate correspondence merely by reference to certain assumptions about the legal status of prisoners. . . . [The government's] line of argument and the undemanding standard of review it is intended to support fail to recognize that the First Amendment liberties of free citizens are impli-cated in censorship of prisoner mail. [at 409]

The Court then appeals to its decisions dealing with the general problem of incidental restrictions on First Amendment liberties imposed in furtherance of legitimate governmental activities. On that basis the Court formulates a stand-ard of review (one subsequently refined in *Turner*), by applying which it invalid-ates the censorship regulations at issue.

Later cases in fact make it clear that the Court quickly abandons its fastidi-ousness in *Procunier* as to whether prisoners hold the First Amendment rights of speakers or expressers; except for *Thornburgh*[39] (see below), little more is heard about the rights of the addressees of prison correspondence. But it is still worth asking the hypothetical question whether, if we suppose that indeed pris-oners who send correspondence are expressers with no First Amendment rights, we have a cogent argument for determining this issue on the basis of a general hearers' rights, a general right to receive on the part of the addressees of such correspondence. The fact situation in *Procunier* licenses no such right. The

---

[39] *Thornburgh v Abbott* 490 US 401 (1989).

Court, correctly, focuses on correspondence addressed to an inmate's wife, rather than, say, to his or her former colleagues at work or play. I doubt that the Court would have been eager to uphold the right to receive correspondence if asserted by a former work partner, or the bartender at the inmate's favourite corner pub. The obvious conclusion is that issues of privacy, rather than of rights to receive, are determining the weight given to intra-familial correspondence. The case is structurally analogous to *Lamont*, in that the expresser has *ex hypothesi* no constitutional right to express. It is normatively similar, in that we have a strong intuition that the regulation is unjustified. The difference is that in *Procunier* the ground of the intuition has nothing to do with freedom of expression.

The other regulations in the prison context which have been held to embody hearers' rights or rights to receive are those which control inmates' powers to request material to be sent to them. Two kinds of regulation have been considered. The first is the so-called 'publisher rule'. This rule, applying in all U.S. federal prisons, permitted inmates to receive books and magazines from outside the institution only if the materials were mailed directly from the publisher or a book club. The rule was challenged in *Wolfish*.[40] By the time the case was decided by the U.S. Supreme Court, the rule had been amended to permit the receipt of books and magazines from bookshops as well as publishers and book clubs,[41] and a further amendment to permit receipt of paperback books from any source was contemplated (*Wolfish*, at 549). Even though the Court was left to adjudicate only a rule limiting the receipt of hardback books, the government still defended the rule—with some considerable plausibility, given the legendary capacity of parcels containing hardbound books to deceive and the ready availability of other ways of receiving the same information. Notwithstanding Marshall J's robust assertion in dissent that it was 'beyond dispute' that 'individuals have a fundamental First Amendment right to receive information and ideas' (at 573), the Court upheld the rule.

Thornburgh presented similar issues. The case concerned Federal Bureau of Prisons regulations[42] generally permitting an inmate to subscribe to, or to receive, a publication without prior approval, but authorizing the warden to reject a publication in certain circumstances, the specification of which is quite detailed. Both inmates and magazine publishers challenged these regulations as a violation of the First Amendment. The Court commented that 'in this case, there is no question that publishers who wish to communicate with those who, through subscription, willingly seek their point of view have a legitimate First Amendment interest in access to prisoners' (at 408), and also in several places referred to the case as one involving prisoners' rights. In deciding the case, the Court applied the standard of review it had developed in *Turner* to uphold the validity of the regulations. Stevens J in dissent charged the Court with failing to

[40] *Bell v Wolfish* 441 US 520 (1979).
[41] 43 Fed. Reg. 30576 (1978) (to be codified in 28 CFR 540.71).
[42] 28 CFR 540.70 and 540.71 (1988).

follow its own precedent of *Procunier*, which he took to be prescribing that considerable weight must be given to the First Amendment interests of 'free citizens', rather than prison inmates (at 422–7).

Granted, the focus of the case is on the formulation of standards for judicial review, not on the underlying normative structure of rights. All the same, I do not follow the reasoning. Publishers' freedom of expression has to do with what, when, and where they publish. It does not comprehend, as the dissent in *Pico* correctly urged, a right to place a publication in a particular place. If the *Pico* dissent is cogent, neither the majority nor the dissent in *Thornburgh* is correct to talk in terms of a publisher's right of access to prisoners, even if the prisoners in question have purchased a subscription to the publisher's magazine. The Court is misled into wrongly analogizing the magazine publisher to a journalist who might well have on press freedom grounds a claim to access to prisoners. In fact, *Thornburgh* is best thought of as a close relative of *Lamont*, and thus as representing a specialized kind of hearers' right. There is something dubious about giving too much discretion to prison wardens to interfere with prisoners' choices of reading material. If we assume *arguendo* that *Thornburgh* sets the correct level of discretion, it does so by balancing appropriately the societal interest in proper prison administration and security against the prisoners' interest in choosing their own reading material. That is certainly an autonomy interest and it has to do with expression. Provided that the narrowness of the right in question is acknowledged, as in the case of *Lamont*, I see no reason not to call it a hearers' right in freedom of expression.

7 WHEN THE AUDIENCE DOES NOT WANT TO HEAR

It is a commonplace that freedom of expression must include in the appropriate circumstances the freedom not to express. Let us consider the implications of a hearers' right that takes the form of a right not to hear. It is difficult to isolate a pure freedom of expression right of this kind, since the right not to hear, or not to receive expression, is closely bound up with issues of privacy. In *Rowan*,[43] the U.S. Supreme Court upheld a statute that gives addressees or householders in their sole discretion the right to request they be taken off a mailing list for what the statute terms 'pandering advertisements'.[44] The publisher applicants contended that the section violated their right of free speech as guaranteed by the First Amendment. The Court eloquently declared:

Weighing the highly important right to communicate, but without trying to determine where it fits into constitutional imperatives, against the very basic right to be free from sights, sounds, and tangible matter we do not want, it seems to us that a mailer's right to

[43] *Rowan dba American Book Service et al v United States Post Office Department et al* 397 US 728 (1970).
[44] 39 USC 3008.

communicate must stop at the mailbox of an unreceptive addressee. Nothing in the Constitution compels us to listen to or view any unwanted communication, whatever its merit. The ancient concept that 'a man's home is his castle' into which 'not even the king may enter' has lost none of its vitality, and none of the recognized exceptions includes any right to communicate offensively with another. [at 736–7]

The significant element here, though, is householder control. In cases where, rather than acknowledging a right not to receive on the part of the householder, the government itself has tried to regulate the delivery of advertising material, the Court has been as eloquent, but unsupportive: 'The "short, though regular, journey from mail box to trash can . . . is an acceptable burden, at least so far as the Constitution is concerned" '.[45] The Court in *Martin* made a similar distinction between government regulation and householder control with respect to in-person canvassing and delivery of literature. The Court, though, at a much later date and after the appearance of constitutional protection for commercial speech, upheld a Florida ban on lawyers' direct-mail solicitation. The Court reasoned that the 'short, though regular, journey from mail box to trash can' argument would be an inadequate response in situations where the mere receiving and opening of the mail would be enough to cause the harm the state had an interest in preventing.[46] The Court took the form of solicitation by lawyers at issue to be of that kind.

A different kind of fact situation where arguably a right not to hear might come into play has to do with telemarketing. I have discussed these cases already in Chapter 3.8 above. As I showed there, the right not to hear is interpreted very much in privacy terms in the decisions that have so far been given. The cases are seen as opposing a freedom of expression right on the part of a speaker against a privacy right on the part of the would-be non-hearer. This is an intuitively reasonable way of presenting the issues in certain cases of this kind. In *Kovacs*,[47] the Court balanced the 'right of free speech' 'guaranteed every citizen that he may reach the minds of willing listeners' (at 87) against 'the need for reasonable protection in the homes of business houses from . . . distracting noises' (at 89). The case concerned an ordinance prohibiting 'loud and raucous noises' from sound trucks on public streets. The Court upheld the ordinance. Notice, however, that, as I tried to bring out in my discussion of *U.S. West*[48] in the previous chapter (at Chapter 9.3 above), to regard such cases as modelling an interest-balancing applicable to commercial expression cases begs all the relevant questions about whether a corporation is entitled to freedom of expression in its own

---

[45] *Bolger v Youngs Drug Products Corp.* 463 US 60 (1983), at 72, quoting *Lamont v Commissioner for Motor Vehicles* 269 F Supp 880 (SDNY) at 883, *summarily affirmed* 386 F 2d 449 (1967) (USCA 2nd Cir), *certiorari denied* 391 US 915 (1968). See also *Consolidated Edison Company v Public Service Commission* 447 US 530 (1980), at 542: 'The customer of Consolidated Edison may escape exposure to objectionable material simply by transferring the bill insert from envelope to wastebasket.'

[46] *Florida Bar v Went For It, Inc* 115 SCt 2371 (1995), at 2379.

[47] *Kovacs v Cooper* 336 US 77 (1949).

[48] *U.S. West Inc v FCC* 182 F (3d) 1224 (1999) (USCA 10th Cir).

person. Even to contemplate that a privacy right of the consumer may stand opposed to the interests of the corporate advertiser shows the hollowness of the idea that the corporate advertiser has freedom of expression as a speaker through borrowing the original autonomy right of a hearer.

8 THE FAIRNESS DOCTRINE

Prior to the use made of the idea of hearers' rights in supporting the commercial expression doctrine, the zenith of the idea in U.S. Supreme Court jurisprudence occurred in *Red Lion*.[49] The name 'Fairness Doctrine' refers to regulatory duties imposed on broadcasters by the U.S. Federal Communications Commission in carrying out its mandate to protect the public interest in regulating broadcasting. In general, the doctrine required broadcasters 'to provide adequate and fair coverage of opposing viewpoints on controversial issues of public importance'. That is, broadcasters could not provide simply entertainment, but had to provide public interest programming; and, when they did provide such programming, they had to ensure that issues were presented in a balanced and fair way. The Doctrine also comprised two subsidiary rules. One required that, in cases where an individual suffered 'personal attack', the individual had to be informed of the attack and given a chance to respond. The other required that, in the case of election coverage, any broadcaster who endorsed one particular candidate in an editorial must inform the other candidates and offer them a reasonable opportunity to respond. The Fairness Doctrine spectacularly survived constitutional challenge in *Red Lion*,[50] even though comparable access requirements in the case of the press were struck down not long afterwards in *Tornillo*.[51] However, the Doctrine came under great criticism during the age of deregulation in the Reagan era. The FCC formally repealed the Doctrine in 1987, and, although a congressional bill reinstating it was passed, President Reagan vetoed the bill. The Fairness Doctrine has not been heard of since.

In upholding the Fairness Doctrine, the Court in *Red Lion* makes two arguments. The first is that the First Amendment cannot be taken to entail an unfettered right on the part of broadcasters to broadcast:

Where there are substantially more individuals who want to broadcast than there are frequencies to allocate, it is idle to posit an unabridgeable First Amendment right to broadcast comparable to the right of every individual to speak, write, or publish. If 100 persons want broadcast licenses but there are only 10 frequencies to allocate, all of them may have the same 'right' to a license; but if there is to be any effective communication by

---

[49] *Red Lion Broadcasting Co v FCC* 395 US 367 (1969).

[50] The case is discussed extensively in Thomas G. Krattenmaker and Lucas A. Powe Jr, *Regulating Broadcast Programming* (Cambridge, Mass.: The MIT Press, 1994), 187–94, 237–75.

[51] *Miami Herald v Tornillo* 418 US 241 (1987). The case is discussed by Scot Powe. See Lucas A. Powe Jr, *The Fourth Estate and the Constitution: Freedom of the Press in America* (Berkeley and Los Angeles, Cal.: University of California Press, 1991), 260–87.

radio, only a few can be licensed and the rest must be barred from the airwaves. It would be strange if the First Amendment, aimed at protecting and furthering communications, prevented the Government from making radio communication possible by requiring licenses to broadcast and by limiting the number of licenses so as not to overcrowd the spectrum. [at 388–9]

The second argument concerns the rights of the public as listeners to broadcasts:

This is not to say that the First Amendment is irrelevant to public broadcasting. . . . [t]he people as a whole retain their interest in free speech by radio and their collective right to have the medium function consistently with the ends and purposes of the First Amendment. It is the right of the viewers and listeners, not the right of the broadcasters, which is paramount. It is the purpose of the First Amendment to preserve an uninhibited marketplace of ideas in which truth will ultimately prevail, rather than to countenance monopolization of that market, whether it is by the Government itself or a private licensee. It is the right of the public to receive suitable access to social, political, esthetic, moral, and other ideas and experiences that is crucial here. That right may not constitutionally be abridged either by Congress or by the FCC. [at 389–90; citations omitted]

According to this latter argument, respect for hearers' and listeners' rights implies not merely that, in cases where government inappropriately restricts access to broadcast expression, freedom of expression requires lifting of the restriction. Such respect also implies that, in cases where private interests inappropriately restrict access to broadcast expression, freedom of expression requires the government in the shape of the FCC to impose appropriate restrictions.

The 'inappropriateness' here is a function of a certain interpretation of the values promoted by freedom of expression. The ideal is not that of a completely unregulated 'marketplace of ideas', but rather that of a marketplace of ideas regulated so as to produce a certain outcome—an informed citizenry able to conduct its affairs, especially its political affairs, in a fair and balanced way. More generally, if the account of the form of civic life desired has a qualitative component to it, the latter argument in *Red Lion* acknowledges that such a goal may require regulation of the marketplace of ideas. Government intervention may be as important as government abstention.

In essence, we have here two competing conceptions or models of constitutional protection for freedom of expression, especially as regards news media. Powe, for example, distinguishes them as the 'right to know' model and the 'Fourth Estate' model.[52] According to the first model, the public has a right to have information and the news media must if necessary be regulated in appropriate ways to ensure that the desired information is forthcoming. According to the second model, borrowing Edmund Burke's memorable image, the news media constitute the 'Fourth Estate' of the realm, operating as an autonomous check on abuses of power by the other three, and able so to function only under

---

[52] Powe Jr, *Fourth Estate*, 233–87.

maximal freedom and minimal regulation. Baldasty and Simpson distinguish a 'Right to Know Model', as exemplified by *Red Lion*, and a 'Debate Model'.[53] The name 'Debate Model' picks up from Brennan J's well-known comment in *NY Times* about 'a profound national commitment' to the principle of 'uninhibited, robust and wide-open' debate on public affairs.[54] Again, the purpose of this model is to urge maximal freedom and minimal regulation of expression.

It is not my purpose at this point in my argument to promote one model of freedom of expression over the other, although clearly my general opposition to the commercial expression doctrine commits me to rejecting the Fourth Estate and Debate models as applied to commercial expression. My point here is this. Suppose that hearers' rights or listeners' rights are correctly interpreted by the ideals of the Fairness Doctrine. Then, a right to receive information will amount to permission to the government to regulate in appropriate ways the operation of the marketplace of ideas, and constitutional protection for freedom of expression will amount to authorizing courts when appropriate to uphold, not invalidate, government restrictions on freedom of expression. If that is so, then hearers' rights (on this construal) are deeply ill-suited to being borrowed by commercial expressers with no freedom of expression rights of their own in order to justify invalidation of restrictions on commercial expression. To put the matter another way, the aim here is not to show that 'right to know' models are the correct way to interpret constitutional protection for freedom of expression, although as a matter of fact I do think they are. The aim is to show that hearers' rights as interpreted by 'right to know' models, whatever their plausibility, take the argument away from, not towards, constitutional protection for commercial expression. The deeper question, which I also will not pursue here, is whether the twin ideals so often appearing in freedom of expression rhetoric of informed discourse and unfettered discourse form a coherent pair.

9 THE LIMITED ROLE OF HEARERS' RIGHTS

The above discussion has revealed considerable heterogeneity to the concept of hearers' rights in freedom of expression. I will chart that heterogeneity and draw some conclusions from it by way of summing up this phase of my discussion of hearers' rights.

First, I introduced and defended the Unnecessary Duplication Principle, the principle that hearers' rights would be significant freedom of expression rights if and only if they were new and independent rights; that is, they should not be used to justify normative results if those results would already follow from the assertion of speakers' rights. The principle had application in one of the foundational cases for the supposed hearers' right to receive information, *Martin*.

---

[53] Gerald J. Baldasty and Roger A. Simpson, 'The Deceptive "Right to Know": How Pessimism Rewrote the First Amendment', *Washington Law Review* 56 (1981): 375 ff.

[54] *New York Times v Sullivan* 376 US 254 (1964), at 270.

There, whatever content attached to a householder's right to listen to what a door-to-door canvasser was saying over and above the householder's right not to open the door if he or she wished turned out to be the canvasser's right to knock on the door under a different aspect. Likewise, in *Edmonton Journal* and *IFAW*, the courts have been misled by speakers' rights in the form of freedom of the press masquerading as hearers' rights. We do not need to appeal to hearers' rights to justify the constitutional protection granted in these cases; we need only appeal to freedom of the press, a form of speakers' right.

The second class of cases where postulated hearers' rights disappear on close examination is those where the right asserted by the hearer is most plausibly regarded as a privacy right, not a freedom of expression right. I include in this category *Martin*, in so far as it stands for a right not to hear by refusing to answer the door to a canvasser; *Stanley* as clarified by its successors, in that it stands for a right to choice of reading or viewing material in the privacy of the home; *Procunier*, in that it stands for the right of a prison inmate's immediate family to receive correspondence from the inmate. None of these cases demonstrate that we need a doctrine of hearers' rights to justify their results.

That leaves three remaining kinds of cases, in which hearers' rights may be meaningfully asserted—(a) claim-rights which impose on expressers a duty to express, as in the case of freedom of information legislation; (b) cases where there are no expressers who are party to the litigation; (c) cases where the claims of hearers are balanced against the claims of expressers in a regulated marketplace of ideas.

(a) There is an important sense in which cases of this type are not cases of hearers' rights *in freedom of expression* at all, precisely because in them duties are imposed on expressers to express. Expression is restricted in these cases, not freed. They are freedom of expression cases in so far as, very often, the party seeking the information is a journalist researching for an article or broadcast. But in that case, the ground for upholding the journalist's claim-right, if appropriate, is freedom of the press. *Pico*, which would fall into this category if the majority were taken at their word, simply seems to me wrongly decided. Doubtless, the school board displayed an unacceptable narrow-mindedness in banning the books from school libraries; but this practical unwisdom is not a failure to respect constitutional rights.

(b) *Lamont*, *Mandel*, and *Vasquez* do stand as cases where the normative appropriateness of the holding is best explained in terms of a failure to respect the rights of hearers to hear or read political expression. My claim, though, is that the political character of the expression is paramount. That is, it is not only possible but also necessary to confine the implications of these cases to the domain of political expression. It does not follow that the position of a consumer unable to find out from an advertisement the price of prescription drugs at a given pharmacy or the languages spoken at a given dentist's office, or the strength of a beer from the label on the bottle, is in the same constitutional position as Prof. Lamont or Mr Jesus De La O. It is true that all are not being given information that they wish to have, because the government is not allowing it to be provided. But it is a large step from the truth of that claim to a general right to receive information on which any would-be hearer may successfully base a constitutional challenge on freedom of expression grounds. Similarly, *Thornburgh* can be taken to stand for a narrow and specific form of hearers' right, one that would defy generalization.

(c) Finally, we have the kind of hearers' and listeners' rights alluded to by defences of the Fairness Doctrine. The normative plausibility of these rights has to be assessed differently from those mentioned under (b) above. The rights in (b) can be accommodated within the traditional picture of freedom of expression as freedom from any government interference in expressing—in these cases, in hearing expression. That does not apply to the Fairness Doctrine hearers' rights. Acknowledgment of those rights requires a shift in orientation from assuming as the implicit ideal an unregulated marketplace of ideas to assuming as the ideal a marketplace of ideas regulated so as to produce a certain result, the roughly equal availability of a spectrum of relevant views on issues of public importance. The merit or otherwise of such an approach to constitutional protection for freedom of expression has been, and continues to be, strenuously debated as itself an issue of public importance. I am not about to settle it here, not even by fiat. My point is simply the conceptual one that such a perspective on hearers' rights will not allow them to be used for the purposes to which they are put by the commercial expression doctrine, to be borrowed by a commercial expresser as grounds for abolishing governmental restriction on commercial expression.

This heterogeneity among the cases supposedly grounding a general hearers' right, together with the justified scepticism as to whether there is any such right, serves to vitiate the U.S. Supreme Court's deployment of the notion in *Virginia Board* as part of its foundation for the commercial expression doctrine. In stating, as it did, that it is 'clear from the decided cases' (at 756) that constitutional protection of communication extends to the recipient as well as the source, the Court listed as precedents names familiar from this chapter—*Lamont, Mandel, Procunier, Red Lion, Stanley, Griswold, Martin*[55]—a conglomerative practice it followed in previous and subsequent cases where supposed hearers' rights were at issue.[56] It is clear that such conglomeration is a symptom of conceptual confusion, not of a clear line of authoritative cases. The Court misrepresents what is clear from its own holdings, that different cases in the list have very different

---

[55] The Court also cited *Thomas v Collins* 323 US 516 (1945), a labour case discussed in Chapter 2 above, and *Marsh v Alabama* 326 US 501 (1946), a case with a fact situation very similar to that in *Martin*, save for the twist that the town whose ordinance was challenged, Chickasaw, was a privately-owned 'company town'. The Court ruled that this element made no difference to the constitutional status of the ordinance.

[56] Cf. e.g. *Houchins v KQED* 438 US 1 (1978), a case concerning media access to prisoners, *Virginia Board, Procunier, Mandel, Lamont, Red Lion, Stanley, Martin, Marsh*, cited at 30; *Procunier* itself lumps together *Martin, Lamont,* and *Stanley*, at 409; *Mandel* lumps together *Martin, Stanley,* and *Red Lion*, at 763.

things to say about supposed hearers' rights, and moreover that very little of what is said grounds the kind of general right to receive promoted by the majority in *Virginia Board*.

The importance of this result must be neither underrated nor overrated. It must not be underrated because it shows that the U.S. Supreme Court's switch from denying to affording constitutional protection to commercial speech cannot be represented as backed by institutional history and precedent. In so representing it, the Court evinces either disingenuousness or confusion or both. On the other hand, the result should not be overrated. All it shows is that, whatever freedom of expression right grounded in autonomy a hearer may have that is capable of being 'borrowed' by a corporate expresser to justify the invalidation of restrictions on its expression, it is not a general autonomy right to receive information, which right accrues to a hearer just because the hearer is a hearer. The existence of a 'borrowable' right must be justified, if it can be, on narrower and more specific grounds, grounds that pertain to the particular kind of autonomy right that, if they had it, a hearer of commercial information would have. The next two chapters will be spent on evaluating whether an autonomy right of this narrower kind can plausibly be held to exist.

11

Commercial Expression and the Self-realization Value

The focus of Chapters 10–12 is on the thought that constitutional protection for commercial expression is justified within the paradigm of autonomy. However, it is not justified through promotion of the autonomy of the corporate expresser itself. Corporations are not the kind of entities to which it is meaningful to attribute autonomy in the moral sense of that notion at issue here. Rather, the thought is that an original autonomy right of the hearer of corporate expression exists in a form to be 'borrowed' by the corporate expresser. Constitutional protection for the commercial expression of corporate expressers, on this argument, is ultimately underwritten from the point of view of normative political morality by this hearers' original autonomy right. In Chapter 10, I undermined the idea that there is a general hearers' right to receive information. We can make sense of such a hearers' right in specific cases and circumstances. However, the best examples from the existing case law involve political expression, or a right of privacy, or a 'regulated market' model for the flow of information. None of these models serves the justificatory needs of the commercial expression doctrine: commercial expression is not political expression; a hearers' right of privacy frequently conflicts with a supposed corporate right of freedom of commercial expression; the commercial expression doctrine seeks an unregulated market in information, not a regulated market. A fresh start is therefore needed, if we are to seek a justification for the commercial expression doctrine rooted in a hearers' original autonomy right to receive commercial information.

At the end of Chapter 6, I distinguished eight theses advanced by the U.S. Supreme Court in *Virginia Board*[1] to justify the extension of constitutional protection to commercial expression in the form in which they did extend it in that case. Of those theses, two (suitably interpreted) implicate the autonomy of the hearer—argument (c), the 'keener by far' argument, in particular in the form in which it was expressed by the Supreme Court of Canada in *Ford*,[2] and argument (f), the anti-paternalism argument. These arguments, if sound, would supply the still unsatisfied justificatory need for the commercial expression doctrine. That is, they would confirm the existence of a specific kind of right belonging to

[1] *Virginia State Board of Pharmacy et al v Virginia Citizens Consumer Council Inc et al* 425 US 748 (1976).
[2] *Attorney-General of Quebec v La Chaussure Brown's Inc et al* [Indexed as Ford v Quebec (Attorney-General)] (1988) 54 DLR (4th) 577.

hearers within the paradigm of autonomy, such that this specific autonomy right could plausibly be 'borrowed'[3] by a corporate expresser to justify constitutional protection for its own commercial expression. Both the 'keener by far' argument and the anti-paternalism argument appeal to the *autonomy* of the hearer. They both claim that constitutional protection for commercial expression is justified because such protection is autonomy-promoting, and specifically hearer-autonomy-promoting. The 'keener by far' argument claims that constitutional protection for commercial expression directly promotes hearer autonomy. The anti-paternalism argument claims that government restriction on commercial expression interferes with hearer autonomy because such restriction is paternalistic; thus removal of the restriction will be autonomy-promoting. The promotion of autonomy is an accepted freedom of expression value. Thus the support these arguments would give, if sound, to the commercial expression doctrine is the appropriate kind of support. Commercial expression is claimed by the arguments to be in itself a source for the promotion of autonomy.

I will consider the anti-paternalism argument in Chapter 12. In the present chapter, I will discuss and refute the 'keener by far' argument. The 'keener by far' argument is one of two versions of an argument for hearers' rights, both of which attach great importance to a 'free flow of commercial information'. Common to both versions is the thought that this free flow is to be given constitutional protection in the form of a hearers' right, because of the value yielded by such a free flow. One version of the argument (cf. argument (e) at the end of Chapter 6) which uses the free flow of commercial information to ground a supposed hearers' right looks, not at the personal value, but the societal value of such a flow. The free flow of commercial information is assumed to be a good, because the free flow of commercial information promotes utility, not autonomy. This version of the hearers' rights argument in effect gives to both expresser and hearer a utility right, not an autonomy right, deriving from the value of the free flow of information, which right it is the mandate of constitutional protection for freedom of commercial expression to protect. I will discuss this argument and its ramifications in Chapter 13 below. Here, I consider a different version of the argument from the free flow of commercial information, one that remains within the paradigm of autonomy.

1 SELF-REALIZATION AND AN INTEREST 'KEENER BY FAR'

The version of the argument examined now is that offered by the Supreme Court of Canada in *Ford*: the Court declared that 'commercial expression . . . plays a significant role in enabling individuals to make informed economic

---

[3] I waive in this and the next chapter the concerns raised in Chapter 10.1 as to whether we sufficiently understand that metaphor. However, it must be kept in mind throughout the discussion in Chapters 11 and 12 that those concerns do nonetheless persist.

choices, an important aspect of individual self-fulfilment and personal autonomy' (at 618). The free flow of commercial information maximizes the opportunities for economic choices to be informed. The 'keener by far' argument
unpacks thus. Informed economic decision-making and choice are 'an important aspect of individual self-fulfilment and personal autonomy'. To foster individual self-fulfilment and personal autonomy is *ex hypothesi* a proper function
of freedom of expression. Those whose individual self-fulfilment and personal
autonomy are promoted are the hearers, the receivers of the freely flowing
commercial information. Constitutional protection for commercial expression,
and thus for the free flow of commercial information, is therefore constitutional
protection for autonomy and self-realization, the autonomy and self-realization
of the hearers. The way to protect this free flow is to invalidate restrictions on
the commercial expression of corporate expressers. It is thus not necessary for
corporate expressers to have in their own persons an autonomy right to freedom
of expression. It is sufficient to protect the free flow of commercial information
that they 'borrow' the right from the hearer, the right that the hearer has from
their autonomy and self-realization being promoted by the free flow of commercial information.

One might call this argument the Self-realizing Consumption Argument. The
idea embodied in the argument is that the ability to make selective purchases in
a free market is a basic freedom of choice that is as essential to individual autonomy, as are any others of the expressive acts traditionally closer to the core of
constitutional coverage of freedom of expression. We do not have much difficulty in seeing constitutional protection for political expression, or artistic
expression, as fitting into the paradigm of autonomy. Our autonomy is fostered
by participation in robust political debate. The same is true for participation in
artistic creation. The Self-realizing Consumption Argument extends the same
line of thought to commercial expression.

Self-realization has been around as a freedom of expression value at least
since the 1960s (see Chapter 1.2 above). Its merits in general as a value are not
in question here. It should, however, be underlined that self-realization or self-
fulfilment (I am not worrying about possible differences between these in this
book) are regularly thought of in relation to freedom of expression as freedom
of expression values *from the perspective of the expresser or speaker*. That is,
one important, even essential, route to self-fulfilment and self-realization is
through self-expression. Thus, freedom of expression as a normative value,
granting as it does normative protection to acts of self-expression, serves to promote self-fulfilment and self-realization. We acknowledge the importance in the
achievement of this goal by self-expression of the expresser being free to choose
the content of his or her own expression: '[it is] the fundamental rule of protection under the First Amendment that a speaker has the autonomy to choose the
content of his own message'.[4] It is not hard to imagine the extension of this

---

[4] *Hurley v Irish-American Gay, Lesbian and Bisexual Group* 515 US 557 (1996), at 573.

argument to the hearer of political expression (we have the autonomy to choose which political message to hear), and to the appreciation of art (we have the autonomy to choose which forms of art or which artworks we appreciate). The argument on behalf of the commercial expression doctrine presently being considered attempts to transfer this autonomy and its contribution to self-fulfilment and self-realization over to the hearer or listener. It is not immediately obvious how the transfer can be secured.

'Commercial expression plays a significant role in enabling individuals to make informed economic choices, an important aspect of individual self-fulfilment and personal autonomy', said the Supreme Court of Canada. One is tempted to add, 'and in making uninformed economic choices too'. The seductive persuasiveness of most advertising I shall consider in Chapter 14. In the meantime, it is perhaps unfair to belabour this point here. False or misleading advertising is not in fact given constitutional protection, as the law presently stands in the legal systems under discussion. In order to be fair to supporters and critics of the commercial expression doctrine alike, we have to focus on commercial expression of the kind that is a candidate for constitutional protection. We have to consider how it may be that expression of that kind plays a significant role, if any does, in enabling individuals to make informed economic choices. There are two different steps to the argument here. The first connects commercial expression to informed economic decision-making and choice. The second connects informed economic decision-making and choice to 'individual self-fulfilment and personal autonomy'. Let me for a while pursue the former idea, while leaving for later sections (this Chapter 11.3–4) the connection between informed economic choice and 'individual self-fulfilment and personal autonomy'.

2 Commercial expression and informed economic choice

It is not difficult to capture the intuitive basis for the claim that commercial expression enables informed economic decision-making and choice. Suppose I know I am going to have to buy some household batteries.[5] I research consumer magazines for reports on batteries. I find out that alkaline batteries give more power for the dollar, but also that there is no significant difference between different brands, so one should buy the cheapest alkaline batteries available. I then turn to the myriad of advertising flyers that come with the local papers, and I discover that Superstore has the cheapest alkaline batteries. So I go there to buy alkaline batteries. That's 'informed economic choosing', and a choice that brings a benefit; I get the most battery power for my hard-earned dollar. The alternative scenario is that I just go to the nearest shop available, and grab the handiest package available. As a result, I run serious risk of getting a less

---

[5] I am writing this a few days before Christmas. I have children. The topic is much on my mind.

powerful kind of battery for my money or paying more than I could for an equally good battery. That's 'uninformed economic choosing', bringing no benefit, but harm. True, the consumer reports I read are arguably public interest expression, not commercial expression. But the shop advertising flyers certainly are commercial expression, and without them I would not know where the cheapest batteries are.

It might be objected that this example trivializes the significance of commercial expression and the free flow of commercial information, and prejudices the argument. The objection is misplaced. It is true that many of the litigated commercial expression and commercial speech cases involve socially important advertising[6]—prescription drugs (*Virginia Board, Western States*), dental, optometric, and ophthalmologic services (*Rocket, Friedman, Grier, Stambuk*), contraceptive products (*Bolger*), compensation for forced sterilization or defective contraceptive devices (*Primus, Zauderer*), environmental policy (*Central Hudson, Pacific Gas, VGT*). But many others involve everyday consumer products—knitting wool (*Ford*), beer and liquor (*Coors, 44 Liquormart, Gourmet*), margarine (*Edible Oil*), cosmetics and hair-care products (*Markt Intern*), housewares and household appliances (*Fox, Hertel*), groceries (*Wileman, United Foods*), toys (*Irwin Toy*). Yet others concern issues where freedom of commercial expression clashes head on with the powerful value of public health (*RJR-MacDonald, Lorillard, Germany, JTI MacDonald, WLF*), and the temptation is strong to dismiss freedom of commercial expression out of hand. It is not irrelevant to the case one might make for the commercial expression doctrine that some cases involve socially important products or services. I will address the issue shortly. But the justification for constitutional protection for commercial expression has to be one which, if it succeeds, succeeds for all kinds of cases. Supporters of the commercial expression doctrine cannot 'cherry-pick' certain cases to rely on, cases which resonate with social importance. No more, of course, can its critics, myself included, be allowed to 'cherry-pick' the trivial-seeming cases or the cases where countervailing social importance weighs in. The argument here will meet that constraint.

3 CONSTITUTIONAL PROTECTION FOR INFORMED ECONOMIC DECISION-MAKING: STEP ONE

Commercial advertising, then, or at least some commercial advertising, does facilitate informed economic choice, in the sense that it affords the opportunity for improved economic decision-making. That fact, though, is only the first step in argument for the commercial expression doctrine. Why might the fact that commercial advertising facilitates informed economic choice be relevant to whether commercial expression deserves constitutional protection? The crucial

---

[6] For full case citations, please consult the Table of Cases.

move has to be to subsume commercial advertising under some appropriate freedom of expression value, it being in general acknowledged that freedom of expression deserves constitutional protection. Merely that informed economic choice brings some benefit to some choosers, or that it fosters some interests of some choosers, will not be enough to secure the move. It has to be shown as a necessary condition for securing the move both that the benefit is invariably brought, and that the benefit brought is the kind of benefit the bringing of which merits constitutional protection under the rubric of freedom of expression. There are immediate difficulties for each of these conditions.

The first difficulty is that it is not necessarily true that informed economic choice is a good to the chooser, that an economic chooser is always better off from the point of view of economic self-interest in preferring informed choice over uninformed choice. Take my battery example. It took me some time to track down the consumer reports, and to plough through the advertising flyers. It could very well be that in so doing I left too little time to pursue some other purpose which would have benefited me more, or served better my interest in being prepared for the holiday festivities. Here, the constraint that the justificatory argument applies to every case has some bite. Cultivating a practice of informed economic choice matters much more in some cases—automobiles, expensive home theatre equipment, housing purchases, one's health-care provider, etc.—than it does in others. In the case of many consumer goods, the time taken to become informed may not be worth it. But if that is so, then informed economic choice is not automatically a good to the chooser, and causal antecedents to informed economic choice, such as the free flow of commercial information, are not automatically goods to the chooser either.[7]

It could be argued, in the alternative, that it must be in any given person's interest that his or her economic decision-making be informed, because, if it is, to that degree overall economic efficiency is promoted, and it is always in the interest of every individual that overall efficiency is promoted. This latter claim, however, is false. Improvements in overall efficiency, other things being equal, may come about in part through individual losses. Some side-constraint on the pursuit of efficiency, such as John Rawls' well-known Difference Principle,[8] is needed to avoid individual losses. The Difference Principle says that social inequalities are justifiable only if the difference in expectation is to the advantage of the worst off. The Principle is, as Rawls emphasizes, a principle of justice, not of efficiency. It is consistent with efficiency in the sense that a perfectly just society is also perfectly efficient; but, where the Principle conflicts with efficiency, the Principle is to be ranked prior to efficiency.[9] Clearly, the Difference Principle as a principle for the design of economic institutions will

---

[7] This variability is a significant feature; it will reappear again in Chapter 13—see Chapter 13.2–3 below.

[8] John Rawls, *A Theory of Justice* (Cambridge, Mass.: Harvard University Press, 1971), secs. 11–13, 44–46.

[9] Ibid., sec. 13.

license considerable government regulation of the economic market, in order to make sure that the least well off are not disadvantaged. As such, defenders of the fundamentality of economic efficiency and a free economic market roundly repudiate the Principle.[10]

The second difficulty is simply that not everything that brings a benefit to a chooser, or furthers the interest of a chooser, thereby and as such merits constitutional protection. The commercial expression doctrine claims: we value freedom of expression enough to grant it constitutional protection; commercial advertising is expression; therefore it too should be protected. More though is needed than this minimal argument, as I have been continually emphasizing in this book. Commercial expression has to be the right kind of expression to be a candidate for constitutional protection. Freedom of expression furthers specific values to which we grant pride of place and which it furthers because of the nature of expression. If it is to be accepted that the free flow of commercial information must be protected by protecting commercial advertising, commercial advertising and the free flow of commercial information must be suitably related to those values that are identified as freedom of expression values. In my battery example, the free flow of commercial information and the resultant informed economic choice allow me to get the most battery power for the least dollar. That is surely a benefit to me of some kind, *pace* the reservations entered in the previous paragraph. But how does it become an issue of freedom of expression? How is advertising the price at which batteries are sold an instance of the value of freedom of expression? We still need this further step to be justified.

In short, while it can be acknowledged that in a general sense commercial advertising facilitates informed economic decision-making, the immediate sceptical response is, so what? How do we get from facilitating informed economic decision-making to meriting constitutional protection under the rubric of freedom of expression? We need an argument with two components: both that in the nature of the case a given benefit accompanies informed economic decision-making, and that this benefit is one that is appropriately promoted through constitutional protection for freedom of expression.

4 CONSTITUTIONAL PROTECTION FOR INFORMED ECONOMIC DECISION-MAKING: STEP TWO

Having provided some context for it, let us then now take up the Supreme Court of Canada's gloss on informed economic choice, that it is 'an important aspect of individual self-fulfilment and personal autonomy'. If the Court is correct,

[10] Loren E. Lomasky, *Persons, Rights, and the Moral Community* (New York: Oxford University Press, 1987), 135–41; Robert Nozick, *Anarchy, State and Utopia* (Oxford: Blackwell, 1974), 189–213.

then we have an argument for the commercial expression doctrine which has the proper mien: commercial advertising is as such instrumental in the promotion of a valid constitutional goal as far as freedom of expression is concerned, namely individual self-fulfilment and personal autonomy. Specifically, commercial advertising promotes the self-fulfilment and autonomy of the individual or person who *hears* the commercial advertising.

In assessing the strength of this argument, let me first note that the Court's claim as it stands is very weak: informed economic choice is '*an aspect*' of individual self-fulfilment and personal autonomy. The Court is not claiming that informed economic choice is necessary and sufficient for self-fulfilment and autonomy, nor that informed economic choice is necessary for self-fulfilment and autonomy, nor that informed economic choice is sufficient for self-fulfilment and autonomy. The Court is wise not to claim any of these stronger theses, for none of them is correct. It is important to see why.

Informed economic choice is not necessary for self-fulfilment and autonomy (and *a fortiori* not necessary and sufficient). Even if a life of informed economic choice is a self-fulfilling and autonomous life, there are many other ways of life that fulfil the self and are autonomous, such that in them informed economic choice plays little or no part. Both in the anecdotal tradition and in reality, some artistic creators and performers pay scant attention to matters economic and still live fulfilling and autonomous lives. Other persons find the life of parenting, or of other forms of care-giving, fulfilling and autonomous, while also paying scant attention to matters economic.

Informed economic choice is not sufficient (and *a fortiori* not necessary and sufficient) for self-fulfilment and autonomy. The Self-realizing Consumption Argument, as I have called it, regards informed economic choice as in itself essential to self-fulfilment and autonomy. Thus stated, the claim needs disambiguating. First, let us remind ourselves of what is meant by autonomy.[11] Autonomy may be thought of, at least in ways relevant to the present discussion, as a capacity or a condition of exercising that capacity. I mentioned above two different attractive accounts of autonomy as a capacity: 'a second-order capacity of persons to reflect critically upon their first-order preferences, desires, wishes, and so forth, and the capacity to accept or attempt to change these in the light of higher-order preferences';[12] autonomy as not merely the ability to evaluate information and choose between options, but also the ability to adopt personal projects, develop relationships, and accept commitments to causes, to be creators of their own moral world.[13]

Each of these formulations shows immediately one problem for the approach to defence of the commercial expression doctrine presently being analysed. One act of expression, or choice of expression, is not in itself going to be an act of

---

[11] See the discussion in Chapter 9.1 above.

[12] Gerald Dworkin, 'Autonomy', in Robert E. Goodin and Philip Pettit (eds.), *The Blackwell Companion to Contemporary Political Philosophy* (Oxford: Blackwell Publishers Ltd., 1993), 360.

[13] Joseph Raz, *The Morality of Freedom* (Oxford: Clarendon Press, 1986), 154.

self-fulfilment or autonomy. The characterizations 'self-fulfilling' and 'autonomous' apply primarily to lives, or substantial phases of lives. Informed economic choices, however, are typically individual choosings, as in my battery example. I do not make a life out of buying batteries, or groceries, or going to the dentist, or drinking beer, even if I do these things many times a year. The free flow of commercial information contributes, if it does, to a number of discrete acts of informed economic choice. How can it be that these discrete acts become knitted together into the capacity or the condition of autonomy?

One answer to that question, of course, is to suppose that the serial, and serious, making of informed economic choices can itself constitute a self-fulfilling and autonomous life of the appropriate kind. In that sense, informed economic choice would be sufficient for autonomy. The conception of autonomy in play here, though, is defined independently; it is a conception of a life of sufficient emotional and intellectual richness such that exercising autonomy as a way of living that life constitutes human flourishing. Thus far more is packed into this notion of autonomy than simply the capacity to make informed economic choices. Argument needs to be made that exercising the capacity to make informed economic choices is a way of exercising autonomy in the sense specified. Such an argument will be difficult to find. The individual human being has many more first-order preferences, desires, and wishes than strictly economic ones, and second-order reflection on those first-order preferences, desires, and wishes will involve considering far more than just the economic status and consequences of those preferences. As Edwin Baker has put it:

Even if supplying information to the listener usually promotes self rule, this 'indirect' support does not distinguish the information's contribution from the contribution made by other resources and opportunities, such as food, shelter, health care, and employment and educational opportunities.[14]

In saying, then, that informed economic choice is but 'an aspect' of self-fulfilment and personal autonomy, the Supreme Court of Canada in *Ford* is not venturing into the territory of claims clearly hard to defend. But can even that more modest claim be defended? Is there any connection at all between autonomy and informed economic decision-making and choice?

Again, it is not hard to offer an intuitive basis for some connection between informed economic choice and a self-fulfilling and autonomous life. Suppose I am an artist operating on limited resources, and I use the batteries I have bought to power a kinetic sculpture that I have designed and built. So it is important to my ongoing life as an artist that I get the best batteries for the least dollar. My self-fulfilment and autonomy come in, however, in the designing and building of the sculpture, and getting it to operate. My act of buying the batteries contributes materially to a life of self-fulfilment and autonomy, but is not a

[14] C. Edwin Baker, 'Realizing Self-Realization: Corporate Political Expenditures and Redish's "The Value of Free Speech"', *University of Pennsylvania Law Review* 130 (1982): 662.

constituent of that life. Or, imagine a counsellor teaching persons in distress how to make more sensible economic decisions than they are presently making—watch for bargains; buy no-name, not brand name, items; buy in bulk; take a bus to the grocery store, not a taxicab, etc.—with the idea that by following this advice they gain more control over their lives and thus more personal autonomy. And the advice works. But autonomy of this kind, while real and of great value, has nothing to do with freedom of expression. Thus, even if these cases give us a sense of how informed economic decision-making can be implicated in the attainment of personal autonomy, they do so without bringing informed economic decision-making under the rubric of freedom of expression.

5 THE 'THICKNESS' OF AUTONOMY

The underlying point is a deep one, that notions such as autonomy, self-fulfilment, self-realization, in the sense in which they matter greatly to human beings and their flourishing, are 'thick' notions. I use the term 'thick' here in a way that is indebted to, but importantly different from, the original use of the term in ethical theory by Bernard Williams.[15] Williams uses the terms 'thick' and 'thin' to differentiate between two ways of thinking about ethical concepts. To regard ethical concepts as 'thin' is to regard them as having little factual import and as capable of being applied to the world anyhow. To regard them as 'thick' is to regard them as containing *ab initio* limitations on the range of entities or situations to which they can properly be applied. Williams in the book mentioned is primarily concerned to explore the consequences of the 'thickness' of ethical concepts for ethical relativism. That issue does not concern me here. I want to extract from his distinction the idea of a concept which carries along with it limitations on the circumstances of its correct deployment, as opposed to one which does not. It might be thought that 'autonomous choice' is a 'thin' concept: anything can be autonomously chosen; one just has to choose it. I hope to show that view is a mistake.

Autonomy, self-fulfilment, self-realization necessarily include as a part the making of choices, and can be negatively affected by interference with the making of choices. But autonomy, self-fulfilment, and self-realization are not just the making of choices, but the making of choices of a certain kind—those which have the appropriate significance or effect—and in a certain kind of context—in the context of formulating, reflecting on and carrying out projects and life plans of some substance. As Cass Sunstein has rightly urged, there is no such thing as an a-contextual entity called 'choice', with the exercise of which the government must never be permitted to interfere.[16] 'The question is not whether

---

[15] Bernard Williams, *Ethics and the Limits of Philosophy* (Cambridge, Mass.: Harvard University Press, 1985), 129 ff.

[16] Cass R. Sunstein, *Free Markets and Social Justice* (New York: Oxford University Press, 1997), 188–90.

or not to respect choice, but what sorts of choices to respect.'[17] If choice was all that mattered, uninformed economic choices could be as autonomous as informed economic choices. Governmental restriction on advertising, even if we acknowledge that it negatively impacts on consumer choice, is the result of political choice, not of no choice. The reason certain kinds of choice—of life partner, of career, of children's schooling, and the like—are thought to be of high value is not simply because they are choices, but because of the kind of choices they are. These choices are constitutive of autonomy, again, not simply because they are choices, but because of the kind of choices they are. If these examples are thought to display a prejudice in favour of the middle class, I readily concede that the decision to cease serving junk food, to buy warm coats instead of expensive track shoes, and the like may have a similar stature.

The prime modern defender of self-realization as the supreme freedom of expression value is Martin Redish. He first defended constitutional protection for commercial speech on the grounds of the contribution of such speech to self-realization five years before the U.S. Supreme Court decided *Virginia Board*,[18] and he is still making the same argument today,[19] especially as regards tobacco advertising.[20] Despite the energy with which Redish promotes his cause, the case is hard to make out. For one thing, Redish talks all the time of 'information' and 'rational self-fulfilment'.[21] Take, however, Redish's favoured case of tobacco advertising.[22] With almost no exception, tobacco advertising with which I am familiar contains little information beyond that which the government has required it to have, and does not exactly appeal to the rational side of human nature.[23] More fundamentally, the argument at the core of Redish's position is defeated by what I am calling the 'thick' character of notions like self-fulfilment, self-realization, and autonomy. Redish is much perturbed, like many supporters of the commercial expression doctrine (see Chapter 1.4 above), by

[17] Ibid., at 189.

[18] Martin H. Redish, 'The First Amendment in the Marketplace: Commercial Speech and the Values of Free Expression', *George Washington Law Review* 39 (1971): 429–73.

[19] Martin Redish, *Money Talks: Speech, Economic Power, and the Values of Democracy* (New York: New York University Press, 2001), Chapter 2.

[20] Martin H. Redish, 'Tobacco Advertising and the First Amendment', *Iowa Law Review* 81 (1996): 589–639; Martin H. Redish, 'First Amendment Theory and the Demise of the Commercial Speech Distinction: The Case of the Smoking Controversy', *Northern Kentucky Law Review* 24 (1997): 553–84.

[21] Martin H. Redish, 'First Amendment in the Marketplace', 472; Martin H. Redish, 'The Value of Free Speech', *University of Pennsylvania Law Review* 130 (1982): 630; Martin H. Redish, 'Demise', 553.

[22] Redish is honest enough to acknowledge that some of his work has been supported by a grant from the R.J. Reynolds tobacco corporation: Martin H. Redish, 'Tobacco Advertising', 589.

[23] One exception might be the recent series of advertisements in Canada with the mien of public service announcements, saying that the tobacco manufacturers urged teenagers not to smoke, because smoking was an adult activity. The manufacturers seemed outraged at the federal government's proposal to ban these announcements: were they not doing exactly what the government wanted, speaking out against under-age smoking? The government of course had realized that one very successful way to persuade teenagers to do something was to forbid them from doing it on the grounds that it (whatever 'it' is) is an adult activity.

the granting of a lower level of constitutional protection to commercial speech. He takes it to be fundamental to First Amendment theory that 'the increased *harm* of the commercial speech in no way alters the *value* of the speech being regulated',[24] in the same way as is true of political speech, for example. 'The category of speech must be deemed to have the same *value*, regardless of the *harm* it causes' (ibid.; Redish's emphasis in each quotation). Redish's claim here has the right shape, in the following sense. If the emphasis is on expression as an aspect of self-fulfilment or self-realization, then expression seemingly will play that role regardless of the consequences of the self-fulfilment or self-realization itself. If it makes sense to speak of the life of a racketeering hit-man as an autonomous and self-realizing life, then whacking the guy who dissed the boss is as much a self-realizing act as completing a sculpture or a book in legal theory, just as far as its constituting an act of self-realization goes. The harmful consequences do not enter into the equation. The price paid for this rightness of shape, though, is that it becomes clear how 'thin' a notion of autonomy and self-fulfilment or self-realization is implicit in Redish's argument. We can separate the self-realizing aspect from the possibly harmful consequences only if we can supply a story of the right kind to 'thicken' up the form of self-realization. In the case of those paradigms of free expression where we do allow the value of freedom of expression to override (certain at least forms of) harmful consequences—political and artistic expression, paradigmatically—we have well understood theories of how these forms of self-realization contribute to human flourishing. In the case of consumer advertising and decision-making, we have no such models.

Redish also asserts that the 'one true value' of 'individual self-realization' is in fact ambiguous: 'it can be interpreted to refer either to development of the individual's powers and abilities . . . or to the individual's control of his or her own destiny through life-affecting decisions'.[25] Redish feels that this ambiguity is a positive feature of self-realization as a First Amendment value, as both interpretations are aspects of self-realization. The two interpretations are, however, as John Valauri has shown in the context of a discussion of Redish's views on tobacco advertising, too distinct from one another for the ambiguity to be fertile, rather than duplicitous. 'The notion of a bad or wrong choice, for example, is an important element of the first interpretation, but is a contradiction in terms under the second.'[26] Even if the proper reading of 'the individual's powers and abilities' is not perfectionist, it is still not within the individual's power to choose whether some course of action—tobacco consumption, for example— contributes to the development of those powers. It is up to individuals to choose to affect their life by such consumption. But to call that 'self-realization' is to adopt the thin sense of 'choice' and of 'self-realization'. Valauri suggests (ibid.) that in practice Redish always opts for the second version when the two conflict,

---

[24] Martin H. Redish, 'Demise', 562.   [25] Martin H. Redish, 'Value of Free Speech', 593.

[26] John T. Valauri, 'Smoking and Self-Realization: A Reply to Professor Redish', *Northern Kentucky Law Review* 24 (1997): 591.

and that is certainly borne out by Redish's emphasis on the self-realizing properties of tobacco consumption. But the first reading is, in my view, the intuitively more plausible reading of self-realization.

The matter of the 'thickness' of the concepts in play here may also be approached from a different angle. Theoretical focus on human flourishing and welfare may try to locate welfare in the achievement of a certain goal. Such an approach is typically perfectionist and objectivist: to flourish, human beings must live a certain way or attain a certain state of goodness. Recently, Martha Nussbaum and Amartya Sen, in different but overlapping ways, have argued that human flourishing should rather be located in the development and exercise of certain capabilities.[27] Capabilities have to do with exercising choice between options. But how are capabilities, choices, and options to be defined? In response to what is perceived as a tendency by Sen to define capabilities too widely, Bernard Williams warns that:

> there is a danger of trivialization here, in particular if one simply generates capabilities from commodities. . . . If we create a new washing powder, 'Bloppo', then we shall have thereby created a new capability, the capability of choosing 'Bloppo'. Indeed, advertisers are always telling us that our freedom or our capabilities are being extended because there is yet another form of washing powder that previously we could not choose because it did not exist, but now we can choose.[28]

Williams believes, of course, that to count the capability to choose Bloppo as a new capability is to trivialize. He is correct, because human flourishing and welfare are 'thick', substantive notions ('thick' in the sense I am using it here). The function of consumer advertising on one level is indeed to make us aware of the range of consumer choices that we have, and, to the degree that information will enter into the decision we eventually make, advertising contributes to informed economic decision-making. But it does not follow that thereby advertising provides us with capabilities in the sense in which, if Nussbaum and Sen are correct, such capabilities are central to human flourishing.

There is, then, a truth to the Supreme Court of Canada's claim that informed economic choice is 'an aspect' of individual self-fulfilment and personal autonomy. The projects of searching for, and after achieving exercising, autonomy, and self-fulfilment may along the way involve informed economic choices, in the sense that the projects will go better with informed economic choice than without. But only some projects will go better with informed economic choice, and then only some of the time. 'Informed economic choice' does not in itself make sense as a project of autonomy and self-fulfilment.

---

[27] See here their own essays in Martha C. Nussbaum and Amartya Sen (eds.), *The Quality of Life* (Oxford: Clarendon Press, 1993), others of the essays in Parts I–III of that book, and others of their own work to which they there refer.

[28] Bernard Williams, 'The Standard of Living: Interests and Capabilities', in Geoffrey Hawthorn (ed.), *The Standard of Living*, The Tanner Lectures, Cambridge, 1985 (Cambridge: Cambridge University Press, 1987), 98; see also Thomas Hurka, 'Capability, Functioning and Perfectionism', in Lawrence J. Jost and Roger A. Shiner (eds.), *Eudaimonia and Well-Being: Ancient and Modern Conceptions* (Kelowna, BC: Academic Printing and Publishing, 2002), 147–50.

6 SELF-REALIZING EXPRESSERS AND SELF-REALIZING HEARERS

As I said a few paragraphs earlier, the Supreme Court of Canada's claim in *Ford* about the connection of commercial expression with informed economic choice and autonomy is a weak one—'an aspect of'—and rightly so. The weakness is inevitable, given that it is the autonomy of *the hearer* with which the Court is trying to connect the free flow of commercial information that supposedly leads to informed economic choice.

Consider the elaboration of my battery example, in which I use the batteries to power a kinetic sculpture. It is easy to see the informed economic choice in that case as deeply connected to autonomy and self-fulfilment. That is because we see the life of the creative artist as typically one of autonomy and self-fulfilment. Note, though, that we would be protecting, if we do, that informed economic choice because of its connection with the act of expression that is the creation of the sculpture. Here, the informed economic choice is instrumental to a valued act of expression; it is not an act of expression itself. The best that could be made of informed economic choices as in themselves acts of expression, perhaps, is to imagine a performance artist for whom somehow making informed economic choices constituted their piece of performance art. Even then, however, it would not be merely the making of informed economic choices that constituted the work of art, but the making of those choices in a given context with an end in mind. Artistic 'happenings' are not just events, and artistic happenings that involve informed economic choices not just informed economic choices.

In the case of the proposed link to the self-fulfilment and autonomy of the hearer, there is an extra link in the instrumental chain. The advertiser produces an expression that contains economic information. The receiver of the information then makes use of it in some consumer activity—presumably a purchase. What is purchased then plays some role in the development or exercise of autonomy and self-fulfilment. But why should all this matter? Why should the contribution of a consumer purchase to the autonomous life of the purchaser mean that the advertisement that was made use of by the purchaser should be constitutionally protected?

One answer might be that self-realization is such a fundamentally important value that anything that contributes to self-realization deserves constitutional protection. Such a principle is far too broad, and obviously incorrect. Self-realization and self-fulfilment come in many forms. As Schauer has rightly noted, once we acknowledge that self-realization as a value creates rights to anything that instrumentally promotes it, a huge and potentially limitless array of positive rights is created. As a result,

because governmental action of any kind almost always is directed towards satisfaction of some important want or need of the population, a right to free speech that rests on the same footing can no longer sensibly operate as a side-constraint against such action in furtherance of the public interest. . . . If all of the suits are trumps, we are in effect playing at no trumps.[29]

A better candidate might be the principle that, since self-expression contributes to either the development or the exercise of autonomy and self-fulfilment, and the promotion of autonomy and self-fulfilment is a proper goal of freedom of expression, the value of freedom of expression requires that anything which is a contributor to self-expression itself fall under constitutional protection for freedom of expression. This principle, however, is simply the 'necessary predicate' argument of *Pico*[30] in a different guise. The thought is that persons have a right to any 'necessary predicate' of the exercise of their freedom of expression right of self-expression—in this context, the advertising which would enable their informed economic choices, which choices make a contribution to their individual self-fulfilment and personal autonomy, which are freedom of expression values. But, as we saw in Chapter 10.5 above, the 'necessary predicate' argument fails conceptually, whatever its success in the case at bar.

In fact the argument in the present context about informed economic choices amounts to '*Pico*-plus'. That is, the principle just stated really claims that anything that is a necessary predicate to a necessary predicate of the exercise of self-expression should fall under constitutional protection for freedom of expression. But, if the *Pico* principle was inadequate, this even broader principle is 'inadequate-plus'. Plenty of reasons can be given for the claim that the expression of expressers needs to be protected for freedom of expression purposes. Separate reasons need to be given for saying that the hearing of expression needs also to be protected. The way in which what I say contributes to my self-realization does not straightforwardly apply to what I hear. But less straightforward ways of making it apply lack therefore the feature essential to the plausibility of including what I say, namely, that the saying itself, but not the hearing, is a key component of the process of self-realization. The hearing, at least that at stake in the free flow of commercial information argument for the commercial expression doctrine, is less directly connected to autonomy and self-fulfilment, and thus the power of the argument from self-realization for its constitutional protection is dissipated.

We have been talking all the while in this section so far as if the connection of commercial expression with individual self-fulfilment and personal autonomy is simply a special case of the general connection between expression and individual self-fulfilment and personal autonomy. But now I want to question even that. How does *the hearer's* individual self-fulfilment and personal autonomy even become a freedom of expression value? The standard argument must go something like this—'Freedom of expression merits constitutional protection

---

[29] Frederick Schauer, *Free Speech: A Philosophical Enquiry* (Cambridge: Cambridge University Press, 1982), 56.

[30] *Board of Education, Island Trees Union Free School District No. 26, et al v Pico, by his next friend Pico, et al* 457 US 853 (1982); see Chapter 10.5.

because expression is intimately involved in self-realization. The self-realizing projects of hearers are affected by what they hear. If the government restricts what hearers hear, then it interferes with their self-realizing projects. Obviously, there are ways in which government might interfere with self-realizing projects that would not be open to constitutional objection. But when they interfere with *hearing expression*, then the constitutional value of freedom of expression kicks in.'

This argument as it stands, however, breaches what has been a fundamental methodological principle of this book, that merely because something is in the ordinary sense 'speech' or 'expression', it is not automatically brought within the coverage or scope of freedom of expression. To bring a purported interference with the hearing or receipt of information within the scope of freedom of expression requires making some assumptions about the background justifying values served by freedom of expression and showing that the expression at issue really does serve those values. This qualification applies especially when the background values being invoked are autonomy, self-fulfilment, or self-realization, since those are, as I have argued, 'thick' values, values with a substance and a content. So, even if it is true that governmental interference with the free flow of commercial information impacts on individual self-fulfilment and personal autonomy, it has to be shown that commercial expression is the appropriate kind of expression, such that the impact of it on individual hearers' self-fulfilment and personal autonomy is the appropriate kind of impact to call up the freedom of expression value and the reasons for constitutionally protecting freedom of expression. The answer, 'Well, commercial expression is expression, isn't it?' is simply not enough, and neither is the claim that restrictions on advertising negatively affect the free flow of commercial information. Of course they do; that's why they are enacted. Why is that a problem?

The commercial expression doctrine now has no way of avoiding a vicious circularity in its argumentation. Remember the context of discussion. I have argued that it is a mistake to conceive of corporate expressers as having *their own* right to freedom of expression. If commercial expression merits protection, it has to be because it is in some appropriate way related to natural persons. The right of natural persons as hearers becomes a candidate basis for recognizing by transference the value of commercial expression. That is because commercial expression is held to have some value for hearers—it may in some cases impact positively, or so we shall assume, on their self-fulfilment and autonomy. It does that by affecting their capacity for informed economic choice. Now, though, we need an argument as to why affecting individual self-fulfilment and personal autonomy by affecting the capacity for informed economic choice, even when it is a form of expression that is doing the affecting, should bring the expression in question within the scope of the freedom of expression value. The standard answers, that the expression is a form of political, scientific, or artistic expression, are ruled out, because commercial expression is none of those. The answer, because it is *commercial* expression, simply begs the question. The question is why we should bring commercial expression under the coverage of the freedom of expression value. 'Because it is commercial' does not answer the question. The answer, 'Because it is expression which affects the individual self-fulfilment and personal autonomy of hearers in the way that commercial expression typically does', is only a more elaborate version of the simple question-begging answer.

7 CONCLUSION

Let me sum up the argument of this chapter. The Supreme Court of Canada offered in its decision in *Ford* the assertion that 'commercial expression . . . plays a significant role in enabling individuals to make informed economic choices, an important aspect of individual self-fulfilment and personal autonomy' (at 618). The assertion, if true, would be important for the project of justifying the commercial expression doctrine. If true, it would give a reason to subsume commercial expression under the rubric of freedom of expression, and specifically under autonomy-related accounts of the value of freedom of expression. That would be important, since the project of defending the commercial expression doctrine will gain much plausibility if it can explain how corporate commercial expression deserves constitutional protection because it fosters a constitutionally legitimate autonomy interest of the hearer of such expression.

I considered the intuitive basis for the Court's claim, that we can easily think of cases where a person makes economic choices that improve his or her life as a result of deriving information from commercial advertising. The basic difficulty with the Court's assertion as a basis for the commercial expression doctrine, however, is just that there is a huge gap between this commonplace (and weak) premise about the role of advertising in consumer decision-making and the desired (strong) conclusion that commercial expression deserves constitutional protection because it promotes individual self-fulfilment, self-realization, and autonomy.

The first point I made (this Chapter 11.3) was that simply bringing a benefit to the chooser was not enough by itself to secure the strong conclusion, since it was not invariably true that commercial expression always brought a benefit to the chooser through creating the opportunity for informed economic choice, and it was also not invariably true that bringing a benefit to someone sufficed to merit constitutional protection for what it was that brought the benefit. I then turned (this Chapter 11.4) specifically to the claim that the benefit brought was the promotion of individual self-fulfilment and autonomy, for that claim at least would, if true, bring nearer the strong desired conclusion. I showed, however, that, whatever the connection between informed economic choice and self-fulfilment, self-realization, or autonomy might be, it could be neither that informed economic choice was necessary and sufficient for those conditions, nor that it was necessary for them. There are many ways of being autonomous other than by exercising informed economic choice.

I then considered what I called the Self-realizing Consumption Argument, the argument that in itself the life of informed economic consumption was a self-fulfilling, self-realizing, or autonomous life. The Argument would, if sound, make informed economic decision-making sufficient for self-realization. However, I repudiated the Argument on the ground that concepts like self-realization and autonomy were 'thick'. They are not just a matter of any old choice, but certain choices; not just a matter of exercising any old capacity or capability, but certain capacities or capabilities. The capacity to make informed consumer choices is not one of those capacities.

Finally, I argued that what might seem to be the main attraction of the Supreme Court of Canada's argument was in fact its downfall. The attraction is that we could, if the argument was sound, explain how the hearer's self-realization, self-fulfilment, and autonomy were related to commercial expression. But the difficulty is this. Self-realization and autonomy are primarily freedom of expression values in relation to the free expresser or speaker. The expresser's or the speaker's self-realization, self-fulfilment, and autonomy are paradigmatically furthered by expressing or speaking. Even so, it is clear that the expresser does not have a right to have constitutionally protected anything that they might need in order to express, but only the act of expression itself. In the case of a hearer or a receiver of information, it is even more implausible to suppose that they may have a right to hear anything which enables them then to perform an act of expression which promotes their self-realization, self-fulfilment, and autonomy. Yet the Supreme Court of Canada argument makes exactly that presupposition.

Finally, I pointed out that, even if we acknowledge that there is some connection between commercial expression, informed economic decision-making, and individual self-realization, self-fulfilment, and autonomy, we still do not have an answer to the fundamental question asked by this book—what is it about *commercial* expression that makes it the kind of expression subsumable under a principle of freedom of expression? The commercial expression doctrine faces a dilemma. The form of autonomous decision-making which commercial advertising certainly affects is economic decision-making. But why should a principle of freedom of expression cover economic decision-making? On the other hand, if we conceive of a principle of freedom of expression as aimed at protecting those forms of expression which do materially contribute to personal self-realization, self-fulfilment, and autonomy, then we have no reason to portray informed economic choice as such a form of expression.

12

Autonomy, Paternalism, and Commercial Expression

1 What is paternalism?

In *Virginia Board*,[1] the U.S. Supreme Court complained about the impugned restriction on drug price advertising in these terms:

There is an alternative to this highly paternalistic approach. That alternative is to assume that this information is not in itself harmful, that people will perceive their own best interests if only they are well enough informed, and that the best means to that end is to open the channels of communication rather than to close them.

Referring to regulation of commercial expression as 'paternalistic' clearly struck a chord not only with the Court itself in future cases, but also with commentators. The characterization turns up again and again as a conclusory criticism of government regulation of commercial expression, the rhetorical zenith being Thomas J's diatribe in *44 Liquormart*[2] against keeping citizens ignorant in order to manipulate their choices in the marketplace. If it can be shown that regulation of commercial expression is 'paternalistic', and if it can be shown that paternalistic legislation is always wrong because it diminishes hearers' autonomy, then an autonomy-based hearers' rights argument for freedom of commercial expression would have some solid ground on which to rest. It is therefore materially relevant to the argument of this book to consider whether regulation of commercial expression is in fact 'paternalistic', and if so a normative mistake, in a way that would call up such an autonomy-based argument. As I shall show, the conceptual issues here are much more complex than the simplistic rhetoric of ivory tower and bench suggests. It is not at all clear that regulation of commercial expression is 'paternalistic'. It is not at all clear that, even if it is, it is then necessarily unjustified. And, finally, it is not at all clear that, even if there are reasons to find such regulation objectionable, they are reasons that underwrite constitutional protection for commercial expression.

The general topic of paternalism has received a great deal of attention in the philosophical literature in the last thirty or so years, not only because of a general concern with the proper limits of the exercise of state power, but also because of concern within the world of health-care about appropriate attitudes

---

[1] *Virginia State Board of Pharmacy et al v Virginia Citizens Consumer Council Inc et al* 425 US 748 (1976), at 770.
[2] *44 Liquormart Inc v Rhode Island* 116 SCt 1495 (1996), 1515–20.

towards and treatment of patients by health-care providers. I will begin this discussion in the present section and its two successors with a brief outline of the *status quaestionis*, before turning to the application of these conclusions to freedom of commercial expression.

The departure point for modern philosophical discussions of paternalism is Gerald Dworkin's well-known (and much anthologized) paper of thirty years ago. In that paper, he characterizes paternalism thus:

interference with a person's liberty of action justified by reasons referring exclusively to the welfare, good, happiness, needs, interests or values of the person being coerced.[3]

I want to highlight three things about this characterization (Dworkin does not intend it as a formal definition). First, note the essential feature that the goal of paternalism is the good, not of the agent, but of the person who is the target of the paternalistic act. It follows that any action—a piece of legislation, for example—which has other goals is not, to the extent that it has those other goals, properly thought of as 'paternalistic'.

Secondly, paternalism is said to involve interference with liberty, since it involves coercion. Dworkin clearly has in mind cases where the law subjects persons to a criminal or civil penalty in order to secure conformity to a behavioural standard; he discusses several times the case of penalties for failure to wear a seatbelt in an automobile. If interference of this kind is essential to paternalism, then paternalism has no relevance to regulation of commercial expression from the perspective of the hearer. Those who could not find out in Virginia at what price prescription drugs were sold, or in Rhode Island at what prices liquor was sold, were not themselves being coerced by threat of penalty. That a fine might have been imposed on an offending liquor store or pharmacy is neither here nor there. Liquor stores and pharmacies have no original autonomy rights in this context. However, as we shall see, to limit the concept of paternalism to coercive interference with liberty fails to cover many of the cases that most exercise ethicists. A wider characterization is needed, and it is the wider one that will ostensibly bring regulation of commercial expression within its scope.

Thirdly, as Dworkin's characterization stands, it is part of the notion of paternalism that paternalism is indeed justified. Such an assumption is of course question-begging, since the normative controversy specifically concerns whether it is, or indeed could be, justified. Substituting 'putatively justified' for 'justified' in Dworkin's characterization can easily solve this problem.[4] But then a more important issue emerges. The emendation makes it clear that the characterization is fundamentally *descriptive*. That is, given this characterization, an action, whether by the state or a private individual, is rightly called 'pater-

---

[3] Gerald Dworkin, 'Paternalism', *The Monist* 56 (1972): 65; Gerald Dworkin, 'Paternalism', in Richard A. Wasserstrom (ed.), *Morality and the Law* (Belmont, Cal.: Wadsworth, 1971), 108. Since the journal is now more accessible, page references here will be to it.

[4] Donald Van De Veer, 'Autonomy-Respecting Paternalism', *Social Theory and Practice* 6 (1980): 189.

nalistic', if it is, because of its factual design, not because of its normative status as justified or unjustified. If it is a matter of non-normative description whether an action is 'paternalistic' or not, then paternalism is not in itself a dirty word. Saying an action is paternalistic is like saying it occurred last Tuesday. It remains to be seen whether, and if so in what way, the feature of being pater nalistic is normatively significant. The conclusory way in which supporters of the commercial expression doctrine throw around the terms 'paternalism' and 'paternalistic' as terms of opprobrium is inappropriate and unhelpful. Now, it may be true that it is always appropriate to be normatively suspicious of any action that satisfies the description 'paternalistic'. If that is true, then it is easy to see how the term can become a term of ethical abuse. All the same, if we are to understand the normative issues clearly, we must be very careful to distinguish between descriptive uses of the term that leave open whether paternalism is justified and normatively loaded uses of the term which prejudice the issue of justification. I will use the term here only in the descriptive sense.

These concerns about Dworkin's original characterization became commonplace in the literature, and he himself soon produced a revised characterization. He argued that:

there must be a violation of a person's autonomy, as opposed to liberty, for one to treat another paternalistically. There must be a usurpation of decision-making, either by preventing people from doing what they have decided or by interfering with the way in which they arrive at their decisions.[5]

He also notes that one prime method of interfering paternalistically is by 'manipulating [some-]one's information set' (at 106). The motivation behind this wider characterization is, *inter alia*, to include cases of medical paternalism—the surgeon, for example, who fails to inform a patient about the risks inherent in a surgical procedure because she feels it will be better for the patient not to know. There is no coercive interference with liberty there, but still a problematic treatment of some sort of the patient, supposedly for that patient's own good. Clearly, we now have an opening for declaring regulation of commercial expression to be 'paternalistic'. Let us use the term 'management' as a normatively neutral term by which to refer to what happens to the flow of information when that flow is regulated. As courts and commentators perceive regulation of commercial expression, such regulation is a management of the free flow of commercial information from advertiser to consumer, and it indeed is. However, it would be a further step (and one which must be justified) from there to saying that such 'management' amounts to 'manipulation' of the consumer's 'information set', and thus to paternalism in Dworkin's wider sense. It would also be a further step, and one in need of justification, to say that any effect such regulation had on consumer decision-making was 'usurpation' of the decision.

[5] Gerald Dworkin, 'Paternalism: Some Second Thoughts', in Rolf Sartorius (ed.), *Paternalism* (Minneapolis, Minn.: University of Minnesota Press, 1983), 107.

If the anti-paternalism argument is to be taken seriously, the wider descriptive characterization of paternalism must be adopted, and we shall adopt it in this chapter.

2 WHAT'S (PURPORTEDLY) WRONG WITH PATERNALISM?

Paternalistic action functions in a context where the presumed background values are freedom, liberty, and autonomy. The moral ideal is one where persons are free to direct their own lives as they wish, to choose their own projects and goals for their lives, to develop and act on their own preferences as to the good for them, and as to how to realize that good. In a complex pluralistic society such as the one in which most readers of this book will live, exceptionless freedom and autonomy of this sort are impossible; the actions of one with inordinate frequency affect others and the actions of others. So the question then becomes, on what basis is individual freedom of action legitimately limited, and especially legitimately limited by the coercive authority of the state? Familiarly, discussion begins with John Stuart Mill's 'one very simple principle' that:

the only purpose for which power can be rightfully exercised over any member of a civilized community, against his will, is to prevent harm to others. His own good, either physical or moral, is not a sufficient warrant. He cannot rightfully be compelled to do or forbear because it will be better for him to do so, because it will make him happier, because, in the opinions of others, to do so would be wise, or even right.[6]

The kind of action characterized here as 'paternalistic' seems obviously to offend against Mill's principle, while the principle itself seems well to capture the idea of what it means to be autonomous and free.

The quotation from Mill, however, contains the germ of two different ideas that emerge in subsequent discussion about what is wrong with paternalism on those occasions when it is wrong. The first is that it is not 'wise'. That is, we have some idea of a proper goal for social behaviour—call it 'utility', for example, or 'welfare', or, even, 'efficiency'—and paternalistic action frustrates that goal. The second is that paternalism is not 'right'. That is, we have adopted some norms concerning rightness as a quality of actions, and, when we compare paternalistic action with those norms, it fails to conform to them. At rock bottom, paternalism is seen as a violation of autonomy, and 'I violate your autonomy if I try to control your behaviour or change your beliefs in ways that circumvent your capacities for free will and rationality—brainwashing, subliminal suggestion, deception or withholding information'.[7] But the ultimate reason for the wrongness of paternalism may be either that a person whose

---

[6] John Stuart Mill, *Essential Works of John Stuart Mill* (ed. and intro Max Lerner, New York: Bantam Books, 1961), 263.

[7] Danny Scoccia, 'Moral Paternalism, Virtue and Autonomy', *Australasian Journal of Philosophy* 78 (2000): 58.

autonomy is violated suffers a deep loss in happiness, utility, or welfare, or it may be that violation of a person's autonomy is wrong as such; violation of autonomy is violation of the intrinsic worth of persons. We will see how important it is to keep these two forms of normative criticism apart.

3 CAN PATERNALISM EVER BE JUSTIFIED?

The question of the justification of paternalism of course is enormous, and enormously complex and contested. I am going to present here only short versions of lines of arguments that turn up with some regularity in the literature. I will be putting them to the test only in the case of their potential application to commercial expression. I will deal first with issues of autonomy, and then with issues of welfare. In both cases, the intuition is powerful that paternalism cannot be absolutely and in all possible cases wrong. Parents control aspects of their children's lives for the good of those same children. Care-givers control aspects of the lives of severely disadvantaged persons for the good of those same persons. We thank, rather than criticize, the person who pulls us out of the way of an oncoming vehicle we had not seen. We (or most of us, anyway) see the point of requiring the use of seatbelts or bicycle helmets, of mandatory health warnings or nutritional information on product packaging. The question is, how are these intuitions to be organized into a principled account of when paternalism is and is not justified?

Why do we intuitively go along with parents exercising influence and even control over their children's actions and choices? We appreciate that, in suitable ways, children are not yet autonomous. They have not lived long enough to have the necessary capacities, both volitional and cognitive, for self-direction. They do not understand much about how the world works scientifically and socially. They find it hard to defer gratification. And so on. Note that, in order for what I have just said to be true, it is not necessary to adopt an objective account of the good for humans. Even if the good for humans is a matter of subjective preference, what I have just said about children holds. Reflection on the case of children and of the severely disadvantaged gives rise to the idea of a voluntariness constraint on paternalistic action. As Joel Feinberg put it, 'the state has a right to prevent self-regarding harmful conduct *when but only when* that conduct is substantially non-voluntary, or when temporary intervention is necessary to establish whether it is voluntary or not'.[8] Such a thesis is commonly called 'soft' or 'weak' paternalism, to distinguish it from 'hard' or 'strong' paternalism that contemplates paternalism being justified even when intervention takes place with respect to fully voluntary choices or preferences. The difficulty with this thesis is, as Feinberg himself points out,[9] that so-called 'soft paternal-

---

[8] Joel Feinberg, *Harm to Self*, vol. III of *The Moral Limits of the Criminal Law* (New York: Oxford University Press, 1986), 12.
[9] Ibid., 13–15.

ism' is not really a form of paternalism. It does not say when a paternalistic intervention is justified; rather, it says only when it would be wrong not to let the intervener off the hook. The voluntariness condition operates as a side-constraint on the justification of paternalism, not as a part of the justification.[10]

Gerald Dworkin in his original article draws a different moral from the case of children. The moral is dubious as it stands, but correct in its implications. Dworkin argues that paternalism in regard to children should be seen as 'a wager by the parent on the child's subsequent recognition of the wisdom of [his parent's] restrictions'.[11] As an account of why paternalism as regards children is justified, the wager theory is weak. As critics have pointed out, if taken literally, it leaves the action counterintuitively unjustified if the child never does come to see the wisdom, or if the child dies young and does not grow up.[12] If taken not literally, but as a form of 'hypothetical consent' theory, deep questions arise as to what, if anything, hypothetical consent can justify. The truth to which the wager idea points, and which I will say more about shortly, is that consent matters to the justification of paternalism. The point now is that, as Douglas Husak has well argued, actual consent is what matters. Notions such as 'hypothetical consent' or 'disposition to subsequent consent' function just as stand-ins for some more diffuse notion of the paternalistic intervention being reasonable. But the point of requiring actual consent is to deny that justifications based on (mere) reasonableness are not enough.[13]

What's wrong with paternalism is that seemingly paternalistic interventions are interferences with, or violations of, the intervenee's autonomy, and we place a high value on autonomy. Paternalistic interventions are, other things being equal, autonomy-overriding. But if in some real sense consent to the intervention is given, then autonomy is not overridden. A person can signal in advance in various ways that at some future time it will be all right to override his then-stated preferences in order to promote his interest or good—again, whether objectively or subjectively defined. Dworkin gives the familiar example of Odysseus and his authorization of interference given to his sailors. 'Here are my car keys. Don't give them back to me, even if I howl for them, if I am too drunk to drive', is another familiar, if regrettably infrequent, example. It is clear though that these are interpersonal examples. How do they apply, or how could they apply, to governmental legislation? In general, Dworkin suggests, 'we give consent to a system of government, run by elected representatives, with the understanding that they may act to safeguard our interests in certain ways'.[14]

---

[10] I will not here delve further into the issue of what makes an action 'less than fully voluntary'; that is a whole topic in itself.

[11] Dworkin, 'Paternalism', 76.

[12] Rosemary Carter, 'Justifying Paternalism', *Canadian Journal of Philosophy* 7 (1977): 135.

[13] Douglas N. Husak, 'Paternalism and Autonomy', *Philosophy and Public Affairs* 10 (1981): 33–4.

[14] Dworkin, 'Paternalism', 78.

We take out 'social insurance policies' (ibid.), by analogy with the 'private' insurance policy in the Odysseus and like cases.[15]

Consent, then, can play an important justificatory role in framing paternalistic interventions as autonomy-respecting, not autonomy overriding. But autonomy-based candidate justifications exist even in the absence of consent. Robert Young draws an important distinction between 'occurrent autonomy' and 'global autonomy'. In general, Young claims, 'to be autonomous is to be free to order one's life in a unified way according to a plan or conception which fully expresses one's own individual preferences, interests and so on'.[16] We can then distinguish, he continues, an 'occurrent' and a 'global' sense of autonomy: 'occurrent autonomy' corresponds to people acting autonomously in particular situations while 'global autonomy' refers to the self-directedness of a person's life in general, 'whether in the broad it is ordered according to a plan or conception which fully expresses his or her own will' (ibid.). Thus a paternalistic intervention may affect autonomy in one of two ways. It may affect 'occurrent autonomy' in that it affects an individual's action or choice of action in some given particular situation. Or it may affect an individual's autonomy in a global way. If I stop someone from taking a sip from a glass of water that has been contaminated, then I am affecting his or her occurrent autonomy. If I negligently injure someone by my bad driving, making that person a brain-damaged quadriplegic, I have affected that person's global autonomy.

The distinction Young makes is an intuitively plausible distinction. Its importance though is not so much in its descriptive accuracy, as in the implications it has for the justification of paternalism. Take the case I gave, of preventing someone from unwittingly becoming ill by drinking contaminated water. Or we might imagine more spectacular cases still—I prevent a person from going out on to a balcony many floors up, which I, but not that person, know to be unstable. These are familiar kinds of examples. Our strong intuitions are that I did the right thing; but I interfered with that person's autonomy, didn't I? So it looks as though we have to choose between saying that autonomy invariably trumps values opposed to it, and so after all I did not do the right thing, and saying that prevention of harm outweighs autonomy, a view that seems to place paternalistic interventions beyond controversy. Young's distinction allows us to escape this fork by saying that paternalistic interventions affecting occurrent autonomy are in principle justified if they protect or even foster global autonomy. The issue in the balcony case and its kin is not the prevention of harm as such, but the preservation of (global) autonomy. Paternalistic interventions may

---

[15] There is still the issue of how in general 'consent' is to be construed when applied to the legitimation of democratic governments, but, since the status of democracy is not at issue here, the issue need not be pursued.

[16] Robert M. Young, 'Autonomy and Paternalism', in Kai Nielsen and Steven C. Patten (eds.), *New Essays in Ethics and Public Policy*, Canadian Journal of Philosophy Supplementary Volume VIII (Guelph: Canadian Association for Publishing in Philosophy, 1982), 57.

thus be occurrent-autonomy-overriding, but global-autonomy-preserving, or - promoting, and thus justified even within the paradigm of autonomy.

A third way of potentially justifying paternalism even assuming autonomy as the supreme value is the following. Suppose that a person has a suitably well developed conception of the good for him- or herself. Note that it has to be suitably well developed: maximal consumption of chocolate ice cream is not a candidate. Suppose too that the person has a suitably well-developed and seriously adopted life-plan to pursue that good. (The same kind of qualification applies— pursuing that good only on the first Tuesday of the month or when there are no poker games on offer will not count.) No other constraints on the content of this good apply. Is it then not plausible to suppose that, even in the absence of overt consent, such a person would welcome paternalistic interventions for the sake of that good? So at least several authors have argued, with some cogency. Richard Fallon claims that 'however much we resent paternalistic interferences, few of us would want our ascriptive autonomy to be treated as an absolute bar to efforts to protect us against our own self-regarding but dangerously ill-considered action'.[17] Dan Brock similarly argues that, if persons are thought of as purposive, rational agents who pursue their own good as they conceive it, then, when they fail to do so, it does not seem rational for them to insist on a right nonetheless to pursue their seeming good, rather than accept that others in this situation know their good better.[18] Autonomy is respected in these cases, because the intervenee chose autonomously the good for the sake of which the intervention occurs.[19]

Even if we stay within the paradigm of autonomy, then, the thought that paternalism must be wrong just because it interferes with autonomy is much too simplistic. If a clear sense can be established in which the paternalistic intervention has received the consent of the intervenee, then the possibility of justification for the intervention exists, consent being an exercise of autonomy. If the intervention affects occurrent autonomy, and has the effect of preserving or promoting global autonomy, then the possibility of justification for the intervention exists. If the intervention promotes an autonomously chosen good, then the possibility of justification for the intervention exists.

Suppose now that we desert the paradigm of autonomy, and consider the possibility of justifications for paternalism in terms of the weight of other values— prevention of harm, for example, or maximization of welfare. There are two ways in which such values may be introduced. One way is to take the value of autonomy as intrinsic, though not absolute, and to treat other values as competitor intrinsic values that will need to be weighed against autonomy in cases of conflict. Since in the dominant liberal world-view autonomy is valued so highly, a candidate justification for paternalism that depends on the intrinsic

---

[17] Richard H. Fallon Jr., 'Two Senses of Autonomy', *Stanford Law Review* 46 (1994): 898.

[18] Dan Brock, 'Paternalism and Promoting the Good', in Rolf Sartorius (ed.), *Paternalism* (Minneapolis, Minn.: University of Minnesota Press, 1983), 247–9.

[19] David Archard, 'For Our Own Good', *Australasian Journal of Philosophy* 72 (1994): passim.

value of autonomy being outweighed by other values will arguably be hard to find.[20] Gerald Dworkin considers, for instance, a line of argument which stipulates that certain goods such as health are goods which 'any person would want to have in order to pursue his own good',[21] and then allows paternalistic interventions whether or not there is actual consent in the name of maximizing possession of such goods for the intervenee. As Dworkin rightly points out, the stipulation is just that. What counts in any given case is whether the intervenee really does espouse those values, not whether philosophers label them as goods anyone would want.

On the other hand, suppose that we do not consider the value of autonomy to be intrinsic, but rather to be instrumental. Autonomy is to be valued because it is a contributor—even a major contributor—to welfare, or happiness, or utility. As Husak pointed out twenty years ago, and nothing has much changed since, there is a general assumption that instrumentalist—especially, utilitarian—justifications for paternalism abound.[22] A case like the contaminated water case, which is after all a case in the normative analysis of which the avoidance of harm figures prominently, is extrapolated to stand for any circumstance in which the harm done to the intervenee in the absence of the intervention is greater than the welfare produced by undisturbed autonomy. The fact that utilitarianism seems to imply such a disrespect for autonomy is of course regularly turned over, and presented as an intuitive objection to utilitarianism: the thought is that any theory which allows autonomy to be so easily toppled cannot be correct as a moral theory. Utilitarians will argue, however, that the appearance of an easy justification within the paradigm of utility for paternalism is illusory. As Richard Arneson points out, the consequences of coming to rely on the dispensation of paternalistic aid are mischievous—a weakening of the general atmosphere of freedom.[23] The potential for abuse of paternalism is enormous, and autonomy ranks very highly as a producer of welfare. But these points, valid as they are, show only that a justification of paternalism on consequentialist grounds has to be carefully constructed; they do not show that such a justification cannot be constructed.

The results of this survey of justifications for paternalism can be summarized. It is a mistake to think that there is a straightforward argument against paternalism: paternalism violates autonomy and is therefore unjustified. It is not automatic that paternalism violates autonomy. Even when it does, and even if autonomy is regarded as of supreme intrinsic value, possibilities for the justification of paternalism exist. They certainly exist if autonomy is taken, not as

---

[20] My comment here depends on interpreting autonomy as linked to 'negative liberty', rather than 'positive liberty', in terms of Isaiah Berlin's well-known distinction (see Isaiah Berlin, *Four Essays on Liberty* (Oxford: Clarendon Press, 1969), 121 ff), and it is of course controversial whether and how far liberalism as a system of value may adopt positive freedom as a goal. I cannot deal with that matter here.

[21] Dworkin, 'Paternalism', 78.   [22] Husak, 'Paternalism and Autonomy', 27.

[23] Richard J. Arneson, 'Mill Versus Paternalism', *Ethics* 90 (1980): 481; Brock, 'Promoting the Good', 254–6; Dworkin, 'Paternalism', 83–4.

intrinsically valuable, but as instrumentally contributing to welfare. It is now time to apply these results to the case of commercial expression.

4 Is REGULATION OF COMMERCIAL EXPRESSION A CASE OF PATERNALISM?

The claim by the supporter of the commercial expression doctrine that we are considering here I have called the anti-paternalism argument. The claim is that government regulation of commercial expression is essentially paternalistic, and violative of the autonomy of the hearers. I have acknowledged that, if this claim can be made out, then we have a good reason for attributing to hearers an original autonomy right available for 'borrowing' by commercial expressers in order rightfully to challenge restrictions on their expression. In the preceding three sections, I have laid out some of the issues that arise when an action, or a piece of legislation, is characterized as 'paternalistic', and is claimed as a result to be unjustified. These issues are complex, and the complexity is certainly enough to show that the characterization of government regulation of commercial advertising as 'unjustifiably paternalistic' will need thorough explication and defence. Sloganeering is not enough. Three conditions must be met. First, government regulation is 'paternalistic' only if it is enacted for the good of the individuals whose information set is being affected. Is that condition fulfilled in the case of regulation of commercial advertising? Secondly, government regulation is *prima facie* unjustifiably paternalistic, on the best interpretation of the relevant normative issues, only if it interferes with the autonomy of those affected in some way. Is that condition fulfilled in the case of regulation of commercial advertising? Thirdly, government regulation is in reality unjustifiably paternalistic only if it both actually interferes with autonomy and does so in a way that cannot be subsumed under any of the accepted forms of justification for paternalism. Is that condition fulfilled in the case of regulation of commercial advertising? These issues will be examined in turn.

The first issue to discuss is whether government regulation of commercial advertising is even paternalistic in a non-conclusory, plain, or descriptive sense of that term. There are two questions here. First, is such a regulation the appropriate kind of intervention in citizens' lives to be a candidate for paternalism? Secondly, is such regulation enacted with the kind of appropriate motive or purpose to be a candidate for paternalism?

As I have indicated already, it is a mistake to think that government regulation of commercial advertising *coerces* the person who is the potential hearer or reader or viewer of the advertising in question. It does not. On the other hand, it is clear that government regulation of commercial advertising does have some effect on the choices and planning and decisions of (at least some) citizens. I want to purchase my favourite brand of liquor at the lowest price available. To do that, I need to know which shop is offering that brand at the lowest price. The government prohibits shops from advertising liquor prices. The government thus either causes me to spend a lot of time in acquiring the necessary information, which time I would not have had to spend if I could have just read an advertisement in the local paper. Or, if I take the line of least resistance and just go to the nearest shop, the government may well cause me to spend more money than I would otherwise have had to spend on the purchase of the liquor. So my choices and decisions are almost certainly different from what they would have been in the absence of the restriction on advertising liquor prices. I stipulate to all that, although the sense of 'cause' here merits inspection.

Recall Dworkin 's 'second thoughts' about the definition of paternalism mentioned above. Does it follow from what I have stipulated that government regulation of commercial advertising must then be construed as 'usurpation of decision-making, either by preventing people from doing what they have decided or by interfering with the way in which they arrive at their decisions', or as 'manipulating [some-]one's information set'?[24] Arguably, such regulation does 'interfere with the way in which [I] arrive at [my] decision'. It may or may not, though, 'usurp [my] decision-making', or 'manipulat[e my] information set'. Obvious as all this seems, we must not beg questions. Not all cases of affecting someone's decision-making or information set are manipulative. If I tell you the correct time when you ask, I am affecting your information set, but not manipulating you. Not all substituting another's decision with one's own is usurpatory. I ask my wife what she would like for lunch, and she says, 'Whatever you decide, my dear.' So I decide. That's not 'usurping decision-making'. 'Of course these aren't manipulating or usurping. The person's asked you; she is consenting.' True indeed, and that shows that the application of terms like 'manipulation' or 'usurpation' to a fact situation is not only saying that an action of a given description has occurred, but also making a normative judgement about whether the intervener's actions are justified. We need a form of words that neutrally describes what the government does when it regulates commercial advertising, and which is not conclusory as to the matter of justification, but which does acknowledge the reality of what is taking place. I shall use the terms 'affects [someone's] decision' and 'affects [someone's] information set' as such a neutral expression.

Government regulation of commercial advertising,[25] then, clearly does affect the information set and the decision-making of hearers or would-be hearers of the advertising. Many further steps in the argument remain before we can conclude that such regulation is an unjustified paternalistic violation of the autonomy of the hearer or would-be hearer.[26]

---

[24] Dworkin, 'Second Thoughts', 107, 106.

[25] I am going to restrict discussion to this range of cases of commercial expression, not only because they constitute the bulk of the cases, but especially because the accusations of unjustified paternalism from the ivory tower and the bench occur largely with respect to cases of commercial advertising.

[26] From now on, I will use 'hearer' to include 'would-be hearer', differentiating them only when the argument requires it.

5 Is REGULATION OF COMMERCIAL EXPRESSION
'FOR THE SAKE OF THE INTERVENEE'?

One essential feature of action that is a 'paternalistic' intervention is that it is for the good of the person who is the target of the intervention.[27] If regulation of commercial advertising is properly to be characterized as 'paternalistic', therefore, it must display this feature. Opponents of such regulation are in no doubt that this condition is satisfied. The U.S. Supreme Court in *Virginia Board*, for example, considers at length the state's reasons for regulating price advertising among pharmacists, claims that these reasons are reasons which promote the welfare and interests of citizens, and that the state's view is that citizens must be protected from the consequences of deregulation of drug price advertising if these reasons are to have their effect in real life.[28] The Court is thus in no doubt that the state's approach is 'highly paternalistic'.[29]

Great care, however, has to be taken with this line of argument. Governments exist to protect and advance the welfare and interests of their citizens, even though the interests are of numerous different kinds and the possibilities for restrictions on legitimate ways of such protecting and advancing are legion. There can be, of course, and indeed is, empirical argument over whether some proposed legislation, or for that matter court decision, really does protect or advance citizens' welfare. But that is not the present issue.[30] The idea of a piece of legislation being 'paternalistic' is that it functions to protect or advance citizens' welfare in some particular way—namely, in a potentially problematic way substituting the state's own assessment of best interests or welfare for that of the citizens. Is that so in the case of regulation of commercial advertising?

It is a commonplace in academic discussions of paternalism that many proffered examples of state paternalism are not really examples of paternalism at all. Joel Feinberg suggests that we have to distinguish between 'conscious reasons', 'deep motivations', 'implicit rationales', and 'true justifications' with respect to a piece of legislation.[31] The reasons that a legislator actually gives for voting for a bill may not be the same as underlying or concealed motivations. What the best rational reconstruction is for the reasons supporting a bill may be different again. In particular it may differ from what some objective perspective reveals to be a true justification for the bill. The idea of being 'paternalistic' may apply in any of these cases, but only the last two are of relevance here. A look at the record of parliamentary or congressional debates prior to the enactment of

---

[27] See the characterization cited from Gerald Dworkin at the beginning of this Chapter.
[28] *Virginia Board*, at 766–70.
[29] Ibid., at 770.
[30] How the force of this point about empirical disagreement factors into the legitimacy of the commercial expression doctrine is something to be addressed anon. See this Chapter 12.6–7 below.
[31] Feinberg, *Harm to Self*, 16–17.

advertising regulations does not reveal legislators expressly claiming to be judging better than citizens themselves what is in the citizens' best interests. They do claim to be doing what is best for the citizenry, but that is not enough to guarantee paternalism. So we have to consider whether the best rational reconstruction, or the best true justification, of some regulation of commercial advertising is that it is for the good of the persons whose information set is being affected, and only for that reasons, and is against their expressed wishes.[32]

Notoriously, when that standard is applied to other kinds of government regulation, it is hard to frame them as 'paternalistic'. Consumer protection laws relating to the design or content of consumer items themselves (not to their advertising), such as laws relating to food and drug purity, or the absence of risk of injury to operator or bystander, are not paternalistic.[33] The best implicit rationale of such legislation is the protection of harm to citizens. The important point is this—not every case of preventing harm from occurring to citizens is a case of preventing citizens from harming themselves. The issue here is what tort law refers to as 'proximate causality'. If I take an instrument that under normal circumstances can be operated perfectly safely—a knife, for example—and I deliberately use it to inflict harm on myself, then I am the cause of the harm. But if I take an instrument—an electric toaster, for example—and operate it in the recommended fashion, but the toaster is so designed that, even if it is operated in the recommended fashion, the device heats up so much that operators are likely to burn themselves, and I do burn myself, then I am not the cause of the harm to me. The toaster, and more remotely but still proximately enough, its designer and manufacturer are the cause of my harm. Government regulation of the design of electric toasters is designed to protect me from harm that is the result of my using the toaster indeed, but is not 'self-inflicted' harm in the way in which my deliberately stabbing myself with the knife is 'self-inflicted' harm. Regulation to prevent the possibility of the latter kind of choice may well be 'paternalistic'. Regulation to prevent the kind of harm I get from the toaster is not paternalistic.

Familiarly, Mill's case against paternalism relies on the identification of a class of actions as 'self-regarding'—that is, of having consequences for no-one but the agent. Equally familiarly, the delineation of such a class is difficult. 'The public interest is always involved, at least to some degree, when persons harm themselves'—the social costs of 'cleaning up, rescuing, retrieving, or repairing' whether within the formal health-care system or not.[34] It may be a nice matter to say at which point the involvement of the public interest makes some given piece of legislation not paternalistic but harm-preventing; but there will be such

---

[32] Husak rightly warns that the 'best rationale' approach to identifying instances of paternalistic legislation risks blurring the distinction between descriptive concerns and justificatory concerns: see Douglas Husak, 'Legal Paternalism', in Hugh LaFollette (ed.), *Oxford Handbook of Practical Ethics* (Oxford: Clarendon Press, 2002), 392. We will have to assume those risks here.

[33] Feinberg, *Harm to Self*, 21; Nicholas Fotion, 'Paternalism', *Ethics* 89 (1979): 197.

[34] Feinberg, *Harm to Self*, 22.

a point. The social costs of 'cleaning up' the effects of harm occurring through not wearing seatbelts in automobiles and trucks, or helmets on bicycles and construction sites, justify enforcement of such practices.

So the question now becomes: how does all this apply to the case of government regulation of commercial advertising? Suppose the state forbids the advertising of liquor prices or prescription drug prices, or places tight restrictions on the format and place of advertising of gambling or tobacco products, or regulates closely lawyers' solicitation. When the state so acts, is it behaving in a manner more like consumer protection legislation, or more like criminalizing attempted suicide (even if we grant, which arguably we should not, that the latter is a case of self-regarding action)? The supporters of the commercial expression doctrine want us to see regulation of advertising as 'paternalistic' in the style of the criminalization of attempted suicide. But the analogy with consumer protection is more plausible. If the case for regulation of commercial advertising being 'paternalistic' is to be made out, it has to be true that the intervention into personal decision-making being solely for the good of the person whose decision-making is affected by the intervention has to be either the best rational reconstruction of the purpose of the regulation or its truest justification. This condition is not fulfilled.

Moreover, the condition is not fulfilled even in the eyes of the courts themselves. The second step of the U.S. Supreme Court's test in *Central Hudson*[35] for the constitutional legitimacy of regulation of commercial speech is that the asserted government interest is substantial. The first step of the Supreme Court of Canada's test in *Oakes* for when it is constitutionally acceptable to limit a guaranteed freedom or right is that the objective is 'consistent with a free and democratic society', relates to concerns which are 'pressing and substantial' and directed to 'the realization of collective goals of fundamental importance'.[36] No piece of challenged legislation regulating commercial advertising has ever failed these tests before the Supreme Court of Canada. The situation before the U.S. Supreme Court is not very different. An asserted government interest[37] has been rejected as 'substantial' in only seven cases since *Central Hudson*.[38] In *Bolger*, the Court rejected a proposed interest in 'shielding recipients from materials that they are likely to find offensive',[39] indeed an interest properly described as 'paternalistic' and as insubstantial, given the weight of freedom of expression as

[35] *Central Hudson Gas & Electric Corporation v Public Service Commission of New York* 447 US 557 (1980), at 566.

[36] *R v Oakes* (1986) 26 DLR (4th) 200, at 226–7.

[37] The Court is procedurally confined to weighing the substantiality of interests actually asserted by the government. It is not permitted to indulge in rational reconstructions of possible interests a piece of legislation might serve.

[38] It follows, therefore, that, in cases where legislation has been invalidated on freedom of commercial expression grounds, the invalidation has regularly been because of a failure to pass the proportionality requirement of the *Oakes* test, or the 'directly advancing' and 'no more extensive' steps in the case of the *Central Hudson* test. This fact is not without its own significance; see Chapter 13.6–9 below.

[39] *Bolger v Youngs Drug Products Corp* 463 US 60 (1983), at 71.

a value. In *Coors*, the Court rejected as substantial a claimed interest in facilitating states' efforts to regulate alcohol.[40] The remaining five cases all concerns aspects of professional advertising by lawyers[41] and accountants.[42] In all of these cases, the state in question asserted in some form an interest in protecting the general public from false and misleading advertising. The Court's decisions striking down the regulations turned on rejecting (with considerable plausibility) the impugned advertising as being in fact liable to mislead. The state's interest was rejected as substantial, then, in so far as it was framed as an interest in regulating what was already determined to be (and arguably in fact was) truthful and non-misleading advertising. Therefore, despite the Court proceeding under the self-description of assessing, and repudiating, a state claim of a substantial interest, the Court is really taking the state to be relying on a right to regulate false and misleading advertising (a right not in dispute) and reasoning that the right has no application to the case at bar. While too enthusiastic a willingness to label advertising as 'potentially deceptive' may be a base from which to launch a piece of paternalistic legislation, the legislation is not paternalistic, if it is, simply because it labels as 'potentially misleading' advertising which is in fact not misleading.

These cases therefore do not refute the thesis that, never mind the rhetoric, neither the Supreme Court of Canada nor the U.S. Supreme Court questions the governmental regulatory interest—even, right—which lies behind the typical statutory control of commercial advertising. Never mind the rhetoric, the two Courts are not in fact treating the legislation they assess as passed on the presupposition that the government knows better than the citizens themselves do what is in the citizens' best interests. The presupposition, rather, is acknowledged to be the proper responsibility of the government to promote the health and welfare of citizens. As Daniel Lowenstein has pointed out, the underlying mechanism in decision theory is entirely appropriate.[43] A series of self-interested individual decisions by rationally maximizing citizens may well result in an overall lowering of aggregate welfare. In restricting opportunities for such self-interested decision making, a government is in principle simply carrying out its obligations to maintain an adequate level of aggregate welfare.

The scent of paternalism is politically intoxicating, both to its opponents and to its supporters. It is possible to miss the above point in both directions. Thomas J in his spirited opinion in *44 Liquormart* goes too far one way. As we have seen (see Chapter 3.2 above), the *Central Hudson* test for the legitimacy of

---

[40] *Rubin v Coors Brewing Company* 115 SCt 1585 (1995), at 1591. The Court however appeared later to accept as appropriately substantial an analogous interest as regards the regulation of gambling: see *Greater New Orleans Broadcasting Association Inc v United States* 119 SCt 1923 (1999), at 1931.

[41] *In re RMJ* 455 US 191 (1982); *Zauderer v Office of Disciplinary Counsel* 471 US 626 (1985); *Peel v Attorney Registration and Disciplinary Commission of Illinois* 496 US 91 (1990).

[42] *Edenfield v Fane* 113 SCt 1792 (1993); *Ibanez v Florida Department of Business and Professional Regulation* 512 US 136 (1994).

[43] Daniel Hays Lowenstein, '"Too Much Puff": Persuasion, Paternalism and Commercial Speech', *University of Cincinnati Law Review* 56 (1988): 1240–1.

government regulation of commercial speech requires the government to meet a lower standard of review than for speech such a political speech that receives full First Amendment protection. Thomas J is opposed to distinguishing commercial speech from political speech in this way. He feels that commercial speech should receive full First Amendment protection, a view of which he continues to be the only active supporter on the U.S. Supreme Court. One argument he uses to defend the view in his *44 Liquormart* opinion (at 1518) is that the *Central Hudson* test implies a condoning of the disparaged paternalistic approach by government. Thomas J's claim is that even to depart from full First Amendment protection for commercial speech is to acquiesce in government paternalism. This thought is mistaken. In the context of current U.S. constitutional First Amendment jurisprudence, where the claim of commercial speech for some protection under the First Amendment is acknowledged, the granting of a lower level of protection may easily be seen as an appropriate balance between a legitimate societal interest in free expression, and an equally legitimate governmental interest in the protection of citizens' health and welfare, and in regulation of the economy. These interests are not in themselves paternalistic, even though specific pieces of legislation may in fact be so. No inference lies from the granting of a lower level of constitutional protection to commercial speech to endorsement of paternalism. Lowenstein misses the mark in the other direction. He argues that the U.S. Supreme Court in fact observes a double standard. Despite the prevalence of anti-paternalistic rhetoric, he claims, the Court is perfectly willing itself to be paternalistic when paternalism is justified. Whether or not that claim is in general true is not here the issue. I want to focus on one of Lowenstein's examples. He takes it that the refusal to extend constitutional protection under the commercial expression doctrine to false or misleading commercial speech is itself evidence of the Court's willingness to endorse paternalism. But it is not such evidence. The refusal to extend constitutional protection to false or misleading commercial speech is as explicable as is the doctrine of the lower level of protection in terms of an acknowledgment by the Court of the legitimacy of the government's regulatory interest.

6 DOES REGULATION OF COMMERCIAL EXPRESSION OVERRIDE AUTONOMY?

It is then highly questionable whether regulation of commercial expression is 'paternalistic'; rather, the best rational reconstruction of its purpose represents it as fulfilling the governmental mandate to promote the health and welfare of citizens, including, but not confined to, their economic welfare. The condition upon paternalism that an intervention be for the good of the intervenee and the condition that, for paternalism to be unjustified, it must impair the intervenee's autonomy are separately necessary. Thus if one of them, and *a fortiori* if the 'intervenee's good' condition, is unfulfilled, then we cannot have a case of paternalism. Since, if the above argument is sound, regulation of commercial advertising does not meet the 'intervenee's good' condition, it cannot in point of logic be 'paternalistic'. If I were to end my analysis there, however, I would doubtless seem to the supporter of the commercial expression doctrine to have reached this conclusion by a kind of philosopher's trick, one analogous to the acquittal of a clearly guilty defendant on a procedural technicality, but without the solid grounding of such an occurrence in principles of fundamental justice. Taking away from me, or making more difficult for me, or quantitatively limiting my options for consumer choice still seems in some way to be affecting my auto-nomy, and as such objectionable, whether it is in some technical sense paternal-istic or not. This impression has to be confronted and dispelled.

It does not follow, of course, from anything so far said that every given regulation of commercial advertising actually does promote citizens' health and welfare, but that is not the issue. Moreover, and more importantly for the pre-sent discussion, any given regulation may tend towards paternalism if it is an intervention in some unwarranted way in the choosing or decision-making of citizens—if, that is to say, the regulation *usurps*, rather than merely affects, decision-making; if it *manipulates*, rather than merely affects, citizens' inform-ation sets. Terms like 'manipulate' and 'usurp' have connotations of impairing autonomy. Let us consider therefore whether regulation of commercial adver-tising can be said to impair autonomy. Bear in mind that, even if it does, it is possible for such impairments to be ultimately justified. We are simply invest-igating here whether it is plausible to characterize regulation of commercial advertising as autonomy-impairing. Given that we are working with Dworkin's wider definition of paternalism, two questions then have to be asked: does reg-ulation of commercial advertising usurp consumers' decision-making? Does regulation of commercial advertising manipulate consumers' information set? I will turn first to the charge of usurping decision-making: in the next paragraphs, I will consider whether the charge can be made out, and in this Chapter 12.7 whether, even if it can, there is some ultimate justification for such apparent usurpation. I will leave the analogous discussion with respect to the charge of manipulating consumers' information set to the next chapter. There are a num-ber of issues regarding the commercial expression doctrine which turn on the thought that such regulation impairs the free flow of commercial information, and it will be best to consider all the issues relating to commercial expression and the free flow of information in one place.

Let us return to *Bolger*, and to the problematic asserted state interest in 'shield-ing recipients from materials that they are likely to find offensive'. What factors contribute to that interest being arguably paternalistic in an objectionable way? One factor is an independent judgement that the information being restricted by government in that case is seemingly of some public importance—information about contraceptive procedures and devices. This factor is, as we have seen, present as well in *Virginia Board* and in many of the professional advertising cases in Canada, the U.S., and Europe. It is not so obviously present in the so-called 'vice cases' concerning alcohol, tobacco, and gambling advertising, nor in housewares sales parties in college dormitories,[44] nor in advertising toys to children,[45] nor in regulation of real estate advertising to prevent racist 'block-busting'.[46] Such public importance draws attention to the contrast between the probability of citizens finding the material illuminating and helpful, and the government's stated belief that citizens are 'likely to find [the material] offensive'. Another factor is the harm from which the government is supposedly trying to protect citizens, the harm of being offended; that ranks very low on the scale of harms protection from which is a candidate for justifying interference with freedom of expression. Such offensiveness plays very little role in other decided cases. It did play some role in *Re RMJ* and in *Rocket*.[47] In the former case, the attorney in question had inscribed in large letters on his business card that he was a member of the Bar of the U.S. Supreme Court, a status in reality of less note than it appears to the uninitiated. The Court commented that 'the emphasis of this relatively uninformative fact is at least bad taste' (at 205), but it declined to find that a reason for upholding the disciplining of the attorney. In the latter case, the disciplined dentists agreed to the placement of a number of advertisements in magazines, extolling themselves as 'New Faces of the Canadian Establishment', and declaring their support for a particular hotel chain. The Ontario Court of Appeal described the advertising as 'distasteful, pompous and self-aggrandizing' (at 679), but nonetheless invalidated the restrictions on dentists' professional advertising. It is easy to feel that it is up to the individual what the individual finds offensive; it is not for the government to assume the probability of those feelings in advance and act to anticipate their occurrence.

Bill New mentions another relevant issue. He argues that 'having little information *in itself* does not impair our ability to reason'.[48] He gives examples of persons lost in the countryside at night, or trapped in a pothole, who nonetheless can reason well on the admittedly little information available. What matters for assessing potential negative effects of legislation on autonomy is how far the quality of reasoning is affected, not simply whether there is some rather than no effect on the information set. That is, New's argument implicitly interprets autonomous decision-making as turning on an opportunity to exercise reasoning to some level of competence and clarity. If that is so, then merely minor modifications of citizens' information sets are not going to threaten autonomy. For this reason, we should question a further case New mentions, of kidnapped hostages. Such unfortunate people New treats as on a par with the lost walkers or trapped pot-holers. So they are in two respects—they are operating in a context of little information, and they are able to reason so as to maximize their

---

[44] *Board of Trustees of the State University of New York et al v Todd Fox et al* 109 SCt 3028 (1989).

[45] *Attorney-General of Quebec v Irwin Toy Ltd* [Indexed as Irwin Toy Ltd v Quebec (Attorney-General)] (1989) 58 DLR (4th) 577.

[46] *Linmark Associates Inc v Township of Willingboro* 431 US 85 (1977).

[47] *Re Rocket et al and Royal College of Dental Surgeons of Ontario et al* (1988) 49 DLR (4th) 641 (Ont CA).

[48] Bill New, 'Paternalism and Public Policy', *Economics and Philosophy* 15 (1999): 69; his emphasis.

welfare within those constraints. These are the only points that concern New in the context of his argument. But being kidnapped constitutes an invasion of autonomy. It would be a stretch to say that the hostages can still act autonomously, because they can reason to find the best thing to do for their welfare in the circumstances. This point shows that what is important about the lost walkers and trapped pot-holers is that they are still able to act autonomously even with limited information. Limited information in itself does not threaten autonomy. Autonomy is negatively affected by something like being kidnapped, not by limited information.

Courts have shown some deference to this point in that they habitually have been more critical of total bans on advertising of some given kind, as opposed to time, place, and manner restrictions. But even so the underlying issue is missed. Even a total ban on the availability of information through advertising is not the same as a total ban on the availability of any information whatever. If the government had made it a regulatory offence for any shop to permit its employees ever to give out information on the prices at which prescription drugs, or liquor, were sold, then we might have a stronger case for saying that the capacity of would-be customers to make autonomous decisions was being eroded. But we cannot say that simply about a prohibition on advertising. The size and depth of the information set is not being sufficiently modified.

We learn therefore two important lessons from these cases. First, the judgment that a given regulation of commercial advertising is suspiciously paternalistic requires to support it more than simply the fact that it affects choice by a modification of the information set. The context of choice—what is up for choice, by whom, where, and when; how much information is unavailable, and how it is unavailable—are of crucial significance. Secondly, the sense of suspicious paternalism relies heavily on the idea that a judgement, or a choice, or a decision, of some kind is properly for individuals to make, in terms of their values and how their lives are affected; the judgment or choice or decision is not for the government to make on the individual's behalf. We must consider now how these lessons play out in the case of government regulation of commercial advertising.

The anti-paternalistic criticisms that have been made in the case of commercial expression fall more or less into two categories—the criticism that government is treating citizens as incompetent when in fact they are not, and the criticism that government is making us incompetent when in fact other things being equal we would not be. It is clear what stake the government might have in such manoeuvres: incompetence on the part of the intervenee is one important route to the justification of paternalistic intervention. The rhetoric of the commercial expression doctrine certainly assumes that both criticisms are justified. I will now argue that they are not justified.

In what way could it be true that in regulating commercial advertising government is treating citizen hearers of the advertising as 'incompetent', in a sense of 'incompetent' that would, if the description were correct, potentially justify

an intervention in decision-making or choice? It would have to be that the decision is one that, *ceteris paribus*, individual citizens have a right to be allowed to
make for themselves, and that government is pre-empting that decision in some
way. Paradigms are familiar. In a recent case in Alberta,[49] the 16-year-old
daughter of a family of Jehovah's Witnesses needed a blood transfusion to save
her life. She and her mother followed their religious beliefs in wanting to refuse
the transfusion. The father, wavering in his beliefs, placed the life of his daughter in the highest place and consented to the transfusion. The court enforced his
consent against the daughter's wishes, deciding in terms of a 'best interests of
the child' test. Although the court found that the common law 'mature minor'
doctrine had been overridden by statute, the court indicated that the girl
nonetheless might not have qualified as a 'mature minor'. It is, however, difficult to attribute to a 16-year-old decision-making incompetence of the kind
needed to justify paternalism. The legislation appears to overinclude this particular person, even if, as the court acknowledges, the law should not be altered
for hard cases. There is a strong case to be made for saying that the father and
the court are on the facts of this case usurping the daughter's decision-making
and impairing her autonomy.

But how is the typical regulation of commercial advertising supposed to conform to that paradigm? Take the case of regulation of gambling advertising.
Presumably, casinos, like any other corporate advertiser, assume that advertising will lead to increased demand for the product or service being advertised,
and thus to increased revenue for the advertiser. Let us suppose that they are
right. So there is some increased likelihood, for any given hearer of the advertisement for casino gambling, that that hearer will choose to gamble. But time
and money spent on gambling are not necessarily in the best interests of the
gambler. Some people may have their values and their lives organized in such a
way that they will not be harmed, and may even be enriched, by gambling. But
many of those who start to gamble as a result of increased advertising will not
be so organized. Their gambling will leave them worse off than they were before
the increase in advertising. These people, though, have a right to choose to
worsen their lives by gambling, just as a person with relevant religious beliefs
has a right to refuse a blood transfusion even though his or her life be worsened,
and even ended, thereby.

Let us suppose that the last sentence states what is true: citizens do have such
a right. That right, though, is not taken away from them by government regulation of casino advertising. Nor is it taken away from them by government
regulation of casino gambling itself. Perhaps it would be taken away, if gambling were made illegal, *and* if no other justification for making gambling illegal
were available. But we are not talking about gambling being made illegal; we are
talking about the regulation of casino advertising. The government is not treating us as unable to take the decision for ourselves whether to go casino gambling

[49] *BH v Alberta (Director of Child Welfare)* 2002 ABQB 371 (Alta QB).

or not when it regulates how casinos may advertise. It is not substituting its decision for our own on whether to go casino gambling. It is not even imposing upon us the values of an opponent of gambling by regulating casino advertising. It is just regulating casino advertising.

It may be said that, as long as government does not make gambling illegal, then any further regulation of gambling—regulation, for example, to dampen the demand for gambling—must be paternalistic and wrong. The general proposition that government has never any right further to regulate a product or service once it has decided not to make manufacture or use of that product or service illegal is clearly false. Government is, one might say, in the business of regulating products and services that are not illegal. As the U.S. Supreme Court itself argued in *Edge Broadcasting:*[50]

If there is an immediate connection between advertising and demand, and the federal regulation decreases advertising, it stands to reason that the policy of decreasing demand for gambling is correspondingly advanced. Accordingly, the Government may be said to advance its purpose by substantially reducing lottery advertising, even when it is not wholly eradicated.

This has not always seemed obvious to supporters of the commercial expression doctrine. There have been references in the U.S. Supreme Court to impermissible 'dampening' of the demand for a product or a service. The prime example is Blackmun J's concurring opinion in *Central Hudson*. He concurred with, rather than joined, the majority decision to invalidate the regulation in question, because he thought the intermediate level of review represented by the four part test enunciated in that case was inappropriate to the facts of the case. He said:

I seriously doubt whether suppression of information concerning the availability and price of a legally offered product is ever a permissible way for the State to 'dampen' demand for or use of the product. . . . This is because it is a covert attempt by the State to manipulate the choices of its citizens, not by persuasion or direct regulation, but by depriving the public of the information needed to make a free choice. [at 574–5]

It is not clear, however, how such an accusation of impermissibility will work. Any form of regulation on the provision of a product or service will 'dampen the demand' for that product or service. Take the familiar example of Prohibition and the ill-fated Nineteenth Amendment to the U.S. Constitution. The attempt to prohibit 'the manufacture, sale or transportation of intoxicating liquors' miserably failed, as a way of 'dampening' liquor consumption by U.S. residents. The manufacture, sale, or transportation of liquor is now far less regulated, but it is still regulated. The issue for the legislature is one of what means of 'dampening the demand' poses the most practical, most normatively reasonable, or most politically acceptable solution, given that prohibition is unworkable. If 'dampening the demand' is the most that can be done, rather

---

[50] *United States v Edge Broadcasting Company* 113 SCt 2696 (1993), at 2707.

than prohibition, so be it. The legitimating reasons that underlie the more drastic proposal underlie the less drastic one too.

Now, how is all that changed by the fact that the legislature now chooses to
'dampen demand' by regulating advertising, and not merely manufacture, sale,
and transportation? What is it about the regulation of advertising as a tactic for
the dampening strategy that suddenly makes such a huge difference to the
issues? One candidate answer of course comes to mind: advertising is expression
and any regulation of expression is impermissible. But that answer is not available at this stage of the argument. One premise of this study is that nothing
follows simply from the fact that the target of regulation is an activity involving
the utterance of words in a language (see Chapter 8 above). *Prima facie*, commercial expression is not expression of a constitutionally relevant sort. We need
an argument to show that it is. We are examining attempts to build such an
argument based on an infringement of an autonomy right of some kind of the
hearer. It achieves nothing to offer an argument in favour of such a right that
assumes we have already shown one to exist.

How else might we proceed? Are there any specific legal products or services
whose further regulation is in the nature of the case objectionably autonomy-
impairing? One answer might be, any product or service whose use is inherently
an exercise of autonomy, or inherently autonomy-promoting. I know of no serious candidate for such a product or service.

Are there ways of regulating legal products or services such that the use of those
ways of regulating is in the nature of the case objectionably autonomy-impairing?
There seems to be a good answer to that question. If a product or service is such
that its enjoyment is a matter of personal choice, and if the way of regulating is
one which burdens that choice, then that way of regulating is in the nature of the
case objectionably autonomy-impairing. The key issue now is, what will count as
'burdening' a choice in the relevant sense? If 'burdening' is taken to imply any
effect on the choice at all, the proposition is far too broad. It is not true that all
effects on choices are autonomy-impairing, any more than it is true (see Chapter
11.3–5 above) that all exercises of choice are autonomy-expressing or promoting.
Unless the product or service in question has a vital material relation to some
overall plan of life, the regulation of that product or service will not be autonomy-
impairing. In the case of the majority of consumer products and services that are
the subject of commercial advertising, this condition will not be fulfilled. It does
not impair my autonomy to have to risk spending, and indeed to spend, more than
I might otherwise need to on buying a bottle of my favourite liquor.

The condition might be fulfilled, however, in the case of health services, such
as the provision of prescription drugs (*Virginia Board*), or of dental services
(*Rocket, Griffin*[51]), or of optometric services (*Friedman*,[52] *Grier*[53]). It is worth-

---

[51] *Re Griffin and College of Dental Surgeons of British Columbia* [Indexed as Griffin v College
of Dental Surgeons of British Columbia] (1989) 64 DLR (4th) 652 (BC CA).
[52] *Friedman et al v Rogers et al* 440 US 1 (1978).
[53] *Re Grier and Alberta Optometric Association* (1987) 42 DLR (4th) 327 (Alta CA).

while looking at these cases more closely, to see how the argument might go there. Take *Virginia Board*. No-one is doubting that personal health, physical and mental, is enormously valuable, and that life is a lot more pleasant with it than without it. No-one doubts that the proper consumption of properly pre-scribed medication is in the appropriate circumstances important for regaining or maintaining health. But it is a long way from there to the thought that regu-lation of prescription drug price advertising impairs autonomy. For one thing, assumptions have to be made about the economic structure of the health-care delivery system in a given jurisdiction. In Canada, for example, where the vast majority of people are insulated by some form of insurance against the full cost of prescription drugs, and prices charged by pharmacies for dispensing differ only within a narrow band of a few dollars, it is hard to say that being able to purchase prescription drugs at the lowest available price is central to personal autonomy. In a pure, free enterprise health-care delivery system, the price of prescription drugs might be more central to autonomy. But, in any case, as in *44 Liquormart* and the price of liquor, forbidding pharmacies from advertising does not mean that no-one can find out the price. It means only that extra steps need to be gone through, which may be a matter only of making a few telephone calls and taking a trip. Imposition of such a task does not impair autonomy.

'But what about the poor and the elderly? Is not the imposition of such extra steps a burden on their choices, an impairment of their autonomy? They can ill afford, literally and metaphorically, to be forced to incur higher than opti-mal costs either for the drugs or for their acquisition.' So an objection might go. Let us ignore the fact that, in any modern developed state, the poor and the elderly are most likely to have free or highly subsidized prescription drugs: there are always the near-poor whom any programme of subsidies will under-include. All the same, the choice still belongs to the individual how and where to purchase prescription drugs. Likewise, the typical intrusive micro-management of professional advertising by professional organizations at issue in such professional advertising cases has, from an objective policy viewpoint, little to recommend it and much to invite criticism. But all that is another mat-ter. I may be put to some inconvenience if I have to make a series of telephone calls to find out how much a given dentist will be charging for a given proce-dure, or, if I am not a native speaker of English, whether the dentist can dis-cuss treatment with me in my own language.[54] But merely having extra steps to go through before making a final choice of dentist or optometrist does not impair my autonomy. Notice again, too, the force of context. In Canada, provincial governments, which have jurisdiction over health, agree with pro-fessional bodies an approved schedule of fees for given services. While typi-cally physicians may not bill over and above this schedule, dentists may do so. All the same, the majority of dentists do not. It is not hard to find out enough

---

[54] Dentists in Ontario, before the decision in *Rocket*, were not permitted to advertise languages spoken.

information to avoid the extra-billing dentist, if that is one's wish. There is no usurping of decision-making here.

The commercial expression doctrine in fact faces a dilemma, in arguing that regulation of product or service advertising impairs the autonomy of the hearer, because it burdens the hearer's choices. On the one hand, if the notion of autonomy is given a relatively 'thin' or formal interpretation, then, while it may be easier to point to occasions where potentially autonomy is involved, it is much harder to argue that it actually is involved, because pure choice as such is very rarely taken away or usurped. On the other hand, if autonomy is given a very 'thick' or contextually loaded interpretation involving, for example, a minimum level of welfare and opportunities for autonomy, then, while it becomes much easier to declare that, for example, the autonomy of prescription drug purchasers is affected by restrictions on price advertising, the price paid by the doctrine is considerable. To build social welfare conditions into the criteria for autonomy paves the way for more legitimate government intervention in social life, not less, in order to create and maintain generally adequate levels of welfare and opportunity. As Husak rightly argues, the legislature regularly has to balance the costs of interfering with autonomy with the benefits that flow from the promotion of autonomy.[55] What the commercial expression doctrine needs, but cannot have, is a way of showing how restrictions on price advertising usurp choice, while taking as a paradigm of choice the kind of autonomous decision-making which all too obviously continues to take place even when price advertising is restricted.

7 EVEN IF REGULATION OF COMMERCIAL EXPRESSION IS PATERNALISTIC, CAN IT BE JUSTIFIED?

I have argued in the previous section that regulation of commercial expression cannot plausibly be regarded as objectionably impairing autonomy through usurping choice. We have seen that one reason regularly given by supporters of the commercial expression doctrine for claiming that regulation of commercial expression is paternalistic and wrong is that it usurps choice. This argument fails. Therefore, despite the prevalence of the rhetoric of paternalism in defences of the doctrine, the rhetoric has still been found to have no basis in reality. Nonetheless, let us suppose counterfactually that the charge of objectionable paternalism did have some basis in reality. We saw in the brief survey above of the topic of paternalism generally that it is accepted that there are valid routes to the justification of paternalism. If any of them have application to the case of regulation of commercial expression, then the rhetoric of paternalism will be further deconstructed and defused. There are in fact two very plausible lines of argument for justifying regulation of commercial expression, even if it is insisted

[55] Douglas Husak, 'Legal Paternalism', 402–4.

that such regulation is paternalistic and is *prima facie* objectionable. The first has to do with the role of consent in the justification of paternalism, and the second to do with the distinction drawn above (this Chapter 12.3) between 'occurrent autonomy' and 'global autonomy'. The latter has more application to the charge of 'manipulation of information set', and I shall therefore discuss it in the next chapter. I shall discuss consent here.

It is a commonplace that the presence of consent negates the charge of usurping decision-making. A patient is in a coma. There is a disagreement between surgeon and family over treatment. A sworn statement by the patient is produced, which authorizes the surgeon in circumstances such as these to use her best judgement. If the surgeon acts as the patient requests, then, even though the surgeon, not the patient, took the decision there is no usurpation of the patient's decision-making or impairment of his or her autonomy. The patient gave his or her prior consent to the surgeon's exercising her own judgement and choice. That's the easy case. As soon as one ventures into the realm of 'I know that this is what he would have chosen if he had been asked', things become more difficult, but still possible. 'We are entitled to assume that this is what he would have wanted, since it is what anyone would have wanted' becomes yet harder, as does, 'I know he will thank me for this when he wakes up (if he does)'.

But these are examples of decision-making issues between persons. In these cases, Husak points out, deontological issues of autonomy weigh more heavily than they do in the case of legislation.[56] In the case of regulation of commercial expression, we are talking about decisions being taken by the state, decisions which have some effect on the decisions of private persons. The issue here cannot be that merely having an effect on the decisions of citizens is enough to make state intervention wrong. New considers the view that 'people simply *cannot* have their lives improved by state action, because state action is bad, period', and comments rightly that 'ultimately this type of case cannot be refuted: it is a matter of belief'.[57] Certainly, some of the more spirited and committed defences of the commercial expression doctrine seem motivated by this belief. But serious politics and serious jurisprudence are not possible without some willingness to reason. I assume such willingness here. So the problem cannot be merely that in regulating commercial advertising government is acting on citizens' behalf and affecting citizens' own decisions. The claim has to be that government regulation of commercial advertising is 'on behalf of citizens' in some distinctive, and thus potentially distinctively objectionable, way. Can that claim be made out?

In general, according to standard liberal political theory, government decision-making on citizens' behalf is legitimated by the fact of the consent of the governed. Not that there are no problems in the interpretation and application to cases of this idea; there are many. But democracy goes on, and we accept that

---

[56] Douglas Husak, 'Legal Paternalism', 391, 401–2. A similar argument is made by Nagel: Thomas Nagel, *Mortal Questions* (Cambridge: Cambridge University Press, 1979), 82–9; see also Guangwei Ouyang and Roger A. Shiner, 'Organizations and Agency', *Legal Theory* 1 (1995): 308–9.
[57] New, 'Paternalism and Public Policy', 82.

citizens' consent is an operative factor however it is to be analysed. But if that is so, why should the special case of regulation of commercial advertising be any different? As Dworkin has suggested, citizens in consenting to being governed can think of themselves as taking out 'social insurance policies': 'what must be involved here is not consent to specific measures but rather consent to a system of government, run by elected representatives, with an understanding that they may safeguard our interests in certain limited ways'.[58] The qualification 'limited' is not to be taken casually, of course, and, as I have already indicated, there is much discussion in the philosophical, legal, political, and economic literature of exactly what those limits are and how they may legitimately function. But to frame the issue as one of suitable limits is importantly different from framing it as *a priori* unjustified because non-consensual.

It is true that I have not given specific, overt consent to Canadian federal government legislation regulating tobacco advertising. Since both in the case of the original Tobacco Products Control Act[59] and its successor legislation[60] I was living in a constituency represented by a member of the opposition, not of the governing Liberal party, it is not even true that my representative voted for the legislation on my behalf. All the same, while political theory may wrangle endlessly over the details, no liberal political theorist doubts that there is some properly available sense in which I have consented to the government taking this action on my behalf. This is not to say that such an action is within those suitable limits to which Dworkin alludes. Whether that is so is a separate inquiry, and in fact is an enquiry to central aspects of which this book is devoted. But it is a mistake to argue that such regulation is choice-usurping and autonomy-impairing, because it affects my choices without my consent. In the sense of 'consent' at play in determinations of democratic legitimacy, it has my consent.

There are two reasons why this line of argument might be thought too simplistic: neither is cogent. First, it may be granted that citizens cannot be asked to consent to every act of government. All we can ask for is our consent to the more fundamental proposed policies, practices, and actions. We do that in electing one party with its particular legislative programme, rather than another party. But there is a very important aspect of our consent at this fundamental level that has not so far been addressed. Canada, the United States and the Member States of the European Community are not just democracies, but *constitutional* democracies (however that term is to be parsed in the case of the European Union[61]).

---

[58] Dworkin, 'Paternalism', 78. I am here talking about legislation generally, and not intending a formal distinction between statutory provisions and the provisions of a constitutional charter or Bill of Rights. Whether the notion of a 'social insurance policy' to which the people pre-commit themselves suffices to render entrenched charters or bills of rights fully 'democratic' is an issue I do not address. For a spirited argument that it would not see Jeremy Waldron, *Law and Disagreement* (Oxford: Clarendon Press, 1999), Chapter 12.

[59] S.C. 1988, c.20.   [60] S.C. 1997, c.13.

[61] See Neil MacCormick, *Questioning Sovereignty: Law, State and Practical Reason* (Oxford: Clarendon Press, 1999) for a thorough discussion of the way in which the governance structure of the European Community challenges conventional notions of legal statehood.

That is, in those jurisdictions there are formal and entrenched documents granting certain fundamental rights and freedoms to citizens, and containing provisions for the invalidation of government regulation that violates such rights. What clearer example could there be of a 'limit' on our consent of the kind relevant here? We may indeed have consented to be governed, but we have made it clear that our consent has limits; specifically and especially, it cannot violate our fundamental rights and freedoms.

All that is true. But consider now how the argument has to continue. So then, the objection goes, we cannot have consented to regulation of commercial advertising, because it is an unconstitutional violation of one of our fundamental freedoms. This step of the argument fails, because it begs the question. The question at issue in this book is whether there is any justification within liberal political morality for the commercial expression doctrine. I am claiming that there is not. To use as a premise in a counter-argument that regulation of commercial expression is unconstitutional is to assume the answer to the question under investigation. That is question-begging. The courts and the commentators who agree with them—the supporters of the commercial expression doctrine—right now believe that freedom of commercial expression should be constitutionally protected. They express that belief in granting freedom of commercial expression constitutional protection, and approving Court decisions that so grant. But those are modes of expression of a belief. They are not arguments that the belief is justified. That is the issue that concerns us here.

A second objection that might be raised to the claim that government regulation of commercial advertising has our consent is this. I do not smoke; I never have. I think it is a disgusting and unhealthy habit. I think that the drain on tax-supported health-care resources that occurs fixing the health problems of people who smoke is outrageous. I think that the tactics employed by the manufacturers of tobacco products to attract people, especially young people, to smoke, and the means they employ to keep them smoking, are outrageous too. So *of course* it is obvious that I have consented to the Tobacco Products Control Act and its ilk; I agree with the legislation. And *of course* it is no usurpation of my choices; I am not going to choose to smoke anyway. But what about my neighbour who smokes, and without guilt or intention to stop? He has not 'consented' to the Tobacco Products Control Act; and anything that makes it harder for him to find out what tobacco products are on the market, and where they may be bought, and at what price, affects his decision-making sufficiently to usurp his choices. Does not his lack of consent ground the charge that regulation of tobacco advertising is unjustifiably paternalistic, because usurpatory of choice?

I have already expressed scepticism that a restriction on the flow of information of this sort really does impair autonomy (and will explore the issue more fully in Chapter 13), but I will not repeat those arguments. The new point is the idea that in some appropriate sense those who oppose a piece of legislation and resent its effect on their choices ground a consent-based argument against the legislation. Dworkin considers this kind of case in his later paper.[62] He considers the example of fluoridation of the municipal water supply, which may be experienced as a paternalistic and unjustified interference with their autonomy by persons opposed to fluoridation: 'It is up to me to decide whether I want to drink fluoridated water; if it goes into the city water supply at source, I cannot take that decision; my decision-making is usurped by the city council's decision to fluoridate the water.' Dworkin suggests that it is reasonable not to require unanimity on a collective decision such as this where the majority interest is important, such as health; the imposition on the minority is relatively minor, such as buying one's own water; and the administrative and economic costs of not imposing on the minority would be very high.[63]

The framework Dworkin proposes for when a legislative scheme may legitimately proceed without unanimous consent seems intuitively plausible, and its potential application to regulation of commercial advertising of interest and of value. The framework in effect embodies the point previously made that, in the case of legislation, the justificatory principles for paternalistic cases shift from deontological to consequentialist principles. For example, it would license overriding the non-consent of smokers, devotees of alcohol, and gamblers to regulation of tobacco, alcohol, and gambling advertising. Husak remarks on the case of mandatory state pension schemes, 'consequentialism best allows us to recognize—and thereby to resist—the horrors of a world with large numbers of impoverished senior citizens—even if that world contains less paternalism and more freedom'.[64] Might not the same be said for a world that contains large numbers of people with lung cancer and other health problems related to the consumption of tobacco products?

True, the framework seems to apply in the opposite direction to microregulation of professional advertising, everyday consumer products, and the like. The negative effects of preventing patients from knowing when their dentists' offices are open, or preventing breweries from putting alcohol content on beer bottle labels, do not seem outweighed by an overall gain in social welfare. So it might seem that a counter-argument to my view might proceed in this way. It is easy to see the *Central Hudson* test for the constitutionality of commercial speech, or the *Oakes* test for legitimate infringement of a *Charter* right or freedom, as versions of such a consequentialist framework. If, then, application of the framework identifies cases of regulation in which the imposition of the regulation on a non-consenting minority is improper, then is it not so that in those cases the choosing and decision-making of that minority has been usurped? I

---

[62] Dworkin, 'Second Thoughts', 110.

[63] He also adds that, where there are economic costs to the minority, they should in fairness be borne by the majority. When I lived in Edmonton, Alberta, the city water was fluoridated. The city, however, set up a tap at the main water plant, which tap would supply water that was not fluoridated. Anyone who wanted unfluoridated water could go to the tap and get the water free. Dworkin's point taken: more or less—there is the inconvenience, the cost of gasoline or taxi fare, of purchasing containers . . .

[64] Douglas Husak, 'Legal Paternalism', 401–2.

have given reasons already for doubting whether the commercial expression cases are on all fours with genuine-looking autonomy-overriding cases like the Jehovah's Witnesses example above. But suppose we concede for the sake of argument that the language of 'usurpation' does apply to the non-consenting minority. To acknowledge that still is not to concede that, *in the nature of the case*, regulation of commercial advertising is choice-usurping. But a conclusion of that strength is what the anti-paternalism argument on behalf of the commercial expression doctrine requires.

Let me issue a reminder. The problem with which we began Chapter 10 was that constitutional protection for commercial expression could not be grounded in an original autonomy right of the corporate expresser, because corporate expressers have no such original autonomy right. So the possibility was then raised that the hearer of the commercial expression might have such an original autonomy right, which the corporate expresser could 'borrow' in order to challenge restriction or regulation of its commercial expression. We then considered what reasons there could be for attributing such an original autonomy right to hearers of commercial expression. The thought was that consumer-hearers have a right to make autonomous choices as to what products or services they purchase, and the typical piece of regulation of commercial expression usurps that autonomy. Now, I am considering the reply that, no, such regulation does not usurp consumers' autonomy, because they have consented to such an effect on their choices; they have consented to be governed by the government that institutes such regulation, and within the mandate of that government is the instituting of regulations of that sort. The claim now is that a government regulation, and *a fortiori* a government regulation of commercial advertising, may quite possibly fail to meet standards which normative political morality lays down for when a lack of unanimous consent is normatively significant, and therefore may quite possibly usurp the decision-making of those who object to the regulation. The claim, if true, shows that there is reason to say that the regulation in question should not have been enacted. But its repeal will have to be left to the democratic political process. The majority will have to be persuaded that, in this case, the imposition on the decision-making of the minority is a cost that it is in the interest of all that they not bear, not merely in their own interest.

Again, it may look to supporters of the commercial expression doctrine as though this latter response in my defence is missing the point. Constitutional rights are often thought to be inherently anti-majoritarian. Their purpose is to protect minorities from the tyranny of the majority. Thus the justified opposition of those who object to a regulation of commercial advertising is, like any other constitutional right, enough to have the regulation invalidated. Let us suppose that the assertion of the anti-majoritarian thrust of constitutional rights is true. The point nonetheless has no application here. Reliance on it in the current debate is as question-begging as it was a few pages above. The question is whether freedom of commercial expression from the point of view of political morality should be recognized as a constitutional right, whether it already is so recognized or not in some given legal system. To use the fact that it is already recognized in some given legal system as a plank in the argument that it should so be recognized begs the question. The *Central Hudson* test as applied under the U.S. First Amendment, or the *Oakes* test as applied to infringements of the Canadian *Charter* section 2(b), or the tests in Article 10(2) of the European Convention on Human Rights may be a good way of operationalizing within constitutional litigation the normative framework suggested by Dworkin's analysis of a few paragraphs earlier. But that these tests successfully mediate the proper norms once a decision has been taken to grant constitutional protection to commercial expression does not show that the original decision to grant constitutional protection was by those or any other normative standards the correct one.

8 CONCLUSION

In this chapter, I have been examining the claim that regulation of commercial advertising is objectionably and unjustifiably paternalistic because it usurps the decision-making of the hearer or would-be hearer of the advertising. I have broken the claim down into two parts—that such regulation is descriptively paternalistic, and that such regulation is objectionably paternalistic. I have argued that neither of these claims can be secured.

One necessary condition for an action being 'paternalistic' is that it is for the good of the individual intervenee. Many apparent cases of paternalistic intervention by governments are not that; the best rational reconstruction of their motivation is a diffuse responsibility to maintain the welfare of citizens. Regulation of commercial advertising is no different. A concern with citizens' welfare in itself cannot be sufficient to make a regulation 'paternalistic'; otherwise, virtually any government regulation will be 'paternalistic', and the term will lose its meaning and force.

I then considered whether regulation of commercial advertising interfered with citizens' autonomy. Not every effect on a choice or a decision counts as interfering with the autonomy of the chooser or decision-maker. I borrowed the expression 'usurp decision-making' to indicate the source of interferences with autonomy. But, if that is the standard, and it arguably is, then regulation of commercial advertising does not 'usurp decision-making'. Hearers of commercial advertising are not being treated as 'incompetent'; they are still being left with the same opportunities to make choices and take decisions. We can certainly sketch parameters for deciding whether affecting choices in some given case is objectionable. I have acknowledged that aspects of the current jurisprudence in the Canadian and U.S. Supreme Courts and the European Court of Human Rights as regards freedom of commercial expression may be seen as operationalizing those parameters in an appropriate way. But I insisted above, and insist again now, that such normative success is beside the point of the present argument. We are considering whether the fundamental assumption of the commercial expression doctrine, that commercial expression deserves constitutional protection from the point of view of political morality, is correct. We are not assessing the rights and wrongs of how courts have actually proceeded, once the decision to protect commercial expression has been taken.

So far I have spent three chapters examining the idea of a hearers' autonomy right that is objectionably affected by government regulation of commercial expression. I have argued against the idea at some length and in some detail, for two reasons. The assumption that there is such a right is central to key arguments presented in support of the commercial expression doctrine. Moreover, the arguments to which the commercial expression doctrine appeals involve the deployment of rhetorically powerful terms like 'right to know', 'paternalism', 'autonomy', and the like. Both of these reasons imply that the project of dismantling these arguments cannot be quick and dirty. If my counter-arguments are sound, then an important conclusion follows. We have discovered no sound basis in normative political morality for the existence of an original autonomy right possessed by the hearer or receiver of commercial expression, which right may be borrowed by the corporate expresser itself to claim constitutional protection for their expressive advertising. A crucial plank in the argumentative platform for the commercial expression doctrine has been shown to be rotten and unable to sustain any weight.

It is also true that my argument against the commercial expression doctrine has not so far confronted what seems to many people the soundest argument for freedom of commercial expression, the argument that regulation of commercial expression negatively affects the free flow of commercial information, which free flow is deemed to be an important individual and social good—so important that it must be constitutionally protected from interference. I turn now in the next chapter to discuss the free flow of commercial information and its significance for my project.

13

The Free Flow of Commercial Information

As I indicated above (Chapter 6), by far the most frequent argument given by courts and commentators for the constitutional protection of freedom of expression embodies a reference to the 'free flow of commercial information'. The general form of the argument is clear:

(1) Government regulation of commercial expression constitutes an interruption of the free flow of commercial information;
(2) The free flow of commercial information is good, both for the individual and for society;
(3) Interruption of the free flow of commercial information is therefore bad;
(4) *Ceteris paribus*, therefore, government regulation of commercial expression should be abolished.

Clearly, many questions can be raised about the argument as expressed in that stark form: what kind of interruption? In what way is such an interruption 'bad'? In what way is the free flow of commercial information 'good'? What kinds of qualifications are built into '*ceteris paribus*'? We have examined in the previous chapter one answer to the first question—the kind of interruption involved is 'paternalistic'; we have rejected that interpretation of the government's purpose, at least as an automatic inference from the fact of government regulation of commercial advertising as such. In Chapter 11 we rejected another thesis, that constitutional protection for commercial expression is justified because it promotes the self-realization of the hearer. But other stories about government regulation remain to be considered, as well as the further, and clearly crucial, assertions about the normative harm and good which regulation of commercial expression involves. All those issues we will consider in this chapter.

1 The free flowing rhetoric of manipulation and induced ignorance

The typical assertion that government regulation of the free flow of commercial information violates constitutional rights is plated with rhetoric—not just the rhetoric of paternalism, but also the rhetoric of 'manipulation', 'censorship', 'induced ignorance', and the like.[1] If we are to assess accurately the strength of

---

[1] For whether there is any deeper significance to this fact than the hollowness of the rhetoric see Chapter 15.2 below.

the arguments in favour of the commercial expression doctrine and based on the free flow of commercial information, the first step must be to dissolve this coating of rhetoric. The underlying argumentative claims can then be properly assessed for their cogency.

The most extreme anti-government rhetoric in a commercial expression court opinion occurs in Stevens J's dissent in *Edge Broadcasting*.[2] The broadcaster challenged federal statutes that prohibited radio broadcasting of lottery advertising by licensees located in states that did not permit lotteries, *inter alia* on First Amendment grounds.[3] The Court denied the challenge. Stevens J analogized the case first to *Bigelow*.[4] He rightly noticed that each case involved a regulation in one U.S. state of information about services available in another U.S. state. He overlooked, though, the public interest difference between the availability of abortions and of lottery tickets. Then in a teratogenic fusion of mobility rights and rights of free expression Stevens J analogized both cases to *Thompson*,[5] a case concerning state regulations that denied welfare assistance to state residents who had resided in the state for less than one year. The point, he said, is 'about one State's interference with its citizens' fundamental constitutional right to travel in a state of enlightenment, not *government-induced ignorance*' (at 2710; my emphasis).

To induce is to lead in, or cause to exist, something that was not previously there; the familiar obstetric sense has this meaning. 'Government-induced ignorance' then must imply that previously citizens were not ignorant, but now as a result of some government intervention they are ignorant. It is not that we cannot imagine cases of a state of mind properly called 'government-induced ignorance'. Take the case of so-called strategic disinformation. Imagine a government afraid that it will lose public support for a military operation far away, against, say, an elusive foe in a heavily mountainous area, if there are likely to be significant casualties to the country's own forces. A war correspondent reports that in some particular attack there was significant loss of life among that country's soldiers, as indeed there was. Any citizen who reads this report has knowledge, or at least true belief, about the number of casualties. The government, however, puts out its own report giving a far lower number; it puts out bulletins designed to destroy the credibility of the war correspondent; it briefs the networks on what a magnificent triumph this offensive was; and so on and so forth. The citizens, being trusting citizens, believe their government. So now they are in a state of ignorance, not knowledge or true belief, and the government has induced that state.

It is clearly absurd to suggest that the U.S. federal government in the fact situation of *Edge Broadcasting* is acting like the government in the disinformation example. In North Carolina lotteries were illegal; in Virginia there was a legal

[2] *United States v Edge Broadcasting Company* 113 SCt 2696 (1993).
[3] Title 18 USC §1307 (1988 ed. and Supp. III).   [4] *Bigelow v Virginia* 421 US 809 (1975).
[5] *Shapiro v Thompson* 394 US 618 (1969).

state lottery. Edge's radio station was located in Elizabeth City, North Carolina, on the border between the two states, but adjacent to the urban area of Hampton Roads, Virginia, from which area it drew over 90 per cent of its audience. Edge wanted its share of the lucrative advertising of lotteries to residents of Virginia, but such a revenue stream was blocked off by federal regulation because of its location in the non-lottery state of North Carolina. How is the federal government inducing ignorance in anyone? For one thing, the government is regulating the expression of others, not itself expressing. For another, in whom is it supposedly inducing the ignorance? It is clear that the residents of North Carolina in Edge's service area were very well aware of the legality of lotteries in Virginia. Stevens J himself acknowledges as much when he alludes to them travelling across state lines in search of lottery tickets. This knowledge is not taken away by the government restriction on lottery advertising; it exists in spite of the regulation. *Bigelow* here is different. It is much less likely that the residents of Virginia, a state in which abortions were illegal, would have known about the availability of abortions in New York, if Bigelow had not published the advertisements in his newspaper. The effectiveness of grapevines should not be underestimated. All the same, such ignorance as the residents of Virginia here possessed was still not 'induced'.

In fact, this passage in the dissent in *Edge* is the only place in court decisions where the rhetoric of 'induced ignorance' can be found, for good reason; the idea is preposterous. References to the government 'keeping [citizens] in ignorance' and 'manipulating [citizens'] choices' or 'manipulating [citizens'] decision-making' are more frequent.[6] The theme of the government keeping citizens ignorant[7] in fact begins with *Virginia Board*[8] itself:

the State's protectiveness of its citizens rests in large measure on the advantages of their being kept in ignorance. . . . The more painstaking pharmacist is also protected but, again, it is a protection based in large part on public ignorance. . . . Virginia is free to require whatever professional standards it wishes of its pharmacists; it may subsidize them or protect them from competition in other ways. . . . But it may not do so by keeping the public in ignorance of the entirely lawful terms that competing pharmacists are offering.[9]

---

[6] The terminology is very frequent in academic commentaries: to compile a list would be tedious and pedantic.

[7] I will turn to 'manipulating' shortly.

[8] *Virginia State Board of Pharmacy et al v Virginia Citizens Consumer Council Inc et al* 425 US 748 (1976).

[9] At 769–70, citation omitted. See also *Bates v State Bar of Arizona* 433 US 350 (1977), 365 (Blackmun J for the majority); *Central Hudson Gas & Electric Corporation v Public Service Commission of New York* 447 US 557 (1980), 579 (Blackmun J, concurring); *Posadas de Puerto Rico Associates dba Condado Holiday Inn v Tourism Company of Puerto Rico et al* 478 US 328 (1986), 358 (Brennan J, dissenting); *Rubin v Coors Brewing Company* 115 SCt 1585 (1995), 1597 (Stevens J, concurring); *44 Liquormart Inc v Rhode Island* 116 SCt 1495 (1996), 1516, 1519–20 (Thomas J); *Greater New Orleans Broadcasting Association Inc v United States* 119 SCt 1923 (1999), 1936 (Thomas J, concurring).

The government most obviously 'keeps people in ignorance' when citizens do not have given information, and the government takes steps to make sure that things stay that way. For instance, a certain piece of information may find its way into government hands, information that relates to a matter of national security. The government takes steps to ensure that the information remains in its hands, and is not released or leaked to the public. That is keeping the public in ignorance.

Such a situation does not obtain in any of the cases in which this expression is used in judicial opinions. The information about the legal services and the fees for them offered by Bates and his colleagues in their legal clinic was not known only to the government, nor had the government taken steps to ensure the information was unavailable to the public. The government had merely proscribed certain ways of making the information known, *viz.*, by advertising. Residents of Puerto Rico were not 'ignorant' of the fact that gambling was permitted there, beer consumers of the relative strengths of different brands of beer, residents of Rhode Island of the prices at which liquor was sold, or residents of New Orleans of the gambling available there. It might be that government regulation made this information harder to obtain, and the significance of that we will assess anon. But it is ridiculous to speak in terms of 'keeping citizens, or keeping the public, ignorant'.

The same is true of the rhetoric of manipulation. The rhetoric is found in exactly the same opinions as that of 'keeping ignorant', with the addition of Kennedy J's dissent in *Florida Bar*.[10] Blackmun J talks about the 'State seek[ing] to suppress information about a product in order to manipulate a private economic decision',[11] and it 'manipulat[ing] the choices of its citizens, not by persuasion or direct regulation, but by depriving the public of the information needed to make a free choice'.[12] In *Posadas*, 'the government seeks to manipulate private behavior by depriving citizens of truthful information concerning lawful activities' (Brennan J, at 351). In *Florida Bar*, the state is 'manipulating the public's opinion by suppressing speech that informs us how the legal system works' (Kennedy J, at 2383). In *44 Liquormart*, the government is 'keep[ing] legal users of a product or service ignorant in order to manipulate their choices in the marketplace' (Thomas J, at 1516). How is the regulation of commercial advertising supposed to be 'manipulative'?

It is not hard to construct examples of intervention in, or management of, a flow of information that is indeed manipulative. Manufacturers of pharmaceuticals may report with enthusiasm the success of a certain drug, while keeping silent about side effects or contra-indications. Children too young to read may be told that a given programme that their parents do not want them to watch is not on television when in fact it is. The plain statement by a lawyer offering his

---

[10] *Florida Bar v Went For It Inc* 115 SCt 2371 (1995), at 2383; he also refers to the ban on direct-mail solicitation as 'censorship', an equal abuse of language.
[11] See *Central Hudson*, at 573.   [12] Ibid., at 575.

services on a contingency fee basis that 'if there is no recovery, no legal fees are owed' may be deceptive, in that clients are still liable for court costs and, unless they are familiar with the technical distinction between costs and fees, may not realize this until too late.[13] We might also mention the political party aide in the U.K. who recommended the release of certain information unfavourable to the government as soon as possible after the 11 September 2001 bombing of the World Trade Center, in order that the news would not be noticed. Little, if any, political 'spin-doctoring' is not also 'manipulation'.

But what does all that have to do with regulation of commercial advertising? The sense that the recipient or non-recipient of information is being 'manipulated' by the manager or restricter of the flow of information is traceable to one fundamental idea, which may take many forms. This idea is that there is some sound normative scheme under which it is proper for the would-be recipient to have the information, and that by being prevented from having it the would-be recipient is in some relevant way harmed.[14] One common way for this general idea to be instantiated is that the would-be recipient is in some way entitled to have the information, and this entitlement is not being respected when the information is withheld. This thought operates most clearly in healthcare-related examples. Given specific actual patients, or citizens in general as potential patients, are entitled to have full information on all the risks associated with the use in treatment of a given pharmaceutical drug or a given surgical procedure. This entitlement is dishonoured when genuine information about side effects or contra-indications is withheld—'withheld', notice, not when risks are falsely denied to exist. True information is simply not given out; it is not that false information is given out. Principles of legitimate political authority imply that government will deal with citizens openly and honestly. These principles are dishonoured when public policy information is withheld or obfuscated.

The difficulty in the case of government regulation of commercial advertising is to find the relevant entitlement or the relevant normative principles. As David Strauss has urged, 'not all government lying, and certainly not all government refusals to release information, are manipulative'.[15] He mentions protection of privacy, conservation of resources, national security as possible examples. Why should things be any different when the government is not itself to be the expresser? If the government denies me the possibility of hearing advertising promoting a state-run lottery, or promoting products which result in consumption of electricity, or promoting professional services of some kind, there is no dishonouring here of an entitlement. Even if I live in Virginia, where there is a legal state-run lottery, I have no *right* to receive the advertising of that lottery in

---

[13] Cf. *Zauderer v Office of Disciplinary Counsel* 471 US 626 (1985), 652–3.

[14] The relativity of coercion claims to background normative schemes is analysed by Berman: Mitchell N. Berman, 'The Normative Function of Coercion Claims', *Legal Theory* 8 (2002): 45–90. Much the same argument would apply *mutatis mutandis* to manipulation claims.

[15] David A. Strauss, 'Persuasion, Autonomy and Freedom of Expression', *Columbia Law Review* 91 (1991): 358.

general, and especially not from a radio station located in a non-lottery state. I have no *right* to know what the percentage of alcohol is in a given beer bottle. I have no *right* to receive tobacco products as free promotional advertising, or to have the chance to acquire a baseball hat or T-shirt with a tobacco brand name on it.[16] It is not even true that I have the right to make consumer or other life-style choices, or even decisions on matters of life and death, under conditions of full information. I do not; no-one has such a right. The more that a decision affects my life, health, and welfare in some profound and irreversible way, then the more forceful is the claim that I have the right to sufficient information materially relevant to making that decision, and therefore the more likely is it that some interference preventing me from having that relevant information will be manipulative. But consumer advertising rarely, if ever, meets such a standard.

Joseph Raz in his well-known essay on 'The Rule of Law and Its Virtue'[17] says that 'one manipulates a person by intentionally changing his tastes, his beliefs or his ability to act or decide'.[18] He also acknowledges that 'it is the business of law to guide human action by affecting people's options' (ibid.). But not all such affecting is manipulative. Raz argues that the rule of law can play a role in ensuring that law respects human dignity and is not manipulative. Violations of the rule of law can result in manipulation in two ways, by leading to uncertainty or to frustrated and disappointed expectations (ibid., 222). The thought is that the virtue of the rule of law is to create an 'open, stable, clear and general' framework of social rules that facilitates the exercise of human autonomy.[19] Uncertainty militates against this 'when the law does not enable people to foresee future developments or to form definite expectations'.[20] Expectations are frustrated and disappointed when people are encouraged to plan by the appearance of stability and certainty, and the law fails them when these impressions are illusory. Raz even suggests an analogy with entrapment: 'one is encouraged innocently to rely on the law and then that assurance is withdrawn and one's very reliance is turned into a cause of harm to one' (ibid.). In these ways, failures to observe the rule of law are manipulative. Despite what the rhetoric of manipulation in the commercial expression context claims, government in regulating commercial advertising is not intentionally changing anyone's tastes, beliefs, or abilities to act or decide. If I am a litigious kind of person, the government is not forcing me not to be one by regulating in various ways lawyers' advertising; it is not forcing me to give up beliefs about an appropriate way to live. The government is not even forcing me not to smoke, or not to drink, or not to gamble, by regulating advertising for these products. It is not forcing me

---

[16] Cf. *RJR-MacDonald Inc v Attorney-General of Canada; Imperial Tobacco Ltd v Attorney-General of Canada* [Indexed as RJR-MacDonald Inc v Canada (Attorney-General)] (1995) 127 DLR (4th) 1, at 12; *Germany v Parliament and Council*, Case C–376/98 (Advocate General's opinion 15 June 2000; judgment 5 October 2000) (ECJ).

[17] Joseph Raz, *The Authority of Law* (Oxford: Clarendon Press, 1979), Chapter 11.

[18] Ibid., 221.   [19] Ibid., 215.   [20] Ibid., 222.

to make do with a different prescription drug from the one I really wanted, by prohibiting pharmacists from advertising prescription drug prices. Nor in any of these cases is the government affecting my ability to act or decide. The typical regulatory framework for commercial advertising in fact fully conforms to the rule of law, in that it provides an open, stable, clear, and general framework of rules. As long as it does that, such a framework cannot be manipulative.

In their final decisions in commercial expression cases, courts have exhibited a marked aversion to total bans on commercial and professional advertising, as opposed to bans which merely regulate more or less severely the style, manner, and availability of commercial messages—regulations, if you like, which dam the free flow of commercial information entirely, rather than those which merely manage it. If Raz's account of manipulation and the rule of law is correct, then one can see where this aversion comes from. Raz is explicit that conformity to the rule of law is a matter of degree and a matter of circumstances (ibid.). So manipulativeness in the case of some restricting of the flow of information will also be a matter of degree and a matter of circumstances. If that is so, then the effect of a total ban on the availability of information of a given kind seems to put the restriction nearer to the point where it might become manipulative than the effect of a partial, appropriately fine-tuned, ban. In the U.S., the four-part *Central Hudson* test, in Canada the application of the *Oakes*[21] test for proportionality in section 1 analysis, and in Europe the effect of Article 10(2) all can be seen as operationalizing in a formal way this intuition about the difference between total and partial bans.

Two points still should be noted. First, if Raz's account of the rule of law is correct, then not even total bans will in fact be manipulative. Secondly, we face the same issue as we did at the end of the previous chapter. It does not follow from the fact that a doctrinal scheme developed within the commercial expression doctrine successfully operationalizes some plausible normative intuitions about proper regulation of commercial advertising, that therefore the commercial expression doctrine is sound. If we are going to grant constitutional protection to commercial expression at all, then a constitutional doctrine that accords with normative intuitions is clearly preferable to one that does not. But we are looking now for a foundation for the commercial expression doctrine in the first place. We are looking to see whether there is any cogency to the charge that regulation of commercial advertising amounts to 'manipulation' of an objectionable kind. If it does, then possibly the way is open to justifying constitutional protection for freedom of commercial expression. But in fact charges of 'manipulation' cannot be made out. If the commercial expression doctrine is to be justified, it cannot be by that route.

All the same, it is undeniable that restrictions on commercial advertising do have some effect on consumer choices and decision-making, and, in so far as the consequences of such choices may or may not contribute to aggregate social

---

[21] *R v Oakes* (1986) 26 DLR (4th) 200.

welfare, such restrictions have some effect on social welfare. Noting this does not end the matter. Three important questions remain to be considered. Does the effect on consumer choice and decision-making amount to a harm of some kind? Does the effect on social welfare amount to a harm of some kind? If the answer to these questions is positive, are the harms in question cognizable as harms occurring in the face of a constitutionally guaranteed right, for example, the right of freedom of expression? In the following sections, we will deal with these questions in turn.

2 DECISION-MAKING UNDER UNCERTAINTY

The formal economic ideal of a perfectly efficient market attributes perfect information to the participants in the market. Whatever value such an assumption may have for the project of theory- or model-construction, its descriptive value is limited. Actual participants in the economic market are always operating under some measure of uncertainty: 'The consumer could be uncertain about any one or any combination of the following: income, product price, product quality, product availability, and, in the dynamic setting, future income, interest rates and inflation rates'.[22] In economic analysis, typically the focus is on uncertainty as to one variable, and the effects of that uncertainty are studied while certainty is assumed as to other variables. This procedure is entirely legitimate for investigating the properties of models, a necessary prerequisite to the application of economics to the real world. But legal frameworks must be employed, interpreted, and applied by actual people in the actual circumstances of life, and the realities must take precedence over the abstractions.

The individual consumer is assumed by economics to be a rational maximizer of expected utility, or rational maximizer for short. The rational maximizer wants, to put it crudely, the best quality for the lowest outlay, where the outlay includes both the price actually spent on purchasing the product and the lowest search costs in finding out which is the best product and who is offering it at the lowest price. 'The best buy will be relative to the costs of diagnosis, product testing, search and processing.'[23] It is not therefore difficult to model simply the apparent way in which a government restriction on commercial advertising affects a rational maximizer in the market. As I have said already, in the case of, for example, a prohibition on advertising the price of liquor, it is not that the information is not available. It is available, but at a cost. Let us follow the practice of assuming certainty about some factors, uncertainty about others. So the consumer knows the range of quality and size of liquor he or she is prepared to

---

[22] C.J. McKenna, *The Economics of Uncertainty* (New York: Oxford University Press, 1986), 2.
[23] Iain Ramsay, *Consumer Protection: Text and Materials* (London: Weidenfeld and Nicholson, 1989), 42.

buy, and knows how much he or she has to spend on both the search and the bottle. The more the search costs, the less there will be available for the liquor. A prohibition on advertising clearly raises the costs of the search, and thus lowers the quality or the quantity of the liquor that he or she can buy, as compared with the case where the information on price and availability is available at a minor search cost through an advertisement in the local paper.

This constrained example gives us a clear sense, then, of the way in which the hearer of commercial expression may have an 'interest' in the 'free flow of commercial information' which is 'keener by far' than his or her 'interest in the day's most urgent political debate'.[24] A restriction on commercial advertising may occasion consumers to end up with a less preferred product than they would otherwise have been able to acquire, because, given the restriction, they pay higher search costs out of a fixed amount of resources than they would have had to pay in the absence of the restriction. The restriction has the effect of imposing *ex ante* a limit on how a rational consumer may trade search costs for product price and quality in maximizing expected utility. If a consumer were engaged in a three-way balancing of search costs, product price, and product quality, all other parameters, including available resources, being fixed, then presumably the consumer would *ceteris paribus* prefer to maximize product quality. The restriction on commercial advertising lowers the available maximum product quality by increasing search costs. The consumer is thus in that specific sense worse off as a consequence of the restriction.

In what sense, however, can a consumer be said to have a 'right' not to be made worse off in that kind of way? The search for an autonomy-based right has been a failure. The government does not violate autonomy merely by structuring our economic choices in this way rather than that. Some special circumstances need to obtain before genuinely there can be a violation of autonomy, and these do not obtain in the case of regulation of commercial advertising. On the other hand, it may well be that we can discover a right here under the paradigm of utility, not the paradigm of autonomy. There might be a hearers' utility right to receive information, a normative position the institutional protection of which justified by reasons of utility.

The central question has to be how typical, or how generalizable, is the model we have considered. The model is highly constrained and highly formal. It makes many assumptions, and the conclusion is relative to the obtaining of those assumptions. The flow of argument therefore has to be top-down, not bottom-up. That is to say, suppose we have indeed identified a specific kind of model where, if a certain kind of government regulation of the free flow of commercial information is in place, a rational maximizer will be less well off than he or she would have been in the absence of the regulation. This model cannot ground an argument that in general, across the board, consumers have a utility right to no

---

[24] *Virginia Board*, at 763.

government regulation of the free flow of commercial information. The case is too specific for that. Any argument for a hearer-based utility right to a free flow of commercial information has to demonstrate in general the utility-based grounds for the free flow. Specific, constrained models like the one mentioned then have to follow from the general grounds as implications or examples.

But that is exactly the point at which problems for the 'free flow of commercial information' argument for constitutional protection of commercial expression arise. No-one disputes the general role played by information in the maximizing both of individual and of overall social utility. As it has been put,

The importance of information to the operation of efficient markets is by now fairly well accepted. Information about price, quality and other attributes allows buyers to make the best use of their budget by finding the product whose mix of price and quality they most prefer. In turn, buyers' ability to locate preferred products gives sellers an incentive to compete to improve their offerings by allowing buyers to find and reward (with patronage) the seller whose offer they prefer. Without such information, the incentive to compete on price and quality will be weakened, and consumer welfare will be reduced.[25]

But the fundamental issue is whether the appropriate requirement in each case is for a *regulated*, not an unregulated, availability of information. Two cases can be considered: the free flow of commercial information in relation to individual maximization of expected utility and the free flow of commercial information in relation to overall economic efficiency. In both cases, it will become clear that 'free flow good, regulated flow bad' is far too simple-minded an approach. I will then assess the implications of that result for the commercial expression doctrine.

3 THE FLOW OF INFORMATION AND FAILURES OF REASONING

The standard economic model of the competitive market assumes not only perfect information, but also perfect rationality, perfect reasoning on the part of the marketplace participant. Clearly, as noted, the typical real consumer operates under uncertainty, under imperfect information. It is still, however, possible to consider within economics the properties of a market characterized by imperfect information. In fact, Joseph Stiglitz has recently argued that the economics of information has been the major source of advances in economics generally in the last part of the twentieth century.[26] All the same, even given any success in modelling market equilibria, or efficient markets, under conditions of imperfect information, questions relevant to the cogency of the commercial expression doctrine remain to be considered. An economic model of a market with imperfect information may be constructed still holding in place

---

[25] Howard Beales, Richard Craswell, and Steven C. Salop, 'The Efficient Regulation of Consumer Information', *Journal of Law and Economics* 24 (1981): 492.

[26] Joseph E. Stiglitz, 'The Contributions of the Economics of Information to Twentieth-Century Economics', *Quarterly Journal of Economics* 115 (2000): 1441–78.

the assumption of perfect rationality, and we will examine the demand for the free flow of commercial information in relation to such models shortly. First, let us relax the assumption of perfect rationality, and assess the possible contribution of the free flow of commercial information to problems presented by imperfect rationality. Can the contribution be presented so that the free flow of commercial information itself will be the solution to imperfect rationality? Can it be presented so that it is the cause of imperfect rationality?

I concede immediately that the notion of 'imperfect rationality' is misleading. No actual person can be perfectly rational, whatever the value of assuming perfect rationality in economic modelling. It is more appropriate to speak, as indeed psychology does speak, of 'bounded rationality', rationality as a capacity to reason with the maximum available effectiveness, given habits of mind that seem endemic to human thought. Ramsay identifies six such habits as suggested by psychological research:[27]

(1) Individuals will tend to use more readily available and vivid information. This factor is especially relevant to in-personal merchandizing and point of purchase information and advertising.[28]

(2) Consumers will process information in the form it is received: an advertisement expressing cost savings annually rather than one expressing them monthly is more effective simply because the former figure is larger.

(3) Consumers when searching for new products or information will refer initially to their previous experience, buying the same brand, even if dissatisfied.

(4) Individuals are poor statisticians and tend to put too much weight on small data samples. They are too willing to accept anecdotal evidence over serious statistics.

(5) Individuals tend to ignore small probability events (e.g., the likelihood of long-term harm).

(6) Consumer search tends to be limited to a small number of alternatives even though a large number are available.[29]

Other forms of inadequate reasoning suggested by commentators focus on the important difference between goods and services whose quality can be ascertainable before purchase or 'inspection goods' (clothing one tries on), those whose quality is revealed by use or 'experience goods' (food, typically), and

---

[27] Ramsay, *Consumer Protection*, 46–7.

[28] The force of this point was arguably recognized by the U.S. Supreme Court in upholding regulation of lawyers' solicitation (*Ohralik v Ohio State Bar Association* 436 US 447 (1978); *Florida Bar v Went For It Inc* 115 SCt 2371 (1995), and missed by the Supreme Court of Canada in its invalidation of regulations on tobacco advertising in retail outlets.

[29] The 'revealed preference' version of utilitarianism will not be perturbed by this result; if a consumer chose a particular bundle of transaction costs and costs of item purchased, then that must be the bundle they preferred.

those assessment of whose quality requires technical expertise and specialized knowledge or 'credence goods' (complex machines or professional services).[30] The ordinary consumer may simply not be able to assess the implications of information provided, even with unlimited time available. Moreover, we are all familiar with the phenomenon of 'information cascade'[31] or 'information overload'; the amount of information before us is simply too much to be processed by the brain, and failures of reasoning result from too much, not too little, information. Bill New and Steven Kelman suggest that even paternalistic regulation by the government would be justified to remedy such defects.[32]

It is clear that an unregulated free flow of commercial information will at best exacerbate, and at worst cause, these difficulties. Much time and money are spent by corporate expressers making sure advertising of their product or service is 'readily available' and 'vivid', and that information in an advertisement is stated in a form that will most entice consumers towards purchasing. Manufacturers spend much time and money cultivating brand loyalty, in order to benefit from the tilt towards previous experience. Statistics can be expressed in a form that is technically correct, but less than fully informative to a person who is not mathematically adept. Consumers are vulnerable when diagnosis and treatment are bundled together in the same provider, as is typically the case with professional services. The sheer quantity of advertising and the intensity of advertising claims is a familiar part of the contemporary landscape, both the literal and the metaphorical landscape.

An unregulated flow of commercial information may also cause failures to maximize utility even in the absence of failures of reasoning. The problem is especially acute in the case of experience goods. If the costs of disadvantages of a particular good or service are hard to uncover, there is little incentive for the seller to provide information. The same is true when the consumer is unlikely to be a repeat player, as in the tourism industry and the real estate industry.[33] As Daniel Halberstam has pointed out, a purely economic approach to regulation of such advertising will be far more subtly tuned than current First Amendment jurisprudence in the U.S.[34]

In addition to these intuitive observations, recent work in information economics has produced a number of technical results at the level of properties of formal models, which results suggest that the free flow of commercial information may work against, rather than for, individual utility maximization. I will mention some examples. In a model of the capital market subject to stochastic

[30] Arthur R. Pinto, 'The Nature of the Capital Markets Allows a Greater Role for Government', *Brooklyn Law Review* 55 (1989): 84; Beales, Craswell, and Salop, 'Efficient Regulation', 505–6.

[31] Daniel J.H. Greenwood, 'Essential Speech: Why Corporate Speech is not Free', *Iowa Law Review* 83 (1998): 1018 n 68.

[32] Bill New, 'Paternalism and Public Policy', *Economics and Philosophy* 15 (1999): 71–2; Steven Kelman, 'Regulation and Paternalism', *Public Policy* 29 (1981): 229.

[33] Ramsay, *Consumer Protection*, 43.

[34] Daniel Halberstam, 'Commercial Speech, Professional Speech, and the Constitutional Status of Social Institutions', *University of Pennsylvania Law Review* 147 (1999): 795.

events, it can be shown that information increases price variability. 'Increased price variability is likely to lead to increased uncertainty about the value of one's endowments, and this is likely to lower expected utility. In one example . . . everyone is better off if no-one is informed than if all are informed.'[35] A model which defines product match in terms of taste as well as price can be constructed in which, contrary to the normal case, informed consumers impart a negative externality onto uninformed consumers; more informed consumers lead to higher prices, since uninformed consumers are the source of price elasticity.[36] In a model of an economy with production and a risk-sharing market, there are circumstances under which more information makes all risk-averse agents worse off.[37] If all agents are weakly risk-averse, then better public information is Pareto inferior in a competitive risk allocation under any one of three specified assumptions.[38]

If we consider broader issues of market failure and market inefficiency, the problems for a straightforward advocacy of the free flow of commercial information are similarly undeniable. The root problem is that information, whether or not it is in the strict sense a 'public good' in the economists' technical sense, has relevantly similar properties. The standard economists' definition of public good[39] turns on the characteristics of such goods as 'non-rival' (the quantity consumed by one person does not limit consumption of the good by others) and 'inexcludable' (if the good is provided at all, it is available for all and none may feasibly be excluded from enjoying it).[40] The difficulty is that 'the purchase, production, and use of information by consumers generate a market-perfecting external benefit to uninformed consumers . . . impl[ying] that too little product information will generally be produced, even in an otherwise competitive market.'[41] To put it crudely, it is not beyond a certain point worthwhile for uninformed consumers to trouble themselves to pay for information. The choices of informed consumers will have an obvious effect on the market in terms of lower prices and improved product quality; but once prices are lowered or quality improved, those benefits are equally available to the uninformed.[42] There are also natural monopoly and free-rider problems associated with information: 'once generated, information can be disseminated at low marginal cost, and

---

[35] Sanford J. Grossman and Joseph E. Stiglitz, 'Information and Competitive Price Systems', *American Economic Review* 66, no. 2 (1976): 251.

[36] Simon P. Anderson and Régis Renault, 'Consumer Information and Firm Pricing: Negative Externalities from Improved Information', *International Economic Review* 41 (2000): 722, 733.

[37] Bernhard Eckwert and Itzhak Zilcha, 'The Value of Information in Production Economies', *Journal of Economic Theory* 100 (2001): 173–4.

[38] Edward E. Schlee, 'The Value of Information in Efficient Risk-Sharing Arrangements', *American Economic Review* 91, no. 3 (2001): 510.

[39] M. Peston, *Public Goods and the Public Sector* (London: Macmillan, 1972), 12–14.

[40] These categories are not empirically brute: see Denise Réaume, 'Individuals, Groups, and Rights to Public Goods', *University of Toronto Law Journal* 38 (1988): 4.

[41] Beales, Craswell, and Salop, 'Efficient Regulation', 503; See also Kelman, 'Regulation and Paternalism', 237; Stiglitz, 'Contributions', 1448; Ramsay, *Consumer Protection*, 38.

[42] Anderson and Renault, 'Consumer Information and Firm Pricing', 721.

buyers can resell purchased information to others. Either factor may lead to an undersupply of information' (ibid.). Beales and his colleagues at the U.S. Federal Trade Commission then point out that advertisers can mitigate the free-rider problem by internalizing some of the gain in the form of higher profits. But, they acknowledge, 'seller-provided information creates other externalities of its own':

positive general information about all brands in a product class benefits every brand, not simply the one generating the information. Similarly, negative information about a competing product class is likely to benefit all substitute products, thus reducing the incentive of any single seller to provide this information.[43]

These problems will again lead to a general undersupply of information.

Other scholars have traced the same set of problems. In one of the classic founding papers of the economics of information, Jack Hirshleifer demonstrated what he called the distributive aspect of access to superior information. 'This advantage provides a motivation for the private acquisition and dissemination of technological information that is quite apart from—and may even exist in the absence of—any social usefulness of that information.'[44] He remarks in a footnote that other markets exhibit the same structural problem (ibid., note 4). Stiglitz showed that, in a product market, improved information that increased the monopoly power of each firm leads to higher prices and lower welfare.[45] Grossman and Stiglitz explored a number of difficulties associated with information in an unregulated market.[46] Among their conjectures are that the more individuals who are informed, the lower the ratio of expected utility of the informed to the uninformed (at 394), and that 'the only possible equilibrium is one with no information. But if everyone is uninformed, it clearly pays some individual to become informed. Thus, there does not exist a competitive equilibrium' (at 395). Their conclusion is that 'there is a fundamental conflict between the efficiency with which markets spread information and the incentives to acquire information'.[47] There are also paradoxes associated with informative advertising in a product market with differentiation. Grossman and Shapiro note the obvious point that, where products are homogeneous, advertising is socially wasteful, but where they are heterogeneous, advertising holds out the promise of improved matching of customer and brand.[48] All the same, there are circumstances when,

---

[43] Beales, Craswell, and Salop, 'Efficient Regulation', 503–4; Stiglitz, 'Contributions', 1456.

[44] Jack Hirshleifer, 'The Private and Social Value of Information and the Reward to Inventive Activity', *American Economic Review* 61 (1971): 561.

[45] Joseph E. Stiglitz, 'Equilibrium in Product Markets with Imperfect Information', *American Economic Review* 69, no. 2 (1979): 343; Ramsay, *Consumer Protection*, 45; Beales, Craswell, and Salop, 'Efficient Regulation', 507.

[46] Sanford J. Grossman and Joseph E. Stiglitz, 'On the Impossibility of Informationally Efficient Markets', *American Economic Review* 70, no. 3 (1980): 393–407.

[47] Grossman and Stiglitz, 'Impossibility of Informationally Efficient Markets', 405; see also Stiglitz, 'Contributions', 1460.

[48] Gene M. Grossman and Carl Shapiro, 'Informative Advertising with Differentiated Products', *Review of Economic Studies* 51 (1984): 64.

even in the case of informative advertising, all that is achieved is the socially wasteful mere shuffling of consumers among firms.[49] There is a fundamental tension between advertising that concentrates on price and advertising that concentrates on the product itself. 'Our result that profits rise with the number of informed consumers suggests that firms would want to engage in product advertising. Produce advertising would benefit firms if they could commit not to advertise prices at the same time. However, firms are unlikely to be able thus to commit themselves, and price advertising may end up destroying the advantages that product-specification advertising creates.'[50]

It is extremely important not to misunderstand the argument I am making here. I am not making the absurd claim that the flow of information has no role to play in the promotion of either maximized expected utility or economic efficiency. Clearly it does. My point is that it is a mistake to suppose that a 'free flow of commercial information' in the sense of an *unregulated* flow of commercial information *ipso facto* conduces to either maximized expected utility or economic efficiency. Problems arise, such that some measure of market regulation is a requirement. Some of these problems arise from the contingencies of bounded human rationality. Others arise at the level of formal economic models. Economic modelling shows, it is true, only formal relations between variables. The interpretation to be put upon the models, and the translation of the models into real economic policy, is always a separate, and a further, step. The thought that in the real world markets need regulation is a political interpretation of a range of economic models; but so also is the thought that the free flow of commercial information is necessarily a good.

Moreover, it can be validly pointed out that supporters of the commercial expression doctrine have not always presumed an entirely unregulated economic market. Right back in *Virginia Board*, the U.S. Supreme Court declared that 'we do not of course hold that commercial speech can never be regulated in any way. Some forms of commercial speech regulation are surely permissible. . . . The First Amendment, as we construe it today, does not prohibit the State from ensuring that the stream of commercial information flow cleanly as well as freely' (at 770, 772). The Court then reinforced this acknowledgment in the first part of the *Central Hudson* test, that the speech under review 'must concern lawful activity and not be misleading' (at 566). The Court typically proceeds on the assumption that, if the commercial speech is truthful and non-misleading, the speech automatically falls within the protective scope of the First Amendment. This acknowledgment, however, does not meet the point at issue. The problems of bounded rationality, of market failure, and the like arise even on the assumption of a flow of truthful and non-misleading information. A simple example may be provided by two recent high-profile cases in Canada from

---

[49] Grossman and Shapiro, 'Informative Advertising with Differentiated Products', 76; Beales, Craswell, and Salop, 'Efficient Regulation', 507.

[50] Anderson and Renault, 'Consumer Information and Firm Pricing', 738.

the securities market.[51] In October 2000 Air Canada gave scripted voicemails to thirteen analysts who closely followed the company. The purpose of the voice-mails was to inform the analysts that the company proposed to take certain charges against earnings in the third and fourth quarters of 2000. The company hoped that these analysts would then reduce their forecasts of earnings, and so the impact on Air Canada shares of the charges would be diffused.[52] Similarly, on 12 February 2001 RBC Dominion Securities Inc., the brokerage arm of the Royal Bank of Canada, webcast an interview with John Roth, then CEO of Nortel Networks Corp, exclusively to RBC's brokers and clients. In each case, the hearers had access to what was indisputably truthful and non-misleading information, but all the same the release of information so selectively counted as a case of market failure. These and comparable incidents in the U.S. led the U.S. Securities and Exchange Commission on 23 October 2000 to issue Regulation FD which *inter alia* prohibits revealing material information only to a chosen few. Air Canada was subsequently fined $1 million by the Ontario Securities Commission for its activities.[53]

In general, courts have acted as though the threshold criterion of commercial expression or speech being 'truthful and non-misleading' is straightforward to apply. The courts seem to have paid the matter the most attention in lawyers' solicitation cases, reflecting perhaps accurately the perception noted above that consumers are especially vulnerable in situations where diagnosis and treatment are bundled. However, even in these cases, largely button-pressing and dis-crepant judgments abound as to whether given examples are misleading or not. The reason is not far to seek. As the thorough analysis by Beales and his colleagues illustrates,[54] it is extremely difficult to define 'misleading' or 'decep-tive' as applied to advertising in a way that generates the kind of clear definition the rule of law requires of legal and regulatory standards. 'False statement of material fact' is too narrow, although such statements do have no economic value. 'Failure to disclose any information which would affect consumer behav-iour' is too wide. Educated intuition cries out for the use of terms like 'mater-ial', 'unreasonable', 'optimal', and so forth; but these terms leave much discretionary power to agencies that must interpret and apply them.

A further relevant general point is this. It may be true that lack of regulation has the potential to lower expected utility and hinder efficiency. But regulation too has its costs. Many of the litigated commercial expression cases, as we have seen, concern professional advertising. Restrictions on advertising in the professions have been until recently very strict. Economic rationales for this

[51] In Pinto's view, the securities market is a special case where government regulation, especially as regards disclosure requirements, is indispensable: Pinto, 'Capital Markets', *passim*.

[52] See Jacqui McNish and Karen Howlett, 'Air Canada Hornet's Nest Could Spur Change', *The Globe and Mail*, 14 October 2000, B1, B7.

[53] Richard Blackwell, 'Air Canada Fined $1-million', *The Globe and Mail*, 28 July 2001, B1.

[54] Beales, Craswell, and Salop, 'Efficient Regulation', 496–501; Ramsay, *Consumer Protection*, 375–87.

strictness have not been difficult to find. Advertising bans insulate existing play-ers from competitiveness and promote market inefficiency, in two ways. First, they constitute entry barriers to new sellers wishing to enter the market, as courts[55] and commentators[56] have realized. Secondly, they deprive consumers and society as a whole of whatever benefits in the form of higher quality and lower prices result from increased competition in the market for professional services.[57] Moreover, because misleadingness is difficult to identify, there is a real danger of over-regulation and resultant inefficiencies.[58] There is the well-known phenomenon of agency capture—the eventual suborning of a regulating agency by the industry being regulated, so that the regulations turn out to be for the benefit of the industry, not the consumer or society.[59] It is a matter of sophis-ticated economic judgement to trade off the economic costs of regulation of the flow of information against the economic benefits.[60] The issues are complex, and do not lend themselves to decision by simplistic principle.

4 UTILITY RIGHTS AND THE FREE FLOW OF COMMERCIAL INFORMATION

Is there then, when all is said and done, such a thing as a hearers' utility right to receive information, a right to receive information grounded in an argument or arguments within the paradigm of utility? It is clear from the preceding discus-sion that this question has no *general* answer. There is no such right, taken as a *general* unitary right. If that is true, then there is no hearers' utility right to the free flow of commercial information, taken as a structural feature of the market. The free flow of commercial information brings with it disutilities as well as utilities, market failures as well as market successes. Instead, there is a patch-work quilt of specific utility rights in specific cases. That is, in some specific cases, there are reasons grounded in utility for not imposing restrictions or regu-lations on the free flow of commercial information. But in other specific cases, maximization of expected utility and economic efficiency requires regulation of the free flow of commercial information to prevent market failures.

Many of the cases of potential market failure arise from the absence of suffi-cient incentive on the part of those who possess information to impart the information. Thus a large number of instances of government regulation of the

---

[55] *Bates*, at 378.

[56] Fred S. McChesney, 'Commercial Speech in the Professions: The Supreme Court's Unanswered Questions and Questionable Answers', *University of Pennsylvania Law Review* 134 (1985): 51; Beales, Craswell, and Salop, 'Efficient Regulation', 514; Fred S. McChesney, 'De-Bates and Re-Bates: The Supreme Court's Latest Commercial Speech Cases', *Supreme Court Economic Review* 5 (1997): 85–90.

[57] Ibid.   [58] Ramsay, *Consumer Protection*, 43.

[59] McChesney, 'De-Bates and Re-Bates', 86–7. And perhaps this is even happening to the courts where the commercial expression doctrine is concerned: see Chapter 15.2 below.

[60] Beales, Craswell, and Salop, 'Efficient Regulation', 501. See ibid., 513–39; Ramsay, *Consumer Protection*, 59–92 for detailed discussion of the merits and demerits of different regulatory strate-gies.

free flow of commercial information are mandatory disclosure requirements. Mandatory disclosures abound in the securities markets. A prospectus for an initial public offering must contain such-and-such information. Information of a given material kind concerning the financial dealings of the company must be disseminated, and disseminated in a particular way. Proper notice must be given of changes of a certain kind to company structure and policy. And so on. The form and content of warranty advertising in the case of consumer products and services is tightly controlled.[61] The form in which the availability of credit may be advertised is tightly controlled.[62] Even though in general it may be claimed that the function of regulations such as these is 'to protect the integrity of the market', it is primarily to ensure that information is available and presented in a form that is comprehensible. Thus the basis for disclosure requirements is ultimately to protect the hearer or receiver of the information. The matter is one of the availability of so-called 'pull information', information a person wants to acquire. Typically, someone other than the person seeking the information is raising obstacles to its acquisition.

Very few of the decided cases of commercial expression, however, concern mandated disclosure of this kind. In Canada, *Ford*[63] concerned a requirement of the province of Quebec that signs in a shop be in French as well as English: without such a requirement, unilingual francophones (of which there will be a significant number in a predominantly French-speaking province) or allophones speaking only French as a second language will not be able to receive the information. Among the advertising regulations at issue in *RJR-MacDonald* were the health warnings that must appear on any tobacco products offered for sale. In *Edible Oil*,[64] the impugned regulation concerned the requirement that margarine be coloured a certain shade of yellow, to make it clear that the product was margarine and not dairy butter—a paradigm instance of a piece of information the seller on its own had no incentive to disclose, but which was materially relevant to consumer utility. In the U.S., the Supreme Court upheld in *Zauderer*[65] the disciplining of an attorney for failing to disclose in advertising that clients may be liable for litigation costs even if no fee were charged. Indeed, the Court's general approach that 'the preferred remedy is more disclosure, rather than less'[66] suggests a tilt in favour of disclosure requirements, even though 'unjustified or unduly burdensome disclosure requirements might offend the First Amendment'.[67] In the context of the securities market, the U.S. Court of Appeal has even commented that 'requiring disclosure of a material fact in

---

[61] Ibid., 450–2.   [62] Ibid., 333–4.

[63] *Attorney-General of Quebec v La Chaussure Brown's Inc et al* [Indexed as Ford v Quebec (Attorney-General)] (1988) 54 DLR (4th) 577.

[64] *Re Institute of Edible Oil Foods et al and the Queen* [Indexed as Institute of Edible Oil Foods v Ontario] (1989) 64 DLR (4th) 380 (Ont CA), leave to appeal to Supreme Court of Canada refused (1990) 74 OR (2d) x.

[65] *Zauderer v Office of Disciplinary Counsel* 471 US 626 (1985).

[66] *Bates* at 375.   [67] *Zauderer* at 651.

order to prevent investor misunderstanding is the very essence of federal secur-ities regulation'.[68] In Europe, mandatory disclosures have been an issue only in the case of health warnings on tobacco products.[69]

In the vast majority of cases of regulation of commercial expression, the 'dis-closure' at stake is one that the corporate expresser wishes to make for its own self-interest, and the regulation impugned is one that prohibits or regulates the disclosure. This is the realm of so-called 'push information', information which people other than the would-be hearer want the hearer to have. Push informa-tion is ill cast as an issue of hearers' rights. It is a commonplace that the presence of advertising in contemporary life is pervasive and largely inescapable. Most advertising is not only not sought out, but also actually repudiated. We record television programmes in order to view them later, not only for the convenience of time-shifting, but also because we can then fast-forward through the endless advertisements. The search is on to develop technology to make VCRs respond to the increased sound levels of television advertising and speed through them automatically. There are recognized 'spikes' in water usage during television advertising as everyone chooses that moment to go to the bathroom or put on tea or coffee. People immediately 'fillet' magazines of all the advertising pages, and settle down to read what actually interests them. The value of caller ID on telephones is not so much to know when friends are calling and so one should answer, as to know when carpet cleaning companies, credit card companies, insurance companies, etc., are calling and one should not answer. Problems of forestry management worldwide would be greatly ameliorated if dustbins throughout the globe did not need to be filled with unwanted print advertising. Corporate advertisers in fact are starting to place less emphasis on advertising in specific commercial breaks that make it only too easy to escape the advertise-ment. They are turning their attention now to product placement, the appear-ance of a branded product in a strategic place in a film, television programme, or even book, where the presence of the product cannot escape notice.[70] No self-respecting self-interested company would be in the business of advertising if all it were doing was reluctantly acknowledging a right of the hearer or receiver to have information. Advertising works to promote the interests of sellers: that is why it is a multi-billion dollar phenomenon. Even though appropriate advertis-ing in the appropriate circumstances is of benefit to the hearer-consumer, it is idle to pretend that all restriction and regulation of advertising must be banned on pain of violating a *hearers'* utility right to receive that advertising.

---

[68] *Securities and Exchange Commission v Wall Street Publishing Institute Inc dba Stock Market Magazine* 851 F 2d 365 (1988) (USCA DC Cir), at 374.

[69] *Germany v Council; R v Secretary of State for Health, ex parte British American Tobacco (Investments) Ltd* Case C–491/01 (Advocate General's opinion 10 September 2002; judgment 10 December 2002) (ECJ).

[70] Roy MacGregor, 'What Canadian Economists should Learn from the First Product Placement Awards', *The Globe and Mail*, 8 January 2003, A 2.

5 THE SUPPOSED DILUTION OF FREEDOM OF EXPRESSION

One of the main uses of the 'free flow of commercial information' argument in favour of constitutional protection for commercial expression seems to have been to assuage a guilty conscience on the part of courts for protecting commercial expression at all. While paying no overt attention to Rehnquist J's (as he then was) well-known barbs about sellers hawking wares and purchasers of shampoo,[71] the U.S. Supreme Court took them to heart to the extent of giving commercial speech 'lesser protection',[72] of regarding it as of 'less constitutional moment' (ibid.), and of permitting it to be regulated with 'less precision'[73] than mainstream protected speech. The Court even acknowledged that:

To require a parity of constitutional protection for commercial and noncommercial speech alike could invite dilution, simply by a leveling process, of the force of the Amendment's guarantee with respect to the latter kind of speech. Rather than subject the First Amendment to such a devitalization, we instead have afforded commercial speech a limited measure of protection, commensurate with its subordinate position in the scale of First Amendment values, while allowing modes of regulation that might be impermissible in the realm of noncommercial expression.[74]

The Court, that is, believed it could arrest any potential 'dilution' of the strength of constitutional protection for political, scientific, or artistic speech by defining the category of 'commercial speech' and confining any lower standard to that category.

The force and implications of any 'dilution' argument against the commercial expression doctrine have to be carefully assessed.[75] The argument can be taken to make an empirical claim: as a matter of fact, if constitutional protection is extended to commercial expression, other forms of expression will be protected less. The difficulty with the argument so construed is that there is no empirical evidence for it. It is over twenty-five years since the decision in the U.S. in *Virginia Board*, and over thirteen years since the decision in Canada in *Irwin Toy*.[76] Yet there has been no obvious erosion of freedom of political, scientific, or artistic expression. Civil libertarian critics of the Supreme Court of Canada have regarded the decisions in *Keegstra*[77] and *Butler*[78] upholding Criminal Code provisions against hate literature and pornography respectively as lessening protection for freedom of expression. Even if they are, they come from the court

---

[71] *Virginia Board* 781 and 787.   [72] *Central Hudson* 563.
[73] *In re Primus* 436 US 412 (1978), 434, 438.
[74] *Ohralik*, at 456.
[75] I acknowledge that I was once far too impressed by it: see 'Freedom of Commercial Expression', in W. J. Waluchow (ed.), *Free Expression: Essays in Law and Philosophy* (Oxford: Clarendon Press 1994), 127 ff.
[76] *Attorney-General of Quebec v Irwin Toy Ltd* [Indexed as Irwin Toy Ltd v Quebec (Attorney-General)] (1989) 58 DLR (4th) 577.
[77] *R v Keegstra et al* (1990) 61 CCC (3d) 1.   [78] *R v Butler* (1992) 89 DLR (4th) 449.

that not long before had struck down sections of the Tobacco Products Control Act in RJR-MacDonald. Civil libertarians in the U.S. are also apprehensive about the chilling of political speech critical of the government since the 11 September 2001 bombing of the World Trade Center in New York. But such chilling has not yet been tested in the courts, and in any case is hardly the result of the commercial expression doctrine.

The dilution argument is problematic in another way as well. One might respond to the U.S. Supreme Court's concerns about dilution as expressed in *Ohralik* as did Callaghan J in *Klein:*[79]

If commercial speech serves a function completely different from that associated with non-commercial speech; if its too-close association with political speech threatens to devalue the latter and the First Amendment; if it is of less moment; if it is entitled to less protection, and to regulations formulated with less precision, than that to which non-commercial speech is entitled; then surely the question arises, why protect it at all?

The obvious response is that the 'dilution' argument assumes that the speech doing the diluting is inherently less valuable—but that is precisely what is being disputed.[80] Such a response might be defended two ways. One way is to reject the distinction between commercial and political expression by arguing that all commercial expression has a political dimension to it. This is the route favoured by David McGowan and Martin Redish,[81] but I have given reasons for rejecting that approach above.[82] The other route is to accept the realities of the 'free flow of commercial information' argument and the values that underlie it, and defend as legitimate the economic focus of the commercial expression doctrine. Protecting commercial speech does not dilute protection for paradigm speech. Rather, it leads to not enough protection for speech implicating economic concerns.[83] The economic character of commercial expression not merely fails to be a reason to withhold constitutional protection. It is in fact a reason to award constitutional protection, and the dilution argument serves only to obfuscate that fact.

This latter route to the repudiation of the 'dilution' argument comports with the results of our investigation into a supposed hearers' utility right to the free flow of commercial information. It is clear that courts in assessing the constitutional validity of regulations or restrictions of commercial expression are engaged in fundamentally *economic* reasoning. The determination that a given governmental interest is substantial, that a given regulation or restriction appro-

---

[79] *Re Klein and Law Society of Upper Canada: Re Dvorak and Law Society of Upper Canada* (1985) 16 DLR (4th) 489 (Ont HCt), at 537.

[80] David F. McGowan, 'A Critical Analysis of Commercial Speech', *California Law Review* 78 (1990): 443.

[81] Martin Redish, *Money Talks: Speech, Economic Power, and the Values of Democracy* (New York: New York University Press, 2001).

[82] See Chapter 1.4 above.

[83] Alex Kozinski and Stuart Banner, 'Who's Afraid of Commercial Speech?', *Virginia Law Review* 76 (1990): 648; Redish, *Money Talks, passim.*

priately furthers that interest in a proportionately suitable way or infringes commercial expression in a proportionately suitable way—these are all ultimately determinations of the appropriateness of a piece of economic regulation. Given that that is so, then some serious questions can be raised about the cogency of the commercial expression doctrine in support of such practices of economic regulation carried out by courts. I will raise three different concerns in this Chapter 13.6, 13.7, and 13.9 below. This Chapter 13.8 constitutes a brief interlude to reflect on the 'marketplace of ideas' metaphor in this context.

6 CONSTITUTIONAL ADJUDICATION AND REGULATION

The first concern is whether courts are structurally appropriate vehicles for economic regulation. Ramsay gives a number of reasons to suggest they are not.[84]

(1) Adjudication is focussed on the rights and duties of the individuals before the court, not on the broad range of policies available on some given regulatory issue.
(2) Courts have limited framework of remedies, compared to a legislature or an administrative agency.
(3) Adjudication is piecemeal, and development of doctrine is incremental.
(4) Courts are passive and reactive; they can only await appropriate cases. Litigation is *ex post facto*, and cases litigated are not necessarily representative of the underlying problem which regulation might be needed to address.
(5) Fact-finding in adjudication is ill suited to broad social facts and general policy issues, and there are difficulties in assembling behavioural science data in the context of any given individual suit.
(6) Adjudication makes no provision for policy review or monitoring of compliance, and the only available feedback mechanism is another, follow-up lawsuit.

These points are well applicable to the case of commercial expression. In order:

(1) The U.S. Supreme Court in *Coors*[85] has great fun pointing out the tension between the government's desire to prohibit providing information about the alcohol content of beer on bottle labels and its general desire in other areas of alcohol labelling and food labelling generally for more disclosure on the part of manufacturers. But such 'twitting with inconsistency',[86] while arguably sufficient to decide the specific case at hand, falls well short of a serious consideration of overall food and drug labelling policy. Likewise,

---

[84] Ramsay, *Consumer Protection*, 74–5. He is summarizing a more extensive argument in Donald L. Horowitz, *The Courts and Social Policy* (Washington, DC: Brookings Institute, 1977), 34–56. I in turn am summarizing Ramsay.

[85] *Rubin v Coors Brewing Company* 115 SCt 1585 (1995), at 1590–1.

[86] C.D. Broad's term for the limits that can be achieved by argument in matters of ethics. The expression is attributed to Broad by Renford Bambrough: Renford Bambrough, *Moral Scepticism*

the examination of the sale of proprietary customer information in *U.S. West*[87] is related strictly to the facts of this case, and cannot address what is essentially an economy-wide issue of privacy and consumer exploitation. The clash between principles of freedom of expression and the Unfair Competition Laws of Germany and Switzerland is well known, but the essentially *ad hoc* decisions in *Barthold*,[88] *Markt Intern*,[89] *Jacobowski*,[90] *Hertel*,[91] and *Stambuk*[92] fall well short of the kind of systematic analysis needed for such a profound issue of normative institutional design. On the other hand, the fact that in the case of professional advertising by lawyers the U.S. Supreme Court has developed something like a detailed regulatory scheme is due entirely to the contingencies of the large number of actions brought by parties with the energy, expertise, and depth of pocket to take them to the Supreme Court.

(2) The case of *RJR-MacDonald* is instructive. The Supreme Court of Canada struck down central provisions of federal policy expressed in the Tobacco Products Control Act, but left nothing in its place. Even though the holding was far from the endorsement of tobacco advertising that its critics feared,[93] the federal government was left scrambling to draft replacement legislation. Only a welcome, and uncharacteristic, degree of reticence on the part of the tobacco manufacturers themselves prevented two steps backwards in this tactic of the fight to preserve the nation's health. Likewise, in cases like *Virginia Board*, *Coors*, and *GNOBA*,[94] the U.S. Supreme Court has struck down aspects of regulatory schemes without any serious attention to the potential problems of a regulatory vacuum.

(3) Consider again the development of doctrine in the area of lawyers' advertising, and consider the position of the doctrine in the early days of its development. Although the U.S. Supreme Court tried hard in *Bates* to lay down some general principles, still the case had to be decided on its particular facts. The Court could not rule in advance on solicitation in pursuit of associational freedoms; that had to wait until *Primus*[95] came along. It could not rule on in-person solicitation until *Ohralik*. It could not rule on regulation of advertising of area of practice until *RMJ*,[96] on fee advertising until

---

and Moral Knowledge (London: Routledge and Kegan Paul, 1979), 85 ff. I have been unable to find it in Broad's published writings on ethics. Given the Cambridge connection, the source is quite likely to be the oral tradition.

[87] *US West Inc v FCC* 182 F (3d) 1224 (1999) (USCA 10th Cir).
[88] *Barthold v Germany* Ser A 90 (1985) (ECtHR).
[89] *Markt Intern Verlag v Germany* Ser A 195 (1989) (ECtHR).
[90] *Jacubowski v Germany* Ser A 291–A (1994) (ECtHR).
[91] *Hertel v Switzerland* (59/1997/843/1049) (1998) (ECtHR).
[92] *Stambuk v Germany* (37928/97) (2002) (ECtHR).
[93] Roger A. Shiner, 'The Silent Majority Speaks: *RJR-MacDonald Inc v Canada*', *Constitutional Forum* 7, no. 1 (1995): 8–9.
[94] *Greater New Orleans Broadcasting Association Inc v United States* 119 SCt 1923 (1999).
[95] *In re Primus* 436 US 412 (1978).   [96] *In re RMJ* 455 US 191 (1982).

Zauderer, on direct-mail solicitation until *Shapero.*[97] Yet other issues lay ahead—on advertising areas of speciality,[98] and statutory waiting periods before initiating direct-mail solicitation.[99] The Court thus took eighteen years to develop incrementally an *ersatz* regulatory scheme that a legislature could have done, and likely done better, in, say, one.

(4) The U.S. Supreme Court's dealings with generic advertising may be cited here. The Court appears to have taken *Wileman,*[100] largely for institutional reasons, in order to resolve a conflict between two decisions in different circuits of the U.S. Court of Appeal (at 2137). The Ninth Circuit, the court below in the instant case, had decided in favour of the fruit producer,[101] but the Third Circuit, in an earlier case concerning a similar scheme for beef producers, had upheld the scheme.[102] In *Wileman,* the Supreme Court also upheld the scheme, departing from its recent pattern of government-bashing and paeans to the free flow of commercial information, as Souter J's spirited dissent in the case made clear. *United Foods*[103] offered the chance for the stars to reappear in their proper places in the constellation, as Stevens J and Kennedy J changed sides to form a majority to reject a generic advertising scheme for mushroom producers. The holding, as we have seen,[104] was an exercise in distinguishing without a difference. Generic advertising exists throughout the agricultural industry. The Court can achieve reform, supposing reform to be needed, only by dealing with parts of the industry one by one as producers in any given part happen to bring litigation.

(5) Struggles with social science data and evidentiary standards have taken place in both the U.S. and Canada. In the trial hearing of *RJR-MacDonald,*[105] large amounts of data were presented by both the government and the tobacco manufacturers concerning the relation or otherwise between consumption of tobacco products and health disorders, and between tobacco advertising and consumption of tobacco products. Nonetheless, the trial judge laid down that 'the connection . . . between health protection and tobacco advertising is tenuous and speculative' (at 512), and that 'the evidence of a rational connection between the restrictions and the objective sought is deficient, if not non-existent' (at 515).[106] The

---

[97] *Shapero v Kentucky Bar Association* 486 US 466 (1988).

[98] *Peel v Attorney Registration and Disciplinary Commission of Illinois* 496 US 91 (1990).

[99] *Florida Bar v Went For It Inc* 115 SCt 2371 (1995).

[100] *Glickman v Wileman Brothers and Elliott Inc et al* 117 SCt 2130 (1997).

[101] *Wileman Brothers and Elliott Inc v Espy* 58 F 3d 1367 (1995) (USCA 9th Cir).

[102] *United States v Frame* 885 F 2d 1119 (1989) (USCA 3rd Cir).

[103] *United States v United Foods Inc* 121 SCt 2334 (2001).

[104] Chapter 3.6 above.

[105] *Re RJR-MacDonald Inc and Attorney-General of Canada; Re Imperial Tobacco Ltd v Attorney-General of Canada* (1991) 82 DLR (4th) 449 (Que Sup Ct).

[106] The second time around, *JTI MacDonald Corporation et al c La procureure générale du Canada* 500-05-031299-975 (2002) (Que Sup Ct), neither side took any chances. The stack of data provided was immense, and the number of intervenor briefs permitted extraordinary. Denis J's limiting his opinion to 196 pages is a remarkable feat in itself.

Quebec Court of Appeal was divided on the issue, the majority accepting that the government had met its burden of proof for establishing such a connection, and the dissent agreeing, albeit less colourfully, with the trial judge.[107] The Supreme Court was plainly perturbed by the issue. McLachlin J (as she then was) writing for the majority was reluctant simply to lay aside the trial judge's finding. Instead, she took his finding to stand for the proposition that there was no *scientific* evidence for a link between tobacco advertising and consumption of tobacco products, but she took advantage of the Court's precedents in *Keegstra* and *Butler* to deem a causal relationship to exist 'on the basis of reason or logic, without insisting on direct proof' (at 97). She even agreed with LaForest J's assertion in dissent (at 52) that the difficulty of drawing hard conclusions from social scientific data argued towards a deference to Parliament's own interpretation of such data (at 91). She simply disagreed with LaForest J on whether the threshold conditions for a justified infringement of a *Charter* freedom had been met. Such an approach essentially eliminates social science data from performing any argumentative role.

The third prong of the *Central Hudson* test which requires proof that a regulation impinging on commercial expression 'directly advances' a state interest imposes an empirical evidentiary burden of some kind. In *Edenfield*,[108] the Court complained that the state had not met this burden in a systematic way: it presented no studies, it adduced no anecdotal evidence, it offered only an affidavit from an interested party which the Court dismissed as conclusory (at 1800–1). The Florida Bar Association in defending its thirty-day waiting period for direct-mail solicitation of accident victims did not make this mistake. It 'submitted a 106-page summary of its 2-year study of lawyer advertising and solicitation', and an 'anecdotal record . . . noteworthy for its breadth and detail' (Florida Bar, at 2377). The material satisfied the majority that the evidentiary burden had been met. Kennedy J in dissent was not so satisfied. He complained that the survey document submitted 'include[d] no actual surveys, few indications of sample size or selection procedures, no explanations of methodology, and no discussion of excluded results. There is no description of the statistical universe or scientific framework . . .' (at 2384). He also dismissed the anecdotal evidence as 'noteworthy for its incompetence', 'selective', 'self-serving and unsupported' (ibid.). His colleagues in the majority responded by declaring that 'we do not read our case law to require that empirical data come to us accompanied by a surfeit of background information' (at 2378).

Both these incidents demonstrate the problems in trying to adjudicate via social science data. If huge amounts of data are presented, neither judges nor their clerks have the professional expertise to make a reasoned assessment, and so the data cease to be able to perform the evidentiary function for

[107] (1993) 102 DLR (4th) 289.   [108] *Edenfield v Fane* 113 SCt 1792 (1993).

which they were introduced. If modest amounts of data are presented, it is only too easy to claim that more could have been presented, and again the evidentiary role of the data is excluded. There is no serious doubt about the propriety of basing regulatory schemes on social science data, whether economic or sociological or psychological. Legislatures and regulatory agencies do it all the time. The irony is that courts are in no position to assess whether a legal standard they themselves have set—the proof of a rational connection between an objective and a social policy—has in any given case actually been met. Thus the legal decision as to whether it has been met cannot be made on the only grounds that are relevant.

(6) The story of *RJR-MacDonald* provides an illustration again of the weaknesses of courts as a regulatory mechanism. Important sections of the Tobacco Products Control Act were struck down, leaving the government no choice but to develop a new statute to replace. This they did: the Tobacco Act. The tobacco manufacturers have now challenged that Act again, losing at trial (*JTI MacDonald*). It took four years for the previous case to reach the Supreme Court of Canada for a final determination, and doubtless the period will not change this time. In the meantime, the Act remains in force, which is fine if you agree with it, and frustrating if you do not.

Both courts and commentators now in Canada have become enamoured of the metaphor of 'dialogue' to characterize the relation of courts and legislatures under the regime of the *Charter*.[109] The thought is that in Canada judicial review under the constitution and parliamentary sovereignty are not to be thought of as opposites, but as complements. The true character of the Canadian legal system is law as the product of interaction between parliament and court. The metaphor, in the context of a defence of the role of the courts in reviewing and, if appropriate, invalidating legislation, goes back at least to Alexander Bickel, who speaks of a 'colloquy' between the Supreme Court and Congress in the U.S.[110] Bickel's idea received scholarly endorsement in Canada even in the early days of the Canadian *Charter*.[111] The recent boost for the metaphor came from Hogg and Bushell.[112] They drew attention to the number of times that legislation invalidated by the Supreme Court of Canada was soon reintroduced in a form which attempted to respect the Court's concerns while equally pursuing the same legislative objectives. In the authors' belief, insistence

---

[109] For references to court decisions see Peter W. Hogg, *Constitutional Law of Canada* (Looseleaf edn., Toronto: Carswell, 2002), 33–12, 44–62.

[110] Alexander Bickel, *The Least Dangerous Branch* (Indianapolis, Ind.: Bobbs-Merrill, 1962), 240.

[111] Anne F. Bayefsky, 'The Judicial Function Under The Canadian Charter of Rights and Freedoms', in Anne F. Bayefsky (ed.), *Legal Theory Meets Legal Practice* (Edmonton: Academic Printing and Publishing, 1988), 157–62.

[112] Peter W. Hogg and Allison A. Bushell, 'The *Charter* Dialogue Between Courts and Legislatures (Or Perhaps the *Charter of Rights* Isn't Such a Bad Thing After All)', *Osgoode Hall Law Journal* 35 (1997): 75–105.

on the priority of either constitution or legislation would obscure the constitutional significance of this interaction. The 'dialogue' thesis of course has an empirical commitment that events properly called 'a dialogue' have actually occurred, and it has been disputed on those grounds[113] and reiterated.[114] The dialogue image may or may not embody a meritorious approach in relation to paradigm *Charter* rights of individuals.[115] It makes no sense at all in relation to governmental regulatory schemes. Such schemes will inevitably need fine-tuning and adjustment in response to the immediate pressure of changing conditions. Multi-year delays while cases wind their way through the court system are of no assistance.[116]

The decision of the U.S. Supreme Court in *Linmark*[117] provides another illustration. The issues surrounding the intersection of race and home ownership in a community are complex and significant. On the face of it, which of a variety of possible policies to adopt is a matter for each community to decide, never mind well established concerns about the role of community standards in relation to constitutional rights. The Township of Willingboro had made a choice to support a measure of racial diversity in the community, and introduced regulations on real estate advertising accordingly. The Supreme Court simply struck down the ordinance and walked away.

7 COMMERCIAL EXPRESSION AND THE SEPARATION OF POWERS

The second issue I shall discuss has to do with overall institutional design in a constitutional democracy. Beales and his colleagues, in considering potential remedies for misleading advertising, emphasize that the benefits and costs of any proposed policy are crucial. They then add in a footnote that this is not meant to imply either that regulatory bodies or legislatures must undertake a full cost-benefit analysis before being allowed to act, or that courts must undertake full such analysis *de novo* when a statute is being reviewed. These are, they say, issues of institutional competencies and review mechanisms that are beyond the scope of their paper.[118] Indeed, these are issues of institutional competencies. It

---

[113] Christopher P. Manfredi and James B. Kelly, 'Six Degrees of Dialogue: A Response to Hogg and Bushell', *Osgoode Hall Law Journal* 37 (1999): 513–27; Christopher P. Manfredi, *Judicial Power and the Charter: Canada and the Paradox of Liberal Constitutionalism* (2nd edn., Don Mills: Oxford University Press, 2001), 176–81.

[114] Peter W. Hogg and Allison A. Thornton, 'Reply to "Six Degrees of Dialogue"', *Osgoode Hall Law Journal* 37 (1999): 529–36.

[115] For an argument that it is see Jennifer Nedelsky, 'Reconceiving Rights as Relationship', *Review of Constitutional Studies* 1 (1993): 1–26; Jennifer Nedelsky, 'Reconceiving Autonomy: Sources, Thoughts, and Possibilities', *Yale Journal of Law and Feminism* 1 (1989): 7.

[116] For assessment of the Supreme Court of Canada's decision in *RJR-MacDonald* in this light see Janet L. Hiebert, *Charter Conflicts: What Is Parliament's Role?* (Montreal and Kingston: McGill-Queens University Press, 2002), 84–90.

[117] *Linmark Associates Inc v Township of Willingboro* 431 US 85 (1977).

[118] Beales, Craswell, and Salop, 'Efficient Regulation', 533–4.

is a commonplace that regulation of the economy is the primary responsibility of the legislature in a democracy, not of the courts. A constitutional court in particular is, in Ronald Dworkin's happy phrase, a 'forum of principle'.[119] Courts deal with issues of principle and with enforcement of rights. Legislatures deal with issues of policy and promotion of utility.[120] Notwithstanding the fact that this distinction is not sharp, it is sound enough. It is acknowledged almost universally that there is a distinction between the government as an adversary to the individual and from whose majoritarian invasion the rights of the individual need protection, and the government as the font of democratic decision-making in areas that pose no anti-majoritarian dangers. I say, 'almost universally', because the commercial expression doctrine stands as an exception.

There is a long history in the U.S. of conceding that the Supreme Court erred in its notorious decision in *Lochner*:[121] in invalidating a regulatory scheme for the baking industry on supposed constitutional grounds, the Court committed the eighth deadly sin of the substitution of the Court's own views for those of the legislature on matters of public policy. The Court itself has alluded to 'the original constitutional proposition that courts do not substitute their social and economic beliefs for the judgment of legislative bodies',[122] and commented that 'in the local economic sphere, it is only the invidious discrimination, the wholly arbitrary act' which calls up constitutional concern.[123] The thresholds set by the *Central Hudson* test in the U.S., the *Oakes* test in Canada, and Article 10(2) of the European Convention on Human Rights permit invalidation of regulations which are a far cry from 'invidious' and 'arbitrary', simply on the ground that courts have different 'social and economic beliefs'.

I am of course not putting forward an original argument here. In his dissent in *Virginia Board*, Rehnquist J (as he then was) famously echoed Holmes J's dissent in *Lochner*[124] in remarking that 'there is certainly nothing in the U.S. Constitution which requires the Virginia Legislature to hew to the teachings of Adam Smith in its legislative decisions regulating the pharmacy profession' (at 784).[125] Thomas Jackson and John Jeffries averred immediately of *Virginia Board* that 'this renovation of discredited doctrine is far more troublesome than commentators have been willing to admit'.[126] The lack of willingness does not diminish the force of the argument.

[119] Ronald M. Dworkin, *A Matter of Principle* (Cambridge, Mass.: Harvard University Press, 1985), Chapter 2.

[120] Ronald M. Dworkin, *Taking Rights Seriously* (2nd edn., Cambridge, Mass.: Harvard University Press, 1978), 22–3, and passim.

[121] *Lochner v New York* 198 US 45 (1905).

[122] *Ferguson v Skrupka* 372 US 726 (1963), at 730.

[123] *New Orleans v Dukes* 427 US 297 (1976), at 303–4.

[124] 'The Fourteenth Amendment does not enact Mr. Herbert Spencer's Social Statics': *Lochner* at 75.

[125] See also his dissent in *Central Hudson*, at 589–90.

[126] Thomas H. Jackson and John Calvin Jeffries Jr., 'Commercial Speech: Economic Due Process and the First Amendment', *Virginia Law Review* 65 (1979): 30–1. For the same argument in the Canadian context see Hiebert, *Charter Conflicts*, 80–4.

The U.S. Supreme Court, despite its support for the commercial expression doctrine, has nonetheless drawn the line at securities regulation. It said in *Ohralik* that there were

[n]umerous examples . . . of communications that are regulated without offending the First Amendment, such as the exchange of information about securities, corporate proxy statements, the exchange of price and production information among competitors, and employers' threats of retaliation for the labor activities of employees. [at 456]

It reaffirmed the claim in *Dun and Bradstreet*.[127] In the only appellate-level case concerning the application of the commercial expression doctrine to expression in relation to information about securities, the court took these holdings to imply that 'securities regulation is a form of regulation distinct from the more general category of commercial speech',[128] and that, given the extent to which the securities market is regulated, 'we do not believe the Constitution requires the judiciary to weigh the relative merits of particular regulatory objectives that impinge upon communications occurring within the umbrella of an overall regulatory scheme' (ibid.). If the court is correct, then it is hard to see how much of the commercial expression doctrine could survive. Restrictions on or regulation of commercial expression always occurs 'within the umbrella of an overall regulatory scheme'—a scheme of regulating the professions generally, of regulating the alcohol industry, the brewery industry, the tobacco industry, the toy industry, the agricultural industry. I am not aware of any impugned regulation of advertising that exists alone as a free-standing regulation independent of any wider scheme. It might be that, once one has bought into the commercial expression doctrine, an exemption for expression in connection with the securities market could be defended. It might be thought that in this case the weighing of the utilities came out especially in favour of regulation, rather than against it. It might be thought that, if hardiness and objectivity are the special marks of commercial expression which allow it to tolerate regulation, all things being equal,[129] expression in connection with the securities market is especially hardy and objective. It might be thought that, if misleading expression is excluded from constitutional protection, there is an especial danger of misleading expression in connection with the securities market. It is, however, far more plausible to see the stance towards expression in connection with the securities market as an acknowledgment of the force of a principle urged many times in this book—that simply because expression or speech occurs in pursuance of a certain activity it does not follow automatically that any regulation of the activity must be examined for potential violations of a constitutional guarantee of freedom of expression. The practice of the U.S. Supreme Court of leaving securities regulation alone, despite the commercial expression

---

[127] *Dun and Bradstreet Inc v Greenmoss Builders* 472 US 749 (1985), at 758.
[128] *Wall Street Publishing*, at 373.
[129] Cf. *Virginia Board*, at 772.

doctrine, has its detractors[130] and its supporters.[131] Both agree that the exemption is illogical on any plausible construal of 'commercial speech'. My argument supports the supporters.

The free flow of commercial information arguably fosters two market goals—aggregate economic efficiency and consumer opportunity to maximize utility. The policy of encouraging advertising *qua* economic policy is certainly intelligible. But, as an argument for constitutional coverage of commercial expression, the argument is question-begging. From the fact that aggregate economic efficiency and consumer opportunity to maximize utility are important, and even paramount, policy values, it simply does not follow that they deserve constitutional coverage, let alone constitutional protection. Nor does it follow that the criteria of economic efficiency and utility maximization are central to constitutional jurisprudence. If a question is submitted for constitutional adjudication, it must be a question that admits in principle of an anti-majoritarian solution. If the issue is whether a supposed right I have to criticize publicly some policy of the government is genuine and is genuinely mine, then whether I have such a right cannot be determined by whether the majority will ascribe such a right to me. Questions of economic efficiency and utility maximization are not such questions. Jurisdiction over such questions is properly exercised by the legislature, as the seat of majoritarian political authority.

8 THE METAPHOR OF THE MARKETPLACE OF IDEAS

The root difficulty in proposing to justify the commercial expression doctrine within the paradigm of utility is that utility maximization and economic efficiency cannot be subsumed under the three traditional liberal freedom of expression values. Commercial expression does not in itself promote self-fulfilment and self-realization (see Chapter 11), nor does it promote democratic political deliberation. It might seem, however, that, since we are speaking of the free flow of commercial *information*, freedom of commercial expression must serve the search for truth. That would be a mistake, and Holmes J's famous image of the 'market-place of ideas' is deeply implicated in this mistake:

But when men have realized that time has upset many fighting faiths, they may come to believe even more than they believe the very foundations of their own conduct that the ultimate good desired is better reached by free trade in ideas—that the best test of truth is the power of the thought to get itself accepted in the competition of the market, and that truth is the only ground upon which their wishes safely can be carried out.[132]

[130] Burt Neuborne, 'The First Amendment and Government Regulation of Capital Markets', *Brooklyn Law Review* 55 (1989): 5–63; Nicholas Wolfson, 'The First Amendment and the SEC', *Connecticut Law Review* 20 (1988): 265–301; Aleta G. Estreicher, 'Securities Regulation and the First Amendment', *Georgia Law Review* 24 (1990): 223–326.

[131] Michael P. Dooley, 'The First Amendment and the SEC: A Comment', *Connecticut Law Review* 20 (1988): 335–54; Pinto, 'Capital Markets'.

[132] *Abrams et al v United States* 250 US 616 (1919), at 630.

The classical justification for freedom of expression from John Milton and John Stuart Mill relied on the search for truth, on the assumption that there was indeed reasoned truth of some kind. As has been pointed out, Milton's 'agon' or wrestling-match from which the stronger truth will emerge victorious is replaced through Holmes's philosophical pragmatism with the 'agora' or trading market of ideas.[133] The fact that the notion of truth seems to provide continuity between Holmes and Milton disguises the fundamental shift in justification that takes place. The classical search for truth is a result-oriented justification for freedom of expression. Information within this justification has either intrinsic value (it is itself the truth) or instrumental value (it conduces to some further truth). The 'market-place of ideas' image as proffered by Holmes constitutes a process-oriented justification. There is no determinant of truth independently of survival in the process of intellectual exchange. The resonances with the rhetoric of laissez faire economics serve only to reinforce the orientation towards process. Within economics, efficiency justifications for policies are sharply, and properly, distinguished from distributive justifications. Efficiency is in this sense a process value.

What emerges from the Holmesian turn to the marketplace of ideas is a justification for constitutional protection of freedom of expression that emphasizes the process of exchange of view, of debate, of expression as something that is worthy of protection in itself. The marketplace of ideas image thus interpreted fits well the process of democratic deliberation. There are supposedly no objectively valid social policies; there are only the policies the people choose. But it does not follow from the fact that the marketplace of ideas image is a vivid image for conveying something profound about democratic politics that therefore the free flow of commercial information in the economic marketplace is an instance of freedom of expression. As it has been put:

Like a snake swallowing its tail, the reality of market relationships is validated through its own metaphorical image. The metaphor [of the marketplace of ideas] invites us first to understand the role of expression through certain presuppositions about the market and then to apply that understanding to the market itself. The weakness of this procedure is that those presuppositions about the market are no longer unquestioned.[134]

To appreciate the force of Weinrib's point, consider a different argument. Aaron Director a while ago[135] and R.H. Coase immediately after *Virginia*

---

[133] David Cole, 'Agon at Agora: Creative Misreadings in the First Amendment Tradition', *Yale Law Journal* 95 (1986): 886; Steven L. Winter, 'Transcendental Nonsense, Metaphoric Reasoning, and the Cognitive Stakes for Law', *University of Pennsylvania Law Review* 137 (1989): 1188–91. Cole and Winter do not agree on how further to parse the metaphor; I will not enter into that debate here.

[134] Lorraine E. Weinrib, 'Does Money Talk? Commercial Expression in the Canadian Constitutional Context', in David Schneiderman (ed.), *Freedom of Expression and the Charter* (Toronto: Thomson Professional Publishing Canada, 1991), 341. See also Stanley Ingber, 'The Marketplace of Ideas: A Legitimizing Myth', *Duke Law Journal* (1984): 1–58.

[135] Aaron Director, 'The Parity of the Economic Market Place', *Journal of Law and Economics* 7 (1964): 1–10.

Board[136] both criticized what they saw as an inconsistency in exalting an unrestricted 'marketplace of ideas' while condoning extensive government regulation of the economy. They wanted the freedom of exchange in the marketplace of ideas to carry over to the economic marketplace. But, as we have seen earlier in this chapter, economic regulation of the economic marketplace is there because it is acknowledged, not only even by but also especially by, economists themselves that the efficiency goals of the economic market cannot be achieved without regulation. The Director/Coase position is motivated by libertarian political goals, rather than professional economist goals. Regulation requires the assumption of a goal that the regulation serves. In the case of economic regulation, the goal is economic efficiency. Absence of, or minimal, regulation comes in as an empirical hypothesis by which this goal can be achieved. As David Strauss has pointed out, the marketplace of ideas image as applied to the process of democratic politics is confusing, in that we have no clear notion of what would count as a well-functioning market, or even how an unregulated market might produce a desirable outcome.[137] But in the case of the 'marketplace' of commercial 'ideas', we do have such a notion—or rather, we have such a notion to just the same extent as we have for the economic market itself, since the marketplace of commercial ideas is just a part of the economic market. It will be a matter of empirical fact whether some given regulation of commercial expression achieves some desired result. The empirical enquiry should not be preempted or constrained by misplaced appeals to rights of free expression.

In the promotion of the commercial expression doctrine, two stages of transformation in the marketplace image occur. This libertarian gloss on the marketplace image is first applied to the marketplace of ideas where, at least in its traditional application to political debate, it has some validity. Then the image is applied in its glossy form to the transmission of information in the economic market, to give that transmission its own layer of gloss. The gloss achieves the misleading assimilation of commercial expression to political expression. The assimilation disguises the fact that it really is in the end, in the case of commercial expression, simply regulation of the economy that we are dealing with.

9 THE ARCHITECTURE OF CONSTITUTIONAL ADJUDICATION

The third set of issues I want to raise about the economic interpretation of the commercial expression doctrine concerns what Frederick Schauer has termed the 'architecture' of constitutional protection.[138] Schauer distinguishes two approaches to rule-making: the particularist approach, which focuses on the merits of each case and develops rules from these, and the architectural

---

[136] R.H. Coase, 'Advertising and Free Speech', *Journal of Legal Studies* 6 (1977): 1–34.
[137] Strauss, 'Persuasion', 349.
[138] Frederick F. Schauer, 'Commercial Speech and the Architecture of the First Amendment', *University of Cincinnati Law Review* 56 (1988): 1181–203.

approach, which considers sets of rules and structures of rules as a whole with attention to the way that rules 'intertwine, overlap and abut' (at 1181). Schauer's thesis is that a general norm concerning freedom of expression, such as the First Amendment, 'if it is to be more than a platitude, must operate to preclude what would otherwise be, taken particularly, reasonable judgments to restrict' (at 1199). He turns this 'architectural' point against the extension of First Amendment protection to commercial speech embodying, as U.S. Supreme Court jurisprudence does, an idiosyncratic standard of review for commercial speech. Offensive speech, child pornography, defamation, invasion of privacy, as well as commercial speech all have separate standards within First Amendment jurisprudence for the upholding or not of legislative restrictions on speech (at 1198), not to mention the standard of review for First Amendment concerns in relation to section 43(a) of the Lanham Act.[139] The 'dilution' argument is reformulated as an argument against excessive subdivision and excessive doctrinal complexity (at 1199). The more complex a doctrine, the less likely it is to be able to function properly as a rule, and the more likely it is that decision-making will become particularistic. But the more that constitutional decision-making especially becomes particularistic, the more likely it is that important constitutional rights will be lost in a mass of case-by-case adjudication. Not that I have anything against case-by-case adjudication.[140] But the result is that a constitutional court then becomes no more, though no less, than 'a great common law court of general jurisdiction',[141] a fate which Robert Nagel has shown to have befallen the U.S. Supreme Court.[142]

As Schauer has shown elsewhere,[143] rules are devices for the allocation of power. The rule-maker has power over decision-makers who have to apply the rules, whether to themselves or others. The rule of the National Hockey League that the puck has to cross the goal-crease line completely before a goal is scored is a device for the League to exercise power over referees, who are barred by the rule from calling a goal for other reasons, for example, that they admire the skill with which a shot on goal was set up. A charter or bill of rights is a set of rules established in some form by a set of rule-makers. It is a device for those rule-makers to exercise power over those whose job it is to adjudicate according to the rules. If the rule-makers are a democratic people or their delegates, then the charter or bill of rights is an exercise of power by the people. Constitutions are thoroughly democratic, a fact overlooked by those who claim that judicial

---

[139] See Chapter 8.3 above.

[140] Cf. Roger A. Shiner, 'Ethical Justification and Case-by-Case Reasoning', in D. Odegard (ed.), *Ethics and Justification* (Edmonton: Academic Printing and Publishing, 1988), 91–108.

[141] Charles W. Collier, 'Precedent and Legal Authority: A Critical History', *Wisconsin Law Review* (1988): 814–15.

[142] Robert F. Nagel, 'The Formulaic Constitution', *Michigan Law Review* 84 (1985): 165–212. Essentially the same point is made by Edwin Baker: C. Edwin Baker, 'Media Concentration: Giving Up on Democracy', *Florida Law Review* 54 (2002): 852 ff.

[143] Frederick F. Schauer, *Playing By The Rules: A Philosophical Examination of Rule-Based Decision-Making in Law and in Life*, Clarendon Law Series (Oxford: Clarendon Press, 1991), 158 ff.

review of legislation on constitutional grounds is undemocratic. Bills or charters of rights are anti-majoritarian, certainly; but they are not undemocratic.[144]

Construed as exercises of power in this way, charters or bills of rights function as they should only when they function as rules. Typically, the language of the clauses has some generality, which effectively delegates some rule-making power to those who interpret them. But this point about the architecture that they need to function aright is sound. As soon as the rules become too subdivided and too complex—too particularized—they can no longer function as rules. Power shifts from the original democratic rule-maker to the decision-maker under the rules, the constitutional courts. If it is true, and I shall not offer an opinion on that here, that constitutional courts in the U.S. or in Canada are exercising, or in the U.K. potentially may come to exercise, too much power, it will not be because of their status as organs of judicial review of legislation. It will be because they have arrogated excessive power to themselves by endless sub-division and complexity of doctrine.

If these 'architectural' considerations have weight, as I think they do, against the development of commercial speech jurisprudence in the U.S. Supreme Court, then they have weight even more so against the Supreme Court of Canada. As I discussed above (see Chapter 4.5), the contextual approach that the Court has adopted to *Charter* decision-making, together with the premise that anything that can be called an 'expression' comes within the coverage of section 2(b) of the *Charter*, means that the Court cannot indulge in anything but *ad hoc* decision-making. Contextualized decision-making is often associated, and properly so, with making judgements in equity. But a court of constitutional law is not a court of equity. Constitutional protections embodied in charters or bills of rights represent broad and impartial protections extended to every citizen as such and as of right, in virtue of their equal dignity as persons. A constitutional protection in the nature of the case, unlike the substantive guidelines for an administrative tribunal, for example, is not something that should be applied to greater or lesser degrees according to the circumstances of the case. We do not think, for example, that there are some groups of people that deserve more protection under section 15 of the Canadian *Charter*, the equality section, than others. If the idea of differing degrees of constitutional protection under section 15 were perfectly palatable, the argument that discrimination by sexual orientation should also be included in section 15 would not even get off the ground. Yet it clearly does, and has been acknowledged to be sound by the Supreme Court.[145]

In the beginning, the U.S. Supreme Court seemed to take the role of information in maximizing utility and promoting efficiency seriously. Even if questions can be raised, and I have raised them, about utility and efficiency as freedom of expression values, at least the Court was trying to do its homework. Latterly,

---

[144] This claim has not gone unchallenged: see Jeremy Waldron, *Law and Disagreement* (Oxford: Clarendon Press, 1999), Part III. But I will not debate the matter here.

[145] *Vriend v Alberta* [1998] 1 SCR 493; *M v H* [1999] 2 SCR 3.

though, in both the U.S. and Canada, the 'free flow of commercial information' has simply become a mantra, to be uttered as early as possible in the decision-making process. Its function is to create an atmosphere of comfort and confidence before the court settles down to the real business of the day, indulging in armchair policy-making under the rubric of the *Central Hudson* test or the *Oakes* test. Armchair policy-making is of course an activity beloved of academicians and theoreticians world-wide. When my friends and I indulge in it over a pitcher of beer in the pub, that's one thing; that's entertainment. But when the highest court in the land indulges in it under the spurious guise of enforcing constitutional rights of the citizen-consumer, that's something else. That's manipulation of the role of the court; that's usurpation of the legitimate powers of the government to regulate the economy.

10 CONCLUSION

The free flow of commercial information is constantly cast in discussions of the commercial expression doctrine as the desirable goal attainment of which is frustrated by government regulation of commercial advertising. As I indicated at the beginning of this chapter, a simple and formally valid argument can be given with the good of the free flow of commercial information among the premises and the evil of government regulation as the conclusion. But such a simple argument left far too many relevant questions unaddressed. The purpose of this chapter has been to identify, and to address, these questions.

I dealt first with a preliminary matter. In the rhetoric of the commercial expression doctrine, talk of the government by its regulation of commercial advertising manipulating citizens, keeping citizens ignorant, and even inducing ignorance in citizens, is widespread. I showed in this Chapter 13.2 that such talk is also conceptually and jurisprudentially irresponsible. 'Manipulation', 'induce', 'keep ignorant' are genuine terms of English, and as such have genuine and determinate meanings. I mentioned some examples of the proper application of these terms. I then showed that the case of government regulation of commercial advertising fell a long way short of conforming to these paradigms. In regulating commercial advertising, governments neither manipulate citizens, induce ignorance in citizens, nor keep citizens ignorant. These claims, so frequently made on behalf of the commercial expression doctrine, are as false and misleading as are many of the advertisements government seeks to proscribe.

However, the commercial expression doctrine is correct in one respect. Government regulation of commercial advertising does have some effect on the free flow of commercial information: it is in some way a management of that flow. So the question is then properly raised: is it a good effect or a bad effect, from the point of view of such valid social goals for public decision-making as economic efficiency, social welfare, or public good? In the language of utility rights, do any utility rights for hearers in general flow from the effect of government regulation of commercial advertising on the free flow of commercial information?

Answers here may take one of two forms. Either (a) any effect on the free flow of commercial information is *ipso facto* bad from the point of view of economic efficiency and other social goals, and so *a fortiori* government regulation of commercial advertising is bad. Or (b) some effects on the free flow of commercial information are bad from the point of view of economic efficiency and other social goals, and some effects are good effects; in so far as government regulation of commercial advertising has a bad effect, it is bad. Whether we explore alternative (a) or alternative (b) turns out not to matter. Neither gives any support to the commercial expression doctrine.

In this Chapter 13.2 and 13.3, I considered some of the results established in the area of the economics of information. The thought behind an appeal to the free flow of commercial information is this. Consumers' decision-making is typically decision-making under uncertainty. Information reduces the uncertainty, and thus promotes better decision-making from the point of view of maximizing welfare or efficiency.

However, research into economic modelling has shown that the generalization that informational content with the free flow of information is inefficient holds only on the assumption of perfect information and perfect rationality in a market. In any actual, real-world market, this assumption will not hold. In that case, the generalization fails to hold. Depending on the specific structure of the market, and given imperfect information on the part of participants in the market, the free flow of information may require regulation if efficiency and social good are to be promoted. An unregulated free flow of commercial information will exacerbate many of the imperfections of both rationality and information that occur in an imperfect market. I give in this Chapter 13.3 a number of examples to show beyond any doubt that alternative (a) above is indefensible from the point of view of serious economics, and therefore that the commercial expression doctrine can draw no support from it.

The failure of alternative (a) shows that there cannot be any general utility right to freedom of commercial expression. Instead, there can at best be, as alternative (b) proposes, specific rights in specific circumstances grounded in the value of utility to freedom of commercial expression. That is, considerations of economic efficiency or social welfare can at best show that this or that particular instance of government regulation of commercial advertising is inefficient, or reduces welfare. But if that is so, then the commercial expression doctrine comes under pressure from a quite different range of arguments. In the remainder of the chapter, I presented a number of these arguments.

In this Chapter 13.4, I pointed out that one range of paradigm cases where it is generally agreed that government regulation of the flow of information increases efficiency is that of mandated disclosures of information. In the case of the securities market, this tendency is marked. It is widely recognized that to permit corporations to withhold information of many different kinds induces too much investor uncertainty for the market to function efficiently. The purpose of government regulation is to protect the investor by making sure the investor has enough information on which to base an informed decision. The purpose of most commercial advertising, on the other hand, is to force on the consumer information that the consumer does not necessarily need, or want, to hear. Thus even if it is true that there are some paradigm cases where more information places the hearer in a better position than less information from the point of view of socially valuable decision-making, these cases are not available to the supporters of the commercial expression doctrine to ground arguments for invalidating government regulation of commercial advertising.

In this Chapter 13.5, I considered the so-called 'dilution argument', the argument made against the commercial expression doctrine that to grant constitutional protection to commercial expression is dangerous, because it will lead to diluted protection for more important forms of expression. I did not endorse the dilution argument so presented. There are two obvious objections to it—first, that it makes an empirical claim ('reduced protection will follow') for which there is at present little or no evidence; secondly, that it arguably begs the question, in that it assumes exactly what the commercial expression doctrine denies, that commercial expression is of a lesser value than other forms of expression. So interpreted, on the other hand, the dilution argument is of great importance to my case against the commercial expression doctrine in the following way. It forces out into the open the acknowledgment that freedom of commercial expression is all about economic reasoning and economic values. Freedom of commercial expression is not about the values with which freedom of expression in general is typically associated. I go on in the remainder of the chapter to examine the implications of this acknowledgment.

Up to this point in the chapter, I have shown two things. First, I have shown that from the point of view of the promotion of economic efficiency or other utility-related social goal, the fact of the matter is that some government regulation of commercial advertising will promote efficiency and some will not; it cannot be claimed *a priori* that all such regulation promotes inefficiency. Secondly, I have shown that the underlying issues here are, and have been acknowledged by the supporters of the commercial expression doctrine to be, economic. The combination of those two points yields a significant result. Discussion in courts of whether a given instance of government regulation of commercial advertising should be invalidated on constitutional grounds is inescapably piecemeal discussion of the merits of this or that instance of economic regulation. If that is so, then the commercial expression doctrine faces a number of objections.

I discussed the first objection in this Chapter 13.6. Theorists interested in issues of institutional design have raised the question whether courts, as opposed to legislatures, are appropriate sources for economic regulation. There are available many sound arguments for the view that courts are not appropriate vehicles. The construction of social policies that maximize utility is hindered, rather than helped, by the institutional practices and constraints placed on courts, as regards which questions are justiciable by courts, what evidence may be considered by courts, what forms of decision may be taken by courts, and so forth. I gave a number of examples to show how these difficulties were manifest in the institutional history of commercial expression cases.

A second objection to courts as places for economic decision-making on constitutional grounds concerns issues of the separation of powers, and the well-known constitutional vice of courts' substitution of their own views for those of the legislature. In this Chapter 13.7, I showed that in the freedom of commercial expression cases courts are doing precisely what the designation of such behaviour as a vice condemns. It may be true that some—even many—of the decisions taken by courts to invalidate government regulation of commercial advertising are good decisions from the point of view of economic efficiency. But that cannot in itself show that the commercial expression doctrine is sound. It does not follow from the mere fact that a court decision secures a good that the issue on which the case turns is properly regarded as constitutional.

A good part of the reason we are tempted to think that, in the case of freedom of commercial expression, these worries about courts taking economic decisions are misplaced is that we are held captive by the image of the 'marketplace of ideas'. In this Chapter 13.8, I deconstructed this image. I showed how it seduces us into thinking that, because ideas deserve constitutional protection, and it is good that ideas are exchanged freely, and there are benefits to free economic exchange, therefore the economic market, including commercial advertising as an aspect of the economic market, should be as well protected constitutionally as freedom of expression. Once it is put that way, the *non sequitur* is obvious.

In this Chapter 13.9, I presented a third argument against the commercial expression doctrine, on the assumption that the underlying issues here were piecemeal and economic. This argument turned on the idea of a proper 'architecture' to constitutional adjudication. The essence of a constitution is that it represents a set of rules, expressed at a high level of generality, which grant to the people whose constitution it is power over the activities of their legislators, who can make rules only within constitutional limits. Constitutionalizing economic regulation in the way that the commercial expression doctrine achieves turns courts into *ad hoc* economic decision-makers and armchair policy-makers. That is not the role, under the best models of institutional design, which courts should be playing.

Despite the favour which the notion of the free flow of commercial information has found among supporters of the commercial expression doctrine, the notion does not in fact provide a platform for any sound argument in the doctrine's favour, on any of the interpretations favoured by the doctrine.

14

Lifestyle Advertising and the Public Good

1 VARIETIES OF ADVERTISING

The discussion in the previous four chapters, especially in Chapter 13, has been built on a pretence. Consider this example. There is a grocery store near our house at which we do not shop very much; the prices are on the high side for the area. The store, however, regularly has discount coupons for dairy products, and usually once a month two-for-one offers on meat. It also has a flyer in the local free community newspaper once a week. The advertisements in the flyer are largely of the so-called 'tombstone' variety, listing simply product name and price, with a few also picturing the product. The flyer is a paradigm example of 'I will sell you X product at Y price'. We habitually scan the flyer when it arrives, to see what (if any) discounts or special offers are available this week, as the quality of the store is as high as its normal prices. The flyer unquestionably provides us with information, and it is information we use to maximize our utility.

But then we open the daily newspaper, and see a full-page advertisement, white type on a grey background, which contains nothing but 'Just Do It', and a logo looking rather like a tick. We drive down the road and see enormous billboards picturing nothing but a sheet of silvery-grey silk, with a slash of bright crimson in the middle. The leucodontic smiles of Canada's gold-medal-winning figure-skating team stare out at us from cereal boxes. And so on. What has any of that to do with the provision of information and the promotion of informed consumer decision-making?

It is simply a pretence that commercial advertising has essentially to do with the provision of information. A great deal—perhaps even almost all—corporate advertising expression does not have anything at all to do with the transmission of information. It has rather to do with the creation of emotional associations, especially associations that will help induce a favourable, and even a desirous, attitude towards the product in question. As Sarah Haan has recently demonstrated,[1] the advertising industry employs sophisticated research in behavioural and cognitive psychology to establish the most successful techniques for directing consumer decision-making towards the preferred products. Advertising

---

[1] Sarah C. Haan, 'The "Persuasion Route" of the Law: Advertising and Legal Persuasion', *Columbia Law Review* 100 (2000): 1281–1305. See also Daniel Hays Lowenstein, '"Too Much Puff": Persuasion, Paternalism and Commercial Speech', *University of Cincinnati Law Review* 56 (1988): 1221–7.

employing such a 'persuasion route', to use Haan's idiom, is very different from advertising which follows the 'information route', as it were, and seeks to affect consumer decision-making simply by providing the consumer with information.

R.H. Coase has made a valiant attempt to deny this difference. He avers: 'Any advertisement which induces people to consume a product conveys information, since the act of consumption gives more information about the properties of a product or service than could be done by the advertisement itself.'[2] The thought makes no sense. If this claim is correct, then the salt with which bar owners liberally coat their free munchies is a vehicle for information, since it causes patrons to consume more drinks. Tobacco manufacturers can guiltlessly kick up the amount of nicotine in tobacco products, since its addictive qualities turn it into a vehicle for information. Coase follows the sentence quoted with the claim that 'persuasive advertising is thus also informative', and that comment is, though still controversial, more to the point. Persuasion, unlike salt on munchies or nicotine in tobacco, succeeds, when it does, by affecting the mind in a way that includes conscious awareness. Whether that is enough to call persuasive advertising 'informative', however, is a matter for further contemplation.

The paradigm examples of persuasive advertising are constituted by so-called 'lifestyle advertising'. The three examples given above are instances. These are advertisements whose content is primarily not informative but symbolic, portraying ways of living in acts of endorsement or advocacy that do not involve discursive promotion of a product. They rely for their effect and for their 'message' far more on visual or auditory imagery and emotional association than on language and explicit content. Further examples are the classic 'Marlboro Man' advertisements, where a clean-cut and fit-looking cowboy is shown smoking a cigarette on a horse amid a gorgeous western landscape; or a recent TV campaign for Molson Canadian beer, showing without language a swiftly-passing kaleidoscope of typically Canadian images and Canadian landscapes, ending with the beer's trade mark logo.

A final kind of advertising may be called 'persuasive-contractual' advertising. By this awkward term I mean a kind of advertising that has features in common with both informational advertising and 'lifestyle advertising'. Two different interests are served simultaneously. Business owners have an interest in making it known to the public that they have certain goods or services available at a certain price: they also have an interest in attracting customers to their business and persuading them to purchase their product. Such an advertisement provides some information, but the weight of the appeal is not cognitive, but persuasive, to emotional longings, desires, and dreams.

Bright lines between these different kinds of advertising will be hard to draw, which strongly suggests that the three categories of 'informational', 'persuasive-contractual', and 'lifestyle' constitute a continuum. My identification of lifestyle

---

[2] R.H. Coase, 'Advertising and Free Speech', *Journal of Legal Studies* 6 (1977): 9.

advertising as a category reflects current Canadian constitutional jurisprudence. In the Quebec Court of Appeal hearing of *RJR-MacDonald*,[3] Brossard JA distinguished three kinds of advertisement for tobacco products:

there is the type which primarily contains information on the relative tar, nicotine and carbon monoxide levels of the brand being advertised; there is the type which is aimed solely at promoting one brand over another based on the effect of the colour, design and appearance of the packaging; and there is the third type which also tries to promote one brand over another but does so by creating an image and associating its consumption with a particular life-style (life-style advertising). [at 383–4]

The Supreme Court in its own hearing of the case adopted this tripartite analysis.[4] The existence of any continuum does not matter to the present argument, for the following reason. I have shown in the preceding chapters that, even if we take as an example advertising which is in the fullest sense informational, no sound grounds exist for the commercial expression doctrine. The purpose of the present chapter is to explore what might seem to be a loose end. A great deal of advertising—most advertising, in fact—is not informational in character, or informational only to some degree. In theory, it might be that a wholly different kind of argument is available for extending constitutional protection under freedom of expression values to forms of advertising that are not, or not primarily, informational. Lifestyle advertising is one such form. I shall now proceed to consider what seems a most tempting argument of that kind. I shall show that it fails, and therefore this apparent loose end is tied up.

In an article on 'Free Expression and Personal Identification',[5] Joseph Raz develops an argument for the value of freedom of expression, not from the point of view of the value of freedom of expression to individuals directly, nor from freedom of expression as instrumental to a social good, but rather from the point of view of freedom of expression as in itself a *public good*. I am going to consider in this chapter whether a 'public good' argument in the form proposed by Raz for freedom of expression generally can indeed be constructed for the defence of specifically commercial expression or speech. I shall present Raz's argument in the next section, before turning to its possible application to freedom of commercial expression.

---

[3] *Re RJR-MacDonald Inc and Attorney-General of Canada; Re Imperial Tobacco Ltd and Attorney-General of Canada* [Indexed as RJR-MacDonald Inc v Canada (Attorney-General)] (1993) 102 DLR (4th) 289 (Que CA).

[4] *RJR-MacDonald Inc v Attorney-General of Canada; Imperial Tobacco Ltd v Attorney-General of Canada* [Indexed as RJR-MacDonald Inc v Canada (Attorney-General)] (1995) 127 DLR (4th) 1, at 98, 100.

[5] Joseph Raz, *Ethics in the Public Domain: Essays in the Morality of Law and Politics* (Oxford: Clarendon Press, 1994), 146–69.

2 RAZ'S PUBLIC GOOD ARGUMENT FOR FREEDOM OF EXPRESSION

1 The Concept of Public Good Revisited

'Public good', taken technically, is, as we have seen (Chapter 13.3 above), a term of art in economics, turning on the characteristics of being 'non-rival' and 'inexcludable'. It is important to emphasize the difference between the *structure* and the *content* of the notion of a 'public good'. The technical account in terms of being inexcludable and non-rival gives formal or structural features of a public good. It is not necessary for a public good so defined to be a good thing from the point of view of some given normative theory. Clean air is often cited as a standard example of a public good. But imagine some planet out there in the Delta Quadrant of the galaxy where the air is totally deleterious to human life forms. Such noxious air, supposing similar conditions of availability, is still inexcludable and non-rival, and so in the technical sense a 'public good', even though it is as a matter of fact not a normative 'good' at all, but rather a major normative harm, on virtually any normative theory of the human good. That specifically clean air, or specifically a supply of potable water, is here and now normatively a good, as well as technically a public good, has to do with the content of the respective public goods. Specifically clean air is a *good* public good because it is, or is perceived to be, of benefit to human beings. It is of course extremely unlikely as a matter of fact that clean air, a supply of potable water, and the like would ever have become the focus of a theory of 'public goods' developed by economists unless those commodities had been from the point of view of some robust, non-economic normative theory good things for humans. If they were not normatively good things, then the classic problem of how to deal with free-riding on public goods would not arise. No human being is going to free-ride on the supply of noxious air in the Delta Quadrant. All the same, there is no conceptual connection between being a public good technically defined and being a normatively good thing for humans.

There is a case to be made for the relevance of the technical aspects of the notion of 'public good' in Raz's argument. He begins the essay we are examining by posing what he calls 'a puzzle' about freedom of expression in the context of liberal democratic culture: freedom of expression is always heavily protected, yet with very few exceptions people's interest in their own individual right to public free speech is rather small.[6] It is rarely exercised (very few actually deliver public political speeches), and rarely affects individual health and welfare. A few pages later, he repeats this theme:

Whatever value the right to free expression has for an individual right-holder derives from his interest in being able to participate in the democratic process. It is, however,

---

[6] At 146; see also Richard A. Posner, 'Free Speech in an Economic Perspective', *Suffolk University Law Review* 20 (1986): 23.

notoriously difficult to show that people have a rational reason to cast a vote in any election with a sufficiently large electorate. [at 152]

Clearly, Raz is aiming to find in the case of freedom of expression as a public good analogues to the free-rider problems associated with the economists' standard public goods. In this latter case, individual utility maximization leads to failures of efficiency and inadequate availability of public goods. Raz offers the 'liberal puzzle' as a parallel. If each individual citizen pursued only what was of private and direct interest to him or her as an individual, he or she would not rank freedom of expression highly, nor, for that matter, the right to vote.

On the other hand, Raz does not, nor does he try to, solve the 'liberal puzzle' as a technical puzzle in democratic theory. Once he has distinguished between the private interest an individual has in freedom of expression and the latter's status as a public good, the 'liberal puzzle' fades into the background. The focus is on the normative question of what kind of 'good' freedom of expression is, and how one can justify its normative centrality to liberalism without appealing to individual private interest. All the same, the status of freedom of expression as a technical public good is essential to the argument. That status is necessary to the free availability of the forms of expression Raz considers being able to promote human flourishing in the way he sketches. However, given the fact that the status of technical public good is in itself value-free, having that status is not sufficient, for any form of expression which has it, to guarantee the valuable character Raz finds in the forms of expression he considers. An independent normative argument is needed. Raz's argument supplies that for the forms he mentions. But he does not mention freedom of commercial expression. The case of commercial expression therefore needs independent examination.

2 Raz's 'Public Good' Argument

Let me first summarize Raz's public good argument for freedom of expression in general. Raz considers five possible responses to his 'liberal puzzle'. Only the fifth argument is relevant to corporate expression. It runs as follows:

a person's right to freedom of expression is protected not in order to protect him, but in order to protect a public good, a benefit which respect for the right of free expression brings to all who live in the society in which it is respected, even those who have no personal interest in their own freedom. [at 148]

Raz now tries to spell out what the 'benefit' is. He points out that freedom of expression is an integral part of democratic regimes, and he lays out two implications of democratic government:

(1) Governmental responsiveness to the wishes of the governed is to be desired only if those wishes themselves are not entirely the product of manipulation by the government.
(2) Other things being equal, the better informed the governed are and the better they are able to evaluate the information at their disposal the stronger the case for heeding their wishes. [at 151]

He claims that these two implications create a public good justification for the defence of freedom of expression: 'For most people the exercise of the right to free public political speech has little value . . . [But] the right is essential for the survival of democracy, and everyone has a great interest in the survival of democracy' (at 152). We are dealing here, Raz says, with the service a right does to a public good. Living in a democratic state is a public good.[7] It is 'non-rival'—the benefit I as an individual derive from living in Canada *qua* democratic state does not in any way impede the acquisition of similar benefits by other residents. It is 'inexcludable'—if it is provided to any residents of Canada, it is provided to all. That is the point, one might say, of democratic rather than authoritarian government.

This example serves to illustrate paradigmatically one way that a right to freedom of expression can be justified by a public good argument, by showing that it plays a vital instrumental role in the maintenance of a public good. The argument, though, is still essentially political in content, and thus will immediately fail to be applicable to commercial expression. However, Raz goes on to cantilever from the democracy example a further-reaching public good argument for freedom of expression. This further argument is not essentially political, and so will be of central concern in this chapter.

The new argument requires the prior establishment of a certain factual background. First, Raz notes that much public expression—on television, in magazines, in books, etc.—is expression of opinions, sensibilities, attitudes, and so forth, which expression adds up to the portrayal of ways and styles of life. He distinguishes two different cases. First (at 154), he takes the example of an economist conveying or publishing economic information. There are two dimensions here, he says, which may have freedom of expression implications—the information the economist provides (which may contribute to the search for truth, for example), and the fact that this public act of information-providing is an essential aspect of, and a revelation of, the economist style of life. To censor or restrict such expression may interfere with the free flow of valuable information, and may be (if it is) objectionable on those grounds. But it also would amount to an interference with the living of the economist lifestyle, a lifestyle of which public expression is an important part. Such interference would thus be objectionable (if it is) for rather different kinds of reasons.

The second case is the large class of expressions that precisely are the portrayals of lifestyles as opposed to the revelation of lifestyles, for example the case of a television situation comedy.[8] These cases have the characteristic that the importance of these acts of expression—the production, the direction, the acting, etc.—does not lie solely in the advancement given to the speaker's interest in saying the things that he or she says. The public act of expression which is

---

[7] I spell out the argument explicitly now. Raz leaves it implicit.

[8] Raz ignores factual issues here about how far the portrayal of lifestyles in TV situation comedies, etc. is realistic. Many critics assert the terminally fantastic unreality of life as portrayed in TV programmes. Out of the philosopher's true love of abstract argument, I waive these worries here.

the performing and broadcasting of the comedy, for the actors in or writer of or director of it, is an essential aspect of their way of life, just as the act of publishing the research paper is an essential aspect of the life of the economist. But because the comedy is a piece of theatre, it is the portrayal of a way of life, the way of life of the characters, which in all likelihood is not the way of life of the actors, writer, and director, and so cannot matter to the latter persons in the way that the comedy matters to those persons if construed in the first way. To put the point another way,[9] the importance of the expression may be held not to lie solely in the speaker's interest in the content of what he or she says. Rather, the importance may lie in a certain diffuse interest various others have in the fact that expressions of a certain content occur.

This interest is as follows. There are three important functions of these portrayals of lifestyles, Raz says:

—They serve to familiarize the public at large with ways of life common in certain segments of the public.
—They serve to reassure those whose ways of life are being portrayed that they are not alone, that their problems are common problems, their experiences known to others.
—They serve as validations of the relevant ways of life. They give them the stamp of public acceptability.[10]

These three functions—the familiarization function, the re-assurance function, and the validation function *stricto sensu*—Raz calls 'validation', collectively and for short. It is a contingent fact that this validating function is so performed, but it is a fact of great importance to the preservation of any culture. Even more is this so in a society with urban anonymity and cultural/ethical pluralism (at 155).

With all this factual background laid out, Raz now gives two normative arguments for freedom of expression as a public good—that is, something which not only has the formal properties of being inexcludable and non-rival, but also is genuinely a normative good. Only the first argument is relevant here; it is the argument from toleration and encouragement of validation (at 156 ff). Through freedom of expression as described, ways and styles of life are validated. A great service is thus rendered to people's well-being, in three ways.

(i) Validation of a way of life helps people's identification with their way of life and so their integration into society.
(ii) Such validation is important for making ways of life real options for people.

---

[9] Raz does not put it this way. In both the U.S. and in Canada, however, great emphasis on the need to eschew content-based restrictions of expression is placed both on the bench and in the ivory tower in typical discussions of freedom of expression. Thus it is important to see how Raz's argument covers content-based restriction.

[10] At 155. Of course, satirical comedies present problems for so straightforward an analysis. I doubt that workers in nuclear power plants derive much validation from the bumbling antics of Homer Simpson. I leave these complications unaddressed.

(iii) Public validation is an essential element in the process of cultural transmission, preservation, and renewal.

This first argument secures, Raz says, only a weak overridable right to freedom of expression. No harm would be done by certain kinds of restriction if the views in question have other outlets.

Thus, 'freedom of expression [is] a public good, a *constitutive* element of a public culture' (at 156). We have here, as in the democracy case, the characterization of a state of affairs that is normatively a *good*. This state of affairs is a 'public culture', a culture in which autonomous flourishing is promoted by the fact that many ways of life are publicly portrayed, fostering the well-being of those whose ways of life are thereby validated; making those ways of life real options; allowing the transmission, preservation, and renewal of rich and robust traditions, forms of relationships, attitudes, and styles of life. Secondly, this good of a 'public culture' is technically a *public* good because it is 'non-rival' and 'incxcludable'. The extent of people's share of the benefits is controlled exclusively by them, by their character, interests, and dispositions—how much they watch TV and what they watch, for instance. This last remark might be thought to ignore the fact of economic inequalities, and their effect on a person's capacity to claim a share of the benefits of a public culture. The point, I take it, is that, if such inequalities stem from official interferences with freedom of expression, then they are unjustified. If they result from other aspects of the design of social institutions, then the issue of their compatibility with a 'public culture' raises normative issues far beyond the scope of both Raz's article and the present chapter.[11]

In short, the public good argument for the value of, and so a right to, freedom of expression is this. A society such that its members, despite their diversity, can readily identify with it makes a unique and special contribution to the well-being of those members. Conditions that in part are constitutive of the continuing existence of such a society are not merely normative goods, but also technically public goods. In a pluralistic society, where lifestyles are many and a wide range of opportunities for identification are necessary, freedom of expression contributes uniquely and materially to the provision of such opportunities. Therefore it too is a public good.

I turn now for the remainder of the chapter to the applicability of this kind of argument to the case specifically of freedom of commercial expression.

3 LIFESTYLE ADVERTISING AND PUBLIC GOOD

The seemingly most plausible instances of advertising which serves a validation function are the cases of so-called lifestyle advertising itself, for they are

---

[11] See John Rawls, *Political Liberalism* (New York: Columbia University Press, 1993), Chapter 8, for some remarks on the relation of freedom of speech/expression to other basic liberties in a well-ordered state.

centrally concerned with the portrayal of a lifestyle. The salient characteristics of such portrayals (following Raz) are the advocacy, endorsing or otherwise promoting of the lifestyle in question; advertising with such characteristics would arguably fulfil Raz's three criteria for the validation function. Meeting the further criteria of being non-rival and inexcludable, the advertisements would then qualify as public goods in both the structural and the normative sense. But this appearance is misleading: I will show that lifestyle advertisements cannot serve the validating function on which Raz's public good argument for freedom of expression is based. The manner in which lifestyle advertisements typically function belies their claim to lifestyle validation. The paucity of information provided about such lifestyles and the manner in which such advertisements affect their intended audience certainly make such advertisements effective in selling products. This utility is gained, however, at the expense of the various forms of validation Raz finds in other public expressions such as television dramas and professional discourse.

The contrast drawn between pure lifestyle advertising and informational advertising relates to information of a particular kind—factual information, directly given. It is hard to deny that lifestyle advertising does communicate a message in some sense: the Marlboro Man invites you to smoke; the Virginia Slims advertisements invite women to celebrate their femininity by smoking. A typical advertisement for designer perfume shows elegantly dressed women in luxurious surroundings. The images are of wealth, romance, and beauty, and the only words in the advertisements are slogans like 'Share the fantasy'. An advertisement for the Jeep Cherokee shows the vehicle on a high mountain shelf, facing an awesome view. The advertisement encourages commuters to buy a jeep instead of a car, and thus have the option of driving up to those plateaus at weekends. All these advertisements convey the message they convey via the portrayal of a lifestyle, and furthermore the portrayal of a lifestyle in a favourable light. Thus to a degree they seem to constitute the validation of a lifestyle. The Jeep Cherokee advertisement, for example, seems to do for Cherokee owners, and the perfume advertisement for elegant ladies who use the product, exactly what *Eastenders* does for people living in the East End of London, in terms of validating their lifestyle. It therefore may seem as though a Raz-style public good argument is available for the protection of lifestyle advertising as it is for portrayals of lifestyles in television situation comedies. I shall now show that this impression is illusory.

Let me reiterate the distinction between two discrete questions:

(A) Is the good (or is there a good) derivable from lifestyle advertising which is a 'public good' in the technical and non-normative sense of being non-rival and inexcludable?

(B) Is there a consequence derivable from lifestyle advertising that constitutes a good thing (a benefit) for the public generally? In particular, if there is a supposed 'public good' derivable from lifestyle advertising, is it really a 'good' that pertains to freedom of expression?

In the case of paradigm public goods—national defence, clean air, cures for infectious diseases, etc.—question (B) is rarely explicitly asked. It is intuitively obvious that the consequences in question are good things; question (A) is simply to identify what *formal kind* of good thing. If advertising as such is at all valuable, then there may be in principle a dimension of good to lifestyle advertising beyond the private good to the owner and other rights-holders in relation to the product being advertised, and the private good to the purchaser of the product. But we have not yet considered carefully the question whether the supposed good is a real one, especially in the present narrow context of public goods and free expression. That is, we have not yet considered carefully whether the values that a Raz-style public good argument finds in, for example, portrayals of lifestyles in television situation comedies and in journal publications are indeed discoverable in lifestyle advertising. Thus, even though I am now focussing more on the claim of lifestyle advertising to be normatively a *good* of a given kind than on its claim to be technically a *public good*—on matters of content, that is, rather than structure—I am still considering only the 'public good' aspect of its claimed worth.

Before we turn to this issue, however, one other case must be noted. As has been noted already, Raz himself draws attention to the way in which the publication of an article on economics by an economist, for example, not only serves the function of providing economic information; it also serves the function of validating the economist's lifestyle, part of which is the publication of articles on economics. Fellow economists may enjoy an awareness effect from the validation of their lifestyle over and above other benefits they derive from the content of the article. Now it seems possible to construe certain kinds of advertising in a similar light, the advertising of individual members of a profession—the lawyer, or doctor, or accountant, or psychologist announcing the availability of his or her services. Such advertising, in addition to its other benefits—making potential clients or patients aware of the availability of the services—may also validate the lawyerly or accountantly lifestyle for other lawyers or accountants, who are after all individual human beings, not faceless corporations. The idea that the Molson Breweries company, or the RJR-MacDonald tobacco company, *itself qua corporation* may have a lifestyle capable of validation is ludicrous: corporations, as distinct from the individuals who staff them, are not the kind of entities that can have a lifestyle. That is not so for a dentist, or an optometrist, as an individual who constitutes a one-person professional corporation, or perhaps a pair, or trio, or suitable manageable number of such who constitute a professional partnership. There the relevant concept of lifestyle validation has a foothold. The idiosyncratic nature of the professional corporation, however, makes it a misleading paradigm for issues of freedom of commercial expression; as I argued in Chapter 9.4, the seemingly individual character of the professional corporation disguises the relevance of the corporate form. Nothing can be generalized from this case, even if a Raz-style public good argument might have some application to advertising by an individual professional person.

As regards the notion that more typical lifestyle advertisements perform the validation function, I have four different counter-arguments to present, which I shall call the Suppression of Interpretation Argument, the Unreality Argument, the False Implication Argument, and the Manipulation Argument. I am well aware that these are not new objections to advertising. However, the context of application is new. I shall consider these in turn.

The Suppression of Interpretation Argument turns on an account of the associational mechanism that underlies the value for advertisers who use lifestyle advertisements. As Richard Moon has shown, 'a lifestyle advertisement is meant to affect consumer behaviour while discouraging conscious realization of this effect'.[12] Moon quotes Roland Barthes: 'Everything happens as if the picture *naturally* conjured up the concept, as if the signifier gave a foundation to the signified.'[13] The perfume advertisement invites readers to assume that the wealth and glamorous lifestyle depicted will be theirs if they use the perfume, or at least the carefree contentment the glamorous bather enjoys. The Marlboro advertisement invites readers to believe that masculine strength and handsomeness, and a healthy outdoor life, will be theirs when they smoke Marlboro cigarettes. Put like that, of course, all these claims are ridiculous. None of those things will happen. The advertisements are successful only in so far as interpretation of the real message conveyed is suppressed in favour of responding unthinkingly to the emotional association. The famous Nike slogan says it perfectly: 'Just do it'. Thinking about the 'it' will interfere with the very possibility of realizing the (unreflectively) desirable goal. Or take the Accenture management company slogan: 'I am your idea'. The suggestion that the management services the company performs are genuinely valuable is expressed in wholly emotional terms. No product (or, in this case, service) X is being offered at Y price.

This very feature of lifestyle advertising, however, means that it is singularly unsuited to performing the three validating functions of expression identified by Raz—the familiarization function, the reassurance function, and the validation function *stricto sensu*. The public good argument for freedom of expression presupposes an 'awareness effect', a level of up-take of the material being read which involves understanding and appreciation, responses which are at least in part in some sense cognitive. There must be appreciation of the lifestyle portrayed as a lifestyle of such-and-such a kind before the public at large can be 'familiarized' with it, or before the stamp of public acceptability can be imposed. There must be conscious recognition of the lifestyle portrayed as being one's own lifestyle before reassurance can occur that one is not alone. Lifestyle advertising works precisely to suppress this kind of interpretative appreciation. Advertisements based on associating images function best when such associ-

---

[12] Richard Moon, 'Lifestyle Advertising and Classical Freedom of Expression Doctrine', *McGill Law Journal* 36 (1991): 115; Richard Moon, *The Constitutional Protection of Freedom of Expression* (Toronto: University of Toronto Press, 2000), 92–6.

[13] Roland Barthes, *Mythologies* (London: Paladin Grafton Books, 1973), 129.

ations are absorbed uncritically, so that viewers will begin, quite unconsciously, to associate the advertised product with some other good they currently endorse. Lifestyle advertising therefore cannot serve the validating function on which the public good argument for freedom of expression is based.

It might be suggested that the previous argument generalizes too quickly. It imposes on all lifestyle advertising such a consumer obliviousness requirement. But such a requirement is seemingly too strong. Persons who already think of themselves as, and perhaps already are, jeans-clad, healthy cowboys riding the big sky country of the West are not being deceived about who they are when they derive self-validation from a Marlboro advertisement. Advertisements can be self-consciously ironic on this score—'Look, we know you aren't going to get into the NBA *just* because you buy our basketball shoes, even though that's what we're telling you'. The advertisement may then exploit the attractiveness of this irony (as film-maker Spike Lee did in his famous commercials wherein he pesters Michael Jordan about his Nikes), which requires that the consumer be aware of it, not oblivious to it, in order to persuade the consumer to buy the product.

This line of argument is cogent, and brings out the extent to which my analysis of lifestyle advertising has empirical presuppositions. That is to say, my claim is not that conceptually the nature of lifestyle advertising is to suppress interpretation. The claim is that as a matter of fact in the majority of cases, and in the paradigm cases, this is how the advertising works. Very few viewers of Marlboro advertisements are actually cowboys; for most viewers, the suppression of interpretation holds. Very few lifestyle advertisements are in fact self-consciously ironic; most deploy the effects of levels of textuality covertly, not overtly.[14] Moreover, in most cases, to the extent that consumer obliviousness is not required, the advertisements will be vulnerable to one or more of the remaining objections I raise, or will simply fail to sell their products, for lifestyle advertisements that fail to sway views with their imagery (thus failing to reap the economic benefits of suppressing interpretation) tend to fall rhetorically flat.

The Unreality Argument is best illustrated by the perfume advertisement and the honesty of its entreaty, 'Share the fantasy'. The lifestyle portrayed is fantastic, not only in the sense that as a matter of empirical fact people often fantasize about living such a lifestyle. It is fantastic, in the sense that it cannot be realized by anyone. Tricks of make-up, of lighting, of photography, and so forth create a false world, an unreal world. Consider the number of times a television advertisement follows a display of the remarkable agility of an automobile with the swiftly-shown proviso, 'Professional drivers; do not attempt'. Like the Cherokee advertisement with the jeep on the mountain-top, the advertisement shows nothing that is ever going to appear in the life-history of anyone who will actually purchase the product in question. To the extent that lifestyle advertising portrays

---

[14] And, if they are overtly ironic, that is likely because some behavioural study has shown the utility of irony as a tool of persuasion.

an unreal or unrealizable way of life, then it cannot serve to validate actual ways of life as the public good argument for freedom of expression demands.

Again, it is important not to overstate the case. Even if the Marlboro advertisement is, as it surely is, an idealization of the life of the modern cowboy (and there still are working cowboys on the cattle ranches of western Canada and the U.S.), still a person who is a cowboy can be aware of, not oblivious to, the idealization and derive self-validation. After all, in the case of the regular TV show with which Raz is concerned, a science-fiction series, for example, while it surely portrays an unreal world, may provide self-validation for persons who are the real-world equivalents of the jobs or personalities portrayed. Presumably, in principle the same could be true of lifestyle advertisements. Once again, an empirical dimension to our argument is presupposed. The force of the argument remains.

The False Implication Argument is typified in the famous Microsoft advertising campaign based on the slogan, 'Where Do You Want To Go Today?' The implication of the advertisement is not only 'inform and empower yourself through our products'. It embodies also the idea that not buying Microsoft's progressive software constitutes resistance to a worthy humanitarian goal— something like: 'Don't deprive your kids of the education they have a right to— buy them the software they need in order to learn'. The advertisement is effective because it links the product with highly favoured values like knowledge, democracy, and pluralism (not to mention power, adventure, creativity, etc.). It is more effective than a simple informed appeal to current software consumers in that it creates a series of powerful, emotional appeals to draw in the sceptics, Luddites, and romantics who have thus far resisted the call to information mobilization. It is an advertisement that appeals to the broadest of our community's values, in the hopes of extending its market to the entire community.

However, it is not difficult to have obvious misgivings about the claims these advertisements make. Society has, after all, done pretty well to fulfil the sort of social goods (such as progress, creativity, sharing of information) suggested in its advertisements without the help of Microsoft. Electronic empowerment is, after some scrutiny, something we all can take or leave. In short, the appeal of the advertisement turns on the false implication that the purchase of Microsoft products is essential to realize valued social goals. The lifestyle of computer literacy and software use is presented in a false light. The public good argument for freedom of expression requires at the very least that the lifestyle portrayed be truthfully portrayed. That typically does not happen in the case of lifestyle advertising.

A different kind of false implication is embodied in a number of advertisements for children's toys. In these, the advertisement begins by showing the toy for what it is, an inert piece of plastic—a flying dinosaur, a space craft, a being of larger-than-life human skills. The child is shown picking up the toy, and then the advertisement uses computer imagery or 'morphing' to give the toy a life of its own. It is shown flying freely, swooping down, attacking buildings, etc. But the toy is not capable of such motion on its own: it has to be held by the child and made to move. The evidence is that, while children 8 years old or more are well aware that they will need to move the toy, younger children are not. They expect that the toy will be able to fly, attack, etc. all on its own. They are disappointed when this turns out not to be true. Arguably, advertisements such as these border on being straightforwardly deceptive, and would fail as contributors to a public good for just that reason. All I am claiming here is that, even if they do not meet standards for deceptiveness in advertising, they fail anyway as contributors to the public good represented by freedom of expression.

The Manipulation Argument is easier to present than to assess. Consider the Jeep Cherokee advertisement. The advertisement seems aimed at commuters already in the market for a vehicle of some kind. If a commuter is also a lover of breathtaking scenery, a way has been shown to satisfy this desire within the purview of one's normal consumer patterns. However, this technique seems little other than lobbying for a shift in one's purchasing patterns, something at least potentially less innocuous than leaving those patterns unaffected. The effect of the advertisement is to link one's love of the mountains with one's choice of vehicles, making the Jeep the means of satisfying the value endorsed. Since the means brought to light is also the product for sale it is legitimate to question the assumption that there is here a beneficial broadening of the consumer's horizons rather than a moulding of her preferences and means of satisfying those preferences. The advertisement creates a market for the product by linking images pleasing to the viewer with the product for sale. The advertisement seems to work by manipulating viewers into having a desire that they did not previously have and on which they then act to purchase the product.

If in fact lifestyle advertising genuinely does manipulate readers or viewers in a way that interferes with autonomous choice by those readers or viewers, then it will not be available as an application of the public good argument for freedom of expression.[15] The benefits from the performance of the validation function of portrayals of lifestyles clearly presuppose a context of autonomous choice, and of persons as autonomous choosers. This is so not only for the middle of Raz's three benefits—making ways of life real options for people. The thoughts that well-being results from identification with one's way of life, and that cultural transmission, preservation, and renewal are goods it is good to promote—both of these thoughts make sense only on the assumption that the identification and the cultural transmission and so forth are not coerced. If it is the case that lifestyle advertising coerces choices, then its claim to validate lifestyles in a meaningful way is vitiated.

The idea that advertising is coercive is not new. John Kenneth Galbraith is well-known for his theory of the 'Dependence Effect', that advertising itself creates the desires that it satisfies, that is, that those desires are dependent on the

---

[15] Cf. Raz's comments on manipulation of political preferences, at 152.

means by which they are satisfied.[16] The claim on behalf of advertising that it leaves all desires as they are and provides only needed information for their maximal satisfaction would undoubtedly be disingenuous, as even my limited discussion of lifestyle advertising has indicated. All the same, the claim that advertising influences readers and viewers in ways that violate their autonomy is hard to make out. Robert L. Arrington has argued that by normal standards of causal determination it is very doubtful that advertising causes anyone to have a desire that by virtue of such a causal history cannot be said to be his or her own.[17] Reese P. Miller suggests a modification of such a view, that, if satisfaction from the acquisition of a product can only come to exist via a false or groundless belief (for example, that unless an engagement is symbolized by an expensive diamond ring, the marriage will not be a happy one), then the advertising engendering such a belief is morally problematic for reasons to do with the value of autonomy.[18]

There is no doubt that, if the Manipulation Argument is to have any cogency at all, then lifestyle advertising of the more egregiously non-rational kind potentially provides the best targets. But the ramifications and complexities of the Argument make it unwise to rely too heavily on it in the present context.

4 Conclusion

In conclusion, I have argued that lifestyle advertising communicates the messages that it contains in a manner incompatible with the presuppositions of a Raz-style public good argument for freedom of expression as a value. Such advertisements fail not because they lack the formal characteristics of being non-rival and inexcludable, but because they fail to perform the validation function needed to show that such advertisements give rise to something good in the normative sense. The argument that they do so give rise depends upon an assumption that the expression that is paradigmatically protected by the argument is informative expression that fosters well-being through an awareness effect on the part of hearers, readers, and viewers. By contrast, lifestyle advertising aims to suppress its awareness effect; it presents unreal lifestyles and false implications of portrayals of lifestyles; in extreme forms it manipulates and interferes with autonomy. It may rightly be pointed out that the argument has the form of generalizing to all advertising of a certain kind, lifestyle advertising, on the basis of certain select examples. This is true. I am relying on the reader's

---

[16] John Kenneth Galbraith, *The Affluent Society* (Boston, Mass.: Houghton Mifflin Co., 1958), Chapter 11.

[17] Robert L. Arrington, 'Advertising and Behaviour Control', *Journal of Business Ethics* 1 (1982): 3–12. For a rejection of Arrington's arguments and the case for saying that advertising does negatively affect autonomy see Roger Crisp, 'Persuasive Advertising, Autonomy, and the Creation of Desire', *Journal of Business Ethics* 6 (1987): 413–18.

[18] Reese P. Miller, 'Persuasion and the Dependence Effect', in Deborah C. Poff and Wilfrid J. Waluchow (eds.), *Business Ethics in Canada* (Scarborough: Prentice-Hall Canada, 1991), 479–88.

perception that the examples chosen are typical, and would sustain such an extrapolation. I am content to do so.

Criticisms of the tendencies of advertisements to undermine rational and autonomous choosing are not new. My aim in this chapter has not been merely to sing another version of a familiar old standard. Rather, I have tried to secure a much narrower point, one with specific relevance to the typical arguments made in favour of the commercial expression doctrine. My aim has been to show that simply being non-rival and inexcludable is not sufficient to consider these instances of commercial expression public goods in the more robust, or normative, sense at issue here. Lifestyle advertising is not capable of being normatively valuable in the specific sense of performing the validation function explicated by Raz as a foundational reason for the value of free expression.

15

Retrospect and Prospect

1 RETROSPECT

In the preceding chapters, a great deal of ground has been covered, both as regards the state of the law in various places and as regards issues of theory and normative justification. This book could not properly conclude without some summary review. I shall provide one here.

The decision of the U.S. Supreme Court in *Virginia Board*[1] is central to the whole enterprise, in that not only the U.S. Supreme Court itself but courts in Canada, including the Supreme Court of Canada, and in Europe took their cue as regards constitutional protection for freedom of commercial expression very much from that decision. There were some later differences. In the U.S., the development in *Central Hudson*[2] of a formal step-wise procedure for assessing the constitutionality of restrictions on commercial speech was an important development. Courts in Canada and Europe developed doctrinal approaches that differed at the level of detail, in order to suit their particular contexts. But all the same, the arguments used by the majority in *Virginia Board* to justify the extension of constitutional protection to commercial speech in that case are fundamentally the arguments that are still used as justifications. The discussion of the case law in Chapters 3 to 5 located subsequent developments in the U.S., and parallel developments in Canada and Europe in relation to *Virginia Board*. In Chapter 2, however, I examined in some detail the arguments for the commercial expression doctrine in their original site in that case. I established two things about those arguments. First, in so far as the Court there tried to claim that its decision was a logical extension of existing institutional trends in precedent cases, the Court was simply mistaken. The precedents to which the Court appealed do not provide sound authority for the commercial expression doctrine. Typically, the Court draws on features of the cases that are not shared by commercial expression in order to attempt to justify its treatment of commercial expression. Moreover, viewed as pieces of reasoning, the arguments actually offered in the cases are full of flaws, and again are far from justifying the conclusions drawn by the Court from them.

---

[1] *Virginia State Board of Pharmacy et al v Virginia Citizens Consumer Council Inc et al* 425 US 748 (1976).

[2] *Central Hudson Gas & Electric Corporation v Public Service Commission of New York* 447 US 557 (1980).

In Chapter 6, I identified in a more systematic way the arguments used in the case law to justify the commercial expression doctrine. Two particular arguments were picked out as being the ones on which most weight turns out to be placed by subsequent judicial opinions and academic commentary: the idea that substantial social value attaches to the free flow of commercial information, and that this social value justifies constitutional protection for commercial expression; and the idea that the free flow of commercial information promotes individual autonomy, self-realization, and self-fulfilment. The focus of the rest of the book, therefore, is on these two arguments as a whole, and on different sub-arguments within them. The goal of my analysis has been to prove that, stripped of the heavy coating of emotional rhetoric that envelops them, these arguments are both invalid and unsound.

Before turning to this task, I both acknowledged and invited acceptance of some crucial methodological assumptions. Some of these were discussed early on, in Chapter 1.4 and 1.5. There, I adopted the ground rules that I would criticize the commercial expression doctrine only on the basis of principles which friends of the doctrine themselves would accept. Although there are a variety of ways in which the commercial expression doctrine can be attacked from outside—from assumptions, that is, which friends of the doctrine would not accept—I chose not to follow those ways. I accepted as a framework for the discussion that freedom of expression is best interpreted as a form of so-called 'negative freedom', and that the values that justify freedom of expression are those of the search for truth, democratic self-government, and individual self-realization and self-fulfilment. In Chapter 7, I distinguished moral from institutional rights, and between two general forms of justification for norms of political morality, via the paradigm of autonomy and via the paradigm of utility. At the end of that Chapter, I also presented the methodological principle that the justification for constitutionally protecting some given form of expression on freedom of expression grounds must be 'top down'. The reasoning must be that the form of expression in question promotes the values which normative theory says are the values that justify freedom of expression. The reasoning cannot begin simply from the fact that in an ordinary sense of 'expression' or 'speech', we have before us a case of expression or speech. I tried to fill this principle out by taking in Chapter 8 the specific instances of the tort of inducing breach of contract, the U.S. Food and Drug Administration regulations concerning the advertising of off-label uses of pharmaceutical drugs, and the right of publicity as test cases. In all three cases, arguments have been made that the controlling law fails adequately to account for the fact that expression or speech is at issue, thus implicating the value of freedom of expression or of speech. I showed that these arguments in the case of inducing breach of contract and off-label drug use advertising failed to observe the 'top-down' principle. The arguments relied solely on the ground that expression is involved, and that ground is insufficient to invoke issues of freedom of expression. The right of publicity provided a valuable comparison case. In the case of this right, the law as it stands pays little attention to the relevance of freedom of expression as a relevant value. There are good reasons within standard freedom of expression theory to call that lack of attention a mistake.

I then turned to examine in detail the argumentation regularly offered to justify the commercial expression doctrine. I began with arguments assuming the paradigm of autonomy—arguments, that is, that assumed the value ultimately at stake in questions of freedom of expression to be individual autonomy. In Chapter 9, I rejected the view that corporations could avail themselves of original autonomy rights, in the sense that they possessed in themselves an autonomy that autonomy rights could protect. I noted that one unfortunate result of the establishment of the commercial expression doctrine is that courts are seemingly beginning in fact to look at corporate expressers in that way, losing sight of the fact that originally the point of the doctrine was to protect the autonomy of natural persons. I considered, and rejected, arguments that corporations are constituted out of natural persons in a way that allows them to bear the original autonomy rights of natural persons.

In fact, despite the *de facto* treatment of corporations as possessors of original autonomy rights, the official position, and rhetoric, of the commercial expression doctrine is that corporations have constitutional rights of freedom of commercial expression in order to promote, or protect, the autonomy rights of natural persons. Corporations 'borrow' these autonomy rights in order to claim constitutional protection for their expression. Corporations' freedom of expression rights are derivative. One central claim in this connection is that freedom of expression as a value subtends a right of the hearer to receive expression. There is an initial intuitive basis to this claim, in that we can construct cases where talk of a hearers' right to receive expression is appropriate. But I argued in Chapter 10, first, that these cases are a motley, a number of different specific kinds of case. It is not possible to get out of them a general right grounded in freedom of expression for any hearer always to have a right to receive expression. I showed, secondly and moreover, that the most compelling instances of a hearers' right either were in connection with political expression, or implied a right to receive of a form that was correlative to a duty to provide expression. Either way, these would be of no help to the commercial expression doctrine, seeking as it does to free the corporate commercial expresser from government regulation.

If the case is to be made, then, for a hearers' right to receive commercial expression, it must rely on reasons special to the case of commercial expression. And indeed the commercial expression doctrine argues that there is such a feature—namely, that the free flow of commercial information from corporation to consumer which freedom of commercial expression would guarantee is valuable because it promotes individual autonomy, self-realization, and self-fulfilment. In Chapter 11, I confronted and rejected this argument. I showed that informed economic decision-making simply does not have the right kind of direct connection with individual autonomy, self-realization, and self-fulfilment for the argument to succeed. While it may often be better for the individual that his or her economic decision-making is 'informed', it is difficult, if not impossible, to show that autonomy, self-realization, and self-fulfilment are as such improved by informed economic decision-making. And the cases where plausibly informed economic decision-making does foster autonomy, it is the autonomy of the individual as expresser which is fostered, not the autonomy of the individual as hearer.

A second issue in connection with the supposed negative effect of government regulation of commercial expression on hearer autonomy is the oft-repeated charge that regulation of advertising is 'paternalistic'. Though frequently and routinely (and eloquently) made, the charge is shown in Chapter 12 to be baseless. There are in the philosophical literature standard accounts of what paternalism is. Regulation of advertising fails to fit those accounts. Many plausible reconstructions can be given of what a government would be about in regulating advertising that would not make such regulation 'paternalistic'. It is not even clear that regulation of advertising overrides the would-be hearer's autonomy in the first place. Even if there might be cases where the regulation was arguably paternalistic, the received opinion in normative political theory is that grounds exist in principle for the justification of paternalistic legislation. It is not hard to make regulation of advertising conform to those grounds. The charge of paternalism is a rhetorical flourish, not a genuinely defensible accusation.

Chapter 13 confronts a wholly different kind of argument for the value of the free flow of commercial information, an argument that its proponents claim will, if sound, underwrite the commercial expression doctrine. The argument is that the free flow of commercial information maximizes social utility, especially economic decision-making of a kind that maximizes economic efficiency. I dealt with this argument in a number of different ways. First, I assessed the dominant rhetoric of the friends of the commercial expression doctrine, that government regulation of advertising 'induces ignorance, or 'keeps the people in ignorance', or that it 'manipulates' citizens by withholding information. I showed that government regulation of advertising is a long way from being analogous to real cases in which such terminology would be descriptively accurate. The rhetoric is just that—rhetoric, powerful though it is. I then considered numerous examples from the professional literature of economics, to show that in that literature it is shown beyond doubt that, in the case of decision-making under uncertainty, it cannot be assumed that an unregulated flow of information promotes economic efficiency or utility-maximizing decision-making. The automatic assumption of the commercial expression doctrine that every interruption of the free flow of commercial information is bad, even in the case of truthful and non-misleading advertising, is just naïve and inaccurate from the point of view of serious economics. I then argued that in any case, even if it were true that invariably the free flow of commercial information promoted economic efficiency, to take economic efficiency to be as such a constitutional value raises deep problems of both a normative and a structural character. It is not clear that principles of democratic decision-making endorse economic regulation by courts as opposed to legislatures. Moreover, given the kind of decision-making regime that structurally economic regulation is, courts as sites of adjudication rather than legislation are ill fitted to carry out such a task. Along the way, I commented on the meretricious character of the metaphor of the 'marketplace of ideas' as a rhetorical force behind the commercial expression doctrine.

There is a further problem with all the arguments for the commercial expression doctrine considered so far. They all rely on the fact that advertising functions as a medium for the transmission of information. Even the briefest of acquaintance with contemporary advertising reveals that to be a wildly unrealistic assumption. The last substantive chapter, Chapter 14, examined a possible argument for the commercial expression doctrine of a different kind from any examined so far. The advantage of this possible argument is that it would not matter that most commercial advertising does not carry information; even pure lifestyle advertising might in principle be worth protecting under the argument examined in this chapter. Joseph Raz[3] offered an original defence of freedom of expression as a value: that it was a 'public good' in the technical economists' sense of the term. So the question seems worth raising whether freedom of commercial expression could be a similar such good. I argued that in fact it does not so qualify. Commercial expression lacks the characteristics which expression must have if it is to perform the public functions that, on Raz's argument, make freedom of expression a public good.

Freedom of commercial expression is a constitutional fraud. It does not have sound grounding in legal precedent. The normative arguments adduced in its favour are without exception invalid and unsound. The arguments wear a mien of plausibility entirely because of the rhetoric in which they are cloaked. The rhetoric has its place, perhaps, in the need to defend citizens from government encroachment on, and interference with, the paradigmatically protectable forms of expression—political, scientific, artistic expression. It really does have no place as regards 'the decision of a particular individual as to whether to purchase one or another kind of shampoo'.[4]

2 Prospect

The deep and unspoken faith of any philosopher writing a work of applied normative theory is that eventually the arguments *matter*. Works of philosophy, even of applied philosophy, are one or more stages removed from actual front-line decision-making. Philosophers can become consultants to front-line decision-makers, and influence them directly in that way. More usually, philosophical writings influence, if they do, the policy designers and

---

[3] Joseph Raz, *Ethics in the Public Domain: Essays in the Morality of Law and Politics* (Oxford: Clarendon Press, 1994), Chapter 7.

[4] *Virginia Board*, at 787, per Rehnquist J, dissenting.

think-tanks, not the policy appliers. In the context of jurisprudence and legal theory, the hope would be to influence legal thought—the legal academy, and the more conceptual thinking of appellate courts (especially, if the gossip is correct, the clerks of appellate courts).

Is it plausible to have such hopes in this case, to make a contribution to the sense that following the trail of the commercial expression doctrine is a mistake? One must be realistic. The commercial expression doctrine is currently well established in the U.S., Canada, and Europe. In the latter two instances, it is true that, with respect to the high-profile issue of advertising of tobacco products, there are signs that courts are now willing to take seriously public health as a goal that will justify overriding of freedom of commercial expression. In the U.S., freedom of commercial speech is very solidly established. It has behind it the backing of deep pockets, and deep pockets well connected to the current governing party. It has behind it a history in the twentieth century, especially in the last decades thereof, of making the First Amendment the centrepiece of political and ideological commitment. That commitment is accompanied by powerful anti-governmental rhetoric from what is, outside the commercial context, the moral high ground. It would be a brave person who hoped any change was imminent.

On the other hand, applied legal theory seemingly has going for it the fact that in some sense philosophy and the law are in the same business—the business of argument and of reasoning. We talk about legal argument, legal reasoning, and legal science. One would think then that, if any first-order discipline—any enterprise X such that there is philosophy of X—were going to be open to the results of theoretical argument, it would be the law. It is, of course, a feature of twentieth-century jurisprudence that legal realism, Critical Legal Studies, feminist legal thought, Critical Race Theory, and the like have brought home how much of the supposed rational character of the law is illusory. But even there the emphasis is typically on deconstructing or unconcealing the choice of premises and assumptions, or on the indeterminacy created by the availability of more than one line of argument. Only the more radical forms of realist scepticism maintain that the claim of law to rationality is spurious all the way down.

Why should the case of the commercial expression doctrine be any different, then? Or should one have especial doubts here that a philosophical demonstration of the invalidity and unsoundness of doctrine matters for the future? I mentioned at the beginning of the previous chapter Sarah Haan's account of modern advertising practices and their relation to research in behaviour management.[5] As her title suggests, her focus on the techniques of modern advertising is not an end in itself. The focus of the article is on the infiltration of such techniques into courts of law, and especially as regards the history of constitutional protection for commercial speech. I take a moment to recapitulate her argument here.

[5] Sarah C. Haan, 'The "Persuasion Route" of the Law: Advertising and Legal Persuasion', *Columbia Law Review* 100 (2000): 1281–1326.

Haan points out the substantial degree to which organizations representing the advertising industry such as the Association of National Advertisers or the American Advertising Federation have submitted *amicus curiae* or intervenor briefs in commercial speech cases before the U.S. Supreme Court. She points to evidence that these briefs have—unsurprisingly, when one thinks about it—deployed the techniques of modern advertising even though they are not on the face of it advertisements.[6] Haan then tracks some specific instances of the influence of such briefs on judicial opinions. For example, in making assessments of whether a regulation furthered a government interest, courts used to assume that advertising would affect demand for a product. Regulation of commercial speech was criticized on the grounds that regulating speech in order to dampen demand for a product was unconstitutional. Such an argument assumes that regulation would indeed dampen demand. However, in the face of public opposition to the idea that it was encouraging teenagers to smoke, the tobacco industry started to emphasize that it was not creating demand, but simply trying to encourage movement between brands. This point, Haan shows, started to appear regularly in advertisers' *amicus* briefs, and it was not long after that before it started to show up in judicial decisions too.[7] Another example Haan gives is this. In the *Edge* case concerning broadcasting of lottery advertising,[8] a brief submitted by *inter alia* the American Association of Advertising Agencies makes the empirical claim that the actual effect of the impugned regulation of lottery advertising is exactly the opposite of what the government intended. There is no empirical evidence whatever given to support this claim. The same applies to briefs submitted by the same organization in *44 Liquormart*[9] about the effect of liquor advertising, empirical claims made with no evidence offered. By the time *GNOBA*[10] comes along the U.S. Supreme Court itself starts repeating these claims as though they are proven facts, and using the claims as sticks with which to beat the government for failing to show that the impugned regulation furthers its stated purpose. As Haan points out, it is not that studies showing links between advertising and demand are unavailable, and clearly the government did not do its own homework very well.[11] But all the same the deployment of advertising techniques was successful. We have noted already the influence of 'information overload' on rational decision-making (Chapter 13.3). In this context, what seemed like a good idea at the time—to ask governments to provide respectable proof that their policies had sound empirical backing—has turned out to create the kind of inundation of facts which impairs rationality and opens the door to non-rational persuasion. Haan reports, for example, a study showing an 800 per cent increase in the number of *amicus*

    [6] Sarah C. Haan, 'The "Persuasion Route" of the Law: Advertising and Legal Persuasion', *Columbia Law Review* 100 (2000): 1306–19.
    [7] Ibid., 1309–11.   [8] *United States v Edge Broadcasting Company* 113 SCt 2696 (1993).
    [9] *44 Liquormart Inc v Rhode Island* 116 SCt 1495 (1996).
    [10] *Greater New Orleans Broadcasting Association, Inc v United States* 119 SCt 1923 (1999).
    [11] Haan, 'Persuasion Route', 1318–19.

briefs submitted to the U.S. Supreme Court from the decade 1946–55 to the decade 1986–95.

The friends of the commercial expression doctrine call upon the professional skills of the advertiser to influence judicial reasoning in more ways than playing games with spurious social-scientific claims. The rhetoric of the doctrine is thick and heavy also, as I have said many times. Its drumbeat is as relentless, and if one is not careful as hypnotic, as in any Brazilian football crowd or heavy-metal extravaganza. We rightfully regard totalitarian control of political expression and broadcasting as heinous breaches of fundamental human rights. But there is a world of difference between Stalinist thought control and requiring mandatory health warnings on the packaging of tobacco products. Not so, it seems to some. On one pass through Martin Redish's article on tobacco advertising,[12] I counted the following: passages where it is said to be merely 'widely thought' that tobacco consumption causes harms or is addictive—five; passages where it is asserted that after control of advertising, control of political speech is next—six; passages where government regulation of advertising is asserted to be 'paternalistic'—twenty-seven; passages where government regulation of advertising is said to involve 'censorship' or the 'stifling' of opposition—ten; passages where government regulation of advertising is said to involve 'mind-control' or interference with citizens' minds—nine; passages where government regulation of advertising is said to involve manipulating citizens—nine; passages where government regulation of advertising is said to induce ignorance—one; passages where government regulation of advertising is said to involve 'keeping the public ignorant'—three; passages where government regulation of advertising is said to involve the 'suppression' of information or expression—twenty-four. One would think we were in *1984*, not 2003.

Perhaps George Wright is correct—it is all about selling words.[13] Perhaps the issue is well captured by the juxtaposition of Redish's title in support (in part) of the commercial expression doctrine and Hutchinson's and Weinrib's against it.[14] Redish, as I have noted more than once, acknowledges that his article on tobacco advertising was written with the support of the tobacco industry.[15] Lars Noah, whose views on the commercial expression doctrine as applied to advertising of off-label uses of pharmaceutical drugs I discussed critically above

[12] Martin H. Redish, 'Tobacco Advertising and the First Amendment', *Iowa Law Review* 81 (1996): 589–639.

[13] R. George Wright, *Selling Words: Free Speech in a Commercial Culture* (New York: New York University Press, 1997).

[14] Martin Redish, *Money Talks: Speech, Economic Power, and the Values of Democracy* (New York: New York University Press, 2001); Allan C. Hutchinson, 'Money Talk: Against Constitutionalizing (Commercial) Speech', *Canadian Business Law Journal* 17 (1990): 2–34; Lorraine E. Weinrib, 'Does Money Talk? Commercial Expression in the Canadian Constitutional Context', in David Schneiderman (ed.), *Freedom of Expression and the Charter* (Toronto: Thomson Professional Publishing Canada, 1991), 336–57.

[15] Martin H. Redish, 'Tobacco Advertising', 589; Martin H. Redish, 'First Amendment Theory and the Demise of the Commercial Speech Distinction: The Case of the Smoking Controversy', *Northern Kentucky Law Review* 24 (1997): 553.

(Chapter 8.2) acknowledges that he intervened on behalf of the industry in discussions of draft U.S. Food and Drug Administration regulations.[16] Who knows how many other academic articles on behalf of the commercial expression doctrine are industry-supported with the authors not having the integrity to admit it? Redish even suggests that government regulation of advertising occurs simply because government is in the pay of opposing economic interests.[17] Regrettably, no industry paid me to write this book.

Maybe, just to be on the safe side, in addition to writing this book, I should hire my own advertising agency.

[16] Lars Noah, 'The FDA's New Policy on Guidelines: Having Your Cake and Eating It Too', *Catholic University Law Review* 47 (1997): 113.
[17] Martin H. Redish, 'Tobacco Advertising', 607.

Bibliography

Allen, William T., 'Contracts and Communities in Corporation Law', *Washington & Lee Law Review* 50 (1993): 1395–407.

Anderson, David A., 'An Errant Tort', *Review of Litigation* 9 (1990): 409–40.

—— 'Torts, Speech and Contracts', *Texas Law Review* 75 (1997): 1499–538.

Anderson, Simon P., and Renault, Régis, 'Consumer Information and Firm Pricing: Negative Externalities from Improved Information', *International Economic Review* 41 (2000): 721–42.

Archard, David, 'For Our Own Good', *Australasian Journal of Philosophy* 72 (1994): 283–93.

Arneson, Richard J., 'Mill Versus Paternalism', *Ethics* 90 (1980): 470–89.

Arrington, Robert L., 'Advertising and Behaviour Control', *Journal of Business Ethics* 1 (1982): 3–12.

Austin, J.L., *How To Do Things With Words* (2nd edn., by J.O. Urmson and Marina Sbisà, Cambridge, Mass.: Harvard University Press, 1975).

Baker, C. Edwin, 'Realizing Self-Realization: Corporate Political Expenditures and Redish's "The Value of Free Speech"', *University of Pennsylvania Law Review* 130 (1982): 646–77.

—— *Human Liberty and Freedom of Speech* (New York: Oxford University Press, 1989).

—— 'Media Concentration: Giving Up on Democracy', *Florida Law Review* 54 (2002): 839–919.

Baldasty, Gerald J., and Simpson, Roger A., 'The Deceptive "Right to Know": How Pessimism Rewrote the First Amendment', *Washington Law Review* 56 (1981): 365–95.

Bambrough, Renford, *Moral Scepticism and Moral Knowledge* (London: Routledge and Kegan Paul, 1979).

Barendt, Eric, 'Freedom of Speech in an Era of Mass Communication', in P. Birks (ed.), *Pressing Problems in the Law* (Oxford: Oxford University Press, 1995), i, 109–16.

—— 'The Importation of United States Free Speech Jurisprudence?', in I. Loveland (ed.), *A Special Relationship? American Influences on Public Law in the UK* (Oxford: Clarendon Press, 1995), 213–32.

Barnett, Stephen R., 'The Right of Publicity Versus Free Speech in Advertising: Some Counter-Points to Professor McCarthy', *Hastings Communications and Entertainment Law Journal* 18 (1996): 593–614.

Barthes, Roland, *Mythlogies* (London: Paladin Grafton Books, 1973).

Bass, I. Scott, Kalb, Paul E., and Berenson, Bradford A., 'Off-Label Promotion: Is FDA's Final Guidance on Industry-Supported Scientific and Educational Programs Enforceable?', *Food and Drug Law Journal* 53 (1998): 193–212.

Bayefsky, Anne F., 'The Judicial Function Under The Canadian Charter of Rights and Freedoms', in Anne F. Bayefsky (ed.), *Legal Theory Meets Legal Practice* (Edmonton, Alta: Academic Printing and Publishing, 1988), 121–62.

Beales, Howard, Craswell, Richard, and Salop, Steven C., 'The Efficient Regulation of Consumer Information', *Journal of Law and Economics* 24 (1981): 491–539.

Berlin, Isaiah, *Four Essays on Liberty* (Oxford: Clarendon Press, 1969).

Berman, Mitchell N., 'The Normative Function of Coercion Claims', *Legal Theory* 8 (2002): 45–90.

BeVier, Lillian, 'The First Amendment and Political Speech: An Inquiry Into the Substance and Limits of Principle', *Stanford Law Review* 30 (1978): 299–358.

Bickel, Alexander, *The Least Dangerous Branch* (Indianapolis, Ind.: Bobbs-Merrill, 1962).

Brison, Susan J., 'Speech, Harm and the Mind-Body Problem in First Amendment Jurisprudence', *Legal Theory* 4 (1998): 39–61.

Brock, Dan, 'Paternalism and Promoting the Good', in Rolf Sartorius (ed.), *Paternalism* (Minneapolis, Minn.: University of Minnesota Press, 1983), 237–60.

Butler, Henry N., 'The Contractual Theory of the Corporation', *George Mason University Law Review* 11 (1989): 99–123.

—— and Ribstein, Larry E., *The Corporation and the Constitution* (Washington, DC: AEI Press, 1995).

Carrington, Paul D., 'Our Imperial First Amendment', *University of Richmond Law Review* 34 (2001): 1167–211.

Carter, Rosemary, 'Justifying Paternalism', *Canadian Journal of Philosophy* 7 (1977): 133–45.

Christman, John, 'Constructing the Inner Citadel: Recent Work on the Concept of Autonomy', *Ethics* 99 (1988): 109–24.

Coase, R.H., 'Advertising and Free Speech', *Journal of Legal Studies* 6 (1977): 1–34.

Cole, David, 'Agon at Agora: Creative Misreadings in the First Amendment Tradition', *Yale Law Journal* 95 (1986): 857–905.

Collier, Charles W., 'Precedent and Legal Authority: A Critical History', *Wisconsin Law Review* (1988), 771–825.

Collins, Ronald K.L., and Stover, David M., 'Commerce and Communication', *Texas Law Review* 71 (1993): 697–746.

Copp, David, 'What Collectives Are: Agency, Individualism and Legal Theory', *Dialogue* 23 (1984): 249–69.

Crisp, Roger, 'Persuasive Advertising, Autonomy, and the Creation of Desire', *Journal of Business Ethics* 6 (1987): 413–18.

Dan-Cohen, Meir, *Rights, Persons and Organizations: A Legal Theory for Bureaucratic Society* (Berkeley and Los Angeles, Cal.: University of California Press, 1986).

—— 'Freedoms of Collective Speech: A Theory of Protected Communications by Organizations, Communities and the State', *California Law Review* 79 (1991): 1229–67.

Davidson, Donald, 'Agency', in Donald Davidson, *Essays on Actions and Events* (New York: Oxford University Press, 1980), 43–63.

Director, Aaron, 'The Parity of the Economic Market Place', *Journal of Law and Economics* 7 (1964): 1–10.

Dobbs, Dan D., 'Tortious Interference with Contractual Relationships', *Arkansas Law Review* 34 (1980): 335–76.

Dooley, Michael P., 'The First Amendment and the SEC: A Comment', *Connecticut Law Review* 20 (1988): 335–54.

Dworkin, Gerald, 'Paternalism', in Richard A. Wasserstrom (ed.), *Morality and the Law* (Belmont, Cal.: Wadsworth, 1971), 107–26.

—— 'Paternalism', *The Monist* 56 (1972): 64–84.

—— 'Paternalism: Some Second Thoughts', in Rolf Sartorius (ed.), *Paternalism* (Minneapolis, Minn.: University of Minnesota Press, 1983), 105–11.

—— 'Autonomy', in Robert E. Goodin and Philip Pettit (eds.), *The Blackwell Companion to Contemporary Political Philosophy* (Oxford: Blackwell Publishers Ltd., 1993), 359–65.

Dworkin, Ronald M., *Taking Rights Seriously* (2nd edn., Cambridge, Mass.: Harvard University Press, 1978).

—— *A Matter of Principle* (Cambridge, Mass.: Harvard University Press, 1985).

Eckwert, Bernhard, and Zilcha, Itzhak, 'The Value of Information in Production Economies', *Journal of Economic Theory* 100 (2001): 172–86.

Emerson, Thomas I., 'Toward a General Theory of the First Amendment', *Yale Law Journal* 72 (1963): 877–956.

—— *The System of Freedom of Expression* (New York: Random House, 1970).

Epstein, Richard A., 'Property, Speech, and the Politics of Distrust', *University of Chicago Law Review* 59 (1992): 41–89.

Estreicher, Aleta G., 'Securities Regulation and the First Amendment', *Georgia Law Review* 24 (1990): 223–326.

Fallon, Richard H., Jr., 'Two Senses of Autonomy', *Stanford Law Review* 46 (1994): 875–905.

Feinberg, Joel, *Harm to Self*, Vol. III of *The Moral Limits of the Criminal Law* (New York: Oxford University Press, 1986).

Feldthusen, Bruce, *Economic Negligence* (4th edn., Toronto: Carswell, 2000).

Fiss, Owen, *Liberalism Divided: Freedom of Speech and the Many Uses of State Power* (Boulder, Colo.: Westview Press, 1996).

Fotion, Nicholas, 'Paternalism', *Ethics* 89 (1979): 191–8.

Fredman, Sandra, McCrudden, Christopher, and Freedland, Mark, 'An E.U. Charter of Fundamental Rights', [2000] *Public Law* 178–86.

Freeman, R. Edward, *Strategic Management: A Stakeholder Approach* (Boston, Mass.: Pitman Publishing, 1984).

—— Pierce, Jessica, and Dodd, Richard, *Environmentalism and the New Logic of Business: How Firms Can Be Profitable and Leave Our Children a Living Planet* (New York: Oxford University Press, 2000).

French, Peter A., 'The Corporation as a Moral Person', *American Philosophical Quarterly* 16 (1979): 207–15.

Fuller, Lon L., *The Morality of Law* (2nd edn., New Haven, Conn.: Yale University Press, 1964).

Galbraith, John Kenneth, *The Affluent Society* (Boston, Mass.: Houghton Mifflin Co., 1958).

Gardner, John, 'Freedom of Expression', in Christopher McCrudden and Gerard Chambers (eds.), *Individual Rights and the Law in Britain* (Oxford: Clarendon Press, 1994), 209–38.

Gergen, Mark P., 'Tortious Interference: How It Is Engulfing Commercial Law, Why This Is Not Entirely Bad, and a Prudential Response', *Arizona Law Review* 38 (1996): 1175–232.

Gibson, Dale, *The Law of the Charter: Equality Rights* (Toronto: Carswell, 1990).

Gilhooley, Margaret, 'Constitutionalizing Food and Drug Law', *Tulane Law Review* 74 (2000): 815–81.

Greenwood, Daniel J.H., 'Essential Speech: Why Corporate Speech is not Free', *Iowa Law Review* 83 (1998): 995–1070.

—— 'First Amendment Imperialism', *Utah Law Review* (1999), 659–72.

Grossman, Gene M., and Shapiro, Carl, 'Informative Advertising with Differentiated Products', *Review of Economic Studies* 51 (1984): 63–81.

Grossman, Sanford J., and Stiglitz, Joseph E., 'Information and Competitive Price Systems', *American Economic Review* 66, no. 2 (1976): 246–53.

—— 'On the Impossibility of Informationally Efficient Markets', *American Economic Review* 70, no. 3 (1980): 393–407.

Haan, Sarah C., 'The "Persuasion Route" of the Law: Advertising and Legal Persuasion', *Columbia Law Review* 100 (2000): 1281–326.

Halberstam, Daniel, 'Commercial Speech, Professional Speech, and the Constitutional Status of Social Institutions', *University of Pennsylvania Law Review* 147 (1999): 771–874.

Harris, D.J., O'Boyle, M., and Warbrick, C., *Law of the European Convention on Human Rights* (London: Butterworths, 1995).

Hart, H.L.A., *The Concept of Law* (2nd edn., by Penelope A. Bulloch and Joseph Raz, Oxford: Clarendon Press, 1994).

Hartley, T.C., *The Foundations of European Community Law* (3rd edn., Oxford: Clarendon Press, 1994).

Hessen, Robert, *In Defense of the Corporation* (Stanford, Cal.: Hoover Institute Press, 1979).

Hiebert, Janet L., *Charter Conflicts: What Is Parliament's Role?* (Montreal and Kingston: McGill-Queens University Press, 2002).

Hirshleifer, Jack, 'The Private and Social Value of Information and the Reward to Inventive Activity', *American Economic Review* 61 (1971): 561–74.

Hogg, Peter W., *Constitutional Law of Canada* (Loose-leaf edn., Toronto: Carswell, 2002).

—— and Bushell, Allison A., 'The *Charter* Dialogue Between Courts and Legislatures (Or Perhaps the *Charter of Rights* Isn't Such a Bad Thing After All)', *Osgoode Hall Law Journal* 35 (1997): 75–105.

—— and Thornton, Allison A., 'Reply to "Six Degress of Dialogue" ', *Osgoode Hall Law Journal* 37 (1999): 529–36.

Hornsby, Jennifer, and Langton, Rae, 'Free Speech and Illocution', *Legal Theory* 4 (1998): 21–37.

Horowitz, Donald L., *The Courts and Social Policy* (Washington, DC: Brookings Institute, 1977).

Hurka, Thomas, 'Capability, Functioning and Perfectionism', in Lawrence J. Jost and Roger A. Shiner (eds.), *Eudaimonia and Well-Being: Ancient and Modern Conceptions* (Kelowna, BC: Academic Printing and Publishing, 2002), 137–62.

Husak, Douglas N., 'Paternalism and Autonomy', *Philosophy and Public Affairs* 10 (1981): 27–46.

—— 'Legal Paternalism', in Hugh LaFollette (ed.), *Oxford Handbook to Practical Ethics* (Oxford: Clarendon Press, 2002), 387–412.

Hutchinson, Allan C., 'Money Talk: Against Constitutionalizing (Commercial) Speech', *Canadian Business Law Journal* 17 (1990): 2–34.

Ingber, Stanley, 'The Marketplace of Ideas: A Legitimizing Myth', *Duke Law Journal* (1984), 1–88.

Jackson, Thomas H., and Jeffries, John Calvin, Jr., 'Commercial Speech: Economic Due Process and the First Amendment', *Virginia Law Review* 65 (1979): 1–41.

Joachim, Scott, 'Seeing Beyond the Smoke and Mirrors: A Proposal for the Abandonment of the Commercial Speech Doctrine and an Analysis of Recent Tobacco Advertising Regulations', *Hastings Communications and Entertainment Law Journal* 19 (1997): 517–62.

Kelman, Steven, 'Regulation and Paternalism', *Public Policy* 29 (1981): 219–54.

Kozinski, Alex, and Banner, Stuart, 'Who's Afraid of Commercial Speech?', *Virginia Law Review* 76 (1990): 627–53.

——'The Anti-History and Pre-History of Commercial Speech', *Texas Law Review* 71 (1993): 747–75.

Krattenmaker, Thomas G., and Powe, Lucas A., Jr., *Regulating Broadcast Programming* (Cambridge, Mass.: The MIT Press, 1994).

Langvardt, Arlen W., 'The Troubling Implications of a Right of Publicity "Wheel" Spun Out of Control', *Kansas Law Review* 45 (1997): 329–452.

——and Richards, Eric L., 'The Death of *Posadas* and the Birth of Change in Commercial Speech Doctrine: Implications of *44 Liquormart*', *American Business Law Journal* 34 (1997): 483–559.

Lee, William E., 'The Supreme Court and the Right to Receive Expression', *Supreme Court Review* 7 (1987): 303–44.

Lennox, Dana Grantham, 'Hello, Is Anybody Home? Deregulation, Discombobulation, and the Decision in *U.S. West v FCC*', *Georgia Law Review* 34 (2000): 1645–700.

Lepofsky, M. David, 'The Supreme Court's Approach to Freedom of Expression—*Irwin Toy v Quebec (Attorney General)*—and the Illusion of Section 2(b) Liberalism', *National Journal of Constitutional Law* 3 (1993): 37–98.

Lester, Anthony, and Pannick, David, 'Advertising and Freedom of Expression in Europe' [1985] *Public Law* 349–52.

Lewis, Anthony, *Make No Law: The Sullivan Case and the First Amendment* (New York: Random House, 1991).

Lomasky, Loren E., *Persons, Rights, and the Moral Community* (New York: Oxford University Press, 1987).

Loveland, Ian, 'Introduction: Should We Take Lessons from America?', in Ian Loveland (ed.), *A Special Relationship? American Influences on Public Law in the UK* (Oxford: Clarendon Press, 1995), 1–23.

Lowenstein, Daniel Hays, ' "Too Much Puff": Persuasion, Paternalism and Commercial Speech', *University of Cincinnati Law Review* 56 (1988): 1205–49.

MacCallum, Gerald C., Jr., *Legislative Intent and Other Essays on Law, Politics, and Morality* (edited by Marcus G. Singer and Rex Martin, Madison, Wis.: University of Wisconsin Press, 1993).

MacCormick, Neil, *Questioning Sovereignty: Law, State and Practical Reason* (Oxford: Clarendon Press, 1999).

Machina, Kenton F., 'Freedom of Expression in Commerce', *Law and Philosophy* 3 (1994): 375–406.

Mahoney, Paul, 'Judicial Activism and Judicial Self-Restraint in the European Court of Human Rights: Two Sides of the Same Coin', *Human Rights Law Journal* 11 (1990): 57–88.

——'Emergence of a European Conception of Freedom of Speech', in Peter Birks (ed.), *Pressing Problems in the Law* (Oxford: Oxford University Press, 1995), i, 149–55.

Manfredi, Christopher P., *Judicial Power and the Charter: Canada and the Paradox of Liberal Constitutionalism* (2nd edn., Don Mills: Oxford University Press, 2001).

—— and Kelly, James B., 'Six Degrees of Dialogue: A Response to Hogg and Bushell', *Osgoode Hall Law Journal* 37 (1999): 513–27.

Mark, Gregory A., 'The Personification of the Corporation in American Law', *University of Chicago Law Review* 54 (1987): 1441–83.

McChesney, Fred S., 'Commercial Speech in the Professions: The Supreme Court's Unanswered Questions and Questionable Answers', *University of Pennsylvania Law Review* 134 (1985): 45–119.

—— 'A Positive Regulatory Theory of the First Amendment', *Connecticut Law Review* 20 (1988): 355–82.

—— 'De-Bates and Re-Bates: The Supreme Court's Latest Commercial Speech Cases', *Supreme Court Economic Review* 5 (1997): 81–139.

McCrudden, Christopher, 'Freedom of Speech and Racial Equality', in Peter Birks (ed.), *Pressing Problems in the Law* (Oxford: Oxford University Press, 1995), i, 125–48.

—— 'The Impact on Freedom of Speech', in Basil S. Markesinis (ed.), *The Impact of the Human Rights Bill on English Law*, The Clifford Chance Lectures (Oxford: Oxford University Press, 1998), iii, 85–109.

McGowan, David F., 'A Critical Analysis of Commercial Speech', *California Law Review* 78 (1990): 359–448.

McKenna, C.J., *The Economics of Uncertainty* (New York: Oxford University Press, 1986).

Meiklejohn, Alexander, *Free Speech and Its Relation to Self-Government* (New York: Harper and Row, 1948).

Mill, John Stuart, *Essential Works of John Stuart Mill* (Ed. and intro by Max Lerner, New York: Bantam Books, 1961).

Miller, Reese P., 'Persuasion and the Dependence Effect', in Deborah C. Poff and Wilfrid J. Waluchow (eds.), *Business Ethics in Canada* (Scarborough: Prentice-Hall Canada, 1991), 479–88.

Millon, David, 'The Ambiguous Significance of Corporate Personhood', *Stanford Agora: An on-Line Journal of Legal Perspectives* 2, no. 1 (2001): 39–58.

Moon, Richard, 'Lifestyle Advertising and Classical Freedom of Expression Doctrine', *McGill Law Journal* 36 (1991): 76–129.

—— *The Constitutional Protection of Freedom of Expression* (Toronto: University of Toronto Press, 2000).

Nagel, Robert F., 'The Formulaic Constitution', *Michigan Law Review* 84 (1985): 165–212.

Nagel, Thomas, *Mortal Questions* (Cambridge: Cambridge University Press, 1979).

Nedelsky, Jennifer, 'Reconceiving Autonomy: Sources, Thoughts, and Possibilities', *Yale Journal of Law and Feminism* 1 (1989): 7–36.

—— 'Reconceiving Rights as Relationship', *Review of Constitutional Studies* 1 (1993): 1–26.

Neuborne, Burt, 'The First Amendment and Government Regulation of Capital Markets', *Brooklyn Law Review* 55 (1989): 5–63.

New, Bill, 'Paternalism and Public Policy', *Economics and Philosophy* 15 (1999): 63–83.

Noah, Lars, 'Constraints on the Off-Label Uses of Prescription Drug Products', *Journal of Products and Toxics Liability* 16 (1994): 139–65.

—— 'The FDA's New Policy on Guidelines: Having Your Cake and Eating It Too', *Catholic University Law Review* 47 (1997): 113–42.

—— 'What's Wrong with "Constitutionalizing Food and Drug Law"?' *Tulane Law Review* 75 (2000): 137–48.

—— and Noah, Barbara A., 'Liberating Commercial Speech: Product Labeling Controls and the First Amendment', *Florida Law Review* 47 (1995): 63–112.

Nowak, John E., and Rotunda, Ronald D., *Constitutional Law* (6th edn., St. Paul, Minn.: West Group, 2000).

Nozick, Robert, *Anarchy, State and Utopia* (Oxford: Blackwell, 1974).

Nussbaum, Martha C., and Sen Amartya (eds.), *The Quality of Life* (Oxford: Clarendon Press, 1993).

Ouyang, Guangwei, and Shiner, Roger A., 'Organizations and Agency', *Legal Theory* 1 (1995): 283–310.

Pannick, David, 'Article 10 of the European Convention on Human Rights', in Peter Birks (ed.), *Pressing Problems in the Law* (Oxford: Oxford University Press, 1995), i, 117–23.

Perry, Stephen R., 'Judicial Obligation, Precedent and the Common Law', *Oxford Journal of Legal Studies* 7 (1987): 215–57.

Peston, M., *Public Goods and the Public Sector* (London: Macmillan, 1972).

Pinto, Arthur R., 'The Nature of the Capital Markets Allows a Greater Role for Government', *Brooklyn Law Review* 55 (1989): 77–103.

Posner, Richard A., 'Free Speech in an Economic Perspective', *Suffolk University Law Review* 20 (1986): 1–54.

Post, Robert, 'The Constitutional Status of Commercial Speech', *UCLA Law Review* 48 (2000): 1–57.

—— 'Reconciling Theory and Doctrine in First Amendment Jurisprudence', in Lee C. Bollinger and Geoffrey R. Stone (eds.), *Eternally Vigilant: Free Speech in the Modern Era* (Chicago, Ill.: University of Chicago Press, 2002), 153–73.

Powe, Lucas A., Jr., *American Broadcasting and the First Amendment* (Berkeley and Los Angeles, Cal.: University of California Press, 1987).

—— *The Fourth Estate and the Constitution: Freedom of the Press in America* (Berkeley and Los Angeles, Cal.: University of California Press, 1991).

Rabban, David M., *Free Speech in Its Forgotten Years, 1870–1920* (New York: Cambridge University Press, 1997).

Rabin, Robert L., and Sugarman, Stephen D. (eds.), *Regulating Tobacco* (New York: Oxford University Press, 2001).

Rainey, R. Randall, and Rehg, William, 'The Marketplace of Ideas, the Public Interest, and Federal Regulation of the Electronic Media: Implications of Habermas' Theory of Democracy', *Southern California Law Review* 69 (1996): 1923–87.

Ramsay, Iain, *Consumer Protection: Text and Materials* (Law in Context, London: Weidenfeld and Nicholson, 1989).

Rawls, John, *A Theory of Justice* (Cambridge, Mass.: Harvard University Press, 1971).

—— *Political Liberalism* (New York: Columbia University Press, 1993).

Raz, Joseph, *Practical Reason and Norms* (London: Hutchinson, 1975).

—— *The Authority of Law* (Oxford: Clarendon Press, 1979).

—— *The Morality of Freedom* (Oxford: Clarendon Press, 1986).

—— *Ethics in the Public Domain: Essays in the Morality of Law and Politics* (Oxford: Clarendon Press, 1994).

Réaume, Denise, 'Individuals, Groups, and Rights to Public Goods', *University of Toronto Law Journal* 38 (1988): 1–27.

Redish, Martin H., 'The First Amendment in the Marketplace: Commercial Speech and the Values of Free Expression', *George Washington Law Review* 39 (1971): 429–73.

Redish, Martin H., 'The Value of Free Speech', *University of Pennsylvania Law Review* 130 (1982): 591–645.

——'Self-Realization, Democracy, and Freedom of Expression: A Reply to Professor Baker', *University of Pennsylvania Law Review* 130 (1982): 678–88.

—— 'Product Health Claims and the First Amendment: Scientific Expression and the Twilight Zone of Commercial Speech', *Vanderbilt Law Review* 43 (1990): 1433–61.

——'Tobacco Advertising and the First Amendment', *Iowa Law Review* 81 (1996): 589–639.

—— 'First Amendment Theory and the Demise of the Commercial Speech Distinction: The Case of the Smoking Controversy', *Northern Kentucky Law Review* 24 (1997): 553–84.

—— *Money Talks: Speech, Economic Power, and the Values of Democracy* (New York: New York University Press, 2001).

Richards, Jef I., 'Politicizing Cigarette Advertising', *Catholic University Law Review* 45 (1996): 1147–212.

Rome, Edwin P., and Roberts, William H., *Corporate and Commercial Free Speech: First Amendment Protection of Expression in Business* (Westport, Conn.: Quorum Books, 1985).

Ryle, Gilbert, *The Concept of Mind* (London: Hutchinson, 1949).

Salbu, Steven R., 'Off-Label Use, Prescription, and Marketing of FDA-Approved Drugs: An Assessment of Legislative and Regulatory Policy', *Florida Law Review* 51 (1999): 181–227.

Schauer, Frederick F., 'Speech and "Speech"—Obscenity and "Obscenity": An Exercise in the Interpretation of Constitutional Language', *Georgetown Law Journal* 67 (1979): 899–933.

—— *Free Speech: A Philosophical Enquiry* (Cambridge: Cambridge University Press, 1982).

—— 'Must Speech Be Special?', *Northwestern University Law Review* 78 (1983): 1284–306.

—— 'Commercial Speech and the Architecture of the First Amendment', *University of Cincinnati Law Review* 56 (1988): 1181–203.

—— *Playing By The Rules: A Philosophical Examination of Rule-Based Decision-Making in Law and in Life* (Clarendon Law Series, Oxford: Clarendon Press, 1991).

—— 'The Phenomenology of Speech and Harm', *Ethics* 103 (1993): 635–53.

—— 'First Amendment Opportunism', in Lee C. Bollinger and Geoffrey R. Stone (eds.), *Eternally Vigilant: Free Speech in the Modern Era* (Chicago, Ill.: University of Chicago Press, 2002), 175–97.

Schlee, Edward E., 'The Value of Information in Efficient Risk-Sharing Arrangements', *American Economic Review* 91, no. 3 (2001): 509–24.

Schneewind, J.B., *The Invention of Autonomy: A History of Modern Moral Philosophy* (New York: Cambridge University Press, 1998).

Scoccia, Danny, 'Moral Paternalism, Virtue and Autonomy', *Australasian Journal of Philosophy* 78 (2000): 53–71.

Sharpe, Robert J., 'Commercial Expression and the Charter', *University of Toronto Law Journal* 37 (1987): 229–59.

Shiffrin, Steven, 'The First Amendment and Economic Regulation: Away from a General Theory of the First Amendment', *Northwestern University Law Review* 78 (1983): 1212–83.

Shiner, Roger A., 'Freedom of Speech-Acts', *Philosophy and Rhetoric* 3 (1970): 40–50.

—— 'Ethical Justification and Case-by-Case Reasoning', in D. Odegard (ed.), *Ethics and Justification* (Edmonton, Alta: Academic Printing and Publishing, 1988), 91–108.

—— *Norm and Nature: The Movements of Legal Thought* (Clarendon Law Series, Oxford: Clarendon Press, 1992).

—— 'The Silent Majority Speaks: *RJR-MacDonald Inc v Canada*', *Constitutional Forum* 7, no. 1 (1995): 8–15.

—— *Legal Institutions and the Sources of Law*, Vol. III of Enrico Pattaro, Gerald J. Postema, and Peter Stein (eds.), *A Treatise of Legal Philosophy and General Jurisprudence* (Dordrecht: Kluwer Academic Publishers, 2003).

Smith, Glenn C., 'Avoiding Awkward Alchemy—In the Off-Label Drug Context and Beyond: Fully-Protected Independent Research Should Not Transmogrify Into Mere Commercial Speech Just Because Product Manufacturers Distribute It', *Wake Forest Law Review* 34 (1999): 963–1055.

Smolla, Rodney A., 'Information, Imagery and the First Amendment: A Case for Expansive Protection of Commercial Speech', *Texas Law Review* 71 (1993): 777–804.

—— *Smolla and Nimmer on Freedom of Speech* (3rd edn., Deerfield, Ill.: Clark Boardman Callaghan, 1996).

Solum, Lawrence B., 'Freedom of Communicative Action: A Theory of the First Amendment Freedom of Speech', *Northwestern University Law Review* 83 (1989): 54–135.

Sparshott, Francis, *The Theory of the Arts* (Princeton, NJ: Princeton University Press, 1982).

Stern, Nat, 'In Defense of the Imprecise Definition of Commercial Speech', *Maryland Law Review* 58 (1999): 55–149.

Stiglitz, Joseph E., 'Equilibrium in Product Markets with Imperfect Information', *American Economic Review* 69, no. 2 (1979): 339–45.

—— 'The Contributions of the Economics of Information to Twentieth-Century Economics', *Quarterly Journal of Economics* 115 (2000): 1441–78.

Strauss, David A., 'Constitutional Protection for Commercial Speech: Some Lessons from the American Experience', *Canadian Journal of Business Law* 17 (1990): 45–54.

—— 'Persuasion, Autonomy and Freedom of Expression', *Columbia Law Review* 91 (1991): 334–71.

Sumner, L.W., *The Moral Foundation of Rights* (Oxford: Clarendon Press, 1987).

Sunstein, Cass R., *Free Markets and Social Justice* (New York: Oxford University Press, 1997).

Tuan, Julie., 'U.S. West, Inc. v FCC', *Berkeley Technology Law Journal* 15 (2000): 353–372.

Tucker, Robert L., ' "And the Truth Shall Make You Free": Truth as a First Amendment Defense in Tortious Interference with Contract Cases', *Hastings Constitutional Law Quarterly* 23 (1997): 709–39.

Tulkens, Françoise, 'Towards a Greater Normative Coherence in Europe: The Implications of the Draft Charter of Fundamental Rights of the European Union', *Human Rights Law Journal* 21 (2000): 329–32.

Turpin, Colin, *British Government and the Constitution: Text, Cases and Materials* (Law in Context, 3rd edn., London: Butterworths, 1995).

Tushnet, Mark V., 'Corporations and Free Speech', in David Kairys (ed.), *The Politics of Law: A Progressive Critique* (New York: Pantheon Books, 1982), 253–61.

Valauri, John T., 'Smoking and Self-Realization: A Reply to Professor Redish', *Northern Kentucky Law Review* 24 (1997): 585–92.

Van Alstyne, William, 'A Graphic Review of the Free Speech Clause', *California Law Review* 70 (1982): 107–50.

Van De Veer, Donald, 'Autonomy-Respecting Paternalism', *Social Theory and Practice* 6 (1980): 187–208.

Vladeck, David C., 'Devaluing Truth: Unverified Health Claims in the Aftermath of *Pearson v Shalala*', *Food and Drug Law Journal* 54 (1999): 535–53.

Waldron, Jeremy, *Law and Disagreement* (Oxford: Clarendon Press, 1999).

Weiler, J.H.H., 'A Constitution for Europe? Some Hard Choices', *Journal of Common Market Studies* 40 (2002): 563–80.

Weinrib, Lorraine E., 'Does Money Talk? Commercial Expression in the Canadian Constitutional Context', in David Schneiderman (ed.), *Freedom of Expression and the Charter* (Toronto: Thomson Professional Publishing Canada, 1991), 336–57.

Wexler, Gary D., 'Intentional Interference with Contract: Market Efficiency and Individual Liberty Considerations', *Connecticut Law Review* 27 (1994): 279–328.

White, G. Edward, 'The First Amendment Comes of Age: The Emergence of Free Speech in Twentieth-Century America', *Michigan Law Review* 95 (1996): 299–392.

Williams, Bernard, *Ethics and the Limits of Philosophy* (Cambridge, Mass.: Harvard University Press, 1985).

—— 'The Standard of Living: Interests and Capabilities', in Geoffrey Hawthorn (ed.), *The Standard of Living* (The Tanner Lectures 1985, Cambridge: Cambridge University Press, 1987), 94–102.

Winter, Steven L., 'Transcendental Nonsense, Metaphoric Reasoning, and the Cognitive Stakes for Law', *University of Pennsylvania Law Review* 137 (1989): 1105–237.

Wolfson, Nicholas, 'The First Amendment and the SEC', *Connecticut Law Review* 20 (1988): 265–301.

Wright, R. George, *Selling Words: Free Speech in a Commercial Culture* (New York: New York University Press, 1997).

Young, Robert M., 'Autonomy and Paternalism', in Kai Nielsen and Steven C. Patten (eds.), *New Essays in Ethics and Public Policy*, Canadian Journal of Philosophy Supplementary Volume VIII (Guelph, Ont.: Canadian Association for Publishing in Philosophy, 1982), 47–66.

Zimmerman, Diane, 'Fitting Publicity Rights Into Intellectual Property and Free Speech Theory: Sam, You Made the Pants Too Long!', *Journal of Art and Entertainment Law* 10 (2000): 283–313.

Index